Kevin Myers

From the *Irish Times* column
'An Irishman's Diary'

FOUR COURTS PRESS

Published by
FOUR COURTS PRESS
Fumbally Lane, Dublin 8, Ireland
email: info@four-courts-press.ie
http://www.four-courts-press.ie
and in North America by
FOUR COURTS PRESS
c/o ISBS, 5824 N.E. Hassalo Street, Portland, OR 97213.

ISBN 1-85182-575-4

A catalogue record for this title
is available from the British Library.

Printed in Ireland
by Betaprint, Dublin.

CONTENTS

SPORT

CONSERVING THE PAST

TROUBLE IN THE NORTH

ROAD RAGE

IRISH POLITICS

RELIGION

WHERE DOES IT GO?

WHEN THE COLUMNS APPEARED

MODERN IRISH LIFE

Summer schools

We are already eyelid deep in summer schools. The MacGill Summer School. The Yeats Summer School. The Humbert Summer School. The Merriman Summer School. The Hewitt Summer School. The Shaw Summer School. The Goldsmith Summer School; for all I know there might be many, many more summer schools.

So it might be a little odd for this column to suggest even more summer schools. Not so if you consider the reason for most summer schools. The Merriman seems to be the most authentic summer school of all. We know virtually nothing about the gentleman after whom it is named, and it seems seldom to have aspired to have been much more than an almighty bash with a bit of cultchoor thrown in. The organisers accordingly never seem to have felt too many restraints about the theme. Firstly because our ignorance of the man who wrote *The Midnight Court* permitted virtually any topic to be considered; and also the latitude permitted by the Merriman ethos was such that there have even been midwinter Merriman Summer Schools.

So either in midwinter or late summer, Merriman could allege that this year it would be about seaweed as a leitmotif in the GAA rulebook or the influence of Thomas Aquinas on Mrs Beeton's *Good Housekeeping Guide* or Sean Ó Riada and the Stealth bomber – the forgotten dialectic.

It didn't really matter, because most of the time people were either too hung over to have the least idea what was being said if they were present or, more probably, were still in bed. From my own experience of Merriman, the papers tend to blur into one another anyway, so that one could have animated conversations in the hall afterwards in which one person was convinced he was talking about Mrs Beeton's *Good Housekeeping Guide*'s influence on stealth technology, while the other was convinced that the subject of the conversation was about the influence of seaweed on Thomas Aquinas. I personally am convinced that I once spent an entire afternoon arguing with one Merriperson that Stealth Ó Riada was responsible for the recipe for GAA seaweed in Mrs Aquinas's *Good Housekeeping Guide*.

It was an argument that I felt – and feel to this day – that I won. Anyway, the simple truth about the Merriman Summer School is that it is admirably full of fun and equally admirably lacking in humbug. But it can afford to be as liberal and as catholic in its subject matter because the nature of the man, and the nature of the revellers, insist that it is so.

Other summer schools are necessarily different. Some summer schools seem to have come into existence because a particular area didn't have a summer school and felt deeply resentful of the crack down in Clare. One senses – doubtless unfairly – that that was one of the motives for the MacGill summer school in Donegal.

Now there are difficulties about the life of Patrick MacGill, difficulties which the MacGill Summer School wisely does its best to ignore. The plain truth is that the mightiest experience of his life, one that dominated him completely throughout his days, was his service with the London Irish in the Great War.

Well, Donegal is Donegal, after all; so we'll just skip that bit, and deal with Patrick MacGill the labourer, and Patrick MacGill the self-educated man and Patrick MacGill the exile; and as for Patrick MacGill who took the king's shilling in the Great War, and tried to – and was rebuffed – during the second; ah, well, next question please.

Then there are the more upmarket literary affairs – Yeats, Shaw, Joyce. Perhaps there is something unsaid still left to be said about any of them; doubtless some American feminist deconstructionist will in due course prove that Yeats was in fact a black lesbian from Harlem, much as, one hears, it is now being claimed that Beethoven was a black man. I look forward to the Merriman version of this: Mrs Yeats's *Good Housekeeping Guide* for black lesbian Stealth bombers in the GAA.

And then there is the Humbert Summer School. And then, indeed, there is the Humbert Summer School; of which I can say no more than, why?

For that is the great question mark over summer schools. Why do some people have a summer school named after them and not others? Why is there no Patrick Pearse Summer School, in which the entire audience sits in profile; no De Valera Summer School where the speakers mumble pieties and keep putting a copy of *The Prince* in their jacket pockets; no Dan Breen Summer School in which everybody shoots everybody else and the survivors are shot by firing squad; no Matt Talbot Summer School, where participants are issued with barbed wire vests; no Father Mathew Summer School at which strong drink is abjured at the first meeting, and the second, and the third, and the fourth; and no Eoin O'Duffy Summer School where everybody dreams of restoring the papal states and struts? Why?

The next Merriman will explain all.

The family that won't go away

It is the breakfast room. Mother, father, son. There is a noise of delicate footsteps in the hall. A polite throat is cleared and the door is pushed open tentatively. 'Hi,' says a little voice. 'Can I come in?'

The father rustles his newspaper (and he means it). 'You mean, *"Hello, may* I come in?"'

'Oh hoy,' says the son, Jonathan. 'Yeah, loike, Oi mean, yeah, roight, come on in, shore.'

'Oh yes, please do come in,' murmurs J's mother, touching her hair. 'Please, you're welcome. It's Zöe, isn't it?'

'Oh maw, Oi tyold yew lawst noight that Zöe and Oi have called it a day.'

'You called it Tuesday, didn't you?' hisses the father, rattling his newspaper.

'Nyow, maw, this is Zara.'

'Hi,' says Zara in a little voice. 'Where will I sit?'

'Haven't a clue. Give up. Where will you sit?' snarls the father.

'Oh don't moind him,' Jonathan assures her. 'He's probably got a humungous hengover, raight, paw?'

'I have got nothing of the kind. Sit here. Have some cornflakes. Rasher?'

Zara utters a little trill of horror. 'Oh no, Oi mean, hyow could yew, Oi mean, animal flesh, how could you put animal flesh in your mouth, Oi mean, Oi never would, well hardly ever.'

The father looks up and sees a knowing smirk exchanged across the table between his son and his latest companion. He snarls his intention of leaving for work.

'Oh surry, paw, but Oi've blocked the droiveway with moy beamer.'

'Beamer? Beamer? Is that your bullnosed Morris?'

'Haw haw haw, paw, haw haw haw.'

There is a sudden gasp, a silence and then a sucking sound as the father withdraws the coffee-grinder from his son's mouth.

There is a reason for this discord at the table. It is this. Young people are no longer leaving home. The sexual revolution is now back to haunt the liberal parents of the 70s. Their children – well, their sons anyway – do not have to leave home in order to have girlfriends stay the night and stay the course, and emerge, smirking insufferably, while enlightened mothers busy themselves with coffee and cheery small talk and fathers smoulder with jealousy.

It's different with the daughters. Daughters cannot yet bring back their boyfriends to spend the night with them and a convivial breakfast with mum and dad. The inexhaustible hospitality of the Irish mother towards her son and his present friend vanishes completely when similar duties might be expected towards the daughter.

'Who are you?' says the mother when she sees the visiting boyfriend; she sounds like two iceflows grinding against one another. 'Kindly leave my house this instant.'

For sons, it's different. The Zöes and the Zaras, the Melanies and the Carlas, are welcome. Dads, mute with anger, might storm out trailing rice crispies, while Jonathan and Zara giggle and Mum asked vaguely, 'More yoghurt anyone?'

'Oh yah, maw, cyool.'

Enormous numbers of young people who once would have flown the coop now remain at home, aided by the apparently inexhaustible appetite of Irish women for motherhood. The ability to have sex without reproach is no doubt one factor, and I'm not talking about the mothers here. But the other great motive behind this change in habit is many mothers' desire to keep mothering.

This is probably one of the great cultural traditions of Irish life, reasserting itself in a new, and quite as powerful a form: mammy still rules the roost, even if Jonathan still sports the night with Zöe or with Zara. Far from the all-powerful Irish mammy vanishing, she has changed her clothes, modernised her attitude, no doubt urges the use of condoms, but is still there to dominate her sons' lives when Zöe and Zara and Melanie and Carla have headed off to their mothers, where dinner, and no doubt sensible contraceptive advice awaits them; for whereas the modern mother doesn't expect her daughter to be a virgin, she certainly doesn't want to see Zöe's swain over the muesli.

Yet there are countless parents in Dublin and elsewhere who long for their young adult children to depart. But the children, no doubt inspired by their friends' households and the infinite maternal hospitability there, decide to stay on – 'Loike, Oi mean, it's reeelly convenient, yew knyow, and moi parents are reeelly cyool, yew knyow, Oi can come and gyo as Oi lyoike, yew knyow.'

So he thinks. It's just that his parents haven't been able to summon up the nerve to tell him to leave – to take his toothbrush, and his abominable clothes, and his nasty sleek car with the car-phone he only ever uses in the driveway and when rounding corners, and to get a flat somewhere and stay there so that his parents can amble around naked in the morning, and eat black pudding and sausages without getting squealy little sermons about animals having feelings too, and maybe, God knows, having sex once in a while without that silly bloody vegetarian wandering in naked and confused and sleepily apologising through her tousled hair, saying, 'Sorry, I thought this was the bathroom.'

It's a problem all over the English-speaking world, the family which won't grow up and go away. You ask QE II, the role-model of the modern Irish mother.

IMMA

There are many divisions in the modern world, but none so complete and unbridgeable as that which rests between the modern artistic community and those outside it. Modern artists seem to be certain that their works are honest and intellectually laudable. Those outside that community gaze in through the glass plate and think it is rubbish – pretentious, unskilled, self-indulgent and frequently despicable rubbish. And those within the community will read sentiments like those and regard them as the buffoonish rantings of a reactionary philistine.

In such matters I am, I fear, a reactionary philistine. I read reviews of exhibitions in wonder and awe, totally and utterly failing to understand what is going on – the recent gallery exhibition in London of artists' bowel movements being perhaps the most splendid example to come to, ah, hand. No doubt I should be grateful that these fine people have found a use for their bottoms. It is not uncommon among small children to take a particular pride in the productivity of their lower alimentary canals and to show the results to visiting bishops or reverend mothers, to their parents' inexpressible delight. But for the moment anyway, such antics, even in repressed and disordered adults, escape my definition of *art*.

With what joy did I read David Hockney's recent attack on art schools for not teaching drawing and for encouraging 'self-expression' as an art-form. Hockney is a sublime genius, the greatest English artist since Turner. Some of his work escapes me completely, but mostly it is quite entrancing, and much of it is spiritually captivating in the way that only great works of art can be.

I am unable to offer a description of art outside my own responses to it. Simply, the object – painting or sculpture – must be so difficult to execute as to be beyond the skills of most of us, and it must speak to some inner self. It must reward, it must bring joy, and it must be enduring. Great art survives. I fear the contents of artists' sit-upons signally fail to meet these criteria.

We do not need to go to London to get that sinking feeling that all is not well in modern art. We are in the era of post-sculpturalist sculpture. Modern portraiture is apparently absolved from the requirements of similarity. The word performance is uttered, and the heart gives a feeble thud and dies.

Herewith are quotes from a press release from the Irish Museum of Modern Art for its Glen Dimplex Artists Award:

> Janine Antoni's work is based on converting everyday bodily rituals such as eating, bathing and mopping and the materials associated with them – chocolate, soap, dye – into sculptural processes ... In 1993 her lard and chocolate cubes installation *Gnaw* was one of the most memorable exhibits in the Whitney Biennial in New York, in which, in the same year, *Lick and Lather*, 14 busts of soap and chocolate, was one of the most acclaimed works ... She is nominated for *Janine Antoni: Slip of the Tongue* at the IMMA ... in which she exhibited works by using her body as a tool, imitating fine art rituals including chiselling (with her teeth); painting (with her hair and eyelashes) and modelling and moulding (with her body). At the exhibition preview, Antoni presented her performance piece *Loving Care*, in which she uses her hair as a paintbrush to cover the floor of the gallery at IMMA with expressionist strokes of black hair dye.

This doesn't sound like art to me, it sounds like showing off, the sort of conduct which when retained beyond the nursery used to be found in vaudeville, not galleries, and certainly not in somewhere like the Royal Hospital Kilmainham which cost £20 million of my money to restore: but not, that I recall, with the stated intention of housing such sillinesses.

It is harder to make any judgment of the works of Mark Francis, which are based on blood, sperm and chromosomes, without seeing them. One is forced to wonder: to what degree does unwarranted and purely fanciful exegesis form the substructure on which these works are able to exist? Listen, 'These works heralded a new departure in his practice, with more densely colonised canvasses suggesting a more threatening atmosphere, perhaps reflecting the fear of AIDS and the so-called flesh-eating bug which gave rise to sensationalist headlines in the UK press in 1994.'

Wherefore the 'perhaps'? Either the flesh-eating bug or AIDS caused him to create 'more densely colonised canvasses' or they didn't.

Jaki Irvine, we are told, 'is one of a number of younger artists who use the media of film, video and sound to explore questions of spatial, temporal and bodily being, which were once the province of sculpture. Her work draws on a variety of sources from Freudian case histories to popular romantic fiction from which she weaves a series of tantalising images, leaving the viewer to construct a plausible narrative.'

Good. But viewers' plausible narrative aside, can the woman sculpt? Can she paint? Is she creating anything in which anyone will be remotely interested in 10 years' time? Or is that irrelevant? And if it is irrelevant, why is such work being presented in a temple of the enduring, the Royal Hospital Kilmainham? Why is it not being presented in a nice Nissen hut somewhere, a temple to the temporary? Because all of this stuff – the mobiles, the performance, the familiars, or heavens, if we're really lucky, a few nicely shaped human bowel movements – is by design and destiny purely ephemeral.

A child smearing chocolate over its face no doubt is a delight to its doting parents; but it is not art, and will not be exhibited in the RHK. Nor should comparably behaving adults be. And there is a further matter. In this age of post-sculpturalist sculpture, when Dublin finally gets round to erecting statues to the good and great is there a single sculptor left who can sculpt a statute without adopting the squatting position?

On the mobile phone

Everybody these days seems to want to give me a mobile phone. My insurance company is offering me one for free. No charge. Just a mobile phone. Open the mail, and a fresh mobile phone offer leaps out at you. A pint of Guinness? Certainly, sir – and have a mobile phone while you're at it.

If it continues like this, mobile phones will be like those little plastic things you used to get in cornflake packets, which seemed to have no purpose in life other than that children collected them avidly. Nobody bought cornflakes for cornflakes' sake, they bought them for these tiny devices which had no known use. Who knows, maybe they were IUDs, and Kellogg's were engaged in a vast conspiracy to supply contraceptives to the women of Ireland, who instead gave them to their children to play with while they were losing their cornflakes to morning sickness.

Nowadays it's mobile phones. They seem like a, well, interesting idea before you actually get one. Those calls from your Hollywood agent. Your banker in Zurich. The coke-dealer off the Cork coast. You might miss them at a vital moment, and instead of the coke-dealer dropping off your consignment at Schull, he vanishes to a ready offer from elsewhere.

On the other hand, an awful lot of people who use mobile phones are quite clearly not the sort one would invite home. Once upon a time such people were known as CBP, darling – comb in back pocket. Nowadays they drive red car-vans to the thump of megawatt music, wear sunglasses, and smoke Camel cigarettes. Women in such vehicles have blonde hair and smoke long-tipped cigarettes, and always use their mobile phones as they corner.

I said at the outset that these people drive car-vans. That is not correct. The vehicles are named after their drivers, and hence are known as van-cars. These van-cars use their carphones everywhere – in pubs, restaurants, parks, possibly funerals, too.

In fact, mobile phones are helpful in that regard. The use of a mobile phone in a pub or restaurant declares the user to be a complete and utter van-car. So there was this compelling argument against having a mobile phone; on the other hand, there might soon be this consignment of coke, bouncing off the West Cork coast.

So I decided to try one of these mobile phones on trial. No rental but I would pay for the calls, which initially seemed a sweet enough deal. What I didn't know was that mobile phones spend money like Ivana Trump. Or that mobile phones are addicts to telephone sex, and spend hours and hours listening to accounts of sexual acts from telephone numbers in Thailand. Or maybe my mobile was accepting reverse charge calls from the Space Shuttle or Challenger Five, somewhere just outside Jupiter.

Certainly the bills which began to pour in seemed utterly unrelated to any calls I was making. I know what I am – a male of the species. My phone calls resemble those radio transmissions in which a million items of information are compressed into a single bleep. Those who hear my phone calls are often unaware that I have made them, such is the pungent brevity of my telephonic style. When I want to ring a telephone sex line in Caracas, I do so from the *Irish Times*, not on my mobile phone.

The bills were simply astounding. I discovered one reason why. A friend's number, which I know for a certain fact was rung only once, appears four times in the itemised bill which I had demanded after fainting at the size of the first bill. Another item suggests that I was talking to a friend for about an hour and a half on a satellite phone.

There can be no reasonable explanation for some of the charges, which might fairly reflect the level of telephonic activity in Manhattan the day war broke out, there was a stock-market crash and Donald Trump was found to be a transvestite lesbian

Australian aborigine called Abigail, but which are and were utterly unrelated to anything I might do, or even want to do, on the telephone. Anyway, the moment the
person I have phoned discovers who he or she is speaking to, they yell, ooops, a small
house fire has just broken out, their grandmother has got into the bath with a two-bar
fire or they have just realised they are in childbirth – sorry darling, must dash, by-eee.

It is not possible for me to run up a large telephone bill. Even the speaking clock
thinks up an excuse and hangs up on me the moment it realises, with a sinking main-
wheel, who has phoned it. I once managed to have a phone call lasting 15 minutes
without the person I called hanging up. How could they hang up? Dropped dead of a
heart attack the moment they heard who it was. Otherwise, my conversations are
short.

Yet here were these bills for hundreds of pounds just rolling in. I got a clue as to
what was going on when my answering machine at home recorded an entire conversation of mine in a pub, but without my telephoning home. It seems my mobile
phone, bored with eavesdropping on my restaurant chat – but believe me, not as bored
as the person I was talking to, sitting there bound and gagged, wide-eyed and weeping: the only way I can keep a companion for the full duration of lunch is by the judi-
cious use of restraints – had phoned me at home. No one was in, my answerphone
clicked into action, and recorded the minutes of conversation which followed.

I don't know how many other calls my mobile phone made. No doubt there were
mobile folk kin in La Paz and Tierra del Fuego, Wellington and Anchorage,
Vladivostock and Pitcairn, who were rung at my expense. Needless to say, I returned
the phone. Others are queuing up to let me have new phones.

What is the trend? Will mobile phones be a fad as passing as plastic yokes in cornflakes? In the meantime, I will probably miss my next coke shipment; and anthracite
too; not to speak of that ton of nutty slack. All bobbing at sea, waiting for me to get
my next mobile phone.

Emdeeville

As new restaurants open everywhere and house prices double between the nightcap
and the orange juice, and as cranes rise menacingly over every rooftop of undemol-
ished Dublin, one god and one god alone is to be found on everybody's lips: it is the
great Persian deity, Inda-naimofuque.

We invoke his name when we turn a corner and yet another computer company
is hard-selling its software, yet another restaurant, specialising in Alaskan-Congolese
cuisine or the culinary traditions of Port Stanley, is opening its door with several hours
of free champagne for thousands. We put our hands to our foreheads and we ask about
the origins of this bounty. That is to say, we cry: Inda-naimofuque, where's all this
coming from?

Suddenly it is as if we are living in a Californian gold-rush boom-town, with virtually no continuities between the croissant-nibbling, Evian-sipping Dublin which is rising before our eyes and the smoky, damp-bricked, rickety-rooftopped Georgian-Joycean rasher-and-eggs-munching Dublin of just the day before yesterday. What happened to that old Dublin? It was there a moment ago, and now it is gone, and has been replaced by bistros populated by people called Mark and Shane and Zöe and Orla who wear sharp suits and sharper hair.

Where did these people come from? Who are their parents? Where did they acquire this confidence to rule the world and trade effortlessly with Frankfurt and with LA? Clink of car-keys as they head for their BMWs.

But the real heart of this new Ireland is not in Dublin, but lies to the west of it. A new metropolis has mushroomed along the Liffey valley. It has little or no contact with Dublin. Its O'Connell Street, its Grafton Street, its heart, its soul, its theatre, its culture, its everything is the M50, from which it takes its name, Emdeeville – M for motorway, D for 50 – as it sweeps all before it, the present and the past alike.

The Persian god, Inda-naimofuque, is invoked at every turn during the growth of this strange crescent city of Emdeeville; as no doubt it was cried with some passion by the millionaire who learned that excavations for his swimming pool in the centreless city of Emdeeville had uncovered 700 skeletons from a medieval burial ground.

But the past is no obstacle to pleasure in Emdeeville. The skeletons within the area exposed have been disposed of, protruding limbs axed off, and the construction of the pool proceeds. Those who swim in those sky-blue waters one day can comfort themselves with the thought that here in Emdeeville the past and the certain future of us all are merely inches away, through those tiles there. Just there. Through the side.

For Emdeeville devours the past everywhere. The ancient settlements of the Liffey – Celbridge, Lucan, Leixlip – have become the population depots for this civilisation, with its two-car households, massive mortgages and absent parents, and its bored boys and girls from nice homes who sniff things behind the bike-sheds and idly hurl rocks at passing traffic, while motorists dodge and screech the name of the Persian deity, Inda-naimofuque!

Here in Emdeeville, the prosperity of Essex has finally come to Ireland – car-ports and shopping centres and vast swathes of estates, dotted with garden centres, shopping malls and bottle-banks – while, on the outskirts of Emdeeville, golf-hotels infect the countryside with a viral rot which rapidly turns farmland pea-green and sterile.

Golf defines this civilisation. The perimeter of Dublin is now a golf course; you can drive a ball in a great arc from Howth to Dun Laoghaire and never leave the circumference of golfcourses which lie between suburbs like seas surrounding an archipelago; but if golf is important for the middle classes of Dublin, it is almost a religion for the citizens of Emdeeville; for is that not what the countryside is for? The playing of golf?

But, this being Ireland, the new and burgeoning civilisation is certainly not godless, for one deity is constantly present as the crescent of Emdeeville covers east Kildare: Inda-naimofuque. It is the constant cry of all the people marooned on the M50 as they head homewards to Emdeeville, in those vast traffic jams the new Ireland now specialises in. Because the odd thing about the land of Emdeeville is that although it is economically successful, its ability to plan infrastructure compares badly with that of Mexico City.

Each morning, each evening, through those great traffic jams which seal the M50 at each end, thousands of motorists intone the name of their lord: Inda-naimofuque.

What else are they to do but call out his name with reverence and with awe? We are seeing a new race, Ireland's answer to Essexfolk emerging: Kildaregirl and Kildaremen are born. They have not yet got an accent, but they will have, just as the DART generated an accent. Their equivalence to Sharon and Tracey will soon emerge; though it is still too early to see what they will be.

In this civilisation, tradesmen are the new aristocracy, even more than they already were in old Dublin. Tradesmen are in such demand to build factories and houses that their favours must be courted with cash on the nail and pots of tea on arrival. Sleepy villages where anglers once browsed in silence on river-banks have become Emdeeville satellite towns, home of the three great commodities of this civilisation – microchips, software and roadrage.

Emdeeville is the new model city of Ireland, the beltway of money, housing developments, swimming-pools, golf-courses, computer factories and leisure-centres, where most of the economic of the New Ireland growth will occur. It is a city without a centre, but it has a coat of arms – a swimming pool surrounded by dismembered skeletons – and it has a motto, a sort of philosophic enquiry, which runs: What Inda-naimofuque Is Going On?

'Cyril's Cinders'

An Irishman's Diary is pleased to bring you today the world exclusive serialisation of *Cyril's Cinders*, yet another best-selling autobiography about an abominable Irish childhood.

What do I remember about my childhood? The same, I guess, as any Irish adult remembers about that time in their lives. Alcoholism, of course. My mother was an alcoholic, and I know now why she was an alcoholic – why, all Irish mothers are alcoholics. It is to hide the pain of Irishness, the pain of life, the pain of existence on an island where every mother is an Irish mother, every mother is an alcoholic, and every mother has a child as miserable as I was. Miserable, forlorn, sad and lonely.

What do I remember about my childhood? I remember my father's cruelty. He was cruel because he was married to an alcoholic, who was alcoholic because she was married to him. He too became an alcoholic because of her great cruelty – and like any Irish mother, she could be very cruel indeed, especially any alcoholic Irish mother, and all Irish mothers are, as we know from the many memoirs selling around the world.

But I was talking about my father, my cruel, cruel father, a heartless man, like all Irish fathers, and made that way I think, by the cruelty of the Christian Brothers, who were that way because of their drunken mothers and their cruel and abusive fathers. In the few moments of sobriety that I remember from my father when I was a child, he would tell me how terrible his childhood had been. In fact it was just like mine. Every morning when I and my 18 brothers left home, with mother beside the sink drinking Domestos and lime, we would wonder whether it was worse being a Catholic because of the B Specials, or worse because of the Christian Brothers.

Each morning, the B Specials would line up outside St Colm's school and machine-gun the pupils. That's why Catholic families were so large, merely to make good the losses suffered in getting to school. Often we 19 brothers would set out for school, but only five of us or even fewer would return each evening, the rest having been slaughtered, *slaughtered*, by the Specials – and that was before the Troubles. It got much worse after the Troubles began.

And at school – well, when I say school, I mean an upturned rusty bucket, because that was school in those days – the Christian Brothers would wait for us to get through the Specials' ambush, and then when the survivors staggered in, they would take down our trousers and beat us with iron rods until it was time to go home again. That was our education, pretty much. The Brothers didn't always beat us right through the day – they would often take a break at noon for a lunch of roast beef and Yorkshire pudding, washed down with fine wines, while the boys would nibble on scutch-grass and rub docks on their bruises, until it was time to be beaten again.

The journey home was worse, because by this time the Specials were drunk again, and often I was the only survivor of 19 brothers who had set out for school that morning. It was terrible, terrible, and what made it worse was that we knew the Specials and the Christian Brothers would do the same to us the next day. And the next. And the next. Believe me, this daily slaughter was very dispiriting for me and my brothers.

Perhaps that was why my mother drank. By the time I got home, accompanied occasionally by a surviving brother, she would have finished the Domestos and would be on the Vim, to which she was partial when mixed with some saddle-soap and a little dash of Brillo. My father would be drunk as well, possibly because it was so cold, for in those days Irish houses had no walls.

Why? Because we were so poor and oppressed. This obviously made us alcoholic as well, and everybody knows Irish alcoholism causes poverty, and Irish poverty intensifies alcoholism. And so it was, my mother, legless on the Vim, my cruel, cruel father, legless on the particular cocktail he fancied, Paddy and Parazone, and me, nursing my bullet wounds and my bruises and gnawing on the armchair for sustenance. On a good night, I could get through an entire Davenport. Other people have tears in their eyes because of piles. Not me. I've got splinters.

Every Christmas, my father would come home with a treat for us all. For my mother, whom he loved in a hard, callous and unloving way so typical of hard, callous and unloving Irishmen, he would normally have a Brillo pad, and for us, he would have a brand new cane, and we would spend Christmas day singing carols while he flogged us.

We knew nothing about sex or nudity. My family did not wash often – it was a *sine qua non* of the deprived Irish childhood that hygiene was largely a greeting reserved for a unit of heredity – and when we did, we put on several layers of clothing to do so.

But those were the relatively happy days; darker times in our miserable Irish childhood lay ahead of us …

(Serialisation of Cyril's Cinders *continues next week)*

'An Abbess Ballooning'

The recent success of Cyril's Cinders, *a harrowing insight into the horrors of Irish childhood, has prompted the author's sister to write her own account of her own infancy, mutilated by sexual repression, alcoholism, the Catholic Church, a harsh, unloving father and an abused and humiliated mother. We are delighted and pleased today to print excerpts from* An Abbess Ballooning.

The greatest message that I remember from my childhood came from my mother. My father was beating her at the time. It was the breakfast flogging which he would administer to the entire family before he would depart – as I discovered later – to have intimate relations with Kelly's heifer, though needless to say in those days we simply thought that sex was what flour arrived in. My mother was across my father's lap, her skirt above her waist, as he was beating her with the poker, 'The lindlords,' she hissed through clenched teeth. 'We are the most distrissful people that ever was known because of the lindlords. Blame the lindlords.'

My mother, of course, blamed the landlords partly because she was a good Catholic, and partly because it was so. The landlords massacred millions of people during the Famine – slaughtered them, mowed them down with machine gun fire, napalmed them, and raped and ravished their way through fields of plenty, exporting food while our poor ancestors chewed grass and licked gravel. No good ever came out of a landlord's house that wasn't in a coffin, my mother used to say, and she was right.

My mother didn't understand that the other enemy of the Irish people was the Church. Well do I remember the priests of our parish chortling over vast banquets and helping themselves to the food of the poor, excommunicating anybody who dared to defy their will. Their tables groaned inside their dining rooms with rich, fat hams, goose pie, suet puddings, wines and the choicest of whiskeys. The nuns were even worse. They revelled in an odd sexual cruelty at the convent school where I was educated.

Educated! The word brings a rueful smile to my face. Educated indeed. The first action of the day by the head nun was to confiscate the lump of turf from each girl as she filed into class. This would later be sold back to our parents as a compulsory purchase scheme (known as peat's pence) to pay for the nuns' holiday in Jamaica. The nuns would then examine our shoes to ensure they would not be so shiny that we could be able to see one another's reflected privates, though of course we were too naïve to understand why the nuns insisted on scuffed shoes.

Naïvety; that of course is the great enduring quality of the Irish people, plus a steadfast stoicism, which enabled us bear the successive burdens of British rule, landlordism, the bishops, the parish priests and the legions of nuns who oppressed us; naïvety was why, after our shoes were examined, we used to permit Sister St Sappho of Fatima to remove our eyelashes, one by one, using a red hot needle. In the interest of hygiene, she insisted; and when our eyelashes were gone, she would yank out the hairs beside our ears.

In class we were made to sit with our hands in full view throughout, and woe betide the girl who wished to scratch an itch. Of course, after the eyelash amputation we were normally in tears when the first lesson began. On most days, this was domestic science, in which we would be taught how to run a home for our menfolk. We were regularly beaten to give us a foretaste of what an Irish marriage was like, with dark hints about what would happen to us when night fell. Of course, we were robbed of our potential as astronauts, physicists, psychiatrists, philosophers or Arctic explorers, for this was an oppressively patriarchal society, in which a woman's future must always be in the home.

Because of the poverty to which we were doomed by landlordism, the British, the monks, the nuns and the bishops, our cookery classes had to make do with make-believe cuisine. We would pretend to weigh pretend flour on pretend scales, and mix our pretend ingredients to make pretend scones in a pretend oven. Well do I remember the not-pretend beating I received from Mother St Tribadism for burning my scones – though of course that was nothing compared with the beating my father gave me for not having any pretend-scones to give him at the end of the day. Still, I was first in the cookery class for my pretend baked ham with pretend apple sauce and pretend baked potatoes, for which of course I received first prize: a trip to Lourdes – pretend, of course.

Instead of going to Lourdes, I was given the privilege of cleaning the convent kitchens, a duty which began at four in the morning. My father accordingly moved our family beatings that much earlier – to 3.30 in the morning, after which I would depart in the darkness to the convent and the rest of the family would retire to bed while my father drank whiskey.

He was normally so hung-over at breakfast that he would have forgotten he had given the rest of the family their morning beatings before dawn, and would administer them again. According to my sister Maria Goretti Immaculata Assumpta Regina Coeli, the only words my mother would utter during this second beating (with three more beatings to come), her skirts over her waist, was 'Blame the lindlords, blame the lindords.'

It might be thought I was the lucky one, but I was not, for Mother St Tribadism, would insist I engage in practices with her which would have been more appropriate between my father and Kelly's heifer. Needless to say, I knew nothing of such things, except that if I resisted her, she would hang me by my toenails from the convent tower.

I would get home at midnight, when my father and I would catch up on the day's beatings, and my mother would piously intone the rosary by the flickering hearth, crying between the Hail Mary and the Glory Be, 'Blame the lindlords, blame the lindlords.' And then the *real* cruelty would begin …

Bienvenue à Irlande

The Bord Fáilte official stood at the quayside, a standard-issue welcoming smile on his face. 'Bonjour, monsieur-cycliste,' he said, 'et bienvenue à Irlande, home du Tour de France.'

'Bonjour et merci. Qu'est-ce que c'est?'

'Ça? C'est – comment on dit-il en français? – rain.'

'Reine? Mais vous êtes une republique.'

'Pardon. Pas reine. Reine means queen, vous eejit. Un moment, pendant je pense. Ah! Un boit from le bleu. J'ai souvenu le mot français pour rain. C'est pluie.'

'Pluie? Cela est pluie? Ce n'est pas pluie, c'est the North Sea en Novembre. C'est incroyable. Cyclant est impossible en such conditions.'

'Non, non, vraiment, on peut cycler, pas de problem, après la pluie a fini, le cyclant est merveilleux.'

'Vraiment? Et comme souvent est-il que la pluie fin?'

'Comme souvent? Ha ha ha! Très amusant! Comme souvent – vous êtes un joker et no mistake, un nouveau Jacques Tati, hein? Vous êtes un wit fantastique, un homme humeureux, a right geg comme ils disent en Belfast, vous êtes …'

'ATTENTION! Dites-moi, comme souvent? Le vrai, j'insiste, s'il vous plaît.'

'Certainment, Monsieur désire le vrai. Il est venu a l'homme droit pur le vrai. Vrai est mon nom moyen. La pluie fin chaque mardi.'

'Chaque mardi? Quoi? Vous tirez mon jambe.'

'Non. Je suis mort serieux. Chaque mardi, á midi. Pour une heure. Et puis la pluie revient. C'est très intéressant.'

'Intéressant? Je suis un cyclist en Le Tour de France, pas un shaggant grenouille-homme. Ce n'est possible cycler en un downpour comme ça. Regardez!'

'Ce n'est pas un downpour. C'est une journée douce, merci Dieu'.

'Un journée douce? Quel sorte de jokeur êtes vous, anyway? Nous cyclerons travers Carrick-en-Suir en un samedi, et presumablement travers la pluie aussi.'

'Mmm. C'est un possibilité. Regard sur le bright-side de vie, c'est que je dit. Toujours le bright-side. Par example, Carrick a très peu de neige en Juillet.

Quelquefois, le soleil presque apparait, et tout le monde est très heureux parce que finallement l'été est ici.'

'L'été? Êtes vous stark raving bonkers? Regardez la pluie-la! Regardez! C'est comme le Möhne dam apres les dambusters ont tombé un Barnes Wallis bouncing bomb contre le mur, et l'eau a vient gushing out, drowning les pauvres bâtards au-dessous. Mère de divin Jesus. Je retourne chez moi, et droit maintenant.'

'Non, non, c'est OK, c'est normal pour ce temps d'année. Restez ici, s'il vous plaît. Nous avons été travaillant très dur pour votre visit. C'est un privilege et un honneur voir vous ici avec nous.'

'Merci. Mais ou sont les autres cyclistes? J'apparais être tout seul. J'ai expecteré beaucoup de competition des autres équipes, mais où sont-ils?'

'Les autres? Ah. J'suis glad que vous avez mentionné ça. J'ai des bon nouveaux pour vous! Vous êtes guaranteé le tricot jaune pour cette jambe du tour de France, parce que plusieurs de votre compatriots ont decidé restez chez leurs et regardez Le Coupe Mondiale instead.'

'Le Coupe Mondiale! Mon dieu! J'ai oublié que c'était sur!'

'Vous avez oublié? Où avez vous été? La lune?'

'Presquement. Sur le spacecraft Mir. C'est horrible, WCs comme les toilettes en Mullingar en 1953, avec le papier de sable, ooooh, sacre brun, et les communications étaient très primitif. Nous avons ecrit à ground control pour instructions, longhand, Basildon Bond, etc. et ils répondrent par smoke-signals, comme le Arapaho. Pas de temps pour idle chit-chat du Coupe Mondiale, je peux dire vous, mate.'

'Ah, puis vous ne voudrez pas avoir entendu! Nous avons arrangé toutes choses pour vous. Les signes en français, les pot-holes sont filled in, pourquoi nous avons even déplacé un roche inconvenient en Carrick.'

'Roche inconvenient? Quel sort de cycliste pensez-vous je suis. Roche est bien passé son prime, il est presque mort. Il n'est pas inconvenient, le pauvre ancien.'

'Roche? Je ne parle pas de Stephen Roche, héro extraordinaire de Carrick, mais au petit roche, un jostling stone ou un pierre-bousculant près du bas d'un column. Il protège le column contre being bashed par les wheels des carriages.'

'Vraiment? Pour moi, et juste pour moi, vous avez déplacé un roche en Carrick? Vous êtes très gentil! Mais c'est très peculière. Vous avez déplacé un roche en une ville où habite le plus celebré cycliste Irlandais, qui est appele Roche! Quel coincidence! Et la ville de Carrick, elle est très jolie, hein?'

'Ah, oui, tres jolie, la plus jolie ville à la bouche du Suir.'

'Et Carrick, c'est un mot irlandais, oui? Qu'est-ce que c'est en français?'

'Carrick? En français? C'est très facile. Le mot français pour Carrick est roche.'

'Je vois. Et vous m'expectez cycler en Le Tour de France en Irlande, moi-même, tout seule, travers une terre en lequel chaque bloody chose est un bloody pierre et le temps consiste seulement de la pluie ordinaire ou la pluie downpour, hein? – C'est un nation de branleurs et branleuses! Complet et utter cons! Au revoir!'

And seeing the last of the would-be competitors for the Tour de France return home, with the Irish leg thereby cancelled, Bord Fáilte fell on its collective knees in thanks that the worst summer in recorded history was not to be broadcast live aound the world. But far more importantly: will the jostling rock of Carrick be returned to its rightful spot?

PREEN!

Good morning and welcome to *PREEN!*, Ireland's newest glossy and most socially discerning magazine! Copies will be distributed FREE to all homes worth £300,000 or more.

Homes worth between £200,000 to £300,000 will be charged £2 per *PREEN!* We will tolerate readers of *PREEN!* from houses worth over £100,000 provided they pay £5 a copy for the privilege of visiting, via our many pages of full-colour photographs, the homes of Ireland's new élite. Newsagents in working-class areas will not be permitted to stock *PREEN!* Special Irish-invented microchip prole-sensors will detect if *PREEN!* is being read by poor people, and will promptly cause it and them to burst into flames.

Not that we are against the poor. Some of our investors are foremost advocates of high taxes to aid such unfortunates, though of course they are not themselves PAYE payers. More importantly, we have our advertisers to consider. Imagine how they might feel if their intimate feminine hygiene products were to be the stuff of idle tittle-tattle from the riff-raff on the bus to Darndale or Kilbarrack.

In order that *PREEN!* visits only the grandest and richest houses in this booming Celtic Tiger wonderland, our editorial policy is the reverse of our British competitors'. They pay the owners of the homes they visit and the marriages they intrude upon. We do the opposite.

You want us to do a spread on your new house, with gold tapped bidets in every room, and leopard-skin wallpaper? Fine; we charge £10,000 a room. You want the wedding of your daughter Zöe, Emma or Chloe to feature in a 14-page spread? You pay by the picture-inch of tulle and back-combed hair appearing in *PREEN!*

BACK! GET BACK! Form an orderly queue there. And stop waving money at me. You'll all make it to *PREEN!* – at the right price, of course. Now, madam, you and your husband have made £20 million pounds from selling mobile phone pouches. Made by slaves in China, bought by you for 3p, sold on at £12. You want *PREEN!* to feature your new seven-acre house on top of the Burren? More than happy to oblige. We can dedicate an entire edition of *PREEN!* for the knock-down price of only £200,000. That is satisfactory? Excellent! So let us begin.

Our tour starts in the one hundred feet by one hundred feet bathroom. Breathtaking! The array of tasteful pastels stretch as far as the eye can see, with even the toothpaste and eyebrow tweezers in matching hues. Very restful. Two car-sized baths, his and hers, carved in ivory. And a perfume-sprayer fills *la salle de bain* with exotic fragrances – attar of roses, Chanel Number Five, eau de cologne and many others pumped from tanks in the attic, controlled by a master-switch beside the WC (which of course will not feature in any of our photographs).

Let me add: You can, for an extra £100,000, have a scratch-&-sniff insert in your issue of *PREEN!* which conjures up the olfactory essence of your dream home for complete and utter strangers. You will? Splendid!

And now *PREEN!* visits the master bedroom – and just look at that bed! The size of Offaly, it is covered in throws from Uzbekistan, Chinese spreads, kilims from Kashmir and prayer-mats from Anatolia. Wide-eyed Victorian dolls with tarantula eyelashes lie in cheerful abandon everywhere, and the west-facing wall is covered in its entirety by a quite breath-takingly wonderful imitation ormolu mirror which, you say, was given to you by your mother – an avid but discerning collector of modern curios.

Splendid! So, for a further £100,000 only we will insert tiny giveaway copies of the mirror in *your* edition of *PREEN!* You'll go for that too? Excellent!

And what a wonderful kitchen! A 20-hob cooker, three electronically controlled fan-ovens, a roasting spit, a barbecue, a dozen eye-level grills, four microwaves, a bonfire for martyring early Christian saints, a special frog de-gutter, a badger-baster, computer-controlled egg-openers and numerous other labour-saving devices, all controlled from a central console! Might I suggest that in the accompanying *PREEN!* text we say that, like all *PREEN!*'s guests, you are an enthusiastic chef and a discriminating gourmet? Excellent!

Now let us open your 10,000 cubic-foot refrigerator which you had DHL'd from California. What splendours! The rare but tasty sealion, of course, occupies much of the space, but look what else is there! Foie gras, haunches of venison, larks' tongues, koala steaks, smoked kangaroo foetus in virgin olive oil, lobsters the size of pit-ponies, 25 different kinds of yoghurt, 47 sorts of fruit ice, 17 varieties of vitamin-enhanced milk, countless mineral waters, and enough champagne to launch the entire US Navy

– Bollinger, Grande Dame, Crystal and Dom Perignon, naturally. But you, of course, drink moderately, work out every morning and read oriental philosophers in your spare time.

We in *PREEN!* believe you. You are a most wonderful person, truly representative of the new Ireland, and that will be £570,000 only.

Banker's order or gold credit cards only, please. Thank you.

PAGES FROM IRISH HISTORY

Remembering '98

In less than a fortnight we shall be into the bicentenary of 1798, and already I get an uneasy feeling, about the simplifications and the glorifications which are on us, as if we have learnt nothing at all about the horrors and the idiot-brutalities of communal violence.

In part the problem is the nature of memory and the requirements of social groups to enjoy a shared and invented past which binds and reassures. This basic need turned the atrocities and the nihilistic insanities of the French revolution into something glorious, a model to be emulated. An entire school of French historiography came into existence to justify what happened during the long dark night into which France descended after the revolution, and which brought flame and war from Moscow to Bantry Bay.

It was the first real world war, and like the later war which enjoyed that name, it had seismic repercussions in Ireland, most of all because of Ireland's deep social instability and its vulnerability to passions and insecurities, which are as closed to us today as those of the poor of Bombay or Calcutta.

We cannot know the minds of the people who took to the pike in Wexford or in Antrim. We cannot know because they probably did not know. All groups are swayed by social forces they do not understand and they are often unaware of.

When we read that in Wexford – of all places – Catholics lived in genuine terror of local Orangemen who, they believed (aided by bogus Orange oaths circulated by Catholic members of the United party) had sworn to wade knee-deep in Catholic gore, we can be sure that this is a society of which we know nothing, nothing whatever.

To present the insurrections of 1798 as a simple rising in pursuit of liberty, equality and fraternity is to ignore the complex and probably incomprehensible realities of the time.

When we read about the pitch-cappings, the floggings, the house-burnings and the murders by yeomanry that took place before the rising, we can be sure that we are looking at a hysterical and dysfunctional society which cannot be judged by the standards of today.

Ballitore, Carnew, Kilcullen, Camolin, Ferns: these blameless peaceful communities were the centres of quite atrocious events. What does it take to pike a man to death? How many times do you stick the pike in? Do you break the ribs, and do you hear them break? Does the victim howl as his innards are penetrated by a steel-tipped wooden lance wielded by a man he has known all his life? Is the pursuit of liberty, equality and fraternity actually the motive for such a deed? Or are we dealing with other forces, before which mortal humans are almost powerless?

Were liberty, equality and fraternity (a splendidly contradictory trinity of concepts) the reason why the glebe house of Mr Burrowes, the Protestant clergyman at Camolin, was torched; why he was shot down after he had offered to surrender to the United men; and why seven of his parishioners, including his 16-year-old son, were piked to death?

Was it philosophic opposition to liberty, equality and fraternity which caused the yeomanry in reply to burn 170 houses, and kill many peasants who came their way? And was it adherence to contrasting philosophical abstractions which caused some yeomanry to stay loyal, and others to desert to the insurgents?

And is it wrong to wish that less, rather than more, of this kind of horror had occurred? Is it wrong to wish that Ireland had paid no attention to the insurrectionary pleadings of the United men, and had remained at peace? Is it wrong to be grateful that many counties did not respond to the plans for revolution? And is it wrong to speculate on what the revolutionaries would have done if they had been successful?

Would they, for example, have instantly introduced a society of liberty, equality and fraternity, justice, peace and plenty – which, oddly enough, never actually happens after revolutions – or would they instead have opted for the Year Zero option, as the French had done, with genocide of the reluctant, the reactionary, the disbelieving?

Or if Bonaparte had landed sufficient forces to impose his will on the millions who wanted nothing to do with wars or revolutions (and what a bloody affair that would have been), would he then have miraculously introduced to Ireland the very kind of society he very conspicuously failed to introduce to any of the many countries he conquered?

Or would thousands of Irish conscripts within a few years not be perishing of frostbite on the road home from Moscow? And will I, yet again, have to endure those dreary witless accusations of 'defending British imperialism' simply for asking such questions?

Probably. No matter. What is certain is that in the coming year we shall hear *Boulavogue* a lot. It is an enchanting tune by a musical genius, Patrick Joseph McCall, and it is a lie. It celebrates how the boys of Wexford at Harrow showed 'Bookey's regiment' how men could fight.

Lieut Bookey and John Donovan from Camolin were isolated from their yeomanry escort – Camolin-men like themselves – near Harrow, and alone and defenceless were knocked off their horses and piked to death by Father Murphy's men – who then went to Bookey's house and burnt it down. To celebrate such a deed in song is pathetic and demented.

Before and after the Famine

No doubt some of you will by this time have experienced the flu' which is currently going the rounds. The body feeling as if it has been roughed up by a combine harvester. The lungs fill up with a strange fluid the colour of ... no, no, I cannot say the colour of what. The brain feels as if it has been hit with a funfair sledgehammer. Thoughts resemble the cerebral processes of grasses. One remembers nothing through the sneezes and the Third Ypres coughing fits. All in all, I finally know what it is to be a veteran of the Great War, aged 101. Horrible.

It takes an extraordinary book to be able to batter through the walls of mucile bovinity which such a flu' induces. Cormac Ó Gráda's *Ireland before and after the Famine* achieved that heroic feat. It is true that much of what I read perished in the vat of sputum which was doing duty as a brain; truer still that much of what I read vanished from my memory as quickly as breath from a razor-blade. Yet nonetheless, Cormac's writing, his lucidity of intellect, were able to penetrate the wet fog of my mind and illuminate undetected, unlit corners.

It is one of the unfailing characteristics of a good mind that it is able to take you by the hand and guide you into areas you would not normally feel at home in. Cormac Ó Gráda's work on the Famine does just that. It is like being in the company of a good pilot or a sound navigator as one passes through the wild waters off an iron-bound coast. One is reassured by an intellectual confidence born of a first-rate brain harnessed to fine scholarship. Even in the depths of the worst individual case of flu' in the history of epidemiology – from which the victim recovered because of a life of extraordinary piety – Cormac's mind and intellectual energy have triumphed.

No doubt most people who have theories about the Famine have never read anything about it since they read Cecil Woodham Smith when they were teenagers. It is still a subject which understandably moves people to anger; and no matter how much virtuous superiority anger bestows upon its owner, it seldom enhances analytical talents. One reassuring feature of Cormac's work is his studied calmness, his unperturbed and imperturbable scholarship. His is a likeable mind. It is a pleasure to be in its company.

It is always good and reassuring to see opinions one is inclined to favour being criticised. Cormac Ó Gráda is particularly good at dissecting the works of revisionist historians of the Famine; being the object of his attentions would sharpen anyone's wits for the fray. The good thing is that one detects no animus in what he says; it is disinterested history and engaged but unpartisan historiography at its best.

One of the most striking qualities of his work is the strangeness of the Ireland he writes about. This Ireland is so unrelated to the Ireland of today that it is clear nobody possesses a knowledge of it through the lore of the family or a sense of their own identity. When one reads a line such as 'the farmyard hen and the duck were contributing more to agricultural value added in 1908 than wheats, oats and potatoes combined, crops which in the early 1840s had accounted for almost half total output,' one realises that Ireland has changed at least twice, unrecognisably, since the Famine. The farmyard hen or duck is not merely extinct in the Ireland of today; so too is the husbandry which went into the raising of fowl and the vast body of lore and veterinarian skill which must have been in existence at that time.

Nothing that we know of from our experience equips us to deal with these times. The lesson should be that the only people equipped to discuss the Famine seriously are its historians. This will not, of course, stop the heated midnight rows about how the British should have done more; should have stopped the export of grain; should have, should have, etc. The point was, they didn't. Why?

My suspicion is that it is impossible to enter the minds of 1840s men and women. Words used then might not mean the same as words used now; indeed, to judge from the mightily pleasant *Pride and Prejudice* on BBC at the moment, the world of the early 19th century is perfectly communicable to us today.

It is not. These are mirages which we take for realities; the reality of Jane Austen's world was that people smelt abominably, had foul teeth and bad breath, relieved themselves into vast unemptied communal chamber pots, wherein resided the goodies deposited by everyone else in the household, and lived lives of crushing, stunning boredom in hideously cold houses surrounded by illiterate, intrusive and dirty servants. You don't get much of that on television, now do you?

Consider one line from Cormac Ó Gráda and pre-Famine Ireland: 'Against the 117 put down to starvation in the 1830s, there were 7,072 drownings, 197 hangings, 3,508 murders, 1,239 deaths from alcoholic excess, 4,349 from burns.'

Now this is truly a mystery world – never mind the intangibles, such as personal hygiene or notions of duty or religious practice or sexual habits, most of which are forever closed to us. We have categories of death here which apparently no longer preoccupy us today. The statistical abstract of 1993 has no category for drownings; 160 years ago, 700 people a year were drowned. Were these suicides? Or was life for an Irish fisherman so appallingly perilous?

About 40 people a year die of burns today, 400 a decade – one tenth the number of such deaths in the 1830s. Quite as striking is the sheer amount of violence in Ireland of the 1830s – more than 350 murders a year, compared to the 20-odd of today. The figure of maybe 200 hangings a year seems, on balance, to be quite low.

The truth is that we *know* nothing of that world. All we can do is grasp at it; and can do no better than to do so in the company of Cormac Ó Gráda's enchanting brain.

The physical force tradition

It is called the physical-force school and it emerged formally and poisonously 150 years ago this week. From the beginning, of course, it was wrongly named: *physical force* is a euphemism for murder. If, from the outset, it had been called the murder-school of Irish independence, no doubt it would have perished within days of coming into existence. But it was not and the heirs of a worthless tradition of murder, which has yielded Ireland nothing in the past century and a half, remain with us still.

The moral basis of the murder-school was delineated pretty well by John Mitchel:

> The vengeance I seek is the righting of my country's wrong, which includes my own. Ireland, indeed, needs vengeance; but this is public vengeance, public justice. England is truly a great public criminal. England! all England, operating through her government; through her organised and effectual public opinion, press, platform, parliament, parliament has done, is doing and means to do, grievous wrong to Ireland. She must be punished; that punishment will, as I believe, come upon her by and through Ireland; and so Ireland will be avenged.

That is as pretty a summation of the psychopathology of the terrorist as you can find anywhere – the personalisation of a political injustice so that ego becomes one with the nation; the demonisation of an entire species, in this case the English; vengeance becomes a therapy and national requirement; and the transformation of political will into a weapon of punishment, designed to do hurt to people, and be morally sure of the rightness of that hurt. It is, of course, a detailed refutation of the Gospels to which most practitioners of the physical-force school have purported to follow; but what matter.

Paradoxically, it was Daniel O'Connell's greatness which enabled the Young Irelanders to make the inroads which they did within the body of Irish nationalism. He was such a towering giant, impassioned, eloquent, brave and the match of any who opposed him, that Irish people could be forgiven for thinking that in his absence, they were doomed to being leaderless helots. In that context, violence was the panacea for the plain man, the man of no property; it was the recourse of the powerless.

It was logically and intellectually wrong. Worse, it suggests a belief in the congenital inferiority of the people of Ireland – that those who lead Ireland and the Irish must necessarily be of lesser mettle than those they must do business with. O'Connell did not believe that. More to the point, he tried to ensure that after his death, others would not believe it.

The Young Irelanders were clearly an attractive and ardent bunch, and dangerously wrong-headed. They themselves did not use violence, and planned no violence

when O'Connell insisted that they conform to the principle of non-violence, enunci-
ated as follows: 'All political amelioration … ought to be sought for, and can be sought
for successfully, only by peaceable, legal and constitutional means, to the utter exclusion of any other,' though this principle did not prohibit 'necessary defence against
unjust aggression on the part of a domestic government or a foreign enemy.'

The problem about the Young Irelanders was that they talked violence; they justified it in the eyes of their uneducated listeners; they larded political language with
violent words, so that political debate became infused with the language of war. The
resonances live on, even amongst the constitutional of today – the warriors of destiny
owe much of what they are to the cabbalistic incantations of the Young Irelanders of
150 years ago.

The journey Fianna Fáil had to make is the journey required of all those who have
dabbled in violence for Ireland. To be constructive, to achieve real progress, to form a
state which reflects the will and aspirations of the Irish people, has required people to
abandon the gun. As I have said on countless occasions before, and no doubt will continue to say into the future, nothing achieved by violent means between 1916 to 1922
could not have been achieved by patient, boring talks.

And that is the charm of violence. Whatever it is, it is not boring. Most young
males who have been in a gunfight find the experience exhilarating. Military forma-
tions create bonds; the death in action of a comrade deepens the grievance and intensifies the emotional commitment to the fray. Bodies call upon bodies; funerals demand
more funerals; and Moloch's appetite grows the more he is fed.

Ordinary people become terrorists – not psychopaths, not the disordered and sad,
not the criminally insane. I have liked most of the IRA members I have met – not
many, it is true, in recent years. And because they call upon a tradition of gun law, few
if any of them feel any remorse for what they have done.

Is that not a terrible thing, knowing what we know about the dreadful things
done by the IRA, that there is no genuine shame over their deeds? Does that not suggest that this is a tradition as intractable and as pathological as anti-semitism in
Germany? No doubt it has not managed the cataclysm of the Holocaust: but what it
has in common with National Socialism is that it suspends the precepts of decency, of
right to life and to livelihood, which lay at the heart of Western civilisation.

Daniel O'Connell knew this – and he knew moreover that his people had only
recently been wooed from the fatal embrace with violence in 1798. That was why he
forced the show-down with the Young Irelanders, to eliminate, once and for all, the
tradition which glorified violence and which studiedly rejected the Sermon on the
Mount. He failed, as we know. Others followed the Young Irelanders – John O'Leary,
Arthur Griffith, Patrick Pearse all cited Thomas Davis as an inspiration. Yet all failed
to achieve what they wanted when using the methods glorified by the Young
Irelanders. Success has come only from using the methods of Daniel O'Connell, outlined 150 years ago this week, and yet remembered imperfectly to this day.

The road to the Somme

Last Saturday the Orangemen of the North were once again celebrating their myths on the 79th anniversary of the opening day of the battle of the Somme.

These myths are not solely of their creation; they are myths which have been subscribed to by default amongst nationalist Ireland and by the Protestants of the Republic. They are myths which have been reinforced too by well-intentioned endeavours by such as Frank McGuinness, who in his attempt to come to terms with the Ulster Protestant identity in his *Observe the Sons of Ulster Marching towards the Somme* has actually helped to buttress myth.

The primary falsehood concerns the nature of the 36th Ulster Division, which was representative not just of the six counties of today's Northern Ireland, not merely of the nine counties of Ulster of the time, but of Irish loyalism generally.

The sacrifices of the ordinary Ulster loyalists of Cavan, Monaghan and Donegal were especially poignant, for they came after it was clear their counties were not fighting to remain in the Union. The Ulster Unionist leadership had agreed to the exclusion of those three counties from the main body of Ulster.

Their future was to lie within a self-governing Ireland; and as fortune would have it, those three counties suffered more heavily proportionately than any of the six counties whose position within the United Kingdom was to be guaranteed.

The 36th did not draw recruits from Ulster alone. Its officers came from every part of Ireland, as the appalling casualty lists in the *Irish Times* were to indicate throughout the month of July 1916, racking little Protestant communities everywhere.

In the coming years, Protestant Ireland in the Republic was to keep secret its grief on that date: to commemorate a day marked by northern Orangemen might have seemed disloyal to the state they lived within.

And so in the absence of public ceremony, public memory of July 1st being a day of tragedy also for southern Ireland faded too.

It was not just the southern Protestant officer-class which lost vastly on that day – ordinary loyalists from the southern counties were serving as plain soldiery in the Ulster Division.

Over 140 men of the Dublin and Wicklow Loyal Volunteers had marched to the recruiting office in Dublin to offer their services when war broke out in 1914, and were enlisted in the 9th Inniskilling Fusiliers serving with the Ulsters.

These men truly have vanished from popular memory, yet no outcome to the war could possibly serve them in any narrow sense. They were loyalists; and out of loyalty served. One quarter of them were to die on July 1st alone.

Their deeds, their feats, their fates on that day are largely unknown, consumed on the terrible slopes before Thiepval Wood or merely vanished in the deep fogs of forgetfulness which have moved in cloudbanks over our history.

A voice calls through that cloudbank – it is of a dying solider of the Inniskillings calling for his friend – 'Billy Gray, Billy Gray, will you not come to me?'

And we get glimpses through the swirling mists of the remnants of the Fermanagh and Donegal Battalion gathering at the Crucifix in the heart of the German positions, under the leadership of Warren Peacocke from Innishannon in Cork, later to be murdered in his home by the IRA.

And somewhere in the midst of the carnage of that day were the men of the southern contingent – almost all of them Protestants and loyalists, and willing to serve their King to the same measure that, not long before, fellow-Irishmen had been ready to serve their Republic.

In all 28 of the southern volunteers serving with the 9th Inniskilling Fusiliers fell in action that July day in 1916. How they died we cannot know. They lay amid the carpet of young bodies, of flesh and bone in the lake of human blood, which covered the German strong-point of Schwaben Redoubt.

It must have seemed to the participants that this was the nadir of European civilisation; except, as we all know, it was not.

News of what had happened to their young men came at harvest time in Ireland. The local postmaster, rather than simply delivering the War Office telegram, would often arrange for a clergyman to take the terrible news to the family.

Philip Orr in his *The Road to the Somme* records the recollections of those at home when the worst was known:

> My mother and I was lapping a field of hay beyond Bleary school … My mother saw the minister up at the house … She just looked steady at him without blinking and said, 'Is it Ted (her brother) or Willie (my father)?' He said, 'I'm sorry to say it's Willie'. She walked along the head-rig back to the house, her back as straight as that of a girl of nineteen.

The news was brought back to Wicklow Protestants that July of the loss of their young men in the battle. These were not sons of gentry but plain farming sons of plain farming folk.

One of those who received the news was Richard Fox, then living at Winegates House. His son, Private William H. Fox, 23771, 9th Inniskilling Fusiliers, had been killed in action somewhere on Thiepval Ridge. He has no known grave.

Though Willie was raised in Winegates, the Fox family home was nearby, in Calary, Kilmacanogue. Then, in common with most Wicklow Protestants, they were loyalists. Loyalism, like the memory of the Wicklow Volunteers, is now all but gone from the county, lingering discreetly maybe to lodge in the private recollections of the past.

But the Foxes are not loyalists now. Johnny Fox TD was the great-nephew of Willie who died on the first day of the Somme; and it was on July 1st, 1995, the 79th

anniversary of his death, that Willie's great-grandniece Mildred was declared elected
TD for the county from which he departed to serve his king and country 80 years ago.

Easter 1916

I believe the Easter Rising was an unmitigated evil for Ireland. Virtually everything to
do with the Rising was horrible, from the homicidal manipulations of the secret society, the Irish Republican Brotherhood, through the events themselves, to the hideous
aftermath of the 'Anglo-Irish war', the civil war, bloody partition, and a legacy of violence and murderous, clandestine covens which haunt us to this day.

No doubt I am mad for deploring the carnage and the suffering and the agony of
1916, all of which, it can probably be argued, enriched Irish life enormously, as did
Solohead Beg, Kilmichael, Bloody Sunday, the destruction of the Four Courts, the
GPO, the Custom House, Beal na mBlath, etc. etc.

I do not see this. I genuinely cannot understand what so many think useful and
historically justifiable. Where I see nothing but horror and destruction, many, perhaps
most of you, see glory, heroism, dedication and the building of a nation.

That was certainly the theme taken by those who organised the celebration of the
1916 Rising five years ago, as if the Irish nation had not existed before 1916, and had
not repeatedly and unfailingly democratically registered its desire for self-government
far more persuasively and more authoritatively than the odd bands of gunmen and
unelected idealists, cited and so lauded in the 1916 Proclamation, ever managed.

There are points I can concede from the beginning. Yes, the volunteers of 1916
were brave, but that was not unusual at that time. European civilisation was being torn
apart by a surfeit of bravery. There was barely a nation in Western Europe which did
not call upon its men to exhibit bizarre, almost wicked, levels of heroism. That the
men and women of 1916 should have been capable of comparable deeds of gallantry
merely makes 1916 part of the lunacy of the period. It does not make it more laudable.

Although much of what happened in the early stages of the Rising was virtually
without any form of bravery, as the term is normally understood, but full of jittery
homicide. Can it really have been the intentions of the planners of the Rising that
impoverished carters should have been summarily shot for not handing over the means
of earning their livelihood in order that insurgents could use them as barricades?

Did the murder of the unarmed police constable Lahiffe by Countess Markevicz
in Stephen's Green constitute a violation of the plan, or was it its quintessence? And
do admirers of that bloodthirsty woman applaud her response to this disgusting deed?
('I shot him, I shot him,' she cried, jumping up and down for joy). And the unarmed
DMP man, shot dead at Dublin Castle in the first few minutes of the Rising – does

not his cold-blooded killing by the Irish Citizen Army suggest that a precedent was being set, which would be followed, and was and is?

The beginning was matched by the end. The last time I wrote about this, I referred to the killings of captured British soldiers – mostly Dublin Fusiliers – at the back of the GPO shortly before the Rising collapsed and I was bitterly criticised. Yet the shootings certainly seem to have taken place, with the details appearing in the first edition of this newspaper after the Rising. That these killings should have been forgotten is not surprising. When people get all weepy about Countess Markevicz, do they remember that she killed a defenceless man in cold blood in a park where now *she* has a statue and he is unremembered?

This amnesia is, perhaps, not surprising. Amnesia is spread like a blanket over the entire affair. Andrew Barry of the 10th Dublin Fusiliers, which had the melancholy duty of suppressing the Rising, told an interviewer in the 1980s that one of his fellow-soldiers later that year had been an insurgent in the Rising, and that: 'he and his fellow-volunteers did not know they were participating in a Rising when they joined what they thought were regular weekend exercises that Easter.'

And this is an aspect of the Rising which is seldom mentioned; when writers tear-fully report of the small band of men who that Easter marched out to take on an empire, it is grand, glorious stuff; but what they do not add is that most of these men had no notion that this was what their leaders had planned. The Irish Volunteers had been called into existence, after all, to protect the lawful gains of the Home Rule Bill; few if any of them joined with the intention of starting a war in the centre of Dublin.

And that is the kernel of my objection to the 1916 Rising – that in all its essentials it was profoundly anti-democratic. The Rising took place within a democracy in which not a single insurgent had bothered to stand for election. The people who were to be insurgents mostly did not know they were to be insurgents until they reported for manoeuvres (which were tolerated by the authorities of Dublin Castle in a fashion I think would have barely been emulated by the insurgents' gallant allies in Belgium).

And, of course, the Rising was a dismal failure … none of the aims were met then, or for decades. A partitioned Ireland, in a condition of perpetual hostility for 40 years, came into existence. The Treaty of 1922 gave little more than had been achieved by John Redmond in 1914. And most enduringly of all, the cult of the gun became sanctified within Irish political life.

All this seems so obvious yet I am accounted a traitorous fool for so saying. I am clearly insane and, like all madmen, am quite convinced I am right. (I am, I am, he cries, as he is led away, sticking straws in his hair. *I am*.)

Michael Collins

Michael Collins is, of course, back in the news again thanks to a film which enjoys a highly selective guest-list. I have not seen the film, belonging as I do to a tiny, tiny band which detests the deeds and legacy of Michael Collins. When I see it I will have to pay for the privilege, but I do know already that the film treats Collins as a hero.

He was no hero in my book. He organised murder and was unable to put back that genie of homicide in the bottle which he had uncorked. We should now be asking hard questions about its originator, and whether it was necessary for him and his generation to resort to violence.

I firmly believe not. And while imposing opinions and values from 1996 on events of 1919, when Collins's squad began its murders, is of only limited use in assessing people in their own time, it is absolutely vital in considering whether such people should be regarded as heroes by our own standards. By those standards, Michael Collins was a frightful man.

Gerald O'Nolan, of Limerick, disputes Garret FitzGerald's criticism of the Collins film for its allegation that the leaders of the Rising were roughed up. He quotes two sources in rebuttal, neither of which says that the leaders were roughed up.

One refers generally to indignities, the other says that Tom Clarke was stripped naked in the grounds of the Rotunda Hospital. No other source says this – none whatsoever – though so many people associated with the Rising gave their view of events in the following years.

Yet even if the allegations were correct, they do not justify murder. Virtually nothing does. To resort to the taking of life requires special circumstances – and those circumstances were not justified when Collins began to send out his gunmen.

This is not to justify the crass and blundering idiocies of the British Government, nor the brutalities and the homicides of its agents. But, after all, nobody is making films saying what fine fellows they were: and whatever he was – and that certainly includes charming – Michael Collins was not a fine fellow. He introduced to Dublin life the rule of the 20-year-old killers – and few things are as terrifying as the righteous murders of a vigintocracy.

The first murder by The Squad occurred eight months before the Black and Tans and Auxiliaries arrived in Ireland. It was of Det. Sgt. Patrick Smith, from Cavan, who was fatally wounded outside his house in Millmount Avenue, Drumcondra. He was a married man and a father of seven, his oldest child being 17 years old.

He had just got off the tram at Drumcondra Bridge when he was shot by several men. The first person to his side was his 17-year-old son, who dragged him into the family home, bleeding profusely. Patrick Smith's wife was away on holiday and his children had to cope with this appalling deed alone. His eight-year-old son ran after the assassins but they were gone, embarking upon a career which would see their cold-blooded murders exalted and praised, and their victims forgotten.

What had Patrick 'The Dog' Smith done to deserve this treatment? He was a policeman, to be sure. But he did not belong to a death squad. He was a member of G Division of the Dublin Metropolitan Police, and did his duty – and merely because we might oppose the execution of such duties does not mean we should murder those we disapprove of.

Once we admit that principle for ourselves, then we admit it as acceptable for others – such as the later murders of 'IRA men' by A, B and C Specials.

I am not saying the security forces were not killing people at that time. But such killings were in spontaneous and occasional affrays, few in number. Times and tempers were heated; what was not needed was warming of those tempers by cold-blooded murder, exemplified by the attack on a group of soldiers attending church service in Fermoy, in which four were shot.

The Most Revd. Dr. Browne, the Catholic Bishop of Cloyne, said of this murderous attack on church-goers: 'I read of no circumstance in the case to mitigate the savage atrocity of the crime. The little band of soldiers had given no cause of provocation … (and) were proceeding in an orderly and inoffensive manner to their religious Sunday service … It was a fearful tragedy, a savage crime, which cried for vengeance from God …'

It was after this atrocity, and the subsequent sacking of Fermoy by maddened soldiery, that the British committed the cardinal and idiotic blunder of outlawing Sinn Féin and suppressing Dáil Éireann. Collins responded by sending out The Squad to murder Det. Daniel Hoey, who had participated in a raid for documents on Sinn Féin's headquarters.

A bachelor who lived in Great Brunswick Street (now Pearse Street) Station, he had just returned from a holiday at his home near Edenderry. He popped into Furlong's shop in Townsend Street and bought himself a glass of milk. As he walked back to his quarters he was ambushed, his killers shooting him through the throat, the chin and the heart.

Murder was spreading through the land. Possibly the momentum was inescapable; whatever it did, the IRA campaign of insurgency did not hasten, but rather postponed, the process of talks, of peace. At the time when poor young Hoey lay dying round the corner from this newspaper, the British Government's Irish Committee was finishing its final report, which it then published.

Another 18 calamitous months had to pass before the report became the basis of the Treaty. As the report said: 'In (our) judgment it is essential, now that the (Great) War is over, *and the peace conference has dealt with so many analogous questions in Europe, that the government should make a sincere attempt to deal with the Irish question once and for all.*' (My italics)

Instead, futile, bloody war followed, whose primary victim was Ireland and its people. Those who brought about that war should not be lightly judged for the calamity they visited on their own land – not least because The Squad's heirs are with us still, and murdering still.

Michael Collins, *the movie*

Just as we hear that Neil Jordan invented a scene in the film *Michael Collins* because of its amusingly murderous resonances with the present Northern Troubles, the censor Sheamus Smith decides to create a special certificate to enable children to watch this filmic anthem to rib-tickling homicide. Dear God in heaven, tell me that I am not alone in finding this bizarre and sickening.

The scene concerned shows four detectives, recently arrived from Belfast to make good the losses suffered by the Dublin Metropolitan Police, gathered in the grounds of Dublin Castle. One of them, MacBride, orders all Collins's associates to be lifted that night. A Dublin detective, Ned Broy (later in life to be de Valera's Garda Commissioner, but in the film to be tortured to death by the British), remarks that it will not be simple.

The four detectives get in the car, and MacBride remarks to them: 'A bit of Belfast efficiency is what they need.' The driver starts the motor, and the car blows up.

Neil Jordan now acknowledges that this is fiction and is based, not on the Troubles of 75 years ago, but on the more recent ones. 'You didn't think it was funny? No?' he asked Philip Johnston from the *Daily Telegraph* adding: 'I did. Look. It was meant to be ironic.'

And this funny and ironic destruction of the lives of Northern policemen, with direct and clearly-stated associations with the murder of Northern policemen over the past 25 years, has been given a special certificate in the Republic to enable children to see it. Do we wonder that Northern unionists look on this State and this society with perplexed hostility, that such a frivolous treatment of the assassination of Northern policemen, clearly a metaphor for more recent murders, should be in a film which has been granted a certificate specifically invented so that as many children as possible imbibe its fabrications?

Yet the censor himself admits that the film contains 'scenes depicting explicit cruelty and violence along with some crude language not normally associated with the Parental Guidance classification.' Well now, well now: and what if some unionist filmmaker was to make a film about how the B Specials 'defended Ulster' from the IRA in 1922 and included scenes of explicit cruelty and violence, and also threw in an entertaining though anachronistic reference to killing members of the Irish security forces?

How would the Dublin Government feel if that 'major cinematic event' (as Sheamus Smith has described the Collins film) was to be given a special certificate in

Northern Ireland so that the maximum number of children in the North could be misled and misinformed by its brutal fictions?

Neil Jordan can make as many inaccurate films as he wants about Irish history. That is his right. But is it the purpose of the Censor's Office in this land, the very office that decided that uniquely in Europe the people of the Republic should not see *Natural Born Killers*, to ensure that as many children as possible in this Republic are exposed to Jordanian distortions?

And not just any distortion; the myths of nationalistic violence – and that includes unionist violence, which in its way is every bit as nationalistic, as foul and even more indiscriminate – are powerful engines today.

No doubt it accords with some general consensus within the Republic that a film about Michael Collins, notwithstanding a container-load of fictions, should be given special treatment, *The Song of Bernadette* of our times. On the Shankill Road, they will no doubt make certain judgments about a society which creates a particular dispensation for a film containing so many patently republican falsehoods.

Film does not lend itself to the complexity of Irish history. It has recently emerged that Dawson Bates, the first Northern Minister for Home Affairs (and widely regarded by modern historians, and indeed by myself, as a deep-dyed, anti-Catholic bigot), in 1922 infuriated Orange lodges and the Ulster Unionist Association by appointing two Southern Catholics as senior officers within the new RUC, the command of which contained 46 Protestants and 12 Catholics.

Bates defended the appointment of Catholics over the legendary horrible, and I suspect murderous, DI John Nixon (who had the backing of the Orange Order), of whom Bates said: 'He has shown a strong party feeling which is unbecoming in a police officer … He has allowed the feeling to develop that there is only one law – that for the Protestants, and in consequence, the Protestant hooligan element is allowed to interpret in its own fashion the laws of the land.'

Nixon had accused the numerous Catholic officers in the RUC of being Sinn Féin supporters, though for the most part they were vehemently anti-IRA. But he was proved right in one case – that of former civil servant Pat Stapleton, who was not merely a Sinn Féin supporter but a spy for Michael Collins. One night, Stapleton vanished with 14 files from the office of the North's military adviser.

What is interesting about Stapleton, a Falls Road Catholic and ex-soldier, apart from what happened to him afterwards – for he seems to have disappeared completely – is that he was able to steal the files because he was a member of the A Specials. The myths most of us have absorbed about this time would have ruled out the possibility of an openly nationalist Falls Road Catholic ever being allowed in the Specials, yet it happened. A bit of Belfast efficiency, no doubt. Truth is stranger than fiction: but when it comes to tribal myth, fiction is always preferable.

I've seen Michael Collins

What can one say about the creatures who run the publicity machine for Warner's, the distributors of the film, *Michael Collins?* Those people who read this column will be aware that I dislike Michael Collins's deeds with an overpowering intensity.

They were necessary only to those who wanted a violent resolution to this island's problems. No such violent resolution is possible. He used violence because he wanted to use violence. He and the Irish Republican Brotherhood did not want simple independence, negotiated patiently and peacefully, and with the democratic approval of the Irish people. He wanted to win a war, having helped start the war, and when trying to halt it, it consumed him.

I deplore his wasted life, his wasted genius, and the moral contamination he spread amongst those he raised and trained to do the vile work of taking human life. But I am aware that I am in a minority, and a much-despised minority too. No matter. But surely Warner's are not so afraid of the opinion of one single despised journalist that, alone of the people who have written about the Collins film – on the basis of the script and my own knowledge of Collins's life – that I should not be invited to the press screening? Ah well. No matter again.

I finally got to see it the other day. Insofar as Neil Jordan and the fine people in Warner's actually give a fig about what I think of the film, I have bad news for them. I think it is magnificent.

I was unable to leave the cinema at its end, so profoundly moved and saddened was I; and I can understand why Neil Jordan has been so personally offended by criticism of the film in Ireland and in Britain. It is a film which shows his passionate commitment to the subject, to the film, to Ireland, and, I believe, to peace.

Many people have remarked on the fictions which occur in the film, and some of them indeed are risible. Abbreviations and contradictions are inevitable in film-making, but there is no excuse for having Ned Broy tortured to death in 1920 when he had another 50 years to live; and I disliked the characterisation of the DMP as gun-happy brutes who tortured their captives and maltreated the injured of 1916 – the kicking of the injured James Connolly by a detective, and the free use of the abusive epithet 'Fenian' by Catholic policemen seems to be simply plain wrong.

But how much more error have I seen in other films, and not realised it?

Possibly film-makers so often engage in such fictive reductionism that they simply take it for granted. And it would be wrong to judge the film purely by those errors which would only be spotted by an Irish audience, especially when each fiction has been contrived in order to convey a more generalised truth. So that though de Valera did not have a direct hand in organising the ambush in which Collins died, in a broader sense responsibility for the Civil War fell so heavily upon his actions and his decisions, that to a degree it can fairly – and filmically – also be said that responsibility for the details of the Civil War must fall upon his shoulders too.

And I detested too the whimsical disposal of four Northern policemen in a car-bomb; their deaths brought gales of laughter in the cinema where I saw the film. For this film has contemporary resonances, though Neil Jordan might not have been consciously fully aware of them: and no doubt the people chuckling with such gusto beside me at the deaths of four bluenose Peelers were probably unaware of what they were doing. I can guarantee that such visceral amusement would not have been evinced if four men so murdered were members of our own Garda Siochána.

But Neil Jordan does not treat other IRA killings so mirthfully, and the slaughter of the Bloody Sunday morning was performed before a silent and appalled audience in my cinema. Nobody could doubt the true horror of such deeds; and though when writing about the screenplay I derided the juxtaposition of Collins's nocturnal conversations with Kitty Kiernan through the brilliantly, brutally filmed breakfast-time massacre, in filmic terms it works – which possibly explains why Neil Jordan makes films and lives in Sorrento Terrace, and I write this and live in Phibsboro (where some of the film, I was happy to see, was shot).

Michael Collins is first of all a deeply powerful movie; firing-squad executions are so commonplace in film that only a rare and distinctive talent can convey anew what a true horror the executions of the 1916 leaders actually were, especially to someone like myself, who detests the profoundly anti-democratic instincts and motives of those behind the 1916 Rising. Neil Jordan manages this superbly. These scenes are graphic without being voyeuristic, and set a visual standard which Neil Jordan maintains throughout the film.

For *Michael Collins* is ravishingly shot, with so many scenes exquisitely and memorably composed, especially the two shots involving Harry Boland and Collins. The Dublin street scenes are utterly brilliant – wet, grey, dirty, Dublin in the rain, Dublin in the doorways, Dublin with paupers and beggars and shining cobbles – Dublin as it has never been filmed before. Real Dublin.

All this said, *Michael Collins* is myth, as Michael Collins himself was myth. This film adds to the mythology, to which I do not subscribe. Quite the reverse. But I genuinely believe that nobody would be recruited for violence by this film, which ends with the despairing slide towards civil war and the enduring divisions which result from violence. Collins was consumed by the beast he helped create; and it was not violence which gave the people of the Republic of Ireland their freedom, but their willpower.

But here I go, sniping at Collins again – played, I should add, with humour, gravitas, passion and often brilliance by Liam Neeson. He deserves an Oscar for this quite wonderful performance. And I was not surprised at the name of the actor given the job of playing Michael Collins's killer – a fellow by the name of Myers.

Typical.

SOME PEOPLE

Discovering Patrick O'Brian

There are certain days, certain moments in those days, which become etched in the memory. They are stored there ineradicably until one faces the appointment with cold clay. They vary in the order of magnitude, these moments. Some might constitute a family calamity, others a moment of pure and uncontrollable joy, and others again something quite trivial, yet which lingers with fierce loyalty: the playground fall in childhood, a night spent trying to sleep in Heathrow, a drunken binge in Belfast.

Somewhere in that spectrum of importance rests the day on which I came across the novels of Patrick O'Brian. Now obviously the discovery of his works does not bear comparison with a family disaster in terms of importance; and nor does it compare with any of those life-transforming moments associated with the discovery that one has actually found a life-partner. But short of that, the moment when I placed a hand on Patrick O'Brian's novel, *The Master and Commander* is incomparably one of the most memorable in my entire life. I say it is memorable simply because I remember it with quite shocking clarity. It was in a bookshop in Belfast. I picked up *Master and Commander*, contemplated it briefly, and for no reason which I was aware of then and can discern now, put it down and chose instead a boxed collection of the first three of the O'Brian series of novels about Jack Aubrey and Stephen Maturin.

It makes no sense that I should have chosen to buy three such books. I had liked the C.S. Forester Hornblower novels in a diffident sort of way, and I had no reason to believe that Patrick O'Brian's would be any different. Logic and common sense should have indicated that I merely try a small sample of O'Brian, but I did not. I bought the lot, went home, opened *Master and Commander* and there, from page one, I was an addict for life.

In the early hours of the following morning I blessed the providence which had steered my hand towards the boxed three-volume set, for had I not another Patrick O'Brian novel to turn to, I should doubtlessly have gone down to the bookshop and smashed my way in to get my hands on the next volume, *Post Captain*. So dawn rose with me engaged deeply in that novel, sleepy but unable to sleep, avid to read but too tired to do so with clarity. Finally, two hours sleep, and up again to Patrick O'Brian, and oh blessed relief, the third volume was to hand when I had finished *Post Captain*.

Unbelievably, *HMS Surprise* was even better that its two precursors. It is quite simply a masterpiece, one of the great triumphs of narrative skill in the English language of recent times. I finished it at two in the morning, sleepless, hungry and forlorn as an orphan. O'Brian had created a complete and entrancing world in which I had spent most of the previous two days. The characters in it had become my friends, the events part of my own life. The great feat of fiction, of transference of the reader from outside the narrative to being a silent witness within it, had been achieved more completely than ever in my experience, apart perhaps from the odd Dickens master-piece.

Departure from that unfolding world caused a kind of bereavement, of loss. It was as if real friends had gone from my life. I was unable to sleep. So I decided to return to the three novels and the friends I had made there; and on their third acquaintance, they were better, more rewarding friendships that they had been after a first reading, and better novels by far; cleverer, more skilful, more subtle, and infinitely more wise than I had suspected. Craft, guile, humour, humanity, brilliant narrative skill, a deep understanding of sexual and of platonic love, and that essential ingredient to a great novel, the ability to engage the reader through the chaff any plot will require, were combined with immense subtlety and wisdom.

On the face of it the O'Brian novels are about the lives of two friends, Jack Aubrey and Stephen Maturin, in the British Navy during the Napoleonic Wars, and in a way this has been their undoing, because they have been assumed to have been war novels, which is rather like saying that Waugh's War Trilogy is about war; well yes it is, *but* …

The two men make improbable friends: Stephen Maturin, a former member of the United Irishmen, a proponent of Irish and Catalan independence, a brilliant and at times chillingly ruthless intelligence agent, a physician, a linguist, a naturalist and a philosopher: Jack Aubrey, an English naval officer, brilliant at sea and a blundering halfwit on land, devoted to his wife Sophie but much given to little peccadilloes in the pelvic line when on foreign shores, without a single political thought in his amiable brain, and quite incapable of the labyrinthine duplicity which governs much of Stephen's life.

All they appear to have in common is a love of music; through music they meet, and music appears as a constant motif through the novels. But their friendship is one sustained by love, and the music is the equivalent to the sexual act; when they play their duets, that is when their minds and their bodies are most perfectly attuned. They achieve a clarity of understanding more perfect than that they would normally expect with their respective wives, who make rare, too rare, but deeply rewarding appearances in the novels: (Stephen's wife Diana Villiers has more sexual charisma than any woman I have encountered in fiction since Gwendolen Harleth in *Daniel Deronda*: I often plan to visit her when Stephen is away on a long cruise).

Mystifyingly Patrick O'Brian's novels have never sold well. It is quite baffling because they are superbly reviewed by serious writers: his admirers include A.S. Byatt, Iris Murdoch, T.J. Binyon. Interestingly enough Charlton Heston is a mad O'Brian enthusiast and does not confine that enthusiasm to a literary collection: he buys the superb originals by Geoff Hunt which are used on the front covers of all fifteen novels published to date.

The latest Patrick O'Brian novel, the superbly named *Nutmeg of Consolation*, is to be published on February 18th. Take my advice. Go to your bookseller and order him or her, at gunpoint if necessary, to order the complete O'Brian canon, and opening up before you will be a world of characters quite as real as those you know personally: Stephen and Jack, Sophie and Diana, and all the myriad minor but nonetheless believable personalities will become part of your own lives, in much the way that Mr Micawber and Pip and Barkus and Sydney Carton and Scrooge and Fagin remain with you for ever. The creation of real people who permanently inhabit the imaginations of those who read about them is the mark of great literature: it is the mark of Patrick O'Brian.

Captain Jack Aubrey and Dr Stephen Maturin

In the recent BBC television play, *A Breed of Heroes*, set in 1971, a British army officer on duty in the North is seen lying on his bed reading a book. The book was the newly-published *Master and Commander* by Patrick O'Brian.

The programme was prompted by the 25th anniversary of the outbreak of violence in the North, and was transmitted the very week that *The Commodore*, the very latest in the series of Patrick O'Brian novels, was published.

We are assured by experts that the 25th year of the Troubles will see an end to those Troubles and that equally the Patrick O'Brian series must soon come to an end also.

To which one can only reply, no doubt: and then add, what, pray, does one mean by the word 'soon'?

These things are relative, as, I recall, Jack Aubrey replies to his friend Stephen Maturin in *The Commodore* when Maturin declares that he is not a strategician, or even a reasonable naval tactician. This is a joke, which all O'Brian fans will appreciate, old though the joke is.

It is a joke which, like those which circulate in the wardrooms where so much of the O'Brian novels are set, can be repeated and repeated and repeated among those who love the stories.

These jokes serve as reminders of the vast and complex world which Patrick O'Brian has created in the near-score of books which make up the Aubrey-Maturin series; and as reminders, they are as powerful and as redolent as smells or snatches of music.

We smile with familiarity, with joy. Here is a world we know, created in the greatest continuous work of literary endeavour in the English language since the Waverley novels.

It is a world O'Brian enthusiasts inhabit from novel to novel, in which that other world – the troublesome, noisome world in which we have to make a living – occasionally intrudes. That O'Brian world has now reached such a state of conclusion, of definitiveness, that it is clear some reviewers think it now Saturday night. And on the sabbath he will rest.

I doubt it. The man is so full of energy, of vigour, of mental sharpness that although he is 81 years old there is no reason to believe that his creative qualities will be blunted or reduced by the immediate years ahead.

These things, as we have agreed, are relative. He is far, far sharper, far cleverer, far more inventive still than P.G. Wodehouse was in his sprightly sixties and Wodehouse wrote on until he was into his nineties.

For those who have not heard of this series of novels, the setting is this: two men, an English sea-captain by the name of Jack Aubrey, and a physician called Stephen Maturin, half-Irish, half-Catalan, befriend one another in the early stages of the Bonaparte wars.

Stephen was a United Irelander and remains a fierce anti-Bonapartist: Jack is a Tory. Both are musicians, each brilliant in his respective professional sphere.

It is an improbable friendship from the outset. Now, after nearly 17 novels, it is now probably the most powerful testimony in fiction in the English language to the love and loyalty which can bind two deeply heterosexual men.

O'Brian is Irish and writes in English, though his first language was Irish.

He is mentioned in no dictionary or anthology of Irish writers, perhaps because he has offended some nationalist canon in centring his tales on the British navy at the time of the Napoleonic wars.

But the more that I think about Patrick, the more I realise that he is not so much Irish or English or even English-speaking as maritime. The sea is the greatest nation of all, and Patrick is its noblest and most prolific laureate.

This essential truth is easy to miss, simply because so many other truths exist at different levels in his novels – the truths of love, of sex, of betrayal, of music, of science, medicine and navigation.

Yet always, there is the sea, the inescapable, inevitable sea, the sea as a fierce, fierce enemy and most obliging of friends, a sea on which a ship must be steered at all times, its sails worked, its bilges pumped, its hands fed.

It is a world of constant toil and threat and uncertainty, on which only the expert, the diligent and the lucky survive.

That between man and the sea is the ultimate relationship. It is without certainty; the balmy and courteous ocean of one day is a maddened killer the next. The conquered next day becomes the conqueror, the slave the emperor. Nothing can be assumed or taken for granted.

Patrick O'Brian and his characters belong to the greatest nation, the universal nation, the nation of the maritime. Few critics have dwelt on this because they fear the description might put people off.

It would certainly put me off. I detest sailing vessels, complicated knots, bizarre and insane rigging howling in a sou'wester.

But this is to misread O'Brian. You do not have to understand anything about Scottish monarchs to appreciate Macbeth; you can share my loathing of the sea, yet still adore the sea-novels of Patrick O'Brian.

For they utterly transcend the nation in which they are set. The last time I wrote about Patrick O'Brian – and I have been writing about him for the best part of two decades – I compared him to Joyce and Proust in the intensity with which he inhabits and writes about his fictional world. I will not retreat from that comparison.

I will go further. I believe in one hundred years' time Patrick O'Brian will be finally seen for what he is – one of the greatest writers in English of the 20th century.

A word of advice. All the people who have on my advice started reading the novels are now addicts, but those who began the series out of sequence agree. You should start at the beginning, with *Master and Commander*.

And for those who have been waiting for this moment for a year: rejoice.

The Commodore is upon us.

Robert Zimmerman

HERE we go again, head into the lion's mouth, into the valley of death charged the six hundred etc. but the reflection which assailed me as I walked down Grafton street the other day was so powerful that I must unburden myself of it before I die of it.

The reflection was prompted by two buskers, if that is the right word to describe people who uninvited bring misery to others and expect payment in return. One of them was pre-woman adult, as I am told teenage girls on certain American campuses must now be referred to, and was singing *Blowing in the Wind*. A few doors away a post-adolescent male was doing something complicated and laborious with his nasal passages; for this too he expected financial return, though it was by no means clear if his task had tune or purpose or was no more than a set of improvised noises vaguely reminiscent of a camel giving birth to a grand piano with the lid up.

I passed on with a set face. There was one person responsible for this phenomenon, now to be beheld in virtually every city in the western world, and, I fear, increasingly in the old communist world, where things, I should have thought, were already bad enough. One person, Bob Dylan.

Or Robert Zimmerman, as he once was and I wish to heaven he had remained. Zimmerman is German for room-man, or chamber-manservant. Long generations of impoverishment and famine followed the Zimmermans throughout their careers in roomservantry, for the moment they opened their mouths, they were fired, so terrible was the noise they uttered.

Occasionally they found employers who were sufficiently deaf not to hear most of the raucous, nasal din, the aural equivalent to fingernails being torn out by the roots on a particularly resourceful black-board, and saintly enough to forgive whatever remnants of noise did escape their deafness. But even they were not saintly enough to forgive the meaningless gibberish which passed for language which the Zimmermans were inclined to shape out of the menagerie of whines and sinus-clearings which did the service of vocal chords in the Zimmerman family even before there were zimmers to wait on.

It was worse than gibberish; it was portentous, pretentious gibberish. Even the most saintly of deaf employers could tolerate the dreadful Zimmerperson noise: what they could not bear was the widely unjustified affectation of deep wisdom.

In dire poverty the Zimmermans went to America. They weren't even allowed in steerage, but were towed on a raft at some distance so that their dreadful keening and ceaseless preachy drones could not be heard by the rest of the passengers. On one occasion the wind shifted and the first class passengers on the portside were treated to a complete night of Zimmersound; when dawn broke, the ship's crew found that part of the ship deserted, the passengers having slipped over the side in order to swim to America in peace and quiet.

Every now and then the Zimmermans were allowed on board to be fed by a stone-deaf stoker, and to clean the heads – the price of their passage – while everybody else squatted on the raft. It was a complicated change-over needless to say, superintended by the stone-deaf stoker who was also, alas, a monoglot Lascar, with at one stage all of the Zimmerfolk on one rope halfway to the raft and the ship's complement halfway back to the ship on the other. It was an exhausted little Lascar at the end of that, I can tell you, and casualties were high on both sides. The Zimmermans arrived in the new world depleted, and even more unpopular than they had been in the old.

Fifty years ago this year, a new and deadly Zimmerman came into this world, with the full repertoire of Zimmerness, only more so. But he had one brilliant idea in his early youth. It was to cease being a Zimmerman, which tended to give the game away, and to be a Dylan instead. Dylan as in Thomas, with echoes of idyll and sylvan and other poetic resonances, so that people ceased to shout, look out, here comes a Zimmerman, let's scram.

And for reasons which have so far escaped the understandings of science, the renamed Zimmerman became hugely popular for doing something for which his forebears in Europe would have been thrown to wild dogs (and frequently were), namely 'singing' in public 'songs' of his own 'composition'. These whining dirges on occasion had, however, one merit: some of them had good tunes which could be diagnosed through their sinusitic clutter by skilled musicians using techniques not dissimilar to the skills of an astronomer making out distant features of the universe with a radio telescope.

We have now had, I learn, nearly three decades of Zimmerman balladry. Funny. It seems longer. But now it is Bob's 50th birthday, and I too would like to give him a birthday present. It is a piece of advice. Stop.

Jeremy Addis and Books Ireland

Books Ireland is one of the publishing miracles of Irish life. Yes, admittedly, it gets some help from the Arts Council, but in the scale of things, that is rather like an engine block being tied to a gasfilled condom and managing to swim to Holyhead. The condom might claim a little credit, but not much.

It is Jeremy Addis, its editor and founder, who must claim the credit. How *Books Ireland* keeps on going defies belief. It is a monthly, sells at £1.25 and is a lavish publication on expensive paper. It carries some advertising, but of the subdued and decorous variety. One only supposes that the rash of armed robberies which have occurred in the Sandymount area where Jeremy lives in recent months has been as a sort of non-Arts Council grant for the maintenance of *Books Ireland,* with Jeremy doing his best Stand and Deliver whenever need arises.

The happy truth is that *Books Ireland* is one of the great publications of Irish life. We tend to take its presence for granted; its absence will not be so blithely ignored (and I note that it, like so many organisations, has been badly stung by the currency upheaval: its published list price for Britain is £1.15 sterling, which suggests that Jeremy's Stand and Delivers will have to be ringing even more often and more loudly over the sands of Sandymount than ever).

The subscription for *Books Ireland* is only £12 a year, a figure so low as to make me shudder with shame. The current issue alone contains 92 book reviews, and sundry other advice and guidance for Christmas presents; the best I can think of costs just £12, and if given in sufficient quantities might bring a long overdue conclusion to Jeremy's felonious career.

Gerard Hanley

What is an Irish writer? How does an Irish writer establish his or her Irishness, if that Irishness does not express itself in the limited range of subjects available for *acceptable* Irishness? If the writer, for example, does not agonise about the Christian Brothers or priests or nuns or the Falls Road or the bloodly shipyards or the desolation of Maguire in his potato patch. If his canvas is bigger than those limited confines, if he chooses to paint in a different medium with different materials and ones which are not evidently Irish, he is mysteriously transmogrified into something un-Irish, something contaminated, something imperfect – something, well, *British*.

The infuriating and incomprehensible complexity of relationships within these islands cuts both ways. The Irish complain, rightly, when the British appropriate Irish writers as British; yet, there is an indignant defence of the recruitment of British footballers to play for the Republic's team – which might yet reach further undignified depths now that no British team has qualified for the World Cup – because of the Irish diaspora 'beyond these shores'.

Yet, often enough those very Irish writers claimed by the British in fact constituted part of a British diaspora which spread through parts of the British empire. Goldsmith, Swift and Farquhar – though perhaps not Sheridan – were part of an exiled community which both identified with the land of their birth – and execrated it too – and yet their spiritual yearning, their grander identification, caused them to cast their eyes across the Irish Sea.

Yet, as the British claim certain Irish writers, the Irish disown, if only by lack of acclamation, other Irish writers – because their themes are not palpably Irish.

J.G. Farrell is one such, Irish and not Irish: in *The Siege of Krishnapur* he wrote about the British empire in a way which did not reduce its participants to wog-flogging caricatures, so there must be something suspect about him. Yet, his portrayal of Singapore in *The Singapore Grip* should have satisfied most of the political requirements of the condition of being an *Irish* writer. He had, however, committed another cardinal sin: in *Troubles*, he actually portrayed auxiliary RIC men as human beings.

Patrick O'Brian also mysteriously lies outside the canon of *Irishness*, for his themes and priorities are not confined to those to be found on a wet island on the edge of Europe. With an identical family background and identical education, had he set his novels in the Ireland of the Famine or the land of the Land League rather than in the British navy, he would *unquestionably* be acclaimed as an Irish writer.

Gerald Hanley is another who, en route, was dehibernicised because of his themes. He wrote about the British empire with extraordinary empathy – and not just with those he served in the British army, but with the colonised too. He wrote that his own ancestors 'had been losers too, and had been enslaved by the same force, a force which invented a mission to cover the human greed of the winners.'

Hanley travelled throughout Africa serving with the British Army and sensed empire and tribe, mountain and sea through his nose and his ears and scanned them all with watchful, remembering eyes. Because he was in his heart both one of the colonised and wearing the uniform of the coloniser, he had a unique understanding of the ways of the African peoples. They would defer to his authority; they would assent to his friendship.

The plural there – 'peoples' – is apposite. He knew more acutely than anybody else the powerful disdains and lofty contempt one African people can feel for another; and none in Africa feels the patrician sovereignty, the lordship of death and of desert and of slave caravan, that the Somalis feel.

Has not one single staff officer in the Pentagon or in the UN force in Somalia bothered to read the most hauntingly brilliant book about the land and its peoples yet to appear in English, Gerald Hanley's *Warriors*?

Hanley knew the Somalis and was intoxicated by them. 'Of all the races in Africa, there cannot be one better to live among than the most difficult, the proudest, the bravest, the vainest, the most merciless, the friendliest: the Somalis.'

Perhaps nobody in the entire continent apart from the Afrikaaners perfected the language of racism quite like the Somalis. Hanley wrote:

> I once tried hard to get the Somalis to give up their contempt for Bantu people at a time when we had Nyasa soldiers in the scattered garrisons of the Somali moonscape. But they broke the hearts of the softer Bantu soldiers. 'We cannot obey slaves' Somalis told me. 'It is impossible for us to live under slave people even when they are in uniform and have arms' ... I knew all this but could not change the Somali feeling of superiority over these chunky, black people from the lush south, nor wipe out the memory they had of a time when these Bantu people were slave material for the Muslim world to the North. That was the trouble, the curse of race, looks, noses, lips, eyes, legends.

Somalis, wrote Hanley, were harder, more durable than other African peoples; indeed, they did not regard themselves as African at all, with their fierce, hook-nosed, handsome features. The Bantus liked discipline, Hanley wrote: the Somalis resented it. 'Every Somali fights to stay himself, a person ... The Somali fumed under discipline and loved the irregular life ...'

Warriors – Life and Death among the Somalis first appeared in 1971, and although a classic, was lost almost beyond recall like so much of Hanley's work. The tragic and dreadful recent events in Somalia, and the futile efforts to compel those who are not to be compelled, can only be understood if you read his masterpiece. It has been rescued from oblivion by the superb publishing house of *Eland*, which makes books to last, tools which can be worked and used and re-used, as this tool by an Irish master should be, to understand the proudest and most fearsome people in Africa.

Winchman John McDermott

I have, upon due reflection, decided to withhold – for the time being anyway – my application for employment with Irish Marine Emergency Services. Initially, it seemed that there was much to recommend such a life. The keen wind, the lashing spray, the gratitude of forehead-knuckling tars as I plucked them from the inhospitable brine; and later, yarns beside a roaring fire, hot whiskeys cupped in hands, as we salty old matelots chatted about the sea and its ways, while our parrots squawked on our shoulders and we rested our peglegs on the communal stool.

It is quite clear, however, that there are aspects to this life which deserve further contemplation. Let us consider the lot of Winchman John McDermott. Winchman was one of the many positions I coveted. No doubt I should one day be lowered into the Steepe Atlanticke to rescue some half-drowned object, only to find that it is Naomi Campbell or Cindy Crawford or Princess Diana or some such plain and dowdy creature; who would of course be suitably grateful.

Perhaps John McDermott had some such notions in mind when he and his crew received the Mayday, the old dot dot dot, dash dash dash, dot dot dot, from somewhere out on the Steepe Atlanticke last week.

You might remember the night in question. I do. It was the night when Co. Kildare swapped places with Meath and much of Co. Leitrim ended up in my back garden.

One obvious place not to be was on the bottom of a cable dangling from a helicopter 60 miles west of the Irish coast in 100 mph winds with the sea lashing at your toenails like crocodiles trying to catch hovering kestrels.

That was what Winchman John McDermott found himself doing, dangling from a Sikorski S 61, while somewhere beneath him the Spanish vessel *Dunboy* had had an engine failure and was, as we nautical types say, broaching to. The night was as black as the inside of a Zulu's wellington in a coalmine, and the wind was shovelling great heaps of sea by the hundred tonne about the place. I, myself, was not so engaged. I was, I believe, drinking a gin and tonic. It is a common mistake not to place a large slice of freshly cut lime in a gin and tonic, *along with a slice of lemon*. No doubt John had this in mind out there above the Steepe Atlanticke that night. Lemon good; lime better; both together, superb. One wonders why this simple truth of gin and tonic is not better known. Ah well.

Anyway, John lowered through this lashing foam and howling gale until he reached the poop. No, that is not what dogs do on Dun Laoghaire pier. It is a part of a vessel, though no doubt there was much poop about the hold where the crew were sheltering from the storm while rivets popped and plates groaned.

If you are going to be a hero, at least may you be a hero surrounded by an appreciative audience, with Naomi, Cindy or Di or some other such creature to admire your intrepidity. All that John found on the *Dunboy* were six-and-a-half brace of Spaniards: Miguels, Diegos, Manuels and possibly even the odd Pedro. But not a Naomi, nor yet a Cindy or a Di.

Up above him, his winchmaster Peter Leonard and the flight-crew, Nick Gribble and Carmel Lyons, were admiring the view while John chose a Spaniard to strap to himself to have hoisted upwards. Thus one Miguel was put on the helicopter; then a Pedro; then a Diego or two. Then, *crack!* The steel winch cable had snagged on the *Dunboy* – no doubt the ship itself was trying to get winched on board the Sikorski – and the hawser had snapped.

Few things in this entire world are as unamusing as whiplike steel, full of energy and anger, lashing around the place; it can cut through concrete like a hot flail through dairy-spread. On this occasion, the hawser flailed upwards, nearly severing four of the five rotor blades.

Carmel, perhaps also screeching an act of contrition, sent out a Mayday. Nick prepared to ditch. Peter Leonard practised the breast stroke. John, squinting upwards in the rain and the gale and seeing the helicopter containing his three friends, plus five bleeding Spaniards, stagger away, apparently doomed, no doubt had thoughts of his own, which probably were predicated on theories on how to finish off the remaining Spaniards, whether or no ...

I think at this point, I was probably enjoying my second gin and tonic. With lime. And lemon. And ice, of course. Naturally ...

Nick Gribble was able to fly his crippled Sikorski to Galway, no doubt with Carmel and Peter doubling as rotors. Time for the Air Corps to get involved.

History does not relate the names of the Dauphin air-crew, but they were and are no less brave than the Sikorski crew; their helicopter is woefully underpowered for hanging round the Atlantic in tempests. It hovered over the stricken vessel (as I believe the expression is) and lowered a line to John McDermott. It snapped. It lowered a second line to John McDermott. It also snapped. It lowered a third line. But it was no good. It is hard to imagine John's feelings as he waved his second helicopter of the night away. These little arrows do things to a chap's soul: and meanwhile, he had eight Spaniards still to attend to. How do you throw eight Spaniards overboard without arousing suspicion? Hmm.

I believe that I, like you, was sound asleep at this time, and was sound asleep too when the RAF Sea King arrived and plucked John from his Iberian interlude, no doubt unbelievably cold, wet, exhausted and miserable and, most of all, alive.

So too were Peter, Nick and Carmel and the Air Corps and RAF aircrew, while you and I slumbered. I have deferred posting my application for a job with IMES until the weather improves. Oh yes, in the meantime, you should, in addition, *squeeze* the lime.

Flann O'Brien

And now, let us honour a man who has enriched us all and helped inspire a generation or more of Irish writers, yet whose name is known to virtually none. Let us say that name, Timothy O'Keeffe, and urge that it be recalled when people mention the name of Flann or Myles.

Without Timothy O'Keeffe, probably very few young Irish writers today would know of the literary works of Brian O'Nolan; indeed, there might not be many literary works to speak of.

It is still impossible to read *At Swim-Two-Birds* without feeling you have entered a hallucinogenic world of logic in its most bizarrely pure form. Substance is illusion; illusion is reality, and all perfectly assembled. It is a masterpiece, and it retains the essential hallmark of a masterpiece – it can never be bettered. Nobody can ever write a novel that is both surreal and superb, and which conveys a literal reality and which can compare with *At Swim-Two-Birds*.

No doubt Brian O'Nolan was aware of the greatness of the work when he completed it. No doubt he relished the moment of publication with all the ardour of consummation. And then other things intervened, the other things being Mr Hitler and the second World War.

Nothing in publishing history compares with the bad timing of the appearance of *At Swim-Two-Birds* just as the publishing houses of Britain were clearing their presses to produce aircraft recognition manuals, books about tank-driving and morale-boosting fiction about the imminent British victory.

Nobody noticed this furtive little publication. It was barely reviewed and even more barely sold. The thoroughness of the disappearance was completed over the coming months. France fell, a cloak of darkness descended on Europe, and trains began to clank east bearing their moaning human burdens.

In such circumstances, the eclipse of a single novel by a single novelist was hardly important. Cities burnt, musicians were gassed and great works of art were looted and transported to Berlin. What loss a single novel? The books would remain unsold and, one day, when peace had returned, could be brought out of storage and sold.

Not *At Swim-Two-Birds*. For in the rain of fire which descended on European cities, and on London in particular, there was one perfectly ironic casualty: Flann O'Brien's novel. Every last copy of it, was destroyed in its entirety.

His next novel, *The Third Policeman*, was rejected. Never the most tenacious of people, Flann O'Brien ceased writing. *At Swim-Two-Birds* was forgotten. Brian O'Nolan concentrated on the column he wrote for this newspaper under the pen-name Myles na Gopaleen. Flann O'Brien disappeared for all time; or so it seemed.

Timothy O'Keeffe was approaching his 12th birthday when *At Swim-Two-Birds* was published. He had been born in Kinsale in 1927 into a moderately well-off family.

The O'Keeffes emigrated to England when Tim was a boy. His brother now lives back in Cork, but Timothy was to remain in England, where his service to Irish civilisation and Irish letters turns out to have been far greater than it could have been had he returned.

After a couple of years in the British Army, he went to Oxford and then entered publishing, in which art he was trained by Sir Robert Lusty. It was while he was an editorial director of McGibbon and Kee that he made his first great, dazzling rediscovery – *At Swim-Two-Birds*, the masterpiece which had vanished from the face of the earth.

How he had discovered the work, we do not know: we do know that he pushed through its publication, and with that event, Irish letters were never to be the same again. He encouraged Brian O'Nolan to write more, and *The Poor Mouth* and *The Hard Life* followed. That he was able to entice such literary endeavours out of the author at this late stage, when alcohol was his complete master, was in itself a major achievement.

And when Flann O'Brien, Myles na Gopaleen and Brian O'Nolan died, Timothy was responsible for unearthing the weird and bewitching masterpiece, *The Third Policeman*. By the time he left McGibbon and Kee, he had also rescued for a broader audience some of the best of the *Cruiskeen Lawn* column O'Nolan had produced under the pseudonym Myles na Gopaleen.

He founded his own publishing house with two fellow-exiles from mainstream publishing, Martin Green and Brian Rooney; but they had begun their business in waters lashed by recession and on the newly-imposed VAT on books. They were hard times.

Yet those who knew Timothy speak fondly of those days: pints of Guinness in Jack Brady's Cumberland Stores, in the Plough or the Irish House; and when the barbarous closing hours of that time ended lunch they would retire to the Colony Club, Timothy's diminutive figure always impeccably clad.

MBO'K provided the first publication of Patrick Kavanagh's *The Green Fool*, rescued from the lost wilderness of the 1930s when a threatened libel action had ushered it into oblivion. Later he published Francis Stuart's *Black List, Section H.*

The catholicity of his literary taste was confirmed when he republished another Irishman who had largely vanished from the public domain. Francis Ledwidge, and who even yet awaits a proper biography and a complete edition of his poems (the Curtayne edition quite deliberately excludes the popular doggerel he wrote for his fellow soldiers).

Timothy got a stroke 16 months ago and died earlier this month. He was buried last Friday, but nobody can bury his lasting achievement for Irish letters. That will last forever; they also serve who only sit and publish.

Stan Gebler Davies

Death sometimes – more often than we care to admit – chooses its companions wisely. In the case of Stan Gebler Davies, death probably got it right. He had got as much out of life as he was going to; and, that being the case, he has been moved on to the next station. We should bid him farewell and not complain that we shall no longer enjoy his irascible humour, his bursts of apoplectic indignation, his whimsical but nonetheless deeply serious Toryism.

Last summer, he marked, rather than celebrated, his fiftieth birthday, in his rented cottage on the coast road out of Dalkey. He did not relish the half-century; nor did he relish the celibate life which circumstance and fortune had so arranged for him. He drank wine through the afternoon and the evening while convoys of friends arrived to wish him well. Such convoys of well-wishers would have gladdened many hearts, but not Stan's, though he remained defiantly cheerful, in a morose and rubicund fashion, as the sun sank and night fell and many, having drunk their fill, departed; and one by one Stan, remaining cheerful and depressed in turn, saw them off.

He never seemed to get drunk, but then those who drink seriously seldom do. Stan drank seriously. He always managed to function, and also managed to write, in a pellucid, mordant and often very clever fashion, even though much wine might have passed his tonsils. Contrary to popular belief, few journalists drink and work. Stan, however, was put on this Earth to reassure those people who think journos are alcos, defiantly churning out copy while three sheets to the wind.

He was an enthusiast in those matters about which he was enthusiastic, obsessive about his women, his wine, his cigarettes, his beliefs. He could be most intolerant of opinions which differed from his own; and, with much drink in him, that intolerance could topple into a boorishness.

So, let us be frank, and not do a Brendan Behan on Stan. He could be a bad drunk. He was, far more frequently, a very engaging drunk who was once upon a time very attractive to women.

Ah now; attractive to women. The baffling and irrational criteria women apply when they say they find a man attractive has long been the despair of the male sex. But most men, even those who insist that women have no judgment in such matters, would have understood that Stan had a certain quality, a raffish, dissolute charm which many women found irresistible, if, on occasion, only briefly. And he easily aroused that most infuriating of qualities within women, that odd maternal compassion which found expression in a most unmaternal passion, made moderately comprehensible for an otherwise uncomprehending male sex by Stan's round and protruding eyes within a face which was once cherubic. There was the lost little boy, very clever but very vulnerable, which endeared him to women. To lots of women.

But looks faded as bottles vanished. He was still able to write, but he grew larger than he would have wished; the more so when lung cancer forced him to relinquish a lung to the surgeon's knife and to give up smoking. Many would have argued that he would not succeed in staying off tobacco. And they were right. He did not. Those fatal obsessive, addictive genes which have been the curse of this race also saw him return to tobacco, in the shape of deeply-inhaled cigars.

But looks seldom engage affection and never retain it. Stan had an oddly destructive quality in his relationships. It was as if he were determined to destroy both his body with his drinking and his affections with his demeanour. He could become infuriatingly cantankerous, boorish, loud and aggressive when he was drunk; that he was so much fun at other times perhaps was little compensation for those who shared his hearth and board and bed.

But he was fun; hugely erudite, witty and sharp. He had presence, too, that other infuriating quality which defies analysis and description but simply *is*. No doubt that presence explained why Stan had so many friends. That presence, that *is*, was no doubt the reason you could detect Stan in a room behind your back – turn, and there would be that roguish glint in his eye, the large and ruined nose, that cheery, indomitable grin, exuding bonhomie, tobacco smoke, alcohol.

He was extraordinarily popular. To this day, I do not understand how he transported himself from one country house to the next. Had I suspected he was driving, I should have fled to Skellig Michael, where they have no roads, until he had run out of petrol. Filling a tank would have been technologically beyond Stan's ken.

Religion. What was Stan's religion? Well, it was sort of Catholic, if in its posher, grander form, the one destroyed by the guitars, clapping hands and tambourines that Vatican II introduced. The demotic, hand shaking circus of the modern Mass would have appalled him. So no doubt he might have been drawn to Catholicism as it exists in the Brompton Oratory in London, or to the loftier forms of smells, bells and spells of anglicanism, where some echoes of the old latinate rite may be found.

In politics, too, he was High. Some years ago he stood for election to Dáil Éireann in the Conservative and Unionist interest in Cork, achieving a vote which was less than the margin of error which exists when the franchise includes the insane, the stupid and the drunk. Still, it delighted him; and delighted, too, the readers of his accounts of his election campaign, which blended an enviably lofty tone with much humour.

Humour. Stan had lots of it. But he wouldn't have had any at all if he had made it into cantankerous, frustrated and lonely old age. His time had come. When ours comes, may we pray we are thus spared the crosses which have now been lifted from the shoulders of Stan Gelber Davies. RIP.

WATCH YOUR LANGUAGE

Chaps, guys and chums

Let us as November 5th approaches consider the damage the event associated with that date has done to a good Irish word, bloke. For the word guy which has done the damage comes from Mr Fawkes of the same name, the gentleman who was framed and executed on the perfectly innocuous charge of attempting to blow up the Houses of Parliament. The Americans, no more than we, do not celebrate the forthcoming anniversary of Mr Fawkes's explosive ambitions towards the House of Commons, but they did absorb the word guy as a synonym for wight, chap, bloke, fellow.

The language engineers who complain about the masculinity of the English language have a point when it comes to casual terms to describe people. They are, of course, deplorably wrong when they attempt to force us to use words like spokespersons and chairpersons, dead words which indicate rather a level of self-conscious linguistic political correctness than either a concern for the vitality of the English language or the etymology of words which they object to and which contain the suffix *–man.*

That suffix does not refer to the sex of the person concerned. It merely indicates that a human being is concerned in the matter. As has been observed ten thousand times before, the word man is genderless: the old root of the word man consisted of two forms with either the prefix – *wer* (male) or *wif* (female), the *ver* being a common Indo-European word for the male sex (as in *vir*, the Latin root which gives us words like virile).

English lost the *wer* form but retained the *wif* form, not merely in the garbled word *woman* from *wif-man* but also in stronger ways too. Even now wife does not necessarily mean married woman. A fishwife is a woman who deals in fish; a housewife is a woman who minds the house (as a husband is a male who is house-bound) and midwife is a woman *wif* who is *mid* (with) the mother at childbirth. An old wives' tale is merely a story told by elderly women (men generally being dead and unable to relate the wisdom of the ages).

Logically speaking, there is no reason why the suffix *–wife* should not be resurrected so that meetings are chaired by chairwives and fires are put out by firewives and organisations are represented by spokeswives and sportswives compete in international contests. But of course, logic has nothing to do with it: and anyway the Genderly Correct are ideologically committed to the dread, dead word person, for whatever reason. The French recognise the essential deadness of the word by using it as negative: the unattached *personne* meaning nobody.

This is not surprising. The Latin *persona* merely means a mask worn by a player, not the player or the individual the player represents. For whatever reason, the maskly moribundity of the word person is retained whenever we try to use it as a suffix. Nobody can use the word chairperson and feel that it retains any colloquial authenticity. It reeks of the language engineering which occupied 19th century English scholars who tried to de-Latinise English with phoney words like folkwain instead of omnibus and folkmoot instead of parliament.

This obsession with the sex of a noun is a purely English language problem. French and German are used to gender applying to all sorts in inappropriate words. By this time we should be aware that a chairman need not necessarily be a male, just as a French speaker does not expect *un chat* to be a tom or *une puce* to be inevitably a female flea. In German, police is feminine and girl is neuter. In Old English, as in German today, foot was masculine, hand was feminine, and eye was neuter; land was male and earth female, sun feminine and moon masculine.

Yet we know, we know, that people attempt to steer language with the same degree of success as a leaf commands the raging tempest; and though the Genderly Correct appear to have won the day with their this-person and their wretched that-person, we can only hope their ponderous neologisms join folkwain and folkmoot in the linguistic has-bin.

Which leaves us with the original query. Why does English have affectionate names for men and not for women? Why do pal, mate, chap, chum, buddy, crony, fellow, cove, guy and bloke not have female equivalents?

Presumably because they derive from once intrinsically male pastimes. Chap comes from chapman, from the Anglo-Saxon ceapman (cheapman) meaning customer. Cove is just a Scottish form of chap, and fellow is similarly derived, from the Anglo-Saxon feolaga, a fee-layer; again somebody you did business with.

Chum and crony are equally male: chum is an Oxford collegiate word, an abbreviation of chamber-fellow, for room-mate. Crony is its Cambridge equivalent, from the Greek *khronios* (time) somebody you spent time with. Mate has a comparable meaning, originally being somebody you ate meat with.

Buddy is simply an American contraction of brother. Pal also means brother, but it has something in common with the word bloke. Pal is a Romany word, one of the few – rum (as in strange) is another – to find its way into mainstream English. Bloke, too, has origins amongst a nomadic people; it is a word from Shelta, the cryptic language of Irish tinkers, and is one of the very few Shelta words indeed to find its way into English (along with gammy, as in leg, and monicker, as in name).

But the Irish word bloke is vanishing before the onslaught of the Anglo-American guy. Within the octave of Mr Fawkes's day, a non-event which spawned the word guy, is it possible to plead a case for bloke before it vanishes for all time? If it disappears completely, I shall be an enormously disappointed bloke, chap, fellow, guy or cove, as will my cronies, chums and pals.

Words at risk

There are those who say that Political Correctness is a purely American phenomenon, and that even there it is a largely derided movement confined to odd university campuses in midwestern states. It is in fact everywhere, and it is almost impossible to argue against many of its manifestations if you are a male.

Man-hatred is the only genus-hatred which it is now possible to express in the general press, provided that male is white and heterosexual. Emma Donoghue wrote an article for this newspaper before Christmas on the nice, safe topical matter of Santa Claus. On the matter of little girls sitting on Santa Claus's lap, she had this to say: 'I have heard too many women's horror stories to like the sight of a little girl on a man's lap.'

For the politically correct, this is the sort of casual observation which also is a key statement. It reveals the kernel of what is politically acceptable to state. Change the words around a little bit, and you have a statement which becomes equally unacceptable but one which would not even have been printed by this newspaper, 'I have heard too many abused children's horror stories to like the sight of a little boy on a homosexual's lap.' Or, 'I have heard too many horror stories about black men to like the sight of a white child on a black man's lap.' Or, 'I have heard too many horror stories to like the sight of a Christian on a Jew's lap.'

Far less objectionable within the canon of PC values is the observation: 'I have heard too many horror stories to like the sight of a black child on a white man's lap.' The essence of PC-ness is chic victimhood. A heterosexual male, one with his penis sliced off in the middle of the night, is most definitely not a chic victim. He is instead a subject of, at best, covert mirth. In the US, his assailant has become a heroine (if that is the right term).

But just so long as the genus-hatred is of white, male, heterosexuals, it is perfectly acceptable to utter such statements, and nobody will object, least of all white male heterosexuals who either absent themselves from the discussion of such matters, or make obliging squeaks of agreement at whatever sins are next to be laid at our door by those who hate us, for fear, I suspect, of accusations of being anti-women, anti-homosexual, anti-lesbian.

There are not many things I am sure about, but I am sure that I am not anti-women, anti-homosexual, anti-lesbian. I am anti-quotas, anti-positive discrimination, anti-genus hatred. But it is impossible for a male heterosexual to express bewilderment and distaste at the antics which went on in American bathhouses, where complete strangers might be rollicking around with a score of nameless strangers and not be accused of 'homophobia'.

Yet vegetarians can express distaste for meat-eaters without attracting accusations of carnivorophobia, lesbians can make whatever genus-hating remark they like about heterosexual men, never mind distaste for their preferences, and blacks can say whatever they like about whites and not be accused of racism.

One of the striking things about the coverage of the wave of violence in South Africa is the use of politically correct terminology. White extremists, like Eugene Terre Blanche's followers, are automatically called racists and fascists. Black extremists, such as the Azanian People's Liberation Front, who kill whites – men and women – merely because they are white, are not called racists or fascists or anything derogatory. They are known as militants or extremists. For racism, in the PC canon, is the white man's disease.

And the white heterosexual man lives in terror of offending the victim-culture which flourishes nowadays everywhere. Certain Americans are now, both here in Ireland and in the US, called Afro-Americans. It is now, apparently, racist to refer to them as black, though the vast majority of them are two complete centuries away from their African homeland, and probably know virtually nothing about it. To call such people Afro-Americans is like calling Richard M. Nixon an Irish-American.

Anthea McTiernan in this newspaper a couple of days ago complained about the participation of men in the feminist debate. 'But women ... women may not disagree. If they do, male journalists begin to spew forth a weary stream of war analogies – battle, fight, taking on – the male language of conflict ironically applied to people barred from the front line by their gender.'

Heaven help the male journalist who began to use the term 'female language' in derogatory terms, if his article appeared. It would most likely find itself in that journalistic peridition know as the spike.

The first casualties – in our weary, male war analogies – in the PC campaign are words. Last year I heard Declan Kiberd refer to the word henchperson. Niamh Breathnach recently coined another and even more gruesome grotesquerie, workpersonship. It is a term which is not only intrinsically odious, it is worse; for the ultimate intention of PC culture is to ascribe responsibility for those parts of Western culture they have not jettisoned to some indiscriminate, genderless, personhood; unless, of course, the author is female or homosexual, in which case the work is celebrated as being by, say, the great gay painter Caravaggio or the legendary lesbian feminist Aphra Behn.

The essence of the PC world is that society can be engineered by behaviour and by language. Fionnuala Kilfeather, co-ordinator of the National Parents Council, urged parents at Christmas to give boys and girls the same toys and games and books which show men and women being equal. In other words, how to create a truly boring but PC childhood.

In England, the Water Research Association has condemned as sexist terms like 'ballcock', 'female joints' and 'bastard file', and warned plumbers they could be prosecuted if they use them.

Almost funny. Almost.

Jargon

It started off moderately enough, this business of Mike and his mobile phone. It used to be Mick, but he spent 10 days in Florida and came back with a tan, an axe-sent and an attitood, saying things like *overly* for over and *cawps* for the Garda Síochána.

'High,' said Mike. Mike is one of these people who always greets you with an altitudinal observation of this kind. No doubt people with mobile phones feel the need to refer to the loftiness of their day.

I suspect this is something to do with mixing in the business community, who have their own language. They *do* lunch. They *pencil* you in. *Three* is good for them. Even when there is not a head of steer in sight, they refer to *bull-markets*. They have fenestral orifices during office hours which enable them to cry, 'I have a window in my day.' And when they can't accept an invitation for something, they make a reference to some obscure Bohemian kingship, often in conjunction with newly cut meadow grass.

'Sorry,' they say, 'No can do. But, hay, I'll take reign-Czech on that.'

Curious. Hay. Prague, royalty, and yet it all has meaning for these business types.

Another expression which they employ individually is one which embraces a group or generality of people upon a person's arrival. That person waves a hand and mysteriously suggesting a fraudulent loftiness, intones, 'High Guise.'

Very strange.

And they talk of *ballpark figures* and *shoestring budgets*. What is a ballpark? Wherefore shoestring?

Anyway, Mike always greets you on his mobile phone with a reference to height, followed by his name. 'High. Mike,' he said on this particular occasion, as usual a model of terseness. 'That is good,' I replied, pleased that his location was sufficiently removed from the ground to enable him seem cheerful.

But there was a curious noise on the line. 'You sound as if you are in a printing press, a device with which I as a journalist am well acquainted.'

'No,' he said. 'I'm sitting in my car outside my office.'

I did not realise then that it is the norm for mobile and car phones to be most used only moments after their user has just left an office where there are banks of working telephones, all which are about ten times cheaper than mobile phones.

But that is the nature of the mobile phone; its owners would prefer to be buried alive and use it beneath six feet of clay at inordinate cost to ring home than to use a nice comfortable ordinary telephone from which you can ring Sydney for pennies. We social observers call it part of the syndrome.

'Good. I am glad that you are able to telephone me from outside your office while sitting your car. You are of course aware that this enables me to telephone you back, anywhere, any time.'

Silence.

'I hadn't thought of that,' he said, sounding worried. 'You wouldn't, would you?'

'Well, not if you don't ring me, telling me that you are sitting in a car outside your office. In all our years of friendship you have never rung me from your office. Desist from ringing me on your car phone while outside your office.'

I thought that had done it, until the phone rang a couple of days later.

'High,' said the voice. It sounded as if it were speaking from an iron foundry.

'Mike. Where are you now?'

'Just drawing up outside my home.'

'Mike, why are you telephoning me from outside your home, putting your neighbours and their pets at risk, when for one-third of the cost you could within seconds be telephoning me from the comforts of your home, without any fear of having to scrape dog-paw from your tyre-treads?'

'I hear what you're saying,' he said, as if that there were a triumph of cognitive skills. 'I have a window in my day right now,' he says, and there is a crunching noise as he demolishes his gate-post.

A silence, costing several pounds a second, then follows, before I hear Mike invoke a large, uncouth man, snarling at him to pass a small assembly of tools.

'Oaf, a kit,' he bawled.

I left Mike to his gatepost, and later learned that he had also managed to entangle a cat in his left axle, which he later disposed of in the dead of night in his back garden. The little old lady next door still makes forlorn clucking noises at her back door each evening, and puts out milk and food, which Mike has to remove stealthily each night to allay suspicion about his crime.

'Do you gobble it up? It seems a high price to pay,' I observed the next time he hailed me. 'Where are you ringing from now?'

'I'm on the big round-about on the Naas dual-carriageway,' he said, unfortunately not completing his sentence before he drove into the lorry in front of him. One does so hate unfinished sentences. To this day I do not know whether he was eating the cat-food.

'Are you well?' I asked when he rang from his hospital bed. He replied with an odd bubbling noise.

'Tap twice if you are waiting for the orthodontist,' I said. He tapped twice. 'You are admirably concise today,' I told him approvingly.

The next time I heard from him he was trying out a new motor car along with, oddly enough, the German Chancellor. 'High,' he cried through his new teeth. 'Test-driving a Beamer, and it's Kohl, you know what I'm saying?'

I assured him that I did. One does, doesn't one?

Dortspeak

There is a voice on an advertisement for Magnum ice-pops which is the most worrying advance so far made by the revolting Dortspeak.

This advertisement consists of off-screen individuals making various ecstatic noises about the virtues of the product before it concludes with the voice of a young female saying in Dortspeak, 'No way, I'm not *sharing* it.'

The basis of Dortspeak is the middle-class Irish accent which has now been substantially overlaid by an Anglo-American argot, in which most vowel sounds seem to be based on a heroic but largely unsuccessful imitation of the English Home Counties with a very large dollop of American words – *no way, kyool, wow, hey, I mean, like, I'm like,* - thrown in, and communication of a kind, no doubt, achieved.

The written word cannot begin to convey the awfulness of the Dortspeak which seems to have taken over southside middle-class schools. It should have been possible to identify earlier the area where this accent was growing and for the speakers of it to be rounded up and kept in one of the larger pens in Dublin zoo, where they could be thrown scraps of meat and could mumble to one another until nature took its due and inevitable course. Alas, this did not happen.

Generally speaking, one cannot be held responsible for the accent with which one speaks. This, I can assure you, I say with real feeling. But Dortspeak is different. It represents an aspiration, It is a rejection of one identity and the embrace of something completely new.

That it is imperfect is merely in the nature of imitation. All imitation is unsuccessful: it does not produce clones but hybrids. The hybrid – and not the original model – then becomes the desirable norm. No doubt a teenager from Glenageary or Sandycove today who started speaking with a Home Counties or a Californian accent would be an object of ridicule, as his parents would have been if they had spoken in the accent their son now speaks in 25 years ago.

Accent swapping is not new. Bob Geldof did it, swapping his Holy Ghost, middle-class accent for the Kool Head-Speak of Dublin roadies of the late 1960s. His voice actually went down-market.

Such linguistic identity-change is not confined to Ireland. I hear that English public schoolboys, especially in fashionable nightclubs, affect a phoney Cockeny accent we may call Eltonese, after the middle-class rock star who made being a working-class hero his particular forte. He was not the first of his class to ape the manners of his lessers. Mr Michael Foot, a former leader of the British Labour Party, used to speak in what he imagined to be a working-class accent; Anthony Wedgewood Benn the same.

But these are either switches of individuals or of groups within a national identity. The unpleasant and disagreeable feature of Dortspeak is the essential aspiration to be foreign.

Identity in Ireland is a complicated business. Having a foreign accent – e.g. English – is sometimes regarded as evidence of being upper-class, much, I suppose, as German was the language of the Czech upper classes. Anglo equals posh (and often equals phoney). But an authentic English accent does not arouse amongst working-class Dubliners and non-Dortspeakers the wrath, the blind and homicidal ire, that Dortspeak does. The only accent to compare with the hostility it arouses is the vernacular of barristers; to which, indeed, in both class and – minus the American dimension – national aspiration, it is closely related.

Which brings us to the Magnum advertisement. The people who made this advertisement are either unaware that the accent used is distinctly new and class-based, and loathed by many who do not speak it. Or, they have made the decision that the sort of people they want to buy their ice-creams – or whatever Magnums are – are the type of people who appreciate Dortspeak. You know, wow, like I mean, Oonagh or Blaithin or Moike or whoever.

Either way, it is a dismal thought. The only consolation is that one can never guess which way these things go. Who knows? The next generation may react and adopt a more Irish accent than the one their parents speak.

I doubt it. I was in Listowel recently, where the spoken language is rich and melodious, a dialect to be cherished not in language museums but as a living language by the people of the area.

I gave a lift to a teenage girl who was hitch-hiking near the village, and was struck by her accent. It was not quite Dortspeak, but it was unquestionably Dublin middle class.

Was she visiting? No, she was from just down the road there. Really? I said. You don't sound local at all.

Oh thank you so much, she said, that's very kind of you. Why? I asked, astonished. Oh because only the stupid, the old, the backward spoke with a Kerry accent, she said. She was *delighted* to hear that she did not speak with one.

The point is this. In her out-going demeanour, she was typically Kerry – as courteous and friendly as you would ever hope to find. Yet to her, that other vital sign of place, of community – the language of her area – was something to be ashamed of.

This tragic attitude is widespread; untrammelled, it could leave the lovely dialects of Ireland to 'the old, the stupid, the backward.' The dialects of English in Ireland are an irreplaceable legacy. They should be cherished, not scorned.

Kevin

Why does a name which has existed for generations suddenly become popular? Let us – purely at random, mind – consider the name 'Kevin', which has an oddly familiar ring about it somehow. This name was made famous within Ireland by the saint of Glendalough, whose celibacy and piety were not remarkable when judged by the personal standards of Kevins throughout the ages, but in comparison with the lewd and adulterous capers of the rest of the contemporary population, seemed wondrously pure.

No doubt the exacting standards of Kevinness inhibited many parents from giving their sons the name Kevin. The battle of Waterloo was not won by Kevin Wellesley, Duke of Wellington. The Home rule movement was not started by Kevin Butt. Kevin Power did not start the whiskey distillery. Kevin Guinness did not found a brewing empire. Kitty O'Shea did not forget her marriage vows in the company of Kevin Parnell. There were no Young Irelanders called Kevin Mitchell or Kevin Davies or Kevin Smith O'Brien.

Other names spread through the world from these islands, the Scots in particular being energetic exporters of their names – Kenneth and Graham, Bruce and Ian, Donald and Stuart and Gavin. Where there were Scottish doublets of Irish names – like Gavin, a mildly mangled, hoots mon version of Kevin, Ian, a caledonianised species of Eoghan, or Donald, a corruption of Donal – it was the Scottish form which became known around the world.

At the start of this century, no doubt aided by a tidal wave of sentimental literature about Irish colleens, the female names of Maureen and Kathleen, Eileen and Sheila, left these shores and took root all over the English-speaking world. But Irish male names stayed resolutely at home. (Curiously enough, even today Northern Protestants have no trouble embracing Irish female names but regard Irish male names like a leper's kiss.)

In the early part of this century, few Irish people chose to give their sons Irish names; Williams and Georges, Samuels and Jameses, Arthurs and Edwards abounded. Scour the newspapers for Cormacs and Liams, Connors and Eamons, Seamuses and Donals, and you seek in vain. I have encountered one Kevin amongst the 35,000 Irish killed in the Great War. One too many, I agree, and a tragedy for the O'Duffy family, but still and all; just the one. Either the Kevins of the time were all cowardly conchies (an inconceivable thought) or they were simply not around.

There were no Kevins in the Easter Rising. No Kevins led flying columns against the dread Black and Tan. One Kevin, and one Kevin alone, seems to have accounted for the popularity of the name subsequently, and that was young Mr Barry, who interrupted his medical studies to bump off a few teenage soldiers and was hanged for his trouble.

Now this, no doubt, accounts for a surge in the popularity of the name Kevin in Ireland. It was patriotic to call your son Kevin. But it remained an Irish name. Its export potential remained zero. All over the world, little boys were baptised Gavin and Kenneth, both Scottish cognates of Kevin; but Kevin remained resolutely an Irish name.

Kevin Gable did not star in *Gone with the Wind*. Kevin Bogart did not make the screen pulse in *Maltese Falcon*. Kevin Stewart did not make anybody weep in *Mr Smith Goes to Washington*. Kevin Cagney machine-gunned nobody in a dozen gangster movies. Kevin G. Robinson did not play the sinister Chicago gangland boss in the same movies.

The same for later generations. Kevin Brando made no appearance in *On the Waterfront*. Kevin Douglas, Kevin Lancaster, Kevin Curtis are equally absent from films of the 1950s. Kevin Presley did not astonish the world with his *Heartbreak Hotel*, Kevin Haley did not *Rock around the Clock*.

The world, other than Ireland, was all but Kevinless. And then something perfectly horrible happened cross-channel. The name Kevin mysteriously spread, possibly by flea-bites, to the very worst of families, to ones which named their sons Wayne, Craig and Glenn. Teachers in England knew that if they had a boy called Kevin in their class, he was the one twisting little girls' arms behind their backs and stealing the lunch-money. Shout 'Kevin!' sternly over the wall of a Borstal, and a thousand hooligans would stop scragging some black kid and pretend instead to be tying their bootlaces.

English Kevins were perfectly horrible; thuggish, idiot Anglo-Saxon brutes. An entire generation of footballing Kevins was born, cloggers every one, save Kevin Keegan, whose family was Irish. Irish Kevins – aristocratic, aesthetic, scholarly every one – were appalled at these English Kevins. How did this happen? For Kevin is very naffness in England.

Amazingly, there was another mystery spread of the name, to America, which had hitherto resisted all Irish male names, even Sean, despite the Connery of that ilk. American Kevins were completely different from English Kevins – they were intelligent, creative and talented – Kevin Costner, Kevin Bacon, Kevin Kline.

How did this come to pass? Why are American Kevins so different from English Kevins? Why is Kevin the only Irish male name which has travelled? And can we not do something to protect the name? If people started selling sheep-dip and calling it Guinness, wouldn't the crowd above in St James Gate do something about it? Is it not possible to ensure that only desirable people become Kevins – Kevin Pavarotti, say, but not Kevin Maradona, Kevin van Beethoven but not Kevin Jagger, Kevin Mandela but not Kevin Archer, Kevin Spielberg but not Kevin Hussein. And why has there been no Pope Kevin? No doubt for the good reason that the Vatican is waiting for ...

Mr

Nothing characterises a people more than the way they address one another. The vocative form, the use of the second person singular or plural, the employment of titles, ranks, status in conversation – they all are burdened with enormous significance which outweighs in importance much else that the speaker says.

There is a problem in Irish-English, which is this: it is still, at all sorts of levels, a learned language, with borrowed social codes and terms of politeness and formality which might have no meaning in reality in Ireland.

Let us, for a moment, contemplate the hippopotamus. When a male hippopotamus wishes to ingratiate himself with an outranking male at the top of the hierarchy, he backs towards him, waving his tail, defecates towards his superior, propelling the contents of his bottom right into the other's face. To the superior, this is most pleasing ingratiation.

The English language supposedly has the equivalent of this behaviour. It is the use of the word *sir*. Yet the reality is that the use of the term *sir* in Ireland generally has none of the implications that obtain in an American usage of the word – indeed, many Americans call one *sir* with alarming regularity, and yet they convey not the slightest hint of intended deference. It is merely a 'have nice day' version of 'hey, you.'

English English probably has as many meanings of the word *sir* as Eskimos have words for snow. There is an enormous, multicoloured gulf between the *sir* with which a barrister addresses a beggar outside the Old Bailey and the *sir* employed by a midshipman addressing an Admiral of the Blue.

We all of us know that for the most part there is something extremely unconvincing about an Irish *sir*, unless it is a means of extracting favours. We are for the most part uncomfortable being called *sir*. We expect it of beggars, for whom it is a term of mercenary flattery. We know they don't mean it in any real terms of respect, and they know that we know. It is an agreed convention, an *A Chara* of the streets.

Both sides probably agree that it is preferable to Hey, you, give us foughin' five, and be foughin' quick about it. Most beggars, even now, do not want to frighten us, and perhaps more to the point, they do not want us to frighten them. The *sir* is a means of establishing a zero-threat way of extracting money. It seems fair enough.

The only occasion you *IT* readers use the term is when you address our beloved editor in a letter. But he knows you do not mean it. It is no more than an agreeable noise, a hippopotamus backing towards his superior, and I can assure you, our editor appreciates it enormously.

The term *Mr* has marginally less rarity. One is called Mr this or that in a hotel; but the mistering is normally done with a jauntiness and a casualness which convey a complete and utter lack of deference. It has implied with it: look we know your first name, and we'd use it, but the house rules here are, strictly no informality, but listen, don't take this too seriously, OK?

It is here we get into trouble. All through the English-speaking world – and for good or evil, this is an English-speaking country – people address one another with relative informality.

By the standards of the French or the Germans, even the staidest of chatelaines in the Home Counties are ranting levellers. English has none of the formalised grammatical politenesses which can make learning and using a foreign language a nightmare. An incorrect *tu,* and undeserved *du,* can produce a freeze which will cause mammals to retreat south for a hundred miles.

Yet not even Australians are as informal as the Irish. Irish politicians and ministers take it for granted that everybody will call them by their first names. Only the President and the Taoiseach and the bishops retain their titles.

Yet the reality of our usages is not reflected in the newspaper usages. The ridiculous *Ms* was imported from America for no real reason other than that it was American. It has changed nothing. Some women in newspapers prefer to be called Mrs, some Miss, some Ms. The importation of a third term has changed nothing. We poor males must struggle on with the single *Mister* to help us.

It was by this term that I was referred to the other day in an article about women and the use of hair-dye, though nobody in this newspaper refers to anybody else by such solemn pomposities. We use first names only.

But a new phenomenon has been creeping into Irish journalism from America in recent years. It is the use of surnames only. This is a revolting and exceedingly un-Irish trend. We do not refer to people by their surnames, other than in terms of extreme joviality, extreme brevity or extreme hostility. In Irish-English, the surname alone, apart from a teamsheet, is one of aggression.

Yet the other day, a report on the imminent retirement of Paddy Downey referred to plain 'Downey'. There is no such person in this newspaper. He is Paddy. To distinguish him from the many other Paddys, and on occasions of extreme formality, we will get quite hoity-toity and refer to him as Paddy Downey. But in reality, he is Paddy, pure and simple. It is nonsense to think of him as anything else.

Throughout the entire GAA he is known as Paddy, and on occasions when about ten thousand Paddies might have gathered in Semple or elsewhere, he is Paddy Downey.

What are we to do about these bogus *Misters,* these truant *Misters?* Style in such matters is not just style. It is substance. It defines relationships and status. It establishes how we regard one another. It emphasises the relative lack or the presence of formal hierarchy. The further importation of American terminology will help us not one bit. Which of course does not mean we won't keep importing useless foreign terms.

Snow White and the Seven VCMWML&HD

Surely one of the most amazing survivals of this age of correctness and infinite sensibility to every disability and every orientation is that of the pantomime. Paradoxically, the most politically incorrect pantomime is the one which is prospering above all others. *Snow White and the Seven Dwarfs* is so popular throughout Britain this Christmas that theatrical agencies are not able to meet the demand for dwarfs.

Dwarf is one of those words which will not lie down and die in the face of disapproval from the political linguistic engineers who have taken over from where our grandparents' governesses left off. That those people who are dwarfs seem to accept the term is irrelevant, though it means both small, as does midget, and also suggests certain disproportions, such as large head and short limbs.

There is not yet a PC term for the reactionary and bigoted term dwarf. Let us start with renaming the most popular pantomime in Britain. What about Snow White and the Seven Vertically Challenged Males With Minor Limb and Head Disproportions (VCMWML&HD)?

It is quite clear that Snow White and the Seven Dwarfs is also seriously sexist, racist and stereotypist in title, narrative and plot. Why does Snow White do the housework while the VCMWML&HD go out and work all day? Can she really be happy cleaning up after men? Is this not domestic tyranny of the most degrading and insulting variety?

It is also clear that the VCMWML&HD cannot all be male or white. They must be yellow, black and brown also, gay, in wheelchairs, visually challenged, female, lesbian and professionally varied, including at least one deep-sea diver and a lesbian welder in a nuclear power plant in Siberia. There has been too much stereotyping of vertically challenged people. They too can be basketball players and tree surgeons.

If Snow White must be female, there is no reason why she should not have been originally a black male from Liverpool who after years of racist and sexist stereotyping had a sex-change operation. Now she is the chairperson of a Collective for Lesbian Chimney-Sweeps in Stockholm where the male patriarchal Clean Air Acts have robbed the sisters of their livelihood.

The name Snow White is both clearly racist and weatherist. Drizzle has no particular colour, is a suitable mixture of many forms of weather and is compatible with rain and with snow, wind and, sometimes anyway, sunshine.

White is clearly an imperialist, colonialist repressive, reactionary skin-tint. Merely the name is enough to remind one of the slave trade, massacres, missionaries, the loss of indigenous cultures, the genocide of native Americans. She, the sister who runs the lesbian collective in Stockholm and fights her gallant war against the male patriarchy, clearly cannot be the colour of the primary oppressor in world history.

Let us call her instead the all-embracing Collective of Repressed Aboriginal Peoples, namely CRAP.

Which leaves us with the number seven. Since this belongs to that family of numbers known as Odd, it clearly discriminates against the numbers which are even. This is a classic example of numerism, in which one half of the numbers of the world lord it over the oppressed and discriminated even numbers. They do this by the violence of their oddness, exploiting the vulnerability of the even numbers' more peaceable ways. It is not coincidental that the innate deficiency of odd numbers is indicated by their sum; any two odd numbers will always come to an even number, which proves the natural inferiority of the odd-number gender.

Mathematically the only way to enunciate the number seven in a politically correct form is to say 6.9 recurring, in which the substantive digit is even and the decimal is only nominally odd, in reality it comes to 1.0, which is both odd and even, and therefore politically acceptable.

We are therefore happy to tell you that Drizzle Crap and the 6.9 recurring vertically challenged varying individuals with quite different but rather surprising and completely unstereotypical job vocations, including an all-in wrestler, a heavyweight champion of the world, a second row forward, a female fighter pilot and a television set, will be opening in their pantomime. Seats are still available.

Two pantomimes quite clearly reveal themselves by their names for what they are – *Dick Whittington* is yet another phallocentric celebration of macho masculinity and heterosexist imperialism. One doesn't have to see it to ban it out of hand as a typical example of gender suppression and the glorification of the phallus as subjugator and tyranniser of the female sex.

And on the other hand, *Puss in Boots* is quite obviously yet another pornographic exploitation of the female body, with the leather footwear symptomatic of the sadistic male impulses towards and tyranny over the female form for the past ten thousand years, as represented in the male objectification of the female form in all art throughout the ages, from the Venus de Milo to the Page Three Porn Victims of Today.

Mother Hubbard is stereotyping women in the most horrendous and patronising way. Aladdin and his lamp is clearly another celebration of the penile form – the phallic symbolism of the lamp from which all power derives would be clear to a sophomore in Indiana University. And *Cinderella*, this year on in the Gaiety, is the most concerted assault on sisterhood by the male establishment in the history of narrative fiction.

So there it is: it looks like *Drizzle Crap and the 6.9 recurring vertically challenged people of all races and of numerous non-stereotypical professions and with mild disproportions in limb and head* again this year. Cripes, isn't the Christmas season such fun?

NATURE STUDIES

Wasp

This is the time of year which feminists should be most sensitive about, when there should be indignant rallies about the fate of their sisters and when decent people everywhere should be rallying to these oppressed females. But there is not a cheep or even a buzz about what is being done to those jolly little ladies, the wasp.

For this is the time of year when they are routinely and insanely massacred; at the merest sight of one of these inquiring females even the boldest of people are moved to imitate a boxing match with an invisible man, swinging and punching and howling; murder is not scrupled at, nor vespicidal stratagems spurned.

Gross illiberalism is applauded, and newspapers are rolled into a fell and furled weaponry which makes decent columnists ashamed that their copy should be so used; we think of the micrograms of ink which we have caused to be printed adding to the deaththroes of our benign and virginal sisters the wasps, worthy sisters all of the order hymenoptera, and, one might, add, intacta; we think of such ink and weep.

In no other walk of life since the Incas were urged to desist from ungentlemanly-like behaviour towards the sexually inexperienced are virgins so routinely slaughtered as wasps are at this time of year. If there were an annual and general round-up of Loreto nuns, if they were routinely swatted as they swooped about their nunly business, if they were lured into vast jampots containing water, there to drown, and if they were sprayed with deadly poisons as they performed their ministry, there would be questions in the Dáil; sisters would gather at street corners denouncing such behaviour as sumptomotic of the oppression of wuminn everywhere; there would be unseemly scenes.

Yet this is the annual lot of wasps, one of personkind's greatest benefactors. Wasps do us extraordinarily good turns, and never even turn up at our front door at Christmas time, bidding us the season's greeting with a hand held out. But for wasps we should be fairly over-run with all manner of parasites. Our gardens would be deserts as fat aphids cavort in the dunes, digesting our roses and our hollyhocks. All sorts of beasts that burrow into our woodwork would be munching through our furniture, silent all but for the little cries of timber as grandad falls through his rocking chair.

There are entire species of wasp whose lives are dedicated to controlling these pests who would otherwise make life on this planet quite intolerable. There is for example a wasp which lays its egg in the egg of an especially nasty beetle which has developed

72

a taste for Chippendale furniture. Entire suites of furniture remain in existence solely because the little wasp grub wakes up when the beetle larva is about to exercise the digestive juices and sets to with knife and fork to make short work of said pest.

And the extraordinary thing is that another wasp, taking pity on the Chippendale chewer, has dedicated its life to laying an egg inside the egg inside the egg, so that just as the first wasp is about to tuck into the beetle larva, the second wasp tucks into it. Amazingly, there is a third wasp which is believed to lay its egg in the egg of the second wasp. This gives nature a sort of balance, and somehow or other, it just seems a little bit more like cricket.

Yet these are the unostentatious wasps, one unlikely to encounter this newspaper in a furled and downwardly swinging condition.

It is the other species, the rather more glamorous Kilkenny-like sister, who is the target for most autumnal wrath. Now it is true that these stripey sisters do show an unladylike appetite for other people's fruit at this time of year. But put it like this. If it were not for the pests these ladies have been out bagging for their loved ones through-out the year, we should not have any fruit at all. Our trees would be bare. Instead, we have many wasps, grown fat on their aunts' endeavours; for generally speaking their mothers have been too busy being queen mothers to go out foraging and it is their mothers' sisters who have gone out to make sure the larder is not empty.

As for the men, do not even speak to me about the men. Sumptomotic, that's what it is. Sumptomotic. They just turned up for the sex and disappeared. It's enough to make a wasbian of a girl.

Now there is, it is true, the matter of the wasp sting. Wasps have stings. But so have bees; yet we do not applaud the murder of bees, and wasps do not sting us more than bees do. They just appear to because their stinging is pretty much confined to those few weeks when the fruit is on the tree and they want their share of the Vitamin C; and they wouldn't sting at all if people didn't try to bite through them when they were eating an apple, or didn't attempt to swat them into extinction while they were harmlessly crawling down a human neck.

The truth is that genocide becomes acceptable this time of year. The Irishman's Diary Equality Committee has met to adjudicate on this one and we have decided that the killing of worker woman wasps is only permitted if an equal number of male wasps can be killed in the same circumstances and in the same amount of discomfiture. Until this can be achieved, the killing of wasps should be suspended. Viva vespa.

Bluebottle

Bluebottle time. One does not even have to leave a window open these days to dis-cover winged and armoured insects hurtling around the place like trainee pinballs.

Never did nature go to so much trouble preparing one of its creations for circumstances which really should have been unpredictable.

The bluebottle, after all, came into existence about 200 million years ago when there was little or no talk about windows, plateglass or office blocks. Yet bluebottles appear to have been invented solely for survival in such circumstances.

Those people who design motor-cycle crash helmets could take a correspondence course from the designer of the bluebottle.

It collides with plateglass windows 20 or 30 times per minute at a speed equivalent to 250 mph. It is rather like a human being stopping the Belfast Dublin Enterprise in full flight downhill near Poyntzpass with her head, every two seconds, pausing briefly to grin, and then repeating the exercise.

Not the least remarkable feature of the bluebottle is the apparent lack of brain damage which it incurs as it dashes itself merrily against the immovably transparent. A bluebottle at the end of the day is every bit as cheerful as a bluebottle at its beginning – the same indefatigable humour, the same defiant chirpiness, the same bubbling inquisitiveness, even though it has spent the day smashing its head on solid objects.

There are other indications that the brain remains incredibly sharp. Anyone who has gone hunting bluebottles with a rolled-up newspaper can testify that they have the reactions of a gunfighter.

Perhaps you might just down a bluebottle at the end of its years, after decades of head-banging and drinking mother's ruin, but otherwise all you do is smash up your newspaper.

I'm not talking about ordinary houseflies now – stupid, slow dithery creatures who do not deserve to be mentioned in the same phylum as bluebottles, the chevaliers of the entomological world.

Killing houseflies is as easy as killing greenfly. It is barely a sport, though I understand that they have meets in the English shires in which hunting folk with pink jackets and pinker noses gather to down the hunting cup before cantering around the drawing room with rolled newspapers in their hands and uttering rude cries as they set about killing houseflies.

At the end of the day the bag is normally impressive – a score of houseflies, three spiders, a woodlouse and even, tragically, a ladybird; but never a bluebottle. The bluebottles have all escaped the muscacidal parabola of rolled newspaper with balletic grace.

It is because of the incredible speed of the bluebottle reflexes that chemical companies decided that the only way to reduce the bluebottle population was by serious warfare. By that time every house in Europe spent the summer in the company of several hundred bluebottles.

The chemical companies produced a poisonous substance which lingers in the air and which even the most intelligent and alert of bluebottles can neither detect nor avoid. The result was ruinous and tragic; millions of bluebottles being poisoned in the most horrible way, their little legs kicking in the air and their wings buzzing in frantic attempts to escape their doom. Even spiders wept to see this calamity.

It was not the fate of the bluebottles which aroused concern. It was the fate of the human beings which was most troublesome.

The pesticides were inhaled by humans and began to affect their DNA. It was when children of parents who had themselves in childhood been exposed to large doses of fly-killer began to develop antlers that medical science, as incredibly shrewd as ever, began to suspect something was wrong.

The final straw was when the children began to shed their leaves in autumn and lined up on telephone wires before flying to Africa. Then medical science decided it would have to find some other means of disposing of bluebottles.

The Diary is happy to tell you it has a solution. It consists of washing-up liquid, a garden handspray, and water. The handspray should be of the variety which has an adjustable nozzle so that it can propel its contents in a stream.

At this point I should explain that bluebottles have a weakness. Unlike us – though not unlike some of the children who were appearing a few years ago – bluebottles breathe through numerous tiny holes in their skin. These holes are protected from water by water-resistant chitin; but as Brother Primavesi taught me years ago, this chitin is dissolved by a mild soap solution.

So fill your handspray with soapy water, and aim its stream at a passing bluebottle. Even an indirect hit will dissolve so much chitin that a large number of holes are clogged and the bluebottle will run out of energy and have to land. Zap it with the spray again: it is doomed. Water clogs its holes; it cannot get enough oxygen, and it simply dies.

Dies, moreover, painlessly; it might even be contentedly rubbing its hooves together in that charming way that bluebottles have, but it is dying. Listen, in addition to not filling the atmosphere with chemicals which cause children to develop apples on their fingers, grow beaks and migrate to the Sargasso Sea, this technique is fun; one actually encourages bluebottles in one's house, rather as hunts encourage foxes.

And then one has all those bluebottle corpses, freshly washed, and free of chemical additive – delicious barbecued, though watch out that their little corpses do not fall through the grill. And will the Diary be the first ever double-Nobel Prize winner?

The rain forest

I don't think for a second that a single tree will not be felled or a single gorilla saved or a single triatomic molecule of ozone preserved by what was done or signed at the Rio Conference.

Indonesia will continue to fell thousands of trees a year and so will Brazil because they want to be regional super-powers and they need the land to grow the food to feed the large populations which regional super-powers require.

What is more, anybody who lives near a rainforest hates it. It is an unproductive, sinister place, full of the most terrible animals who are never happier than when laying eggs in your eye or biting your hand off or burrowing into your chest cavity and making a nest or infecting you with diseases which cause paralysis, lunacy and death.

People who live next door to rainforests actually want to live next door to green fields with cows and sheep and sweetcorn and beans and maybe the odd tree with a few birds singing in it and possibly a monkey or two – but not more than that because monkeys are horrible creatures which steal food and shriek at you and hurl kaka at you when you pass beneath them.

It's only people like us who get all sentimental over rainforests. *We* don't have to worry about monkey-kaka getting in our hair, though we get hysterical enough at the behaviour of seagulls; *we* don't have to worry about insects that want to raise their young under our toenails; *we* don't have to go to bed wondering whether some flying beast of the night is going to come out of the rainforest when dark has fallen and turn our haemoglobin into a six-course banquet, finished off with maybe a mouthful of testicle;

we don't have to take precautions against black pit vipers slinking into our beds in the dead of night and administering to us enough poison to exterminate the population of Longford;

we don't have to check under the lavatory seat every time we use it that there is not some spider whose life's ambition is to bite us somewhere exceedingly precious indeed, causing us to die, barking with agony and in a straitjacket after months of torment; *we* don't have to wonder whether that rumbling noise is not termites making off with our house, and that the reason the armchair is proceeding very slowly across the lawn is that it is being taken away as a snack for the termite queen;

we don't spend our lives in constant anxiety that our children are going to be plucked from the back garden by vultures and taken away to an invulnerable and wholly inaccessible nest high in the rainforest canopy, there to be fed bit by bit to nasty, hairy looking beaked reptiles covered in scraps of feather, the vulture young, which ornithologists all over the world want to have protected but the locals would like to see hunted down until the last one is ritually throttled by delighted villagers;

we don't have to worry that every time we feel an itch it is not in fact a young insect actually escaping through your skin from the subcutaneous nursery its mother made for it and its sibs in your belly some months ago, which perhaps helps explain why you are down to three stones in weight, are the colour of pus, your teeth are falling out, and you have been confined to bed for the past six months; *we* don't expect to be attacked by huge carnivores which spend their days in the rainforests plotting murder and come out at night and tear you limb from limb;

we don't have to lie awake in mortal terror lest a bat land on our face during the night and suck our eyes out while we sleep; *we* don't have to contemplate the prospect of blood-sucking butterflies; *we* don't have to worry that whenever we fall into a river some tiny fish is not going to swim into our urethra and once there secure its position by barbs which only feel like redhot needles, that's all, no worse than that, and which can't be removed by any means known to modern science, never mind the primitive horrors which pass for medicine wherever you get rainforests;

we don't ever have to think that it is possible the vegetable you have on your plate might very well want to eat you more than you do it, and has very possibly already consumed the only child left after the vultures, the carnivores, the bats, the spiders and the various insects had their dinner at your family's expense; *we* don't have to walk for weeks to get a newspaper, or a plate of chips, or a new suit to replace the one eaten by ants, or shoes to protect yourself from the giant foot-eating ladybird or a hat to protect your ears from the ferocious attack of the sabre-toothed sloth or a cannon to ward off the attentions of giant lungworms.

It's possible that I have not made myself clear, that I have been ambiguous, indecisive, hesitant in my use of language. A common failing of mine. What I'm trying to say, but not communicating properly, is that rainforests are horrible places, people hate them, and chop them down at every opportunity, whether or not people in places like Ireland assure them they shouldn't.

And that's why I don't think the Rio conference will achieve anything.

My Phoenix Park

Oh tasteful thief, that you should have chosen the one book that I have been sent this year and truly valued. How did you claim your booty, you velvet-fingered, soft-padded creature gliding through the *Irish Times* newsroom when the world sleeps? The riches of an abandoned office lay before you, yet what detained the eyes and the attention of this silken felon? None other than my newly acquired volume of the plantlife of the Phoenix Park. And what could rival that subject – what Beethoven symphony, what Leonardo, what George Eliot novel, compares with the greatest masterpiece in all of Dublin? The thief cannot take home the Phoenix Park, but he or she can take home a book about its history and its plants, its grasses and its trees. And leaving all else behind, the thief that night stole off with my beloved volume of the botany of the park.

What matter. I have the park, each day of the year, and at this time of year, almost to myself, for one of the peculiarities of Dublin people is that they think the park is for bright summer days.

It is not. It is for every day of the year; it is for when the days are long and hot and meadow larks yell giddily from on high, the vast herd of deer browse through the yellowing, seared grass and heat shimmers in great waves across the Serengeti of the Fifteen Acres. In the great mass of woodland which covers much of the park small birds croon their territorial anthems; warblers, dunnocks, robins, blackbirds, and that great mimic, the thrush, conjuring up the songs of half-a-dozen birds as well as its own dizzy improvisations, a glorious din of chuckles, melody, woodland noises and random sound effects.

Sparrowhawks hurtle through the trees and across the Fifteen Acres. Swallows and swifts swoop too, shrieking with murderous intent through twilight, as insects rise and it is feeding time; what spectacular calculations enable these incredibly daring flights to intermingle at closing speeds of 120 miles an hour only inches above the ground, around trees and deer and astonished humans?

Even when many people decide to walk the park, their large numbers are swallowed up in the vastness. The great stands of broadleaf, surely one of the great plantations of tree in Ireland, shimmer their countless greens; green upon green, emerald upon emerald, oak upon oak, ash upon ash – great symphonic movements of shades of green, blended with silver and brown and that great unifying family of shade.

Leaf upon leaf; the filigree of the ash leaf and the threefold broadswords of the chestnut and the curvilinear subtlety of the oak and the great masses of leaves of trees of unknown names, which my thief, the whore, no doubt now knows, and I no doubt, never shall.

No matter. Some things it is better not to know; some things, even the commonplace tree which I see every day, perhaps is enhanced by mystery, that namelessness which retains origin and history within its vast and shady discretion.

The year advances. The chestnut nourishes broods of conkers which come to spiky ripeness and are discarded. Children scrabble beneath the trees for their favours. The chestnuts have already begun to change their leaves; an iridescent clan of colours begin their parade, gaudy, luminous, magenta and orange and russet and gold and isabella and a thousand tints which have no name because each is as unique as snowflake for its brief existence until it is gone.

When one walks the park as night draws in, one wonders; how can winter be durable, with days so short and the magnificent foliage stripped from the trees and bleak grey skies hovering only slightly overhead, sometimes yielding to reveal a weary sun making a limp promenade over the southern horizon?

A nightjar churrs in the spinney I call jays-wood and then is gone, to join the swallows and swifts feeding their fill among the wildebeest and hartebeest of Zimbabwe. Oh how can one bear the prospects of winter after the majesties of summer and autumn?

Easily, easily; for the park achieves a fresh glory in the winter – that almost horizontal light picking out the sublimely delicate tracery and filigree of the dense capillaries of twig, leafless and dark against a winter sky. Illuminated in the dense mass of woodland by shafts of sunlight is the bark of beech and birch, shining, almost glowing on a winter's day.

Many of the exotics are gone, but stalwarts remain. No bird's song is more beautiful or indefatigable than the robin's, and fresh visitors have arrived – fieldfares and redwing from Scandinavia, and more modestly from our own shorelines, oystercatchers, probing and browsing through the wet grasslands near the old magazine.

And then the benedictions of the snow, that virgin expanse covering the Fifteen Acres marked solely by the delicate inquiry of deer's cloven feet. In that cold you can induce wild robin to feed from your hand; in that snow you are untroubled by sight or sound of other visitors. The park is yours and yours alone.

December 21st, the fellest day of the year, comes and goes. That day the sun rises shortly before 9 a.m., is gone shortly after four and it is dark by 4.30 – a day of Finnish dismalness. A month has now gone since that miserly allocation of daylight – less than eight hours of it. We are now embarked upon that glorious journey towards June 21st, when the sun rises before five and it is still daylight at 10.30 – 3½ minutes' daylight gained each 24 hours till then.

Already since that grisly day in December, a day is about 100 minutes longer and the splendours of spring approach – crocuses and daffodils are already pushing through the soil. Buds are on trees. Winter can rant and rage; can throw blizzards at us and lay carpets of frost upon our cars and lawns. Yet he knows; his is a retreating army, and the marvels of spring in the park lie ahead.

Oh have your book, thief: for I have my park, and that is my paradise.

Greengage summer

It was a greengage summer, Mrs Kennedy Smith [the United States ambassador], a greengage summer. The greengage was introduced here by Sir William Gage two centuries ago. It rarely comes to full fruit in this meridian for the summers are not hot enough, or dry enough to permit this exotic plum to clothe its seed in the sweet-green flesh which makes it so prized. It comes to fruit in a rare summer – a greengage summer.

It was the summer when Brian Clark died, and we gathered in Powerscourt Church of Ireland church to remember him. Nobody in that church will forget the heat that day, the sun bursting through the windows in the way it only burst through church windows in childhood.

That evening we all stood in Brian and Brenda's back garden and drank wine and ate sausages. The sun went down on the smouldering mountains and the air was full of the rich tang of cindered turf and charcoaled gorse, and we remembered Brian and knew that we would remember the summer of his death, this greengage summer.

Outside Wicklow smouldered, fires crawling through the gorse and bracken for mile upon mile of mountain. Maybe now we shall see again the heather on the Wicklow of my childhood, glowing a wondrous purple at sunset, a purple that I spent fruitless hours trying to capture with my watercolours in that distant year, that other greengage summer of long ago.

This was the summer of the rugby world cup. We approach the new season now with the grass scorched off the rock hard pitches. Soon the smell of dubbin and wintergreen and old sweat and ancient encrustations of Palmolive soap will be filling the noses of returning players as they prepare for weeks of torment running off the fat and sloth laid down during the endless barbecues of this last summer, this greengage summer, Mrs Kennedy Smith, this greengage summer.

It was the last summer of innocence for world rugby. From now on rugby players will be paid. It is inevitable. Bow to the inevitable. Bow to the inevitable rain, when it comes, or the snow, or, this summer, this greengage summer, Mrs Kennedy Smith, the sun.

What an addictive thing it is, the sun, Mrs Kennedy Smith, and its frame, the blue blue sky. You are used to that kind of thing, Mrs Kennedy Smith, from your Boston childhood. We are not. The hazy-lazy days of summer are something Americans sing about. We do not. We are guaranteed no such thing. We normally steal the odd hour of sunshine here, the occasional afternoon there. For you, summer is a meteorological season of heat and sea bathing and boats and slobbing around in sneakers and sloppy joes.

For us, summer is the name we give the period of cloud between the clouds of spring and the clouds of autumn.

Except this year, Mrs Kennedy Smith, except this year, the year of the greengage summer. Each morning we woke and the sun was there in the sky, as miraculously to our eyes as the land was to Noah's. Day after day of it, week after week, month after month. We have seen nothing like it – indeed, I doubt very much if Europe has seen anything like it since Sir William Gage brought the little green fruit here.

Then, of course, we had warmer weather. Tobacco grew in Cork, vines flourished throughout Munster, and greengages grew green and sweet in that era of greengage summers.

We have tended to console ourselves in our diet of grey climate that we would be bored by Californian weather. Mrs Kennedy Smith, let me tell you something in all confidence – this is nonsense, the adult equivalent of the gibberish children shout, their fingers to ears, to prevent themselves hearing what they do not want to hear.

Secretly we are a mediterranean people. We yearn to gather lobster pots from warm seas, to finger olives on the tree, to watch the vines grow heavy as autumn approaches, to see with pleasure how the greengages grow on the greengage tree. Mrs Kennedy Smith, the greengages grow on the greengage tree.

We grow feckless in this greengage warmth on these greengage days. Nobody at their office, nobody at their phone, the weekend in the west suddenly stretching into a week, a stolen month; and why not?

Octogenarians will be remembering this summer, Mrs Kennedy Smith, in the final decades of the next century, and speak longingly of this season now, this greengage summer.

I saw insects I never remember seeing before, and my flowers flourished in a way they have never flourished. My apples ripened in the sun and were ready to be eaten by August, and such a crop, Mrs Kennedy Smith, such a crop, and not knowing country lore, I do not know how to store them.

But they are fine apples, crunchy and sweet and juicy.

Though they do not compare, Mrs Kennedy Smith, with the apples I scrumped – that was the word we used where I spent my childhood in Leicestershire – from the orchards then, that greengage summer. No apple tastes so sweet and fine as that childhood apple purloined illegally, an imagined dog sinking its teeth into your heel as you clamber over the wall, your shirt stuffed with fruit.

Then safe from the attention of orchard owner or orchard owner's dog, I sank my teeth into that forbidden fruit, on that greengage summer of long ago.

Though even that apple did not compare with some greengages I had the other day, beautiful, beautiful greengages, their sweetness spiced with mischief, the juice enlivened by felony.

Mrs Kennedy Smith, may I ask you a question? Do you know you have a couple of greengage trees hanging over your garden wall in the Phoenix Park? Though they have not now as many greengages upon them as once they had, these greengage trees this greengage summer.

For someone, this greengage summer, has scrumped your greengages. And I know who it was who, upon a greengage summer's evening, ate those green greengages from your greengage tree; and I know who it was ...

Spider-time

This is the season of the spider. She greets us each morning in our wash-hand basin, grinning cheerfully beside the hole she has just crawled up. Or she stands expectantly in the shower hoping to share the morning cascade; and maybe, when you are both thoroughly clean, you will let her crawl up your leg and find somewhere nice and warm to snuggle into, where she will be comfortable and not be seen.

Yet curiously, you will most likely not permit this commonplace decency, though you have no firmer friend than the spider. There is no greater evidence of the existence of a benign god beaming down on us from her celestial web. One day she will ask us to join her in her divine gossamer – and when you inquiringly stoke one of the outer struts of her web, will she beckon you with a few affable limbs, or will she dart out, bite you through the neck, and suck all your vital juices from you?

It all depends on how you have behaved in this world. Dear reader – I ask you frankly: have you permitted a spider to go prospecting about your person for some-where warm and snuggly to spend the day and maybe digest that scrumptious blue-bottle which otherwise would have been driving you mad? You haven't? Oh shame: does not your heart curl up with remorse within you at your churlish ingratitude?

There is no more enduring testimony to the fecund inventiveness of father nature than the spider. Do you know there are some 30,000 species of spider? Such bliss! Oh, do you not long to have one of each in your bedroom, exploring your toes, making webs in your slippers, feasting on small birds upon your pillow?

And listen, my sisters, for it is you who seem to fear the spider most of all: are you not reassured that the spiderly world that you behold is almost entirely female? The males, as in the human world, are a contemptible, worthless bunch, insignificant, beneath attention; small, unmotivated creatures who perish soon after sex, unlamented and forgotten.

Whereas the female spider now –

> When Cob the brooding spider sits unmoving on her silk;
> Her children wait patiently for more of mother's milk.
> A cream which is extracted from an unwilling bewinged pail,
> Oh, indeed the female of the species is more deadly than the male.

Spiders are everywhere on this planet. No more diverse form has been found – on alpine peaks and in arctic crags, in deserts and in tundra, in pools and high in the atmosphere, the spider seams and sews, casts nets and weaves vast garments through the air. Some gather prey by hunting; others net their dinner with a lattice of quick-drying spit. Know the feeling well.

Women of Ireland, come here to me: does it not please you to see the gossamer glory of an autumn morning? Does it not thrill you that that great light and luminous tent stretching through a meadow at dawn is one of the great structures of the world, and it is all of women's devising?

Attend more closely. Were there any spiders in Beijing? And if not why not? Is the spider not the greatest artist, engineer, beguiler of us all? In only one regard is the spider deficient. The spider is a poor singer. Also, I am told many lady spiders have an attitude towards sex which leaves much to be desired. No matter. I am unlikely to couple with a spider, no matter how great my desperation.

In all other regards the spider is our great benefactor. My windows are festooned with webs where hurtling bluebottles have come to a pinioned end, their husks hang-ing like carcasses on a butcher's window. For there is no more ecologically sound fly killer than a spider. Perfect recycling of fly matter with no chemical residues.

Have you the least idea how we benefit from a spider's appetite for flies?

An acre of Meath grassland will house two million spiders and all of them busy extracting pesky insects from the planet, which would otherwise be in your tea, hair and soup.

Not just in Meath does the spider toil so beneficently – take that spider you find in your bath. It did not come up the plughole. It hates plugholes as much as you do and, like you in similar circumstances, it cannot climb up the smooth porcelain sides. So do not wash it down the plughole; it will drown, instead of being able to prowl through the house while you slumber, stalking and killing weevils and carpetmites which make you scratch and sneeze. If it wants, let it crawl up your leg in the shower. It will soon find somewhere nice and comfortable to nest and then you can ignore it.

For the spider is even more your friend than your dog: you do not have to take it for walks and it does not bite the postman. Or even postwoman, being a female.

You can even eat spiders. The British arachnophile, W.S. Bristowe, went a-courting with his young doxy through an English meadow, savouring the delights of fresh spider. They pronounced orbweb spider, *Araneus quadratus,* the tastiest, with a rather nutty flavour. An unusual way to win the hand of a young lady; still maybe it's worth a shot –

'Ma'am, could I interest you in a small banquet of leggy arthropods?' no doubt are the words to woo a woman to one's bed. And after one has made love, one could lunch lightly on a collation of common garden spiders, with perhaps a little dessert of money spider done in mousse and covered in a black widow sauce, pausing occasionally to floss their little legs from between one's teeth.

A warning here. If you are banqueting in your marital bed with someone other than your spouse, do make sure to brush up all the little limbs afterwards. Those little leglets are a dead give-away. Divorce courts accept them as evidence.

But other than in dietary matters, Hearken right well – *Guard your spiders well: then shall you live long and know contentment all your days.*

Bats and CJH

Charles J. Haughey might not go down in history quite the way he might have wanted – the man who united Ireland, turned the country into an Irish-speaking industrial giant and a regional power with an ocean-going fleet and an Army before which the nations of the world (the Brits especially) trembled.

But he might well be remembered as the man who seriously endangered the bat in Dublin. This is not criticism. Charles Haughey was the man responsible for the revitalisation of Dublin City. No other Taoiseach we have had would have had the energy or the vision or the willpower to bring about the regeneration of the Temple

Bar area, and the creation of the special tax zones which caused such huge capital sums to be invested in parts of the city which had seen no useful economic activity in a generation or more.

When CJH became Taoiseach some 16 years ago, there was barely a restaurant in the city centre worth eating in. When a good restaurant opened in Powerscourt Townhouse in the early 1980s, it closed because there simply was not a market for high-quality food in the city centre.

It looked as if the old city of Dublin was doomed. The entire focus of social and economic activity was shifting southwards towards Dun Laoghaire.

Worse than the simple movement of capital and social activity towards the southern suburbs was the sense of despair which gripped the city and those who lived there; no hope, no rescue, the future seemed evident. Large tracts of land and old brickwork were becoming the home of buddleia and fern and crime.

What CJH achieved as Taoiseach was to reverse that trend in its entirety. And the beneficiaries have not just been in Temple Bar; the regeneration of the central northside area is well under way.

No doubt there are criticisms – most people who have looked at some of the flats which have been built might regret building regulations were not more emphatic about minimum sizes; and there are real fears that many of the apartment complexes are simply ready-made tenements.

But a more certain criticism is that the reconstruction of such vast amounts of central Dublin has destroyed old roofs; and old tiled roofs are what bats love as nesting places.

I should declare a special interest here. I do not like bats; I love them. They were invented by the Lord on his most perfect day: they are animal perfection.

Some people have had the good fortune to have had a bat trapped in their hair; would that that great good fortune might one day come my way. I know of people who have had a bat land on their faces while they slept.

Such bliss! To wake up being kissed by a bat is infinitely superior to waking up being kissed by Namoi Campbell or Julia Roberts.

No doubt bat conversation is limited in variety, largely consisting of squeaks and indignant trills. To our ears, this means little; but to bat ears it is pure Mozart. And even for those who do not speak bat, an evening watching bats hunt is an evening spent close to paradise.

No bird can manage the startling changes of direction a bat can manage, turning a sharp right-angle on a point at speed, as if a nail had been hammered into a bat wingtip. I once saw a bat being taken on the wing by a sparrowhawk in north-central Dublin; it was an astonishing sight – only the sparrow-hawk's huge velocity enabled it to catch the bat as it turned to evade its hunter.

Of course that night I mourned the batkins in their little roost, waiting for their parent to come back with a feed of scrumptious moth-*mousse* and a few score mosquitoes. Maybe the batkins died. That is nature; meanwhile a brood of baby sparrowhawks were tasting their first bat stew, neatly vomited up by mum or dad.

But it is highly unusual for a sparrowhawk to catch a bat; their time-ranges barely touch, and it is a rare hawk and an unlucky bat which come to the conclusion that I saw.

For the most part, bats are without predators in the air; though in their homes, cats find them quite tasty, and will feast on batkins at Christmas – stuffed with chestnut and lightly grilled in garlic butter, they are surprisingly agreeable. Their bones are delicate and perfectly digestible.

Yet it is not as foodstuff that I hail the bat. It is as entertainer and air cleanser that the bat comes into its own; it is a joy and a wonder to watch the bat patrolling the skies, taking insects which might just view your neck as a dinner plate.

People say that bats are blind, but that is mere envy. Bats are not in the least blind; in addition to having their audio-range finding and detection equipment, bats are perfectly capable of threading a needle. We are uneasy in the presence of such talent, such intelligence.

Certain bat enthusiasts have trained bats as domestic pets – their droppings are perfect, compact little pellets which are clean and easy to clear up, and are quite good as roof insulation, though it would take quite a while for one bat to produce the volume of droppings required to keep a house warm.

A small perch will suffice once you have domesticated your bat. It will feed on grubs obtainable from an angling shop, and will reward your kindness by gobbling any mosquitoes which enter your living room, turning them within 24 hours into roof insulation.

If you are squeamish about handling bats, your wife will no doubt oblige you; and if you are really worried about how it spends the night, she will let it roost in her hair while she sleeps.

But the obliging wives of the capital will not provide the entire bat population of Dublin with homes. Might not Dublin Corporation, or the developers who after all are making so much money from the tax-free zones, establish batteries on the tops of all new buildings in the city?

The bats of Dublin are one of the city's greatest joys. We should take their future seriously.

Phoenix Park II

It was about this time of the year, Lady Day in August, that we once heard a nightjar in the Phoenix Park. So far as I know, it is the most northerly sighting of that lovely bird. It behaved exactly as it should, perching along and then athwart the branch of

the tree, churring as it did; just as night fell and the moths began to come out to provide the crepuscular night-jar with its dinner. I have not seen it since.

Once I put up two corncrakes there, surely the closest to Dublin city centre they
have ever been. Pheasants are common-place, especially in a few choice acres where I
go and virtually nobody else does.

There are sparrowhawks and falcons and the occasional kingfisher and, on certain
odd summer days, the swallows swish by one's feet and dart over the shoulder as if they
are performing high-speed inspections.

In winter the oystercatcher, a handsome little nun of a bird, comes in great flocks
to browse on the grasslands, arriving together, squeaking news of somewhere suitable
to graze as they wheel in from Poolbeg, their alternative home.

The indifference of most Dubliners to the presence of this park is one of the great
wonders of the age. For it is a paradise, each season of the year, and each day of its
season. On wet days in winter it is sublime, because it belongs only to the few souls
prepared to brave the winds and the rain; and then you can walk its grasses and its
woodlands firmly of the opinion that it is your estate.

There is not a day in the year when the signs of life are not evident in the trees of
the park; no sooner are the last of the leaves gone than the buds of the new season present themselves, holding out hope as night encroaches upon daylight, advancing in
both directions towards noon, leaving a few hours of daylight around the centre of the
day.

That day when day is barely day is as far removed from this day, Lady Day in
August, as we are today from what seems like only yesterday's spring fevers of April
when the swallows arrived. Between now and the shortest day of the year lies the last
residues of summer.

The swallows will be going in about a month, just as autumn advances. The park
is an unbelievable paradise in the autumn; more conkers to be found than all the children in the world can want, and a spectrum of colours for which there are no words;
and the stealthy advance too of the wintry smells of loam and soil, abolishing the fresh
green smell of growth.

In midwinter, the park achieves an odd glory; because funnily enough, trees are
often at their best without leaves, and seen in the long straight light of the winter sun,
they became magnificent pieces of architecture, gleaming blackly against the vast skies
which tower over the park.

That is one of the great and haunting beauties of the Phoenix Park – the vast vault
beneath which it lives. Those who live in the city forget the spectacular scale of the
arch which joins the horizons. For much of the year it is overcast; but virtually every
day will provide some break in the clouds, when a huge theatrical production will be
presented by sun and sky and cirrus, columns of sunbeam and wisps of cloud and odd,
nameless colours whirling before vanishing for all time, to be replaced by fresh, freshly
minted colours which will soon vanish too.

It is impossible to tire of the numerous walks in the park; merely to follow a route in the opposite direction from usual is to see fresh wonders – the delightful skyline of Dublin, the green of Rathmines townhall, the numerous church spires and steeples; or the Dublin hills, surmounted by the Hellfire Club, as visible from the park as the park is visible from it.

And both places have been attracting the kind of visitor which neither needs – gangs of youths drinking through the night, and leaving hundreds of beer cans behind them. I visited the Hellfire Club the other day – it is in a disgusting condition. Is it ever cleaned up? Like Phoenix Park, the Hellfire Club is one of the places tourists to Dublin visit – what a marvellous image they must take away with them.

I do not know what to do about these people. If they took their beercans with them when they left, I would say, do nothing. Leave them be. They are doing no harm. But it is not that simple, certainly not in the park, where there has through the summer, especially during the dry-season, been an increasing amount of fire-setting. Freshly cut and dried hay has been burned; so have trees been set on fire.

What to do about the worthy gentlemen who get up to these capers? I haven't a clue. Maybe a period of late-night patrols by intrepid gardaí or Army Rangers – for it is certainly not a job I would do – could curtail the late night revellers. Or at least make them take their empties with them.

They, at least, are anonymous. I am sick of complaining about the plastic tape left by the grooms of the polo-players. Is it not time for the Park authorities simply to say, No polo unless you leave the fields clean? New money might not recognise duty; but it will certainly understand the meaning of homelessness.

The park is more than a park. It is one of the great archaeological digs through Irish history. It was an abbey, and where there was an abbey, there were probably a well and a holy site before it. The tenants of the abbey worked the strip-farming system, and the undulations left by their agriculture ripple over the playing fields even now.

The choicest homes in Dublin in time became the homes of the papal nuncio and the American ambassador. I am unlikely to be president; and even more unlikely to be US ambassador here. A frightful shame. To compensate all those who love the park and will never live there, could not some publisher commission a *Book Of The Park*, with essays on the history and the buildings, the wildlife and the plants, of Dublin's great jewel? Please?

Hibernamus in Hiberniae

The nights are cold now, and they are longer, but the shortness of the days is offset by their beauty. The hedgerows are losing their leaves with the reluctance of children undressing in a cold bedroom, and around them the great broadleaf trees are touring the colours of the rainbow before going naked for the season which becomes us best: winter.

Summer in this country is a fraud; it is an annual perjury, made grievous by our witless innocence as we buy our suncream and charcoal. We should yearly curse our infernal, eternal stupidity, and not the summer weather, which is what it is – fickle, drab, cloudy and bleak. Yet we have been compensated most gloriously this year by a quite wondrous autumn; perhaps it is simply that it is my first autumn in the country, but I don't think so. Splendid day has followed splendid day.

Blackberries, the hedgerow pearls, are normally uneatable at this time of year, their sugar content low because of the poor sunshine, though the tradition has it that they have lost their flavour because the devil has pissed on them. This year, Lucifer has kept his bladder under control; or maybe it is just that the autumn sunlight has been so strong that the blackberries are now, finally, when they should be past their prime, actually at their best. The berries of mid to late summer, normally delicious, were wan things, tasteless and unripe; but this October, the brambles are laden with juicy fruit, and crab apples, elderberries and sloes have reached a late but plump harvest.

You can make a lovely jelly from the sap of boiled crab apples – perfect with pork – and of course you can drink the juice of sloes, but only after a year's immersion in gin, to celebrate the last Christmas of the 1990s. I have never heard of elder-gin, but this most glorious of autumns I will make some, and taste it in a year's time, and then maybe fall down dead.

It might well be one of those etymological coincidences that the two Latin words, *Hibernia* for Ireland and *hibernus* for wintry, are so close; or on the other hand, the ancient Romans, knowing a thing or two, might well have allowed one word to be influenced by the other. Few places must have seemed more abominable to the Latinate spirit than that wet island on the edge of the known world in winter. They even came here, messed around for a while in Kildare, and then fled. Even parts of Scotland seemed superior to Ireland in winter.

They are an intelligent people, the Italians, but they have their off-days. Ireland is at its best in winter, when every fine morning brings a fresh surprise and the flat sunlight illuminating the black shiny bark of leafless trees creates a landscape of bewilderingly beautiful sculptures. Freed of most of their summertime duties of work, country people are able to relax in the winter and engage in the sports Italians would pay fortunes to be able to enjoy over such vast, uncrowded spaces.

The swallows are gone, of course – though I saw one unfortunate last weekend; doomed, doomed – and our skies are now filled with wheeling mobs of jackdaws, rooks and crows. Few things are as evocative as the gathering of corbines at nightfall, their plaintive, beckoning voices ringing out through the dusk as they communely seek a roost. Thrushes forage in large mobs through the winter grasslands, and if we are lucky soon they will be joined by redwings and fieldfares from Scandinavia, proof that winter has arrived there.

Winter officially begins here when the clocks change, on the closest Saturday to October 21st, two months short of the mid-winter solstice, though they return to summertime a full three months after the solstice. Why this should be so is one of the mysteries the British astronomer royal might be able to explain to me; nobody else can. Nor can anyone else explain why we so slavishly follow English clocks: we did not when we were part of the United Kingdom yet we do today, though there can be no logical reason why Donegal should dance to the time set in Greenwich, 700 miles to the south-west.

Now there are moves in Britain to create two time zones there, simply because the chronological needs of Dover are not the same as those of Orkney. Are we going to have to wait, once again, for the British to take the initiative on something before we, once again, ape their ways?

No matter what the clocks may say, now we are moving towards our true season, the season to which our cuisine and our habits and our clothing incline us. Summertime is a heresy, the false prophet of a deluding schism which invariably leads us into a forlorn and godless wilderness, from which we escape with relief, sadder but seldom wiser. Forget summer. Ahead lie the wet and blustery glories of winter: wildly wagging gundog tails disappearing into the brake and horses' rearquarters vanishing over tall, uncropped hedgerows; buttery scones and hot whiskeys; squirrels skittering through trees; and always, always, from winter's first day, the tiny buds of the coming spring. Rejoice: *hibernamus in Hiberniae*.

SPORT

Night golf, swimming

This column has in the past referred to the worldwide derangement commonly known as golf. The people who resort to this practice are either those poor souls, the barking mad lunatics who have been let out into what is known as community care, there to gambol or caper as they see fit – and what they see fit to do is to chivvy an inoffensive white object around the countryside – or are victims of such advanced senile dementia that the best and simplest thing to do is to slip some strychnine into their Complan, or fix the brakes in their bathchair.

One hardly knows what to make of the news from Australia of the invention of a form of the game which I hesitate to speak of in mixed company. It is night golf. With or without chaperones, I cannot say. Knowing golfers, probably not. Their shamelessness diminishes us all.

Yet my problem is this; it is possible that the night-time game of golf will so exhaust the golfers nocturnally that they will be unable to appear in daytime and, like badgers and stoats and other offensive beasts of the night, will retire to their noisome little nests. While the rest of civilisation is enjoying the benedictions of the sun, golfers, stoats and in Australia, where this all began, Tasmanian devils rest in their fetid burrows.

The added advantage of night-time golfing is that it is completely without televisual appeal. But yes, I admit this is true also of day-time golf, but there are other things to see when day-time golf is on the air. For reasons which have so far not been explained by science, golf is played amongst some of the most beautiful scenery anywhere; so if you are compelled to watch television day-time golf, you can at least watch the beech trees being beech trees.

Night-time golf does not even possess this compensation. All there is to be seen is a luminous ball and a luminous club-head. Club-head strikes ball. Ball whizzes off into the distance. Ball falls into hole normally occupied by golfers, stoats and badgers. Game over. Not even the most perverse of television producers could possibly see any potential in night-time golf.

Alas this is not the case for swimming, an even more deplorable sport for the spectator than golf. At least the scenery in golf changes; different events occur. If one is very lucky, a golfer is struck by lightning and is turned into a piece of charcoal, but that sort of luck is unusual. I know of people who have watched golf avidly over several decades in the fond hope of seeing a golfer turned into barbecue-fuel, and never seen it once.

But there can be other diversions. There are, of course, always beech trees being beech trees, never mind those enthralling occasions when a mashie niblick fells a passing eagle or albatross (golf courses, to judge from the reports of golf writers, are densely populated with improbable forms of birdlife).

But in swimming there is no such diversion; swimming is quite the most baleful sport yet devised. Identical swimmers, wearing identical hats, and virtually invisible in the wake they create, plough backwards and forwards at about a fast walking speed over half an acre of mild chloric acid. If it was a little bit stronger we might be afforded the pleasure of seeing some of the swimmers dissolve, leaving maybe just a couple of teeth in the bottom of the pool and with possibly even a criminal investigation to follow.

Every single race is to all intents and purposes identical; nationality, age, sex, size, all are vanquished in the swimming pool: it is all shoulders, splash and whirling heels, and then back down to the other end again, with more brainless, deafening cheering than you would find even in a massed stadium of braying, rabid golfers on glue.

Something odd occurs to my brain when I turn on television and there is competitive swimming on; it turns into a sort of shark-infested porridge; where most of it becomes inert and glutinous, and the rest of it is in agony.

Apparently they use people as swimmers. There is no real evidence that they are actually living breathing human beings who eat and breathe and love and go for walks like the rest of us. They might as well use towed mannikins to equal effect.

All of which leaves this column in that curious vessel a quandary, for the Irish Amateur Swimming Association has requested me to prepare to participate in National Swim Day on June 5th.

What to do? One is not against swimming. There is a great deal to be said on its behalf, if you happen to have found yourself on the *Lusitania* or the *Titanic* at an inopportune moment; and doubtless it is wonderful therapy for people who need to recover from an accident. But that does not mean we should make a sport out of it, any more than one makes a sport out of tourniquet-tying, or open heart surgery, or hysterectomies or prostate surgery in the medical world; and nor is there an equivalent sport for getting out of crashed cars or burning airliners or houses on fire.

One hates to be churlish, so the least and also the most I am prepared to do for the Irish Swimming Association is mention that this National Swim Day exists, and that I will be too busy to participate, having a prior commitment to play golf that day.

Golf and tennis

Oh dear, it is that time of year again when the double scourge of golf and tennis are at our throats and chewing. The one metaphorical glimmer of light on the summer's horizon is that after a month of rainlessness (at the time of writing) the rain is pouring down; can it possibly be that the sporting divinities have decided that enough is enough, it is time both to water the gardens and to rain off these desecrations of human endeavour? Why not? Fate is sometimes merciful.

Was it not an abrupt change in the weather which ended the Black Death, and another which ended the Great Fire of London. Two months of rain to wash away the abominations of golf and tennis, and meanwhile doing wonders for my garden, might yet restore me to the bosom of the Church.

It would not if I thought the hereafter was going to consist of golfers and tennis players. Yet despite the horror and loathing in which all decent people hold these two species, they are surprisingly different in all but the certainty of their rendezvous with the fires of hell.

Golfers deserve those fires for their sweaters alone: if one found oneself sitting in the same railway carriage as somebody wearing such a sweater you would be readily forgiven for pulling the communication cord. It is not widely known but Irish Rail guards are equipped with portable firehoses to wash out any stray golfers found about the place; they have a range of 15 yards and each firehose reservoir is good for 10 average size male golfers and up to 20 smallish females: there are special rates for golfing families, you will be happy to hear.

It is possible that you will be unable to get to the communication cord, either because you have been blinded by the sweater, the golfer is between you and the cord, or the golfer has begun a golf-conversation with you ('And there I was, staring at an albatross, bunkered at the seventh, my mashie niblick's crankshaft gone, with the colonel dead and the Gatling jammed …'), and you are experiencing brain-fusion. In this case, step out of the railway carriage. It means certain death, but that is infinitely superior to being cooped up with a golfer all the way to Cork. (There is, by the way, a little known ordinance, tacked on by the great John Redmond to the Home Rule Act and never repealed, which exonerates all railway passengers from any crimes they might commit in the company of golfers, excluding the sabotage of docks and treasonable conversation with the enemy, but certainly not excluding murder.)

It is one of the deep flaws in the argument for equality between the sexes that women demand to be equal members of golf clubs, whereas I wake up each morning blessing the day for beginning without my being a member of a golf club; may it end the same! For the women golfers' is a peculiar argument; the logic of which I have never quite understood. I have failed to perceive a comparable demand for equality of membership of Mountjoy Jail.

But though I dread – to the point of having my pharmacist make up special suicide pills – sharing a railway carriage with golfers, I concede that personally they seem relatively blameless individuals.

Malice appears to be absent from their faces. They gaze blankly from the pages of that part of the newspaper reserved for their suffocatingly tedious pastimes, vacant smiles on their faces, their eyes indicating that their brains are working as feverishly as a halibut's on a slab. In short golfers, though bores, seem a decent enough lot. The same cannot be said for tennis players. The nastiest and most graceless of sporting types seem to have been tennis players. Some of the worst cheat, bully, bamboozle and lie; they shout, they scream, they grunt, and they have combined the hymn of benediction perfectly with the essential Descartes: 'Tantrum ergo sum'.

You want convincing that tennis players leave something to be desired? Can any sport produce names to equal those of Nastase, McEnroe, Connors, Hewitt and Navratilova, without rummaging through its lesser membership among the inmates of death-row?

At least in tennis the female sex shows clear and irrefutable evidence of its superiority over the male. To do certain things badly – eating one's children, say, or bookburning, or massacring symphony orchestras – is evidence of superiority over those who do it well. So women tennis players are to be applauded for the appalling quality of their tennis.

Watching them stand on the back line lobbing the ball at one another, one is put in mind of those knitting circles in Donegal or the Hebrides, the women ravelling wool and chanting one of the colourful work-shanties which go with such activity. Perhaps there are hitherto unknown tennis work-songs which Navvers and Sabbers rhythmically chant to one another from backline to backline and which folklorists are itching to record.

One sees that women tennis players, though incapable of playing either in the same category as men, or even the same number of sets, are demanding equal money. I agree with them. Anybody who strives so hard to do something for which they are wholly unequipped deserves handsome financial reward.

This summer I trust that Wimbledon Lawn Tennis Club will, on the same principle, inaugurate the Porpoise and Dolphin Singles competition: and perhaps it is time that Guinness Peat Aviation abolished the pischophobic policies which have not allowed cod, herring and haddock their rightful places in their piano competition; and surely the hour has come when the *Irish Times*/Aer Lingus literary awards accepts entries from grapefruit.

Hours of women's tennis – though it will seem like months – awaits us all over the coming weeks. There is one blessing. Television has not discovered the ultimate horror – women's golf. I suspect that makes women's tennis seem almost unbearably exciting in comparison. Oh good shot, Navvers, old girl.

Jack Charlton and Eamon Dunphy

Jack Charlton sat in his hotel room in Istanbul last night, his head in his hands as Maurice Setters outlined the latest news of the improbable setbacks to his already injury-ravaged squad. 'Wot did you say' appened to Niall Quinn?' he moaned.

'Hit by a low-flying bird, boss,' muttered Maurice Setters.

'A low-flying bird!' cried Jack. 'A low-flying bird! By 'eck, what sort of sofy 'as'e becoom if 'e can be stopped playing by a tiny little phookin bird.'

'It was an ostrich, boss.'

There was silence in the room for a while. 'All right,' Jack sighed.

'Why the phook can Paul McGrath not play?'

'Bitten by a dog, boss.'

'Bitten by a dog? Bitten by a dog? Are you taking the phookin' piss out o' me, Maurice. I'm in no yuma for jokes, Maurice, I'm tellin' you. What soart of phookin' dog, soom bleedin' pooch, I suppose?'

'An Anatolian sheepdog, boss. The biggest and fiercest dog in the world. There's no chance of him playing boss. None.'

'When will the boogah be able to play, then?'

'Not sure, boss, It depends on his leg.'

'When it gets better, you mean?'

'No boss. When they find it.'

Jack Charlton breathed deeply. 'Oh I don't know why I bother. I reelly don't. And remind me why Packie Bonner can't play.'

'Religion, boss. His religion won't let him on Wednesdays.'

'Religion? Religion? But 'e's a phookin' Catholic, i'n't 'e?

The 'ole phookin' squad's Catholic. Met the Pope, di'n't 'e?'

'Kissed the ring. Saw it with me own eyes. Catholics can play football any day they like. Mebbe they can't use condoms on Wednesdays, but they can play phookin' football.'

'Sorry, boss. Things have changed. He was sitting next to a Tenth Day Latter Day Witness on the plane. Tenth Day Latter Day Witnesses believe in the decimal week, boss. Decimal coinage, decimal weights, decimal measures, 1992 and all that. He converted Packie. Packie is now a Tenth Day Latter Day Witness. He refuses to play on Wednesdays, their Sabbath.'

'Where is 'e now?' muttered Jack, his hands on his face.

'He's out with Roy Keane trying to convert Istanbul to his religion.'

'Roy Keane? You don't mean Roy Keane …?'

Maurice Setters nodded dumbly. Again there was silence in the room.

'Well, you may as well let me 'ave all the news, our Maurice. What players of the original squad do we have left?'

'Of the original squad, boss? Of the original squad, boss, we have, precisely, ah, none.'

Jack Charlton sat on his bed looking like a man who has just downed a pint of Guinness only to find a dead mouse in the bottom. He rubbed his chin.

'Is there a plane out of this phookin' city tonight?'

'It's not that bad, actually, boss,' declared Maurice brightly. 'Reinforcements have been arriving in from Ireland.'

'Reinforcements? Wot reinforcements? There are no uninjured Irish footballers left in the entire phookin' world.'

'That is true boss, that is true. I did not actually say there are footballers. Some of them are retired footballers, and others are just hopefuls.'

' 'Opefuls? Wot 'opefuls?'

'Prudence and Primrose Entwhistle are what you could call hopefuls, boss. They say they are from Kingstown.'

'Well, I've chosen Scots and English and Welsh to play for Ireland. No 'arm in a couple of Jamaicans.'

'And a number of former internationals have stepped forward, boss. Charlie Hurley, Ambrose Fogarty, Jackie Carey. In fact, with the latest arrival, we've got a full team.'

'Brilliant Maurice. Phookin' brilliant. I knew I could rely on you. This latest arrival, 'o is 'e?'

'Eamon Dunphy, boss,' said Maurice in a low voice.

There was a sound of a pencil snapping.

'Doonphy,' hissed Jack through clenched teeth. 'Phookin' Doonphy.'

And that, my lord, is how Maurice Setters came to depart through the unopened window of a 20th-floor bedroom in Istanbul, seriously injuring the Entwhistle sisters, who were distributing Bibles and rescuing stray cats at the time. I therefore seek a postponement of today's match.

Granted.

Rugby at Lansdowne, 2001

And so after the final home match in the international rugby championship of 2001 at Lansdowne Road and both spectators had gone home, the coach, manager and captain as always gave their press conference.

'We're disappointed, naturally, with the result,' said the coach. 'We were hoping for a win in our last home match of the international season. The boys have all worked hard over the year, and we had reason to believe that we could do it.'

'However, we were unlucky. We didn't play well on the day, the ball didn't bounce for us and the conditions did not suit the sort of rugby we like to play. Still, we can take some consolation from the fact that we got points on the board. We can build on the positive aspects to our performance, and hopefully go on to greater things ...'

At that point he was hit by a cabbage. 'Yes, well, I can understand that some of you are a little disappointed,' he continued, dodging an elderly orange. 'But you have to look on the positive side of things. Ouch. Any questions?'

There was a long and incredulous silence while the various journalists strove to compose themselves. Yvonne Judge was the first to manage it. 'Some people might observe that the opposition today was not particularly strong. Croatia has negligible rugby traditions. This was their first international, and they knew so little about the game that they arrived with 11 players.'

'Well that's my point,' replied the coach. 'It's very difficult for our lads to play against unpredictable teams like Croatia.'

'Look, the Croatians even put a player in goal,' Yvonne replied a trifle testily.

The coach slapped his knee. 'Exactly! Now how can you play rugby against a team which has a player standing between the posts the entire time? It stands to reason difficulties are going to arise.'

'They knew so little about the rules of the game that they kept heading the ball' one objector cried.

'We hadn't encountered tactics like that before. No wonder we lost all the line-outs,' the coach continued in rather hurt tones. 'I wish you wouldn't emphasise the negative aspects. Remember we scored a try.'

'That was in the first minute, before Croatia had realised they could use their hands,' howled one journalist. 'We hardly ever got into their half again, even though Croatia used only soccer tackles and played a four-four-two formation.'

'Now that's my point. We have never experienced rugby played like that, and we took some time to settle in. And the size of their players didn't help.'

'Their tallest player was six foot, and he was the guy in goal. He only touched the ball four times, when he thought he was making saves, and then he was penalised each time for throwing the ball forward. Four scrums under their posts, and we lost the lot. Unbelievable.'

'Look, our scrum had never faced an opposition which lined up in a wall 10 yards back from the ball with their hands over their private parts and a goalkeeper dancing behind them shouting instructions. Our lads found that very disconcerting. Goalkeepers shouting instructions should be outlawed in rugby. I intend to raise the matter at the next meeting of the international board.'

'But it's not just today's match we're talking about. We haven't won a match in years. The last match was no better than today's.'

'Well, Tibet proved to be stronger than we had expected. Frankly I was amazed at how well they played.'

'How well they played? Their scrum consisted of the Dalai Lama and some fellow who kept hitting a gong, yet they still managed to score two push-over tries. They outran our players even though they all wore orange robes. Even their yak managed to score a try in the corner.'

'Yes, well, we've looked into that. Yaks are illegal. They shouldn't have been playing a yak.'

'Albania didn't have a yak, and they beat us hollow,' one mournful voice from the back pointed out.

'Yes, but they had Mother Teresa in their second row. She proved to be a more powerful scrummager than we had expected. A strong runner too, and excellent in the line-outs. Quite a handful.'

'But is it not just countries like Albania and Croatia which are now stronger than us. We lost every match on our South American tour last summer. Tierra del Fuego walloped us. The Falklands massacred us.'

'Yes, well I'm not all that sure about the legality of fielding a team which included three merino and four Scottish Blackface.'

'And a collie,' added the mournful voice from the back. 'Yet their flock still managed to push our scrum back. Barbados annihilated us, and they thought they were playing cricket. Scored 10 tries for no wickets and then declared, and even then we couldn't score. Even when they went off for tea we still couldn't score. I think that was the worst moment in my entire career as a sports journalist.'

'The good news is that we are confident about our summer tour. It is to New Zealand.'

At that point the coach was knocked unconscious by the simultaneous arrival of three turnips, several tomatoes, and nearly one hundredweight of potatoes; and the journalists went home with the one appalling thought in mind – that we still have France to play, in Paris, after Irish officials had presided over the English humiliation of the French.

Mercy.

Tyson

How mad are we all? If we could watch men having sex-acts together on television, how long would it be before Ministers denounced such spectacles and the government moved to end them? Instead, we merely watch men beating the brains out of one another, and politicians fawn to be seen in the company of the brain-smashers. It is sick.

When Stephen Collins won whatever championship it was against Chris Eubank in Millstreet the other week and then said he would like to fight Nigel Benn next, how many of his cheering admirers remembered that Benn's last opponent, Gerald McClellan, began his fight as a boxer? No more. Now he is a mangel worzel.

This is the essence of boxing. The absence of animus between the boxers is irrelevant. Soldiers feel no animus against the men they kill. It is the boxer's intention to end his fight by knocking out his opponent.

No doubt a nice scientific victory over 12 rounds is pleasing enough; but how much better is it to be able to talk of a storming knock-out in the tenth! No doubt a thousand tiny blood vessels have been popped in your opponent's brain; no doubt ten million brain cells have been turned into protoplasmic goo. But that is the fight-game, and we are all adults here, are we not?

Sure, free men make decisions to fight. Fair enough. Free men could also take a decision to fight with broad-swords. This is called duelling and is outlawed. Boxing once was. Now it is not. No doubt this is a measure of our freedoms.

This does not make it right. Forget all the talk we have been hearing about what a nice bunch of people boxers are. Just because they are nice does not mean they do not possess instincts which are dangerous and unhealthy and should be kept in cages in a zoo.

What sort of people do we think most killers are? Do we think they are people who beat their wives and assault children and smash up pubs and break beer bottles in strangers' faces? They are not. For the most part they are decent ordinary people who possess the particular quality which separates them from the rest of us – to disregard the inviolability of the human body.

I remember meeting a Protestant paramilitary leader in a Belfast pub. Sitting at a table next to us was a nice young man who was drinking a soda water with his mother. The lad had a few words with us. He was charming and very friendly, and gave me an amiable nod before he left, helping his mother with admirable care and concern through the door.

'That lad scares me,' said my companion. 'He's the most natural killer I've ever come across. Doesn't drink, doesn't smoke, is kind to everybody, loves his mother, is popular with girls, has a good job, has lots of friends, works hard, and kills without a thought.'

That nice young man had been responsible for the murders of half a dozen Catholics, one of whom was a driver of a milkfloat. The lad had waved him down early one morning while the rest of the city slept and asked him for a lift up the Springfield Road. So they proceeded up the Springfield Road that silent dawn, chatting and delivering milk; until my young friend reached the point where he wanted to get off, when he turned and shot the milkman in the head and went home for an early breakfast.

He would have made a good boxer.

Do you understand how meaningless it is to say how nice boxers are? What sets them all apart is not their physique or their skill or their speed; it is the willingness to do terrible damage to another human being's brains, and to train hard and brutally to that end. And the boxer does not train just to win but to knock his opponent out. He trains to do brain-damage.

We should be grateful to Michael Tyson that he is free this week to remind us of what boxing is all about. Tyson is a truly foul human being, the double beneficiary of his colour and the colour of the woman he raped. Had he been a white man who raped a black woman he would have got the savage sentence which his savage deed deserved and audiences would have hissed him. Had he been a white man who raped a white woman, feminists would have been picketing the jail which held him as he emerged.

But Desiree Washington had the misfortune to be black, and somewhere within the bar-code of US justice there is the presumption that a black woman who goes into Mike Tyson's room at three in the morning has a shrewd idea of what's going to happen.

She had not; but she has now. And the feminists have been silent about her appalling fate because it is not politically correct to denounce a brutal violent woman-violating thug who is black. Mike Tyson – oh forget his unhappy background; lots of people have unhappy backgrounds – is an authentically evil person, who trains to hurt, and who enjoys hurting, and who will be soon hurting more, and being rewarded more than any other 'sportsman' in history for his trouble.

Tyson is a boxer. Only the weak-minded think there is anything other to boxing than the ability to inflict maximum damage to another human being within the Queensberry choreography. It is the capacity to inflict more hurt on another human being in cold-blood with fists than the rest of us can manage with weapons in anger. It is a disgusting and foul profession, beyond the sanction of law because those who fight are free men.

We have recently had the ridiculous situation where a film in which violence is *simulated* was banned; yet real brain-shattering violence is on our television screens almost nightly, and is applauded by our leaders if the victor is Irish. This is idiocy.

There is a simple way of driving this foulness from our screens – by taxing punitively the owners of dishes or cable-systems which can receive them. Nothing, of course, will be done.

MEs make great footballers

Whatever else happens we must hope that Jack Charlton resigns as Irish soccer manager, if only to put an end to that woeful advertisement for Monaghan Creameries, the one which reaches its climax with some earth-shattering query from a Charlton-interrogator along the lines, 'Well Jack, what do you think about the Cup?'

'Wot coop?' asks our genial Geordie, 'I dreenk ma Monaghan meelk outa a glass.'

I would dearly love to know what advertising agency was responsible for this precious, priceless evidence of the spread of BSE amongst humans. The authors of such crassness, such leaden, dung-brained attempts at humour, deserve all the notoriety they can get.

Advertising copy-writers all over the world would cluster around them in mute congratulation, slapping their shoulders in speechless admiration. Even in Tibet and Rwanda, Kampuchea and North Korea, where the copywriter's art is in its infancy and where inexperienced copywriters are often infantile and cumbrous – yes, even in those forlorn outbacks of copywritery, they have never managed anything so otiosely lame and cretinous as *Well Jack, what do you think about the cup?*

What Cup, I drink my Monaghan (or Lhasa or wherever) milk out of a glass.

I will at least say this of that ad: it has ensured that I never, ever again drink Monaghan milk. I would rather let my bones crumble from osteoporosis, I would when thirsty prefer to lick wet tar or to suck the spit from the mouth of a dead pig, than let a teaspoon of Monaghan Milk pass my lips. Otherwise, I'm sure it's grand stuff.

I still regret that Bob Paisley, a true gentleman and the greatest British football manager of all time, did not get the Irish job 10 years ago, for two reasons. The first is that he would have had too much class to utter the banal Monaghan milk tripe. The second is that he believed in football as a source of joy and an expression of athletic artistry.

But he could have achieved only so much, again for two reasons. The first is the inane British footballing culture of which we are part, all thumping leather, 110 per cent commitment, and low-skilled, lumpen-proletarian brainless energy, which does not long survive against the intelligence and skill and sheer footballing comprehension of mainland Europeans.

We hoof the football around much like Monaghan cows: our milk advertisements match in trite naivety the football our young men will inevitably play within a football culture run by life's NCOs rather than life's officers.

This has nothing to do with class background, everything to do with a dislike of genuine applied intelligence.

Possibly Mr Keegan in Newcastle and Mr Robson in Middlesboro might improve things – but it is hard for intelligent and thoughtful exceptions to prosper amid the largely brainless muscularity they will encounter over an entire season of English football.

The lessons they learn to survive in such parade-ground brawls will hardly serve them well when they encounter staff-college trained gentleman from Ajax, Juventus, the two Milans, and Madrid – men with toes that can perform open heart surgery, and brains like chessplayers'.

There is another thing, a cultural thing. Ireland produces left-sided midfield players galore, loads of outstanding centre-backs – but no strikers. That personal arrogance, that consummate, greedy, non-sharing quality, is not, I suspect, appreciated within the Irish male working-class culture where soccer has its home.

The artist who shares the ball, who distributes it brilliantly around the park, is much appreciated – *viz.* the Careys, the Dohertys, the Bradys of this world: sublime, silky generous players.

But the striker who specialises in the selfish and momentary economy of converting the energies of many into a personal triumph by his egotistical brilliance is distrusted. Possibly that kind of wayward, individuality is too Protestant, too individual, not teamish-enough – perhaps too capitalist, too ME.

The trouble is MEs make great footballers. Pele, Best, Eusebio, Cruyff, and before them, di Stefano, Puskas, Matthews, Finney. They were all MEs.

Jackie Charlton hates MEs. But Paisley loved them. So did Matt Busby, who revelled in them, creating two glorious teams of MEs – Whelan, Byrne, Edwards, Taylor and Pegg *et alia*, and then, a decade after Munich, Charlton, Best, Law, Crerand, *et alia*.

May Charlton's successor in Ireland love MEs too, and infuse a respect for ME-footballers through Irish football. Otherwise we are in for a diet of Monaghan-milk football – obvious, slow-witted and pitiful.

CONSERVING THE PAST

Dublin old and new

The imminent transformation of Grafton Street, with Switzers and Brown Thomas and Marks and Spencers performing a kind of cumbrous and elephantine gavotte, all resulting, it seems, in the death of the name Switzers, sounds another death-knell (as we original writers would put it) in the old Dublin. Soon the great commercial institutions of the city, if they are to be measured by the high street names in existence from St Stephen's Green to the Parnell monument, will be identical to those in any English provincial city, and the traditional names of Dublin trading houses will be gone for all time.

Perhaps it is the nature of the modern city that this should be so; that there is a template which imposes its will on urban commercial development regardless of local taste. I doubt it. Dublin was not made a better or wiser place by the loss of city centre hotels, such as the Wicklow and Jury's, the Hibernian and the Russell; indeed, history has shown that the destruction of city centre hotels was a grave error. Fresh hotels like Blooms, the Conrad or the Westbury, of course without the encrustations of style or tradition, have had to take the place of the older institutions which were demolished in those thoughtless fits of destructive suburbanisation which every now and then has grabbed the city.

Grafton Street has been taken and held by cross-channel or multinational conglomerates. Its surrounding streets have been colonised by expensive domestic accessory boutiques which sell wooden spoons and striped flour jars for the price of a small car. If one comes out of those streets with one's wallet intact, one feels the same sense of astonished relief experienced by travellers who emerge alive after a journey on foot through central Bosnia.

O'Connell Street, with its length of American burger bars, justifies another Easter Rising, just so as the British can put a few gunboats up the Liffey and then blow the wretched place apart. One does not have to be a resident of Dublin to feel this. Visitors to the city, who have heard so much about the gracious splendours of this wide Georgian thoroughfare, are generally appalled by what they see: hundreds of yards of rundown New York, replete with the grisly smell of burnt animal fat and decorated with thousands of discarded paper wrappings.

Yet not far from the stark sub-transatlantic horrors of O'Connell Street dwells an old Dublin which even now is a joy to walk around: I suspect it is virtually unchanged in the past 20 or 50 years and the kind of shops which existed then flourish now. It is the stretch of the city which dwells on lower Henry Street, Mary Street, Parnell Street and Capel Street. The sort of brass fittings or kitchen shop which off Grafton Street would require you to hold up a post office on pensions day merely to acquire a door knocker or a tea towel, in the Capel Street area still guarantees bargains. The most fascinating hardware and ironmongers shops still thrive mysteriously in this corner of Dublin: locksmiths, chandlers, cutlers, glaziers, jewellers and other little outlets which probably date from the time of the Williamite revolution manage to flourish in a reticent, tasteful fashion. The High Street glitz of the main thoroughfares will make a brief fortune and go bang, like a super-nova; from the Capel Street area one gets the sense of generations at work – quiet, diligent people who have inherited their business from parents who in turn inherited it from theirs, and the greatest ambition of the present incumbents is to make a sufficient income, to take pride in their work, and when the evening comes, to pass their humble little enterprise on to the next generation.

Foolishly, I recently went looking for paint in one of those outer-suburban DIY complexes, and all I could find were the sort of ill-looking pastels favoured by National Lottery winners for their newly constructed neo-Georgian 15-bedroom bungalow. I toured the paintshops off Grafton Street, with comparably dismal results.

And then somebody mentioned Dods of Mary Street, and I duly went there. It was a pure joy – more colours than exist in a solar system, and with staff members who seem intensely knowledgeable about paint. Their manner was not that of the over-friendly fools who make up with congeniality what they lack in knowledge, nor was it the grovelling obsequiousness of the toady, but instead they possessed a quality which has almost vanished from Dublin shops: an interest in doing a good job as well as possible. I do not know who owns Dods: whether it is a Dod or a Dods or several people called Dod. But anybody who wants to be reassured that somewhere in Dublin there is an outlet which still prizes old fashioned professionalism, and which employs staff on the principle that they should be of some use to the public and therefore should actually know something about the objects they are selling, will benefit from a visit to this shop. So many of the staff of suburban DIY outlets seem to be recruited from the ranks of the chronically imbecilic as a form of occupational therapy: it is the norm in such places to have a six-inch bolt pressed into your hand if you ask for a lavatory cistern or a wire-cutters if you ask for four gallons of white emulsion, and you can count yourself lucky indeed if you emerge without a 30-foot ladder when you went in to purchase a towel-rail.

No such experience awaits you in Dods; or indeed in any of the funny little outlets around Capel Street. And the best-value but oldest antique shop in Dublin, Duffy's, is just around the corner, in Parnell Street, It is advisable to go fully wrapped up. Browsers have been found on the second floor, burrowing a hole in the snow which has never thawed from the blizzards of 1963, and waiting for the St Bernards to arrive. The Duffy brothers themselves are carved from the material of arctic lichen and go round in shirt sleeves when even diesel freezes.

Do yourself a favour. Drift away from the fashionable and pricey areas of Dublin and spend a few pleasurable hours doing your Christmas shopping in the Capel street area. It is the last shopping district in central Dublin which is unmistakably and truly Dublin. We should cherish it as we cherish our Georgian squares and our ancient monuments: it is old Dublin, living still.

John Henry Foley and O'Connell Street

We should, no doubt, rejoice that John Henry Foley's majestic work, *The Mother*, is returning to Ireland; if only the grounds for rejoicing were broader than they actually are! The truth is about as narrow as it can be. The new owner is a private individual, though I do not complain about that: but for that person, the sculpture would have remained in England. The National Gallery, which might have been expected to take an interest in such things, did not even bid for the work. One hardly knows what to say.

But this reality reveals a broader reality. We do not care for Foley. Most people in Ireland have probably never heard of him. He was an artistic sculptor of genius, probably the finest in the United Kingdom in the 19th century. If he were a writer, he would no doubt be much feted in public memory. But he was a monumental sculptor, and so he is forgotten. And that neglect is best symbolised by the fate of his greatest public monument, his statue of Daniel O'Connell in Dublin.

O'Connell Street has been ruined, its spacious avenues visually obstructed and its great statues obscured, by the ill-advised plantation of London plane trees. I recently contemplated a photograph of the crowds of people who had gathered on O'Connell Street for the Eucharistic Congress 60 years ago. The photograph was taken, needless to say, by that other great neglected Irish artist, Father Browne SJ.

O'Connell street was then treeless. It is no wonder that earlier generations used to boast about O'Connell street being the widest thoroughfare of any capital city in Europe. True or not, what was true was that it *seemed* to be the widest main street of any capital. Its proportions were so perfectly phrased that it added to what was then a very petty metropolis indeed a grandeur and an elegance far beyond the general aspirations of city-design.

Yet for all that, it was not extravagantly grand for the rest of the city; it was not a ten guinea haircut on a two-and-ninepenny head. Of course, it had the advantage of Nelson's column with its perfect height and sublimely tapered obelisk column. In strict dimensions, the column might have been said to have been too large. But when Johnson designed it, he did so with his perfect eye for spacial relationships. That vast and improbable monument did not dwarf the street or mock its scale; the width of the street remained undiminished by the square granite bulk of the base.

O'Connell Street was then, of course, the capital street of the capital city. It had the major entertainment centre in Dublin in the metropolis in the Metropole-Capitol cinema complex, which included the Princes Bar, perhaps the finest pub in Dublin. It takes city management of grotesque myopia and incompetence to destroy that complex; it would take a perfervid nationalism of the most virulent kind to contemplate, never mind rejoice in, the destruction of that column. Dublin nonetheless was up to such heroic challenges and met them easily.

The Metropole complex was destroyed, the Princes pub sold abroad, and in their place a shop for British Home Stores erected, the irony of the vandalism concealed beneath the figleaf of the title under which the company traded – BHS. And the great work by a great Irishman, Francis Johnson, was reduced to patriotic rubble amid the jeers of the mob.

In all of Dublin architectural history, there can be few more lamentable chapters than the double blows inflicted on the broad grace of its main boulevard. But a third assault was planned, and planned with the best intentions. It was the plantation of London planes along the length of the street.

Even to condemn the plantation of trees is to invite a reflex reaction from the unthinking that one is anti-tree. Well, I am. I am against trees in the wrong place; and London planes are very emphatically the wrong trees in O'Connell Street. Indeed, I would go so far as to say that they are simply the wrong trees anywhere these days.

London planes came into their own because they could survive the fumes and fogs in coal-burning cities, and people needed to have trees amid the atmospheric filth which existed then. Those days are gone. We have clean air. Moreover, we no longer have a city-centre poor population who need to see trees on O'Connell Street, otherwise they would never see trees at all. It is not necessary to have London planes for human reasons.

The argument is overwhelmingly in the reverse. We actually need not to have trees, especially of the scale of London planes, on O'Connell Street. They do nothing good for the city at all. Nothing. Their vastness and the walls of shadow they create conceal the monuments along our main colonnade of statuary. Foley's great statue of O'Connell is dwarfed or concealed by the ugly bulk of London plane in summertime; the rest of the statues are rendered completely invisible until you stand next to them. The entire perspective of the statues is obliterated. We have lost the greatness of our greatest street to the mediocrity of the London plane.

The plane is big and ugly. It cannot even support the passerine birdlife which people associate with trees. Small songbirds do not perch on it, presumably because of the conformation of its twigs and its inhospitable habitat. And in our climate, we do not need trees for shade from the sun in the summer. For those who need the reassuring touch of *rus in urbe,* there is no reason why small trees, compatible with the requirements of songbirds, should not be planted in open spaces in the city.

The truth is that at the moment, the London planes in O'Connell Street and elsewhere in Dublin conceal our spaces and our buildings, our skies and our statues. Yet who in public life will have the nerve to propose the right course of action – that we cut them down? Then we can again rejoice in the art and the genius of John Henry Foley.

As the writer said to the bishop

THE only two questions which should interest any of us about Bishop Eamonn Casey do not touch upon his pelvic capers with the comely young Murphy woman who, I am overjoyed to see, has been back with us again. One is reminded of the remark from Mr Bennett in *Pride and Prejudice* – 'You have delighted us long enough.' Indeed.

Anyway, she now tells us that it is time for the bish to come home: 'Nothing Bishop Casey has done merits his exile. He has been reconciled with our son. He has served the people of Ecuador well. I now ask that he should be encouraged and supported to come home quietly and humbly, his privacy respected.'

No doubt. I always thought the bish's downfall began way before he became entangled in the sumptuous embrace of the luscious young Murph. And that brings me to question number one. If the bish is allowed to return from Ecuador, what reparation would he offer to make for the sacrilege done on his orders to Killarney Cathedral when he was a very young bish indeed. Killarney was one of the great Victorian cathedrals of Ireland, its plasterwork a magnificent wedding-cake of gorgeous and triumphal Gothic. It was Pugin's finest work here.

Age-wise, the winsome Annie has already outlived Pugin by nearly 10 years. It is unlikely that she – or any of us – will leave behind anything to compare with the sumptuous majesty of Killarney Cathedral, its oaken pulpit, its marble altar, the last of Pugin's works before he went to make the acquaintance of another architect whose imperfections often seem to outshine his triumphs. Witness the bish. Witness our Annie.

When the bish was bish in Killarney, aside from his busy social diary, he was also much engaged in the business of ransacking the cathedral. The stunning plaster was ripped out to expose the bare core, which was never meant to be exposed.

The altar was excised and destroyed. The huge, hand-carved and magnificent pulpit was removed like an impacted molar and taken away to be broken up.

Ireland in the wake of the second Vatican Council has seen many architectural outrages. Many fine churches had their Victorian essences ransacked and ruined by gauche, unfeeling hands – not just, I suspect, for liturgical reasons.

Some other and less definable urge was, I think, at work, related to that other and co-synchronous movement in Irish Catholic architecture, the building of non-church churches.

It was an interesting movement. From the 1960s onwards, architects all over Ireland were given commissions to build churches which looked like anything but churches. On balance, church design had changed very little in 1,500 years.

A monk in Glendalough or Gougane Barra, whisked in a time machine forward through the 19th century, would have taken one look at the great churches being constructed at that time – Killarney, or the wonderful cathedral in Thurles, or St Mary's in Tuam, and he would have said: 'Yes, that's a church. Yes, that's a church. Yep, that's one too.' 'And what the bloody hell is that?' he would have said, as he spotted a wigwam or a cube or a huge steel-and-concrete butterfly, which is what churches became in the 1960s.

Why? What psychic disturbance within the Catholic Church caused its prelates to commission churches which went to very considerable trouble to look like anything other than a church? Why should an organisation which clung to a continuity of design through schisms and heresies, wars and reformations, papacies and rival papacies, have chosen the 1960s to redesign its churches?

Was it expressing an artistic rejection of the style of the church buildings which it had lost in the Reformation? Was it attempting to create a new style of church which nobody could mistake for a Protestant church (mainly because it was too ugly, though ugliness was presumably not the intention of those who sought ecclesiastical styles which resembled crashed aeroplanes, emptied dustbins and crumpled newspapers).

The bish does not seem to have had a crashed aeroplane in mind when he ransacked Killarney. Instead, he appears to have had a more conservative though no less vandalistic ambition – to conjure from the sublime Pugin marbles and plaster a pastiche medieval abbey. Ruin was thus visited on a masterpiece.

Now, what is Annie Murphy compared with the desecration of one of the great Victorian churches of Ireland? Nothing. She produced a bouncing baby boy, a fact we should all rejoice at – another human being on this planet; hallelujah! – and there's an end of it.

We all, I am given to understand, were brought about by approximately the same process. I am also told that it can be quite pleasurable too; no doubt something for a declining old bachelor like me to look forward to. Maybe the bish could give me some technical advice on what to do when the big moment arrives.

But on balance, the fact that the odd bishop does what most other people do anyway should not be the source of anger or bemusement or indignation. It was what the rest of us have not done – namely, the destruction of Killarney Cathedral – which should be of concern.

I might add that the last time I was in the cathedral in Galway, the next happy diocese to enjoy the bountiful good and expensive taste of the bish, I was unable to find the memorial window to the Connaught Rangers. Did the bish get rid of it too?

It wouldn't be all he took from Galway. He also made off with £70,000 from the diocese, which he returned only when his little game was rumbled. I would like to hear a little more about the Garda investigation into this, what charges are pending etc. as they would be against any of us for trousering 70 whackeroos of somebody else's boodle. And that was question two.

Otherwise, welcome back, bish.

Church vandals

Does the Catholic Church today – at any level – care about the churches which it has inherited from the past century and which it is now busy reordering to suit present – and possibly temporary – liturgical needs? And is it not a little strange that most of the churches being vandalised today, and which have been vandalised over the past 25 years, were constructed by and within a society which was emerging from the social holocaust of the Famine?

Why is nobody perturbed that the extraordinary sacrifices made by the ordinary people of Ireland to build these churches at the worst time in their history should be so forgotten not merely by the present custodians of these churches, the priests and the bishops who are certainly no better than they ought to be, but also by the career Faminists, for whom the Famine is almost a badge of identity and perpetual proof of Britian's perfidy?

That the clergy generally do not seem to worry about the sacrilegious vandalism of modern liturgical trends is one thing. No doubt they have higher things on their minds than the beauty of beautiful things raised to honour their Redeemer. No doubt they are arranging the next folk-Mass, complete with banjos, ukuleles and soupy young girls singing *Blowin' in the Wind* during the communion, with maybe a John Denver number during all the jolly handshaking, to be too worried about the achievements of dead priests and dead peasants.

But what about the career-Faminists, the ones who go on and on and on about post-colonial guilt, and who are full of the angst and agony and anguish left by 10,000 years of oppression: why are they silent as the works and the triumphs of those who emerged from the catastrophe of the Famine, yet still raised great churches and formed beautiful things, are brought to ruin amid modernist, ephemeral tat?

It almost passes belief that the uproar which has engulfed the Catholic Church in recent days has not been about the institutional vandalism of its priests and prelates as they ransack Victorian masterpieces, but over the peccadilloes of the clergyman Michael Cleary. It is 10 years since I was first told that he was not a celibate. Nothing could concern me less. The man was a hypocrite. That was Cleary's real offence, though I myself found his ceaseless glad-handling and egregious bonhomie somewhat odious.

But it is no reflection on the Catholic Church that a priest behaves so. To err is human and Michael Cleary was human. It is however a grave reflection on the Catholic Church – and what passes for debate within its ranks – that the destruction of its churches has merited barely a word of discussion.

It was splendidly salutary that one of the notes the late Cleary received was from the architectural Visigoth Casey, who was no slouch in the paternity line, but whose main crime – uncondemned to this day by the Catholic hierarchy – was the destruction of Killarney Cathedral and the magnificent and unique Pugin Plasterwork. Craftmanship ruined today is craftmanship which cannot be recovered. While day and night divide, we will not see the like of Pugin's Killarney Cathedral again. Casey did that. Casey – uncondemned and uncontrite barbarian. And also a dad.

We have had perhaps millions of words printed about Casey, father, and Casey, fornicator; but the Catholic Church cannot and does not deplore the birth of another soul. But nothing can undo the ruin done to Killarney Cathedral – yet just about the only words written to condemn this putrid deed have appeared in this space.

As it was in Killarney, is it to be so in Carlow also? Thousands of words have already appeared about the priest Cleary, who loved a woman and behaved more as a man than a priest than perhaps he should. But his offence is marginal. The offence of church-wreckers – the offence to those in the past who by their husbanded pennies and by their artistic skills were able to bequeath to this generation the churches of Ireland, and the offence to those in the future who will be deprived of the beauties of that legacy - is not marginal.

Yet far from the proposed £1 million 'restructuring' plan for Carlow Cathedral – which will of course mean the removal of the pulpit, altar rails and font – being the topic of heat and fury, the subject is barely discussed, and when it is, the point is missed. Objectors are quoted in this newspaper as saying that the proposed changes cost too much and the money should go to the poor.

No doubt money should always go to the poor: yet it was money from the poor which built the churches of Ireland in the first place. One million pounds on renovations might indeed be too much. But it would not be too much if it was right to spend it; and it cannot be right to spend one million pounds, not on saving the building, but undoing the works of beauty paid for by the poor of Carlow in the aftermath of the Famine years.

The pathetic justification offered by the Bishop of Kildare and Leighlin, Dr Laurence Ryan, for the proposed alterations is that they will 'alter the cathedral in line with requirements of Vatican II'.

Rubbish. Complete and utter rubbish. Vatican II did not enjoin people to destroy the works of art created by the unimaginable sacrifices of our forefathers and fore-mothers. All over mainland Europe Vatican II is observed, but the great and triumphalist churches of the Counter-Reformation remain unmolested. The churches of Ireland enjoy no such immunity to modernist vandalism.

Other hands will one day join in these churches; other eyes will see what we have left and note where we have brought ruin; and other tongues will frame the curses reserved for those who have destroyed what we had no right to destroy.

Abandoned churches

The old churches of Ireland are the treasuries of the countryside. Catholic or Protestant, they are repositories of the history of the little platoons whose history is so often forgotten, whose tale is never told. Perhaps uniquely in Europe, the churches of Ireland carry the tales of the communities who worshipped in them, however thinly.

One of the saddest developments of recent decades has been the fate of the Protestant churches of Ireland. That many must cease to be Protestant because of declining populations was no doubt inevitable, but was it inevitable that these churches would be de-roofed and left abandoned rather than be taken over by the Catholic Church?

Was it inevitable that the Catholic church would get into its bright collective head to overthrow one and a half thousand years of church construction and instead construct monstrosities which resemble satellites with extended solar panels, wigwams and lampshades?

What great cultural amnesia was at work here that the churches of apse and nave, of sanctuary and transept and choir should be replaced by multi-coloured theatres, complete with folk guitars, hand-clapping and tambourines?

Even the drabbest Church of Ireland church – and by heavens the mid-Victorians built more than a few of those – represents its community more faithfully than these gaudy floodlit palaces which have Las Vegas rather than Glendalough as their model.

Few churches in Ireland have such a terrible tale to tell as the Altar church in west Cork, where browsing some years ago I met a fellow browser, whose face was rather familiar, and whose magenta cloth suggested that he was no undernourished parson. It was in fact Dr Donald Caird, Archbishop of Dublin; and together we stood in the long grass and contemplated the graves of the Protestant dead.

I did not know then that Altar is the other name for Teampal na mBocht, which was built in the heart of that part of Cork where the Famine struck most cruelly. I sensed something there, in the bleakness of the place and the ubiquity of stone, in the grey light which filled the air.

Some places never escape the legacy left to them by calamity. Such talk is magic-talk, non-sensical, illogical; but I have sensed a similar sinisterness in Verdun, and it chilled my blood, just as, I suspect, the blood of the visitor to Teampal na mBocht must lose its warmth.

Altar, as the church is now called, was the scene of the strangest stories of the Famine, the mass embrace of the Church of Ireland by 600 local Catholics who built the church with their own hands over the winter of 1847 and were worshipping in it by the spring of that year.

Naturally, this departure of the faithful from Rome caused consternation, and there was a vigorous attempt by a priest by the name of Mr John Murphy to resecure the souls for the Catholic Church.

In most parts of Ireland where Catholics converted to the Church of Ireland during the course of the Famine – sometimes through ill-advised and much resented soup-plus-proselytism, sometimes simply in recognition of the vigorous attempts by Protestant clergymen to keep the hungry alive – as the crisis passed the converts realigned to Catholicism, like iron filings re-orientating themselves when a magnet is removed.

But not in Cork. The people who became Protestants remained Protestant, despite much local bitterness and the generation of an extraordinary obloquy which soon knitted into the folklore of the place.

Eoghan Harris's play 10 years ago about this extraordinary community aroused much controversy when it was presented at the Abbey; rewritten and represented, it opens tomorrow in Galway as part of the Arts Festival before it moves to Belfast and the Shankill Road.

The play - now called *The Apostasy of Matthew Sullivan* – is being staged by Goodtime Productions, who have, I gather, sold their cars, their children, their under-wear and have agreed to share a single toothbrush between the lot of them in order to raise the money they need for this. No Arts Council money, no Hands-across-the-Border boodle has been made available for them; as yet.

Yet many of the Protestants of Cork who either felt uneasy or, by God, were *made* to feel uneasy in 1922 fled North. Some settled in Down and Armagh, others no doubt found jobs in Belfast and vanished there, their tales untold. For all the unionist pref-erence that the story of Northern Ireland be told as a discrete narrative, largely untouched and untouchable by events outside it, the inescapable truth is that Ireland as an island is bound together.

The history of Cork and the history of Ballymena might march to different drums; but those drums pick up one another's rhythms, or drown one another, or hear some new and alien beat which influences their own. Here is a clear example of com-monality of injustice and justice, starvation and charity, bigotry and tolerance.

It is good to hear that Ms Avril Doyle, the Toast of the Terrace in her UCD days, has provided £2,000 for the staging of this play. At least we can now hope that the players of Goodtime Productions each keep their own toothbrush; possibly the order concerning uses of lavatory paper might even be rescinded.

Ecclesiastical art

This column has, in recent times, referred to the fate of many Catholic churches in Ireland under the influence of Vatican II – pulpits ripped out, altar-rails removed, great marble altars wrecked or ruined by liturgically correct reconstruction.

It is of course not the first time that the Catholic churches of Ireland have been subject to radical interference to suit contemporary moods. The previous occasion was called the Reformation.

Yet it is easy to forget the vigour of the counter-Reformation in Ireland, as represented by the Jesuit Church in Back Lane, Dublin, which Richard Boyle, Earl of Cork, described as 'being ... galleried with rails and turned ballasters ... with many other chambers, of all things most fair and graceful, like the banqueting house at Whitehall'.

This information comes from the catalogue of the recently opened exhibition, *Ecclesiastical Art of the Penal Era*, written by the exhibition organiser, the architectural historian, Joseph McDonnell. No more important exhibition of Irish religious art or artefacts has opened in recent years; and those who so lightly and thoughtlessly contemplate ransacking churches to suit some modern whim might contemplate the endeavours of their forbears labouring during the Penal Laws to collect great works of art for their Church and their churches.

No doubt such works of art today would be regarded as reactionary, outmoded, out of touch with modern attitudes, and might even find their way onto the junk heap that claimed so much of the interior of Killarney Cathedral and other modernised churches.

Those who would wreck the treasuries of churches so painfully gathered in the last century and earlier might visit Maynooth during this month, and there learn, if nothing else, modesty.

It is clear that the Catholic Church in Ireland, even at the height of Penal proscription, did not just think of itself as a humble church of hedge-priests, reciting the Mass on the Mass-rock and then vanishing. This was the church of great merchants and Old English, Norman and Gaelic lords. They did not have modest notions about themselves, their church or the way they worshipped. They belonged to the long bright day of the counter-Reformation which flickered throughout the deepest darkness of the Penal days.

Throughout the penal days the Catholic Church in Ireland remained recognisably a European church. By aspiration and attitude it reflected the certainties which animated the Catholic Church elsewhere. It accumulated artefacts, either by direct commission from Irish artists, or by purchase abroad of works of art, to reflect the piety of its leaders and their belief, intensely inspired by counter-Reformation, in beautiful things being a proper reflection of their love of God.

These artefacts survived. They have survived in churches, in the hands of religious orders, and in quiet and forgotten little wardrobes and closets of convents all over Ireland.

Joe McDonnell has not merely brought to public attention a great and forgotten treasury of Irish religious life; he has provided indisputable proof that the Mass-rock version of Irish Catholic life in the 18th century is inadequate and probably a self-pitying fantasy.

One of the works which Joe has discovered – the home of which must obviously remain a secret, so priceless is it – is Corrado Giuquinto's *Adoration of the Magi*, which is quite simply one of the greatest artistic masterpieces in Ireland today. It actually lives in a little convent somewhere, which has been its home since it came to Ireland during the Penal days. Its purchasers had no modest notion of themselves; or indeed of how to worship God with worldly things.

There is an elegant irony in the appearance of Ruben's *The Descent from the Cross*. This painting is housed in the Dominicans' of St Saviour's Priory in Lower Dominick Street in Dublin, a house which has embraced modern liturgical folk Mass mumbo-jumbo with such enthusiasm that it has all but abandoned the old sung Mass which was one of the glories of the old Catholic Church.

Time and again one comes across the role of convents in the protection of these old masterpieces, especially of textiles.

One can imagine sisters of the wardrobe over the years lovingly stroking brocaded chasubles and silk chalice veils neatly folded in vast wooden drawers.

And these items in particular suggest the determined confidence of the priests – the men who wore or used these items were clearly going to celebrate the Mass in style.

These were garments made by great craftsmen and craftswomen; and though at times the men who wore these chasubles, or used these chalice veils might be hunted by priest-takers, and might on occasion live in dread of their lives, the extravagance of their vestments suggests a swaggering indifference to state hostility.

Some of these sets of vestments are true works of art. The Kirwan vestments, made in France – possibly Lyon – and donated in 1781 by Mary Kirwan, whose brothers Ignatius and Dominic, were Dublin merchants, are triumphs not only of seamstress art but also of composition and of colour harmony.

And there are the monstrances and ciboria and reliquary crosses – these again show a confidence and pride which I am convinced , were part of Irish Catholic life through the period of the Penal Laws and which enabled the Catholic Church to survive that epoch. The Dublin monstrance of 1735, the O'Connor monstrance of 1772, are quite dazzlingly beautiful *Irish* works of art, as is the Channel Row silver chandelier of 1729, made by the Protestant silversmith John Hamilton in Dublin.

The existence of such a treasury, scattered throughout the religious houses of Ireland, was completely unknown until Joe unearthed it.

We should rejoice at its uncovering; and ponder upon the church, its men and women, who assembled it.

Alu-fenestreers

What happens to people before they are allowed to become aluminium-frame window installers, the alu-fenestreers? Are alu-fenestreers sent on a special desensitivity course at the same college where those worthies responsible for mock-stone cladding are educated, where they can learn to violate every artistic principle, every notion of architectural sympathy, every fundament of beauty? No ordinary talent can create such ruinous horrors as that perpetrated on thousands and thousands of houses all over Ireland. No ordinary school of vandalism is at work here. No ordinary cultural desecration is done by these admirable craftsmen. What we are dealing with here is a rare genius indeed.

Dublin is fortunate enough to possess some elegant 1930s art deco houses. I do not know who built them, but I am forced to marvel that the capital possessed builders at that time of particular elegance and style and vision. The houses are not like so many of the edifices erected today by today's quite splendid generation of housebuilders who manage to combine a dozen different architectural and cultural styles in a single building, all of them incompatible.

These art deco houses have a singular integrity. From chimney-pot through to glazing bar they follow coherent rules about line and beauty. They are of a piece throughout. Each detail consorts with and complements all other details on the house. Once got right, it is not necessary to elaborate on or change these details. What they were is what they should remain.

Indeed, this is true for much of the housebuilding done in Ireland up until the 1960s when something rum happened to builders. They seemed to have got at the sauce and have never been quite the same since. For generally speaking, if the artisan cottage builder of the 19th century constructed a cottage in a certain way, there were artistic and practical reasons for doing so. Housing plans had a logic to them and a convenience, whether in the great stone barns built by the Victorians or the mock-Tudor fantasies concocted by Edwardian architectural confectioners, and certainly in the elegant art deco houses of the 1930s.

The other day I saw a line of them. They had been marvellous creations with beautiful curvelinear windows with neat glazing bars and doors which matched the themes evident in window design. I say *had been* because that is the appropriate tense – only one house had retained the original windows, and that house alone allows one to say what little gems of perfection had once existed there.

The gallant alu-fenestreers had got at the rest. Instead of the curvelinear windows, made, I imagine, from steel, there are now angular aluminium constructions which have destroyed the essential softness of the original design – they look like sections of market-garden glass frames bolted almost at random onto unrelated housing facades.

Visually it is like a poke in the eye with a burnt stick – and one house even rubs vinegar into the injured eye with *mock Tudor* glazing bars.

What was a lovely line of 1930s houses now looks like an architectural knackers' yard. And the awful thing is that it would have been as easy to get it right as it was to get it expensively wrong, though I am unconvinced that the few days of really cold weather we get in a year need the costly defences provided by double-glazing. No doubt you get your costs back within, oh, 50 years or so: but you have reduced elegant house facades to dismal travesties.

Which gets us back to our original point. Where do they get the people who go on to become alu-fenestreers? Who runs the crash-course in desensitivity which many of them appear to come through, *summa cum laude?* No doubt there are numerous artistic alu-fenestreers, but where are they? Why do they not embark upon a programme of extermination of those who are ruining the good name of the ancient craft of alu-fenestration?

Dublin is not alone in its misfortunes at the hands of the double-glazing Alu-fenestreers. All over Ireland, even in places like Kinsale which cherish their visual identity and which go to great lengths to preserve the old, the swashbuckling alu-fenestreer has been at his fell capers. There seems throughout Ireland to be a curious blindspot towards windows. Why? Windows – their location, their size, their design, their glazing bars – define the building they serve. They are not mere transmitters of light and inadvertent losers of energy – they are the key visual device to a building.

Yet our jolly alu-fenestreers seem to be unaware of this essential truth, especially when they are given their head and let loose on new bungalows, which they adorn with panoramic windows the size of a cricket pitch. But it wasn't merely because of heat loss that builders limited the size of their windows. There are other, human considerations. First, large windows do not make a room brighter, for the simple reason that they also let out light again. Second, such windows abolish privacy. Third, windows should suit the room and walls they serve – *serve* being the operative word. Windows should be subservient devices. Fourth, there was an agreeable reticence in the old days about flaunting your wealth and which we might well emulate today, if only for purely selfish reasons of security. Fifth, such windows are virtually impossible to keep clean and exercise a curious fascination for bluebottle corpses, which migrate to them from all over the world. Sixth, birds hurtle against them, leaving little pink skullprints mid-pane and crumpled corpses below. Messy. Seventh, what you will see on most days when you hope to gaze at a panorama extending from Bantry Bay to Malin Head is in fact a wall of rain trickling down vast expanses of plate glass, obliging you of course to draw the curtains and remove the window entirely. Thus your darling fenestreer ends up achieving nothing, except, of course, enriching himself and confirming his reputation as a centaur: half-man, half-beast.

The Loop-Line Bridge

How very pleasing that the future of the perfectly dire Loop Line at Butt Bridge is finally open to doubt. It is not the only monstrosity in Dublin, but it is just about the oldest one. It manages both to be ugly and to obscure not merely one of the great 18th century buildings in Dublin, the Custom House, but also one of the few very fine 20th century buildings, Busarus.

When my colleague Frank McDonald was writing about the Loop Line at Butt Bridge recently, he suggested that a replacement could be constructed with only a fortnight's interruption in transriverine traffic. Hmmm. Even if it were possible to build the proposed slim and elegant bridge in such a short time, the disruption resulting would nonetheless still cause an epidemic of burst blood vessels as battalions of snarling madmen tried to cross the river. No matter. We could do with a few less madmen, and the construction of an elegant bridge as a means of weeding them out merely serves to land two halibut with the one worm.

The issue of the Loop Line at Butt Bridge does prompt one parenthetic question: Is it not possible for some bright entrepreneur to run a car ferry-service between say, Howth/Sutton/Clontarf and Blackrock/Dun Laoghaire/Dalkey? Would drivers not willingly amputate their feet with a rusting tin-can, never mind part with a few pounds in ferry-fare, rather than having to inch the length of the coastal road, their teeth tearing lumps out of the steering wheel? We gave the world the *Titanic*; are we now incapable of running a ferry-service across Dublin Bay?

Meanwhile, as we are getting rid of the Loop Line bridge, we should be turning Liberty Hall into Liberty Level. Liberty Hall is not just ugly; it is also dangerous. It was largely constructed from a glue made of flour and water, with the result that its large windows regularly flutter away from their moorings and redesign the physique of passing pedestrians below.

Might not the removers of the Loop Line bridge, while they are directing their hammers at that monstrosity, in the backswing, sort of accidentally-on-purpose, not level Liberty Hall as well? All of mankind would be grateful, not least those unfortunates in the building itself, squatting in their overheated yet draughty offices, with seeping walls and hardboard instead of the sheet plateglass which had flopped out one night and fallen behind a Loop Line support, extensively altering the anatomies of a copulating teenage couple, who now know the meaning of window-pain.

Upriver, O'Connell Bridge House is a masterpiece of hideousness, a complete concrosity. That it should ever have been allowed to dominate O'Connell Bridge and the Liffey passes all understanding. The world would be a far better place were it to be ground into powder and fed to orphans. The same tempting fate should surely be reserved for Hawkins House behind it, and Dublin's city centre could revert to Georgian dimensions.

The violator of some of that Georgian elegance, the Loop Line at Butt Bridge, as you know was supposedly named after the leader of the Home Rule League. Paris has a similar construction, Le Pont de Mai, which Catholics declare was named after the month dedicated to the Virgin Mary, and communists because of the revolutionary implications of May day.

As it happens, both bridges owe their names to similar causes. When the committee to discuss the construction of the new railway bridge over the Liffey met some time late in the last century, the architect who had accepted the commission to design it, a barbarian much in love with the ferrousity of rivets and welding, unrolled his plans.

'This is, gentlemen, my masterpiece, the greatest work of my lifetime!' he cried, gesturing at his design of an elongated metal box which would conceal the grace and elegance of the Custom House, with only the latter's cupola appearing modestly over the top of the bridge. Revolted, the committee, patriots to a man, contemplated the atrocity in stunned silence, while their all-powerful chairman, a creature of great personal magnetism, began to choke.

The symptoms of extreme emotion being rather similar, the architect mistook the committee's wordless horror for speechless admiration. 'Thank you gentlemen, thank you. I am flattered, deeply flattered, that you should have been so moved by my project. The only question now is, of course, what should we name it?'

A silence of uncertain longevity settled upon the company, while the appalled chairman feverishly worked on his collar. He was speechless, for he could not express the deep revulsion at what he saw. He pointed a wild finger at the drawing and spluttered, 'But ... but ... but.'

'A brilliant suggestion, sir,' agreed the author of this pontifical monstrosity. 'That great patriot Isaac Butt will be most pleased. Might I congratulate you upon your wisdom and your political sensitivity.'

'Hear, hear,' murmured a couple of the chairman's toadies, who never missed an opportunity to concur with compliments about the great man. The vote to name it Butt Bridge was passed without division, even as the chairman fell into an apoplectic coma.

Meanwhile in Paris, a similar chairman of a similar committee was similarly loosening his collar in similar disbelieving horror at the plans from a similarly abominable architect; and on the threshold of a similar coma, he spluttered, '*Mais ... mais ... mais*'. And communists and Catholics instantly and unprecedentedly agreed: '*Ah! Magnifique! Le Pont de Mai! Quel homme!*'

Golf-courses

Evening was settling in nicely on the skyline as a mixed foursome wended its happy way from the 18th green. The old lime tree cast a shadow the length of a church spire across the flower-beds, where bees were beginning to pack their bags and return home for the night. The Oldest Member was sipping a small gin and ginger as he placidly viewed the advance of twilight and the end of another splendid day's golfing.

'Ireland,' he observed to the only other person seated on the veranda, a pale young man attired with one of those violent essays in tastelessness which the golfing world terms 'sweaters', 'was not always so favoured with golf courses, my boy, I remember a time – and a dark and terrible time it was too – when it was possible to go several miles without seeing a single course.'

The young man blinked and started, realising to his dismay that it was he who was being addressed. His jaw fell several notches. He began to rise. 'I, er,' he spluttered as he did so. 'I've just remembered that I've a fearfully pressing engage …'

The Oldest Member waved him down with an implacable hand. 'Not a single golf course for mile after mile,' he continued. 'Not one. They were dark, deadly days.'

'I had no idea that it was so late,' continued the pale young man, plucking distractedly at the thinning locks above his furrowed brow. 'I really must be goi …'

'You would like me to describe that era which preceded the happy epoch upon which we are now embarked? Very well. But only if you are sure that you have the time. I would hate to impose. You young people today …' he chuckled gamely. 'No time for an old codger like me.'

'It appears, after all, that I have,' replied the youngster with a certain philosophic weariness as his buttocks descended to the seat of the armchair. 'Might I buy you a drink?'

'Woof', replied the oldest member. 'A gin and ginger would be most agreeable, thank you. Now,' he said, as the pale young man gestured to a waiter, 'what does the term Mellifont mean to you?'

'Mellifont? Par 75. A stinker of a dog's leg on the eighth. Bunkers and sandtraps which would settle Rommel's hash on the 11th. An absolute brute of a lake beside the 13th green. The 18th's not too bad, so long as you allow for the deceptive slope into the dog-pond beside the spinney waiting to catch your tee-shot. Once went round it in 95.'

The Oldest member slurped gently at his gin and ginger. 'You are a fortunate young man to have such enchanting associations with the name Mellifont. You cannot know, you cannot possibly know, what the name means for those of us of an older generation. Tell me: have you every heard the expression, "abbey"?'

'Why yes I have, as a matter of fact,' said the young man with more than a hint of exasperation. 'We of the younger generation are not completely stupid, you know. It's the name of a rather nice little inside-putting practice arena in the centre of Dublin. And wasn't it the name of a Swedish pop group?'

The Oldest Member drew thoughtfully on his gin and ginger, 'Abba,' he said. 'The Swedes were called Abba. But you have no other associations with the name abbey?'

The young man thought for a while before shaking his head. 'No, I don't think so. Why? Should I?'

The Oldest Member shook his head delightedly. 'Absolutely not, my boy. I am proud of you. Now. Another question. What does the term Clonmacnoise mean to you?'

The young man shuddered. 'It means that I'll be lucky to hole in under 100. Once I was back in the clubhouse on 180 after I sliced into the Shannon and had to use a number five iron all the way back from Banagher.'

'My dear fellow, you are going up and up in my estimation. And such dreadful things they say about young people today. Tell me, has the name "Glendalough" any association for you?'

'Only bad ones. The 17th hole. A par four, so they say. Ha! It once took me 25.'

'Gougane Barra?'

'A doddle. Even with my handicap.'

'St Canice's?'

'Once got a birdie on the 11th.'

'Do you know why this course is named New Grange?'

'Not a clue.'

The Oldest Member sighed a contented sigh. 'It wasn't always a golf course, you know. Nor were the others, not until the 1990s, when all over Ireland, local councillors decided to convert this country into Europe's golfing capital. Tell me. Have you ever heard of archaeology?'

'Does it mean coping with the long grass beside the fairway, as is, rough-knowledge, hence, RK-ology?'

The Oldest Member sighed an even deeper sign of contentment. 'My. The Celtic Tiger did a good job,' he murmured approvingly.

TROUBLE IN THE NORTH

The stench of Weimar

'*Guten morgan, mein Fuehrer,*' I said softly as I entered the room. That noble old gen-tleman lay on his bed snoring gently. 'It is time for your morning wash.'

His eyes opened and I watched as he came gradually to life. He smiled briefly as I wiped a trickle of saliva from his mouth and then coughed the soft, productive cough of old lungs. Yet life burned within him as he murmured his daily inquiry, the only one that has been on his lips since the bunker: How goes the struggle?

'Well, *mein Fuehrer,*' I answered as I began to sponge down his wizened old frame. 'It is not like the good old days when our legions ruled from Calais to Odessa, and from the dunes of Libya to the floes of the Arctic. Nothing will ever be like that again.'

'Have faith, my loyal one,' murmured the great man from his pillow. 'Have faith. It is true that they were great days, true, too, that they are gone. But they will be back, just as one day, when my doctors have perfected the medical techniques necessary, I will be back in a younger, fitter body, back to take my place at the head of the German nation.'

He coughed again, a more painful racking sound, and I lifted him up, raising his skeletal ribcage so that I could pat his back and massage the phlegm out of the bronchial passages.

'You will be back, *mein Fuehrer.* You will be back. The signs are good all over Europe. The wretched Slavs are slaughtering one another again. Mere cut-throats, *mein Fuehrer.*'

'Do not underestimate the value of cut-throats. I raised some fine SS Divisions from those Slavs.'

His smile illuminated the room as this noble old soul cast his mind back to the greatest days Europe has known. I drew back the blankets and placed him on his seat-of-ease. But his bowels were as unproductive as ever, and his bladder managed no more than a trickle.

'An unfruitful task, eh, my faithful one,' chuckled my beloved leader. 'Never fear. The day is at hand when we may discard this old body and your duties will be less onerous than they are now.'

'No duty is onerous serving you, *mein Fuehrer.* Such duties are pleasures.'

I confess my heart glowed when he bathed me with the look of affection such as few have ever known. He patted my hand, and murmured those immortal words: '*Ein Reich, Ein Volk, Ein Fuehrer.*' We both fell silent, and I am not ashamed to say that tears trickled down both our faces as we thought of the good times that were gone.

'Come, my little one,' the *Fuehrer* jestingly rebuked me. 'This is no time for womanly tears. You say the news is good. Tell me more.'

'Well, *mein Fuehrer*' I began, raising each of his white and bony feet and wiping them with a warm, damp towel. 'In the new united Germany there are attacks on Slavs and on the Polish scum. Fortunately there are few Jews left there, but there have been attacks on some of those, and on their graveyards.'

A happy chuckle emanated from the far end of the bed as I powdered the beloved one's feet. 'But strangely enough,' I added, 'the best news is from Ireland'.

'Ireland? What good news can emanate from that wretched wet island?' he inquired gruffly. 'The one place in Europe which I never planned to invade.'

'Well, *mein Fuehrer*, your old allies are back in business with a vengeance.'

'My old allies? The IRA? That rabble?'

'Things have changed, *mein Fuehrer*. They have become the most proficient killers in Europe. Not merely proficient, but utterly, utterly ruthless.'

'I like that. It is a vital quality. But how ruthless are they?'

'Completely ruthless, *mein Fuehrer*. They bomb hospitals, blow up children, mass-murder Protestant workmen, and assassinate politicians they disapprove of. They enforce their rule in the areas they dominate by smashing limbjoints with magnum bullets and concrete blocks. Their Protestant opponents are quite as ruthless. It is a pleasure to bring such good tidings.'

'You interest me, my faithful one. These sound like the material for *einsatzgruppen*, those fine young men who cleansed our east with steel. But a readiness to kill for national socialism is not enough. One, national socialists must have support, and two, their bourgeois-democrat opponents must be too pusillanimous to take them on.'

I confess at this point I almost leapt with excitement. 'That is my point, *mein Fuehrer!* That is why the omens are so good. Firstly, the IRA does have support. And as far their bourgeois-democratic opponents – ha! Why, recently the IRA abducted a citizen of the Republic, tortured and murdered him, not for giving information to the British, but to the police in the Republic.'

'Foolish. Very foolish. For I suppose the Irish Government rounded up every known IRA sympathiser in the area, and hounded the entire organisation into silence?'

'No, *mein Fuehrer*,' I crowed, almost hugging myself with glee. 'They did nothing. Nothing. The killers are free, no member of the government even went to the dead man's funeral, and the main debate in the Republic is not how to deal with the IRA, but whether or not the Republic will be able to get a contract with Libya, the country which has repeatedly supplied the IRA with all its weaponry.'

That noble old gentleman smiled. 'Ah, I detect a familiar odour,' he murmured as I straightened his blankets. 'It is the stench of Weimar.'

I leaned over and kissed his pale and furrowed brow. 'Weimar,' I whispered joyfully. 'Weimar.'

Loyalist paramilitaries

One really does need to be reminded every now and then of the astonishing, mind-boggling psychopathological stupidity of Protestant paramilitaries in the North. Whatever one might say about the Provisionals – and I believe on occasion I have muttered an aside about them – and however ludicrous their view of the world, sustained by a political analysis which would not pass inspection by a 10-year-old, there is at least a coherence to what they do. They want the Brits out by fair means or foul, and since fair means are too unattractive and require thought and analysis and that irritating little thing called democracy, they settle for foul.

Oh true, true, every now and then they lose the run of themselves and, quite forgetting their Tonean precepts of Catholic, Protestant and Dissenter, they start butchering Protestants, a sort of instinctive inclination which they, like good pitbull terriers which hardly ever eat a child, are normally able to contain. But boys will be boys ... However, for most of the time they stick to their target, which remains a satisfyingly large constituency.

But the occasional psychopathological indulgence of the Provisionals is the staple of what the Protestant paramilitaries do (and do because the community from which they are drawn presumably does not find such deeds all that offensive).

Earlier this year a young Catholic woman visiting a disabled and elderly Protestant in north Belfast, in order to cook for him, was murdered by the Ulster Defence Association. Since she was the softest of soft targets, without any political or paramilitary connections, it seems barely possible that anybody could have thought her a target. But she was a Catholic and the UDA is the UDA, and only people who have met the UDA can understand how someone like her might be considered worth killing.

The UDA conforms to all the clichés of Alabama rednecks. Firstly, they are for the most part unbelievably stupid. All over the world this century people have set themselves up in the herrenvolk, the ubermensch, the chosen people. Nobody has embarked upon such pretensions from a similar basis of racial claptrap, religious bigotry and such uncouth, inviolable but violent stupidity as the Northern Protestant paramilitaries. These people are truly, astoundingly *thick* – thick, nasty, brutish and violent.

I have been in the company of UDA and UVF men roaring with laughter as they have discussed bombings, romperings (savage beatings) and killings; I imagine concentration camp guard reunions are something similar.

Thick, nasty, brutish and violent is probably a moderate description of the qualities of the men who shot Robert Shaw the other day. Robert Shaw's killing presumably took some planning for the TNBV gentleman who arranged it, though he was such an obliging victim it seems hardly necessary. He had no paramilitary links, was a Catholic living in an overwhelmingly Protestant town, was overweight, had heart problems, was just recovering from major surgery and used to park at the sea shore while friends dug for lugworms. On the day he was murdered he was actually asleep near the lugworm diggers when the thick, nasty, brutish and violent killers took his life.

What do the community from which these killers come think about this murder? Well, let us judge from the fate of John McIver, a Scots-born Catholic who abandoned his catholicism just as soon as he could. A Glasgow Rangers supporter, he served with the British army in Northern Ireland and in 1975 settled in east Belfast, passing himself off as something he was desperate to be – a Protestant.

Somebody in east Belfast discovered his Catholic background. In a crowded Protestant club one night last year he was knifed to death, the attack being so savage that his blood fountained all the walls and his killer. There was just one door to the clubhouse, staffed by a doorman. One hundred people were present that night, yet there was not a single eye-witness to the killing.

Still, it is not all bad in the North. The good news from there is that a UDR woman is to act as the maid of honour in the marriage between a Catholic woman from Derry and a Protestant man from Belfast. The bad news is that, between them, they have killed 19 people, which is how the happy event is to come about.

The blushing bride at the wedding is to be Anna Moore, Northern Ireland's most capable female terrorist, if capability is to be measured in terms of dead bodies one can claim to one's credit. Miss Moore was responsible for the Droppin' Well bombing, which killed 11 British soldiers and six civilians. On the McGlinchey/O'Hare scale, she rates at hurricane level.

Her winsome bridesmaid is Susan Christie, a UDR corporal who cut her boyfriend's wife's neck with a filleting knife and then stabbed herself in the leg in order to substantiate a claim that the murder was the work of two strangers.

And the groom in this splendidly ecumenical affair is Robert Corry, a Protestant paramilitary serving life for murder after bombing a Catholic pub.

The three met in Maghaberry prison, where Miss Moore and Corporal Christie share non-cellular accommodation in which they prepare and eat their own meals.

Anna Moore comes from an interesting family. A divorced lady, her sister, her two daughters, her boyfriend and her cousin are all convicted terrorists.

She and her husband-to-be are both born-again Christians, and both have renounced violence. Their wedding reception will be held in the jail, where there will be sausage rolls but no alcohol and no conjugal rights.

It all sounds so splendid that one rather regrets these discoveries of born-again Christianity were not made 19 lives ago; and I do trust, for all concerned, that Corporal Christie does not take a shine to Mr Corry. She apparently does not handle competition well.

Tiochfaidh ár lá

'*Mr Corrigan, the IRA has slaughtered nearly a dozen people and maimed many more in a bomb attack on the Remembrance Sunday commemoration in this town. What have you to say about this?*'

'Excuse me, no comment. No comment.'

'*Mr Morrison, have you any comment to make on the killing of the three people in Gibraltar?*'

'This is yet another example of British murderous tyranny. Britain cannot rule the occupied Six Counties without recourse to murder and atrocity. We have had 800 years of British oppression in this country, 800 years of British violence and murder, and here is a typical example of the British murder machine at work – three dedicated young republicans murdered in cold blood, just innocent young Irish people about their own business, slaughtered by the trained assassins of the Special Air Service. But they cannot cow us. They cannot make us lie down. The war of resistance to British oppression and occupation continues. It might not be in this generation that freedom comes. But it will come. It will come. *Tiochfaidh ár lá.*'

'*Mr Adams, what comment have you to make on the Warrington bombs which blew a town apart on Valentine's Day, killing two small children and injuring scores?*'

'I feel very, very sad. This is a tragic day for the people of Warrington, for the families of the dead and injured, for the people of Ireland and for the republican movement in particular. We never wanted this war. It was forced on us by the violence of British presence in Ireland for 800 years, by the violence of partition and sectarian oppression within the Northern Ireland state. Republicans are peace-loving people. We did not choose the path of violence. It was chosen for us by the British war machine and its unionist cohorts. We want peace in Ireland and peace between the islands of Britain and Ireland. But there can only be that peace when the British acknowledge the historic wrong done to the people of Ireland and withdraw their war-machine and so allow the peoples of Ireland decide upon their future.'

'*Mr Adams, that does not get away from republican responsibility for this bombing. My question is, how can you justify it.*'

'And my question to you is this: why did the Warrington police not clear the town High Street as the Active Service Unit of the Irish Republican Army had asked them to do? Why did the Warrington police ignore the clear five-minute warning of the bombs? Why were the people of Warrington allowed to remain so close to the scene of what the Warrington police knew would be a scene of devastation? We are saddened, greatly saddened, at the events in Warrington. But the republican people of Northern Ireland know what suffering is. Our hearts go out to the people of Warrington, and we know better than most people who ultimately is responsible for the Warrington disaster – the British Government and the police authorities of the town of Warrington.'

'Mr McGuinness, what is your reaction to the latest attack on a Catholic pub?'

'These attacks are organised and made possible by covert agents of the British war machine in order to cause the maximum division within the Irish people. This is a measure of how desperate the British war machine has become that it now takes war to innocent Irish people, Catholic and Protestant, who are out together having a quiet drink on a Saturday night. The republican movement condemns this attack and all sectarian attacks. The Protestant people may rest assured that they have nothing to fear from us, the republican movement. We want to live in peace with them, as they would like to live in peace with us. It is only the poison of the British presence which causes the divisions between the two peoples of Ireland.'

'Mr McGuinness, you say that these attacks are the work of agents of the British government. So how is it possible that so many arrests have followed the loyalist attacks?'

'Because the British war machine knew all along what its dupes would be doing and it is then able to engage in a public relations exercise by arresting those dupes after they have done the British Government's dirty work.'

'Are you saying the loyalist backlash is a creation of the British Government?'

'That is exactly what I am saying. The plain, decent Protestant people of Northern Ireland do not want this way any more than we do. If the British withdraw, let us sit down and hammer out an agreement about how we, Catholic and Protestant, are going to live in the peace and prosperity which is the birthright of every Irish person, Catholic and Protestant and which we all so fervently desire.'

'Mr X, as leader of the IRA, how can you justify the execution of alleged informers and thieves by the IRA?'

'Nobody in the republican movement likes this sort of thing. It distresses us greatly. Republicans are family people. We have wives, husbands, children. We did not choose the killing business. It was chosen by the British and forced on us. We merely accept our historical duty to defend the rights and the integrity of the Irish people. We are a guerrilla army. We have to defend ourselves against traitors within the community we are sworn to protect. It is our disagreeable duty to take stern measures against those traitors. If there were some other way, believe me, we would take it. But I would ask one other question. How did the French Resistance, or any resistance to the Nazis, cope with traitors? With far more ruthless measures than we have ever contemplated, believe me. And today they are the heroes of France. *Tiocfaidh ár lá.'*

Assorted, notional highlights brought to you by An Irishman's Diary covering the last twenty years of Section 31. From now on, God help us all, we get the real thing on our airwaves – fantastical, illogical, as historically bizarre as the Book of Mormon, all heathen gibberish intoned over a field of death.

The Birmingham Six

Can it be that the wrong film has been made? Can it be that the most astounding and fascinating story to emerge from the numerous wrongful convictions and imprisonment in Britain of Irish – and indeed English – people on IRA charges remains largely untold?

Perhaps the story remains untold because it is literally incredible.

The story is of a 13-year-old boy whose father, an ex-British soldier, was a member of the Tory party. His mother was an active campaigner for the Conservatives. The family sported Union Jacks and a Churchill statue in their living room.

The boy's brother had failed to get into the London police because of poor eyesight, and he himself nurtured profound ambitions to join the British army. Yet this lad found the massed ranks of the entire British legal establishment aligned against him, with various experts being recruited from different military and forensic establishments all over Britain.

To add a further incredible dimension, Lord Havers, the foremost legal figure in England who was to be implicated in the wrongful conviction and imprisonment of this boy, was later to be the legal adviser and protector of the greatest villain in recent British financial history – Robert Maxwell.

The boy is Patrick Maguire, son of Annie Maguire, and the question remains: why did the police up to the highest level, the British Director of Public Prosecutions, successive British Home Secretaries, Attorneys General, and law lords galore go to such trouble over a mere 13-year-old boy?

Patrick Maguire was initially imprisoned in 1976 for possession of nitroglycerine. He was 13 when the alleged offence had taken place, 14 on conviction. No 14-year-old has every been imprisoned in 25 years of trouble in Northern Ireland, so why Patrick?

No doubt it helped that the crucial evidence against him was prepared by a laboratory technician with two months' experience, who was only a few years older than he was. David Wyndham was just 18 when he performed the forensic tests on the swabs taken from Patrick's hands and those of his family and from his mother's rubber gloves.

No doubt it helped that the forensic scientist for the prosecution in the original trial had argued that only nitroglycerine could have turned up positive in the tests done on the swabs, but admitted just as the judge began his summing-up that other chemicals could have tested positive.

No doubt it helped that the initial swabs were destroyed and so could never be retested in any appeal. No doubt it helped that the vital swabs could have been contaminated by lazy handling when they were sent for testing at the Royal Armaments Research and Development Establishment.

No doubt it helped that a lab technician at RARDE told the court during Patrick's trial of just one experiment she had performed during the investigations, and did not disclose the details of two other experiments she had performed.

No doubt it helped that Walter Elliott, a forensic scientist, just happened to neglect to tell the court that it was possible to contaminate hands with nitroglycerine through a third agency.

No doubt it helped that a scientist involved in testing the swabs, only in hindsight said the positive results from the swabs were 'disturbingly unique' and that at the time, 'we just did not believe it, quite honestly ...'

Now, the only interpretation I can place on that observation is that the swabs had been deliberately contaminated by some unknown person to ensure that the innocent Maguire family would be convicted.

Patrick, a stripling of 13, did you every get the feeling that they were out to get you?

Prosecuting the Maguire family was the future chief Law Lord, Lord Chancellor and Master of the Woolsack, Lord Havers. Presiding over the case was the future Master of the Rolls, Lord Donaldson. The little figure we see peering over the dock, along with the rest of his family, is little Patrick Maguire.

And so it was that the Maguire family finally left the dock – Patrick Maguire, an ex-soldier and his wife Annie, two stalwart members of the Conservative Party, for 14 years; Giuseppe Conlon, a former Royal Marine, William Smyth and Patrick O'Neill for 12 years; Vincent Maguire, 17, to five years; and last and most certainly least, Patrick Maguire, for four years.

Among the many illustrious people who concerned themselves in this case was David Mellor, who as junior minister at the Home Office told Gerry Fitt that there was no reason to intervene in the decision of the courts, nor to set up a scientific inquiry into the case.

Guiseppe Conlon, as we know, died in jail. The Maguire family was released in dribs and drabs and finally cleared, as ungraciously as possible.

Last September, Patrick Maguire was cleared of assaulting policemen. The prosecution collapsed when the policemen in question gave differing accounts of the supposed assault. Patrick told the court he had been arrested as he left a pub and handcuffed.

He was put in a police van and there savagely beaten. 'There were at least four officers in the van and I didn't want to lie like a dog on the floor. The punching and kicking stopped soon after we drove away.'

The magistrate cleared Patrick without comment.

And the date of this alleged police assault on Patrick Maguire? It was just hours before three other policemen began their trial for conspiracy to pervert the course of justice in the trial of the Guildford Four, the very case which began this farrago of wickedness and injustice. And in that trial, they were found not guilty.

Lee Clegg

Lee Clegg. I might as well refer to the matter of Lee Clegg, since everybody else in the entire world has done so. Should he be released? Probably. Why? Because I am far from convinced that murder, in its full and premeditated sense, was what Clegg had in mind that autumn night four years ago. That said, I have to add that the fine gentlemen of the Parachute Regiment have been working long and hard on getting a Clegg. Now they have got one, they should not be surprised.

The Parachute Regiment is by far and away the least successful British army regiment to have served in Northern Ireland. Other regiments might have suffered more casualties; none has served as such an efficient recruiting sergeant for the IRA. Wherever they have arrived in the past quarter of a century, they have brought misery, violence and brutality.

One night in Ballymurphy many years ago, I was stopped by paras. They told me that I had two minutes to leave the estate, or otherwise they would shoot me. Just then, I saw that a few feet away four paras approached a middle-aged male pedestrian. There was no warning. They simply clubbed him unconscious with their rifle-butts, laughing as they did so. Blood gushed in geysers from his scalp.

I picked the man up and put him in my car. A para sergeant looked very closely at me and said: 'If we see you again around here, you're dead.' I took my new and battered friend to the Royal Victoria Hospital, where for reasons beyond my understanding, they refused to admit him. I waited until about 3 a.m. until they had patched him up and I could take him home again.

As we left the hospital, we met a teenage family friend of his, to whom I gave a lift back to Ballymurphy. I need not tell you whom we ran into. 'You again,' said my nice para sergeant. 'I thought I warned you ...'

We were taken out of the car and lined against a wall. My beaten friend was rebeaten, kicked and abused. My new friend – about 16 – was repeatedly kicked and punched. Me, perhaps because of my nice accent, they did not kick, merely manhandled as I lay spreadeagled against that wall in Ballymurphy for about half-an-hour, while paras bawled abuse and threats into my ear.

What happened to that 16-year-old boy? Did he join the IRA, as I suspect I would have done if I had been him? Is he now dead in Milltown Cemetery? Did he find himself doing 15 years on terrorist charges because of what happened to him that night?

I wrote a letter of complaint to the GOC Northern Ireland. He replied 'Dear Myers,' and suggested that I contact the RUC. Very useful. Very, very useful.

One mere contact, of the kind that thousands and thousands of Northern nationalists took for granted wherever the gentlemen in red berets were around. Other encounters were more conclusive. On the night of internment in 1971, the paras had a shooting gallery in Ballymurphy as Catholics attempted to flee their homes before a loyalist assault. Nine, including one Catholic priest, were killed.

The next year, the night the IRA ceasefire ended, similar para shootings in the Ballymurphy area claimed another half-dozen or so lives, including those of a four-year-old girl and another priest, Father Fitzpatrick.

It is hard to be sure, but if you include the 13 shot dead on Bloody Sunday, the paras have killed probably about 40 people in Northern Ireland, virtually none of them terrorists. This constitutes about 15 per cent of all people killed by the security forces in the Northern Ireland troubles. Scores and scores of British army battalions have done duty there, most of them leaving without taking a single life. The three battalions of the paras could make no such claim.

For example, Paras killed George Johnstone, a police reservist, at a road-block after he had a disagreement with them; no doubt it was not dissimilar to the disagreement I might have had with them had I been drinking. Paras shot dead a schoolteacher, Liam Prince, near Warrenpoint, and then raided his home. Once they discovered what sort of home it was, they assured his family that Liam was alive and well.

Liam belonged to a police family. His father was a police officer; so was his brother. His application to join the force was awaiting processing when he was shot by paras after they said they had come under fire from his car.

Oh yes. That one.

The paras are a special regiment. Their culture is a sergeants' mess culture – loud, unreflective, bullying. As soldiers, they are anachronistic reactionaries – a battalion parachute drop is as useful in war as a cavalry charge. Yet that is what they are recruited and trained to do, along with much unthinking ferocity.

The disease of unreasoned violence is endemic to parachute regiments. The Canadians have just disbanded their parachute regiment after paras on UN duty – God help us – were found guilty of torturing and murdering a Somali, and actually videoing the entire process.

If the British want to have a regiment like this – and they do, apparently, though their recruitment processes are wasteful, stupid and brutal and must lose the British army many good recruits – that is their business.

No doubt they will come in handy when the Argentineans make a grab for the Falklands again. Until that time, could the paras not be kept in a cage on Stornoway and be thrown lumps of raw meat or whatever they live on? No doubt, when the time comes they will be in a suitable mood to reclaim windswept, sheep-cropped unpeopled and uninhabitable islands. They have proved to be incompatible with civilised life in Northern Ireland. Whatever happens to the peace talks, please, no more paras.

Martin McGuinness, the poet

How gratifying to learn that the everlastingly boyish personage of Martin McGuinness has been writing poems about sea trout. I had often wondered what he lay awake thinking about at night, his charming blue eyes blinking at the ceiling. Now I know. Sea trout.

Sensible fellow. He must have a lot on his mind. He is probably wiser to think about sea trout than some of the other things which might disturb a fellow when the sun is down and the spirits of the slain foregather and lament their abbreviated lives.

He might, were he so disposed, think of his fellow-Derryman, Patsy Gillespie instead. Patsy Gillespie? You have forgotten Patsy Gillespie? No doubt many people have. Mrs Gillespie hasn't, and I'm sure Martin McGuinness hasn't either.

Patsy Gillespie was a canteen worker in a nearby British army base. It was no secret. Everybody knew what he did for a living.

Four years ago last October, IRA volunteers broke into Patsy Gillespie's home in Derry and taking his family hostage, abducted him and took him by a back road into the Republic, where they strapped him into a van loaded with explosives. Patsy was ordered to drive the van to the British Army checkpoint at Coshquin. He was told that his family would be killed unless he obeyed orders. An IRA squad followed Patsy as he drove his van to Coshquin. As he drove the van into the checkpoint, one of the IRA men triggered the bomb.

Five young soldiers and Patsy died in the explosion. Patsy had a funeral, but the coffin was empty, because there was no body. It was vapourised in the blast. Pieces of shredded human torso were found scattered all over rooftops.

Far better to think of sea trout.

Certainly better than to think of what went through Patsy Gillespie's mind as he drove to his doom. What a choice to give a man – unless you become a suicide bomber for us, we will murder your family. And the man who tied Patsy to the van and looked him in the eye, knowing that soon Patsy would be no more, tell me, did he report on the experience? Did he say what it was like to gaze into the eye of a man who was being sent on such a mission from which there can be no return?

Better by far to think of sea trout.

And then there is the tape-recording, the tape-recording of Patsy Flood. Patsy Flood was a member of the IRA in Derry. He was killed before Patsy Gillespie's involuntary foray into kamikaze bombing. Patsy was also an informer. And Patsy was kidnapped and held for nearly two months while his wife, Liz, was repeatedly lied to and lied to, given constant reassurance that her Patsy would soon be returned to her.

But that was never to be. Never. That Patsy was as doomed as the other Patsy was, from the moment the IRA got their hands on him. Patsy the informer admitted to his work for the RUC within a day of his capture. Nonetheless he was kept alive for seven more weeks, and a confession admitting to informing was tape-recorded.

Have you heard that tape-recording, Martin, the whimpering voice of a man who knows he has an appointment with the masking tape, the black plastic bag, the gun? Have you? Some people have. It seems the recording was made not long before Patsy was made to dress in a boiler-suit, and his hands were tied with the tape and a bag put over his head, and he was taken to the Coach Road Junction, not far from Newtownhamilton, and a rifle was put into the back of his head and a single shot was fired, shattering his brains and skull.

So far as I know, Patsy's last recording might still be in existence. But better to think of sea trout.

Perhaps it is possible to hear a recording of Kevin Coyle's last will and testament. Kevin appeared at a Sinn Fein press conference in Derry just 10 years ago, saying he had been approached by the RUC to become an informer. How warmly he denounced the RUC for their impertinence. To little avail. Because the very next day he was abducted, interrogated and, not altogether surprisingly, found guilty of the offence he had already confessed to.

He too was hooded, bound and shot. But we all agree, sea trout are nicer things to think of.

Better than thinking of the fate of Ruairi Finnis. Ruairi was born in 1970 and was a true child of the Troubles. Like so many such children, he was also an RUC informer. He was discovered by the IRA, abducted, interrogated and sentenced to death. No doubt another tape-recording was made of his pitiful final noises, for he could have been in no doubt as to his fate. His hooded body, shot through the head three times, barefoot and pathetic, was found in the Creggan four years ago.

Ah no. Think of sea trout. Think of sea trout.

Just who is Martin McGuinness, laureate to the humble sea trout? Well, everybody who has met him seems to like him. He is modest, quiet, honest and sincere, or so I am told, a devout and pious Catholic who is passionate about getting the Brits out.

He has twice been convicted of IRA membership in the Republic. He told the court: 'I am a member of the Derry Brigade of Óglaigh na hÉireann and am very, very proud of it. We fought against the killers of my people. Many of my comrades were arrested, tortured or killed. Some of them were shot, while unarmed, by the British Army.'

Shot while unarmed, eh? Oh the rotters. And Patsy Gillespie? And Ruairi Finnis? And Kevin Coyle? And Patsy Flood? And the other 40 or so 'comrades' who have ended their days in plastic bags and boiler suits in some leafy country lane?

Better by far to think of the fate of trouts than touts.

Conference time

This traditionally is the time of year in Northern Ireland when journalists would fall mysteriously ill, phoning their offices with the croaking excuse that they were terminally afflicted, do not expect to see them again. 'I'm dying so I am, bloody well dying. Never felt worse in my life', only to recover within the week. The reason? The Ulster Unionist Party annual árd-fhéis was drawing nigh.

There might be words in the English language to describe the ennui, the numbing of all cerebral powers, the brain-crushing boredom which results from spending a wet winter weekend in some deserted seaside town in Northern Ireland, but I do not know them. Nor do I know the words to describe the sensation induced by being in the company of Hazel McFettridge, Elspeth M'Whinnie, Oliver Cromwell Chichester-Clark, Dawson Trimbleside, Stelfox Crumbleweed and Drew Drew for hours and hours and hours on end for an entire weekend. By the sea, in wintertime.

Believe me, until you have experienced Portrush in November, you probably think bleak is a make of china ornaments.

Normally at an Ulster Unionist conference, *God Save the Queen* was sung every hour on the hour before motions applauding the B Specials, the Ulster Defence Regiment and the 36th Ulster Division were passed without division. In between, there would be a unanimous denunciation of a state called Air-ah, followed by a fresh blast of *God Save the Queen.*

The conference would break up halfway through the afternoon for a refreshing cup of the beverage which cheers but does not inebriate. Hazel, Madge and Elspeth discussed how well Her Majesty looked on television recently and compared their own dear royal family with *nasty* Mr Hume and *nastier still* Mr Haughey. And as for *that Gerry Adams ...*

Hazel, Madge and Elspeth's hats, which seem to contain a bowl of fruit each, bobbed in unison as their wearers contemplated *that Gerry Adams.* Then it was time to return to the conference and have a vote on The Debt Ulster Owed to Sir James Craig of Immortal Memory, before everyone stood to attention to remember Ulster's Glorious War Dead. Then followed a few hymns – no more than 97 verses of *Rock of Ages*, 70 verses of *The Old Rugged Cross*, and of course *Abide with Me.* Dinner would follow – a ham salad followed by trifle; *quite delicious,* opined Sadie McInkblot, but I do hope that wasn't sherry I tasted.

Muriel McHedgerow shuddered in horror. *Don't Sadie,* she said, horrified. Then delegates again would attest: *this* we *shall maintain,* before looking at their watches, murmuring good gracious, *look at the time, nearly ten o'clock – time for bed.*

Good night, Myrtle. Good night Oswald. Good night Cuthbert. Good night Sammy. Good night Sammy. Good night Sammy.

In the hotel bar there would be silence – a deserted, crushing silence. On the beach, the journalist who had drawn the short straw was neatly folding his clothes before wading into the ice-cold sea, and not intending to return to them or the conference, ever.

An SDLP conference, on the other hand, could be relied on to keep the barmen busy till breakfast. Poker schools would ply a brisk trade, while men from the Glens kept a cautious eye on men from the Black Tyrone and for the hard wee loughmen from the Montiaghs, with fists carved from bog-oak.

In the bar the journalist was ordering 15 large Paddies, and 15 pints of Guinness to go with them, 15 Pernods to go with the pints and the Paddies, and 15 bottles of Carlsberg Special to wash the Pernods down. And that was just for the delegates' wives.

The journalist was scurrying backwards and forwards to his company and wondering how on earth he could slip this one by on expenses, before realising with a sinking heart that the Fermanagh delegate was repeating the order just in case the bar shut.

'The bar's not going to shut', says the delegate from South Derry. 'Agh, I know, but just in case.' 'You're right', says the man from South Derry, 'There Sean, same again.'

West Belfast, not to be out-done, repeats the order. The journalist lowers his head and begins to weep. Through his sobs, he hears South Armagh double West Belfast's order as he realises that it is already his round again and he has before him 45 untouched drinks. In the far corner, one delegate is breaking into *Roddy McCorley*, while another appears to be trying to get off with his wife. *Roddy McCorley* falls off his chair and slides under the table; and with similar ease, his wife and friend slip off towards the rooms.

At dawn the hack can be seen tearing off his clothes as he stumbles down the beach, firmly intending to swim to the Faroes. The delegates shortly afterwards stumble downstairs with faces which resemble the innards of the Muraroa Atoll. Roddy McCorley is asleep under the bar, Mrs Roddy McCorley has a big smile on her face: and a certain blonde journalist is removing the barricade she erected against her bedroom door, outside which a snoring, recumbent figure is testimony to the sedulousness with which he prosecuted his unsuccessful siege:

Some of the things you are not told about Northern party conferences.

What peace process?

Is that enough for you? Are you happy now? All you who bullied the doubters with cries of Brit-lovers, war-mongers, Provo-bashers; you who kept us off RTE airwaves so that we would not doubt the validity of this 'peace-process'; you who forced the Sinn Féin-Hume consensus down everyone's throats; you who tolerated no dissent and heard no other voices but that of winsome northern nationalism; you who achieved the very pan-nationalist front the unionists most feared – are you satisfied now?

Who are the architects of this abysmal mess we find ourselves in? Within just over a week two gardaí were Kalashnikoved in Limerick, Sinn Féin recorded its highest ever vote in Northern elections since 1918, and the centre of Manchester was destroyed; and yet still we heard the clarion call that lines of communication to the authors of these horrors must be kept open. In fact, keeping Gerry Adams in business, incredibly, now seems to be the business of our elected politicians. Listen clearly. Talk of a split is a Sinn Féin-IRA *ruse de guerre* to cause confusion and sow doubt. There is no split. None. And there will be none.

Meanwhile, let us count heads. Who got us here? Gerry Adams did, along with his semtexing chums in the Army Council of the IRA. Well done lads. Nice job. But we'd expect this of you. You're only doing what you've always done. You've read your *War of the Flea* and those other texts of terrorist-guerrilla war, and you're good at sowing doubt in the political centres you are opposed to. In fact, you're brilliant.

Who else is responsible for this monumental folly, that the State should bend a knee to Cain and feast with him in high places? The first was John Hume, widely regarded as the god of Irish nationalism; the great statesman who sees his way so clearly through the problems of Irish life; whose hand can steer Irish nationalism into a lasting accord with Irish unionism in which neither side dominates and fairness governs all.

Excuse me? This is rubbish. John Hume is John Hume, not the Archangel Gabriel, dropped in from outer space, free of the prejudices and aspirations of his tribe. He is *quintessentially* a man of his tribe. That is why he is utterly detested by Northern Protestants. He is clever and articulate and fluent.

And at the moment, he is silent. Last week he was asked about his position towards Sinn Féin's silence over the murder of Jerry McCabe. He repeatedly declined to condemn Sinn Féin's attitude. For he never condemns Sinn Féin. Why is this? Has Sinn Féin got something over him that we are not being told about? Why has he got to be palsy-walsy with these fine fellows the whole time? Disagreements are the stuff of political life. And if Sinn Féin has something over him, is it one of the engines for the peace process?

Peace process. Ha. What is this peace-process? These people kill whom ever they want and wreck cities, and we're told by the likes of Bertie Ahern and others that we mustn't boycott them; though they boycott whomever they want, just as they are this minute boycotting the Northern forum because it is full of unionists.

We know that the absurdly named 'peace process' has no basis intellectually. Sinn Féin-IRA were brought in from the wilderness so that their aim, a Britless united Ireland within the lifetime of a British government, could be achieved by peaceful means. This was garbage; but this, aided and abetted by John Hume, Tim Pat Coogan, Jean Kennedy Smith *et al* was the main thrust of the 'Peace Process', as seen from Sinn Féin's eyes, the only eyes that count. Why the jubilation amongst Sinn Féiners at the time of the ceasefire? Because they thought negotiations were underway that would bring about a united Ireland within the next few years.

Now they know this will not happen. It cannot happen because the northern unionists will not permit it. No discussion. Instead of concentrating on that central truth, we have allowed the Sinn Féin leadership to be feted as if it were the deliverer of peace rather than the tactical suspender of its fascist war. This frivolous witlessness reaches an apogee in the astonishing decision of the Arts Council to give a grant to one of the most sinister IRA terrorists of all, Danny Morrison.

Face this truth about the IRA. It is green and it is Nazi. Judge it by its record. No wonder Gerry Adams was the first to urge, let the past be the past, and by-gones be by-gones. We are here today standing on the stepping stones of the very by-gones we are told are not important. We can make no judgments about the future, and the present is the accumulated past. No past, no present. Got it?

The past tells us that the IRA wants the surrender of democracy to the power of its guns; it will stop at nothing less to achieve its ends, regardless of what the people want. This is not an aspiration which can be reasoned away over the coffee-table. Individuals might have a change of heart, but not the IRA. It is what it is, an armed organisation fighting for a Brits-out, united Ireland.

No doubt Gerry Adams wants an end to the war; but he has not abandoned his aspiration to end the northern state against the wishes of the people who live there and of the people of the Republic. His 'peaceful' ambition is to take from the unionists what they will not surrender peacefully.

Do you understand this? There is no middle line, no meeting-place between unionists and those who wish to de-unionise them against their wishes. Worse, no declaration of a ceasefire will now persuade the unionists to talk to Sinn Féin. The 'peace process' is finished. Only naivety sustained it for so long. We are up to our necks in the direst trouble, and all options are hard. Decency and self-interest demand that we cannot allow this State to be a safe haven and headquarters of the IRA and our courts the playthings for their wily counsel. It is, alas, time to air the beds in the Curragh.

Gerry Adams

Most of you will not have heard the interview with Gerry Adams on the BBC Radio Four *Today* programme. Sections of a pre-recorded interview with me about the Gerry Adams biography, *Before the Dawn*, were broadcast by Radio Four before the Adams interview with John Humphreys, which ran:

Humphreys: But you're saying that you were never responsible in any way for anybody's death, even though Kevin Myers himself has an account of how you were heard in an Irish pub …

Adams: Well, Kevin Myers.

Humphreys: ... telling somebody to go and kill somebody.

Adams: Well, Kevin Myers is patently telling lies in ... in that context ...

It's not often that I agree with Gerry Adams, but here he was nearly telling the truth; though the word *lies* is perhaps a little strong. For it is untrue that I overheard Gerry Adams ordering anybody to be killed. What I said in a *Spectator* article two years ago, though not in my radio interview, was that I had been in a pub in Andersonstown when a fight broke out between two men, one of whom was beaten terribly.

I was meeting an IRA contact who told me that it was time to leave; an IRA unit had arrived to sort the problem out in that rough-and-ready constabulary-way they have. I left, and walked past Gerry Adams talking to a group of men outside. I wrote in the *Spectator* that I heard Adams say: *'Shoot him.'*

I wrote then that I did not think these words meant that anybody was to be killed; my assessment was that the man was to be knee-capped – and I wrote two years ago, as I write now, that it is more than possible that the words were instantly revoked and the assailant's kneecaps were not even tickled by the cold breath of gunmetal.

Let us admit something further; maybe Gerry Adams's words were all in jest. But those two words, 'Shoot him,' were uttered. This I know. And there is no point to the story other than this. Gerry Adams had authority with the IRA in those days; he certainly had authority with my friend, who regarded him as a figure of awe.

What I do not understand is this: why does Gerry Adams deny he was in the IRA? For I admit that I have made a grave error in my assessment of Gerry Adams; though I detest much of what he stands for, and I detest armed republicanism in all its forms, I recognise that he is personally committed to ending, not merely this phase of the armed struggle, but also the tradition of armed republican conspiracy. This requires great courage. It would be churlish not to recognise and honour such courage.

He is doing this from within the ship of armed republicanism. I think his efforts are doomed; but they are worth making. If he were to bale out, he would have no control over the vessel as it ploughs its futile and bloody furrow through a boundless sea of war. He is, if you like, taking the responsible and statesmanlike action; and his credibility, and his power, depend entirely on the fact that he was authentically in the heart of the republican struggle, *that is, he was in the IRA.*

Does this vitiate what he is doing now, trying to end the armed struggle? It does not. It adds stature. For me to argue that the IRA use of violence is wrong is meaningless, mere twittering. But for someone like him, trying to end violence as a means of securing republican aims, is quite another. His is a voice with power from the depths of the armed struggle. His audience is the real audience which conducts the war, and will stop it when it is persuaded to. That persuasion will come not from outside the republican movement, but from within it.

Alas, I do not believe that Gerry Adams has the persuasive powers to convert the militarists to peaceful means. They understand only guns; and the more guns fail to get what they want, the more guns they use. The generals of the IRA are like the stereotypical generals of the Great War; if certain tactics do not work, keep on trying them. So instead of one-ton or two-ton bombs, the IRA is now playing with 10 tons of explosive.

Ten tons of explosive – have you the least idea what 10 tons of explosive would do to a city like London, with its thousands of acres of plate glass and its hundreds of thousands of employees toiling behind those vast and shining cliff-faces? No police force in the world is organised enough to evacuate such numbers of people from the blizzard of glass shards which sweeps streets after a city bombing. Twice, the IRA has brought this form of warfare to English cities this year: the toll, 500 injured and two dead.

And there will always be this toll, always, while the IRA chooses to let off bombs in city centres with limited warnings. Why such limited warnings? Because the bombs could be defused if the warnings were longer. And it is all so purposeless, for there is no causal connection between what the Provisionals want and the means they employ to get it.

Bomb the heart out of London; slay Cockneys by the barrow-load; bring fire and ruin to its commercial heart – and you will not make a ha'pence worth of impression on the Northern loyalists, the fine fellows who gave us Drumcree. Their position is non-negotiable; and if they are expelled from the United Kingdom, they will not ease their exile by entry to a united Ireland. It simply will not happen.

The militarists in the IRA live inside some logic-distorter which prevents them from seeing this simple but central truth. They regard the British presence as some malign magnet which orients Northern loyalists away from their true identity. This is nonsense. Everything we learn from the Northern unionists tells us it is nonsense. I believe Gerry Adams now accepts that it is nonsense. Let him say so – and say it, moreover, as a man who was what I believe him to have once been – a commander of the IRA in Belfast.

Political symbols

Here we go again. The incorrigible failure to understand other people's passionately held beliefs seasonally asserts itself, yet regularly manages to catch us unawares. When we are braced for the storm, it does not erupt; when the seas look placid, we are suddenly hit by a tidal wave.

Drumcree and the Orange insurrection of last summer took most people by surprise; what was generally regarded by nationalists as a festival of bigotry was seen by unionists solely as an overdue assertion of oppressed rights and subverted identity. Are we capable of distancing ourselves ever so slightly from the seasonal emotions which propel us into such fevers?

This question is relevant now because the poppy is upon us again. Last November, Northern Ireland went through paroxysms of anger over the refusal of BBC newsreader Donna Trainor to wear a poppy on screen. She said she would wear neither the poppy nor the shamrock, since they were seen as symbols of division in Northern Ireland.

The word that counts here is 'seen.' It is that use of the word which weakens her argument; because it means that other people's misinterpretation of what you do is an essential guide to your conduct. The veto of strangers becomes your own rule book of behaviour. But even that act of conciliation achieves little. For in Northern Ireland, and to a lesser degree in the Republic, the act of doing nothing, of staying neutral, is seen as taking sides in one way or another – most especially in the matter of wearing vegetables of identity.

There can be no more honourable or enchanting symbol than the shamrock. It not merely is a reminder of the debt the Irish owe to an outsider – probably a Briton – and of the deep power of Christianity on the life and lives of Ireland and the Irish; it is also a symbol widely used through both sections of the Irish people.

It is the symbol of the IRFU, which straddles both traditions magnificently. It is in the badge of the RUC. It was in the emblems of the 36th Ulster Division. On the face of it, it should be a completely neutral symbol of Irishness, available equally to Orangemen and to nationalists.

But we know that is not so. Protestants in Northern Ireland are uneasy with the shamrock. For whatever reason, it reeks of Fenianism, of Taiguery, of the Pope. It is acceptable as an institutional emblem, intertwined with the harp or the crown; but, as a personal decoration, for many Protestants it is a threat.

It is Catholics in the North who wear shamrock and celebrate St Patrick, authentically, as their own. If you doubt it, try walking into a Shankill Road pub wearing shamrock on St Patrick's Day; but notify the local hospital of your blood-type first. Better still, get measured for a suit; you'll wear it just the once.

Should one capitulate to that grotesque misinterpretation of a truly blameless symbol? No, absolutely not. For the shamrock is not a symbol of triumph or of victory; it is an innocent expression of an innocent identity, unstained and unsullied. If other people have a problem with that, then that is other people's problem; one might have to be prudent in the company of their unreflective muscularity, but to allow their misunderstandings about the shamrock to influence what you wear in a television studio is simply absurd. There is no end to such capitulation.

Such remarks about the shamrock will be patently obvious to Irish nationalists. What will not be quite so obvious is that similar remarks can be made about the poppy. In its origins, it is quite blameless and a-political, which is what makes it so different from the Easter Lily of republicans, which celebrates a violent political event.

The poppy was born out of the carnage of the first World War; the day on which it is worn is not a day of victory, nor is the poppy an emblem of victory, but of a day of peace, of war finally ended.

The reason for wearing the poppy was not to celebrate victory or war, but was like any flag day, a money-raising process. In this case, to raise money for the care of the millions who were maimed.

No doubt much of the language associated with Poppy Day irritates many nationalists. Irish people watch the ceremonies of the Cenotaph in London and find no echoing chord in their hearts; all that strut and grandeur, banners and flags. So British. So royal. So foreign.

But it is time to make the journey into another heart. People remember their losses in different ways; intensely ornate ceremonial is foreign to Irish habits and is mystifying to the Irish psyche. But merely because we have trouble empathising with such practices doesn't mean the motives behind them are not authentic. Britain's losses in war this century exceed one and a quarter million; is it surprising that such blood-letting demands ceremonial, if only out of guilt, a desire to repay the unpayable?

Echoes of that British ceremonial are to be found in British Legion commemorations in the North. For many unionists, Armistice Day provides an opportunity to declare who they are. No doubt that understanding of the meaning of the poppy is shared by others from the opposite side, which is why the IRA blew up one Remembrance Sunday parade nine years ago and – conveniently forgotten by their apologists – tried to blow up another in a remote part of Fermanagh on the same day.

If I say the shamrock is a divisive emblem of republicanism, am I correct? No, I am not. Equally, the poppy is not an emblem of Britishness or of Orangeism, though some choose to make it so. As the historian Jane Leonard has shown, poppy sales in Dublin in the 1920s exceeded those in Belfast. The poppy is a sign of remembrance of the dead of the world wars and a means of supporting the living maimed.

The shamrock is a sign of Irishness and a memorial to the christianisation of Ireland. Only the intolerant misinterpret; and only fools bend their knee at the intolerance of others. To honour St Patrick and to remember the thousands of Irish dead of two world wars are not incompatible deeds; they are public and civilised professions of the complexity of our history.

Alice

Alice was reading the newspaper by the fire. The Mad Hatter was attending to some millinery, the March Hare was playing billiards, and beside the big grandfather clock the Queen of Hearts was sawing the White Rabbit's head off.

'What does "measured military response" mean?' asked Alice thoughtfully.

'Well, exactly as the speaker says, I imagine,' observed the March Hare as he chalked his cue. 'Saying what you mean and meaning what you say are the same thing, you know.'

'I know nothing of the kind,' said Alice, rather hotly. 'We had this conversation before, and when I said that, the Mad Hatter retorted that that was the same as saying, "I see what I eat is the same thing as I eat what I see".'

The Mad Hatter looked up from his needle. 'That was in Wonderland,' he said sadly. 'Things were different in Wonderland. And Behind the Looking Glass too – remember the Looking Glass, Alice? Happy days, happy days.'

'Well, if this is not Wonderland, and it's not Behind the Looking Glass, where am I?' Alice asked in a plaintive little voice.

'This is a new adventure,' murmured the Queen in quietly triumphant tones as her saw cut through the rabbit's neck and the head fell onto the carpet. 'And one in which I am in my element. This adventure is called "Alice in Peace Process Land", where nothing is just as it seems.'

'I am quite used to that in my adventures, you know,' said Alice, a little impatiently. 'I'm not a complete fool.'

'Maybe you are,' said Tweedledee as he sailed through the door. 'And maybe you're not,' said Tweedledum behind him. 'For if you were a fool, you wouldn't know you were one,' chimed in Tweedledee. And Tweedledum added: 'And if you weren't a fool, contrariwise, you wouldn't know foolishness enough to recognise it. That's logic.'

'Oh,' said Alice, a little faintly. 'I didn't realise that's what logic was.'

'Don't be surprised at what logic does in this place,' said the March Hare. 'The men who used that term, "measured military response" no doubt think it's logic. Logic in Peace Process Land is a universal quality possessed by everybody, right or wrong.'

'Is it?' asked Alice in a small voice, and sounding quite appalled. 'So there's logic in calling the butchery of a half-a-dozen perfectly innocent civilians on the outside a measured military response to the murder of a man inside a jail, is there?'

'Yes,' said Tweedledum. 'Yo,' said Tweedledee.

'And for military, I should read non-military?'

'Precisely,' said the Queen, popping a rabbit eye into her mouth.

'And I read here,' continued Alice, waving a newspaper, 'that people in Peace Process Land meet according to the Mitchell principles, and everybody disavows violence and promises to disarm for ever and ever. So that means these UFF-UDP thingummies have broken their word, so they'll be out for ever, yes?'

There was along, studied silence in the room, before the dormouse, who had crept in unobserved, remarked sleepily: 'No, not quite forever. Six weeks actually. That's a long time for a dormouse, you know.'

'Six weeks?' cried Alice. 'That's only a week per murder. That's monstrous! What does the Dublin Government say about these killings of blameless Catholics by loyalist fascists, pardon my French.'

'No pardon needed, my dear,' said the Mad Hatter, snipping a stitch with his teeth. 'There now. Well, the Dublin Government's Minister for Foreign Affairs says yes, he'd welcome back the political representatives of the killers, once six weeks have elapsed.'

'I see,' said Alice. 'Is that the way of it, that participants in the peace talks can go on a killing spree half-way through the talks, and after six weeks they can come back into the talks, and everybody's lovey-dovey again, is it?'

'Pretty much,' agreed the White Queen, looking up from her snack.

She wiped her mouth with her sleeve and it came away stained crimson. 'That land of the peace-talks is full of people like me, who sup at the bowl of blood and call it logic. We must be placated. If we are not at the talks, we kill again. That's why democrats must let us have our way. Always.'

'But you were at the talks, you swore you wouldn't kill again, and you did,' said Alice levelly.

'We were provoked,' sniffed the White Queen.

'So even though you broke your word by murdering, you'll still be allowed back to rejoin the talks to repeat the same promise you have already violated by murdering?'

'Not murdering, my dear. Engaging in a measured military response, which is now concluded,' said the White Queen. 'And after a six-week sanitation period, we'll be welcome back, according to that nice David Andrews – so handsome, isn't he, so statesmanlike.'

The Queen of Hearts looked down at her bowl and let out a little cry of joy. 'Oh, I just love it when the blood starts puckering, don't you?'

'And how long will a peace built on such rules last?' asked Alice, of nobody in particular. There was a long silence, broken only by the soft munching sound of tiny rodent bones as a threshing tail vanished into the Queen's mouth.

She belched. 'Dormouse. Yummy.'

Wrong, totally and utterly wrong

Wrong: totally and utterly wrong, wrong, wrong. It's an unsettling, disorienting thing finally to realise that the prediction about which I have written thousands of words turns out to have been complete rubbish. Many other questions are no doubt raised by the recent Stormont deal, and these might very well show that some of my predictions have been correct, but that is scarcely relevant. What is relevant is that what I said would never happen, a unionist-SDLP-Sinn Féin accord, has come to pass.

It is a fact; an undeniable and glorious fact, and I am gloriously, magnificently, totally wrong.

I was wrong not merely in my assessment of what Sinn Féin would do and how the Unionists would react to a proposed deal with a republican movement that is still awash with Semtex and Kalashnikovs, but also about the intentions and goals of the two main Sinn Féin leaders, Martin McGuinness and Gerry Adams. They were in fact prepared to do what I was sure they would not or could not do – that is to settle for far less than the IRA began this war to achieve.

This was an exceedingly brave and difficult thing to do, and it would be contemptible not to give credit where it is due. Blessed indeed are the peacemakers, and even more blessed for persevering in the face of doubts and sneers from such as myself. Their place in history is assured, and for bringing us peace, they deserve that place.

But, as it would be wrong not to give credit to John Hume, and to those two men in particular, Gerry Adams and Martin McGuinness, for managing with great patience and adroitness to bring the greater part of the republican movement round to their strategy of advance by peaceful means, so would it be wrong to forget what the IRA has been up to for the past 25 years.

No cause deserved or justified the feast of homicide and misery which the IRA and others placed on the table of the Irish and British peoples. I sense already a rewriting of history, as if an honourable cause has found a new and honourable means to an end. A comparable rewriting of history followed earlier passages of violence, and so fed an appetite for war, as if war had been a friend to Ireland and to the cause of independence. The complete reverse has been the case. This is the bicentenary of the 1798 Rising, which is already being marked by some fairly brainless celebrations of a truly terrible time in our history.

The Easter Rising of 1916 was transformed by mythic rewriting into something noble and uplifting, though it caused appalling suffering to the plain and unconsulted people of Dublin and was an assault on democracy by a conspiracy within a conspiracy – and not one of those conspirators had ever bothered his head to present himself beforehand to the electorate. From 1916 emerged the wars of 1919 to 1923, which were littered with atrocious events of every description, and which brought low the names of Britain and of Ireland. Incredibly, that calamitous period was soon to find numerous apologists, and the cold-blooded murder of unarmed men before their wives came to be glamorised and romanticised.

One great and enduring truth emerged from all these episodes of homicide and communal violence: the cause which called for such deeds, such sacrifices, for ruined lives and for economic despoliation, was never advanced by them. Not an inch. I have written many times how little an advance the Treaty of 1921 was on the Home Rule Bill of 1914: only an investment of a lake of human blood before and after the Treaty conceals this central truth. Peaceful means, patiently and persuasively followed, could have achieved in 1919 or 1920 what murder and ruin brought about years later.

Violence failed; but those who ruled the new State had been men of violence, and history was rewritten and reconstructed to justify the failed and bankrupt means they had employed. The bloody fantasies of one generation fed the appetites of later generations and the virtues of violent conspiracy were exalted and honoured.

The dreary cycle of murder, of repression, of state and terrorist brutality, of organised stupidity masquerading as duty, began again even as the RUC was being disarmed and the civil rights programme was being implemented in 1970. Where do we even begin to tell this tale, of murder upon murder, massacre upon massacre, atrocity following upon atrocity, of screaming men being tortured to death and of young mothers being secretly buried by torchlight, until it seemed that Ireland alone in all of Europe was doomed to live in some perpetual dark age of moral primitivism and homicidal boastfulness? The tale is too terrible to tell; so terrible that a veil is already been drawn over the suspension of individual and corporate conscience which caused such wicked things to be done.

That is why now is the time not just to praise and thank the peacemakers, and I do, and to ask forgiveness for doubting them when the hour was darkest and they needed help, not derision; but it is also the time to remember the purposeless, idiotic war they both waged and ended. We will be doomed to relive this nightmare if we ignore or choose to forget the truly abominable nature of the events of the past 30 years.

Never again, dear God, never again.

Doubts

For the first time in 80 years, the people of Ireland tomorrow vote together on their future. That we have got so far is indeed a miracle, and confounds a great deal of what I repeatedly predicted; which is good. Being shown to be wrong when you have offered a steady diet of gloom is mightily pleasing indeed.

My delight at the Good Friday accord lifted my spirits at the time, and I wrote nice things about Martin McGuinness and Gerry Adams, and I will not unwrite that which I have written. But the issue is not about individuals, and never was. It is about historical movements, about powerful familial cultures, about profound senses of identity, about public, often taunting, celebrations of tradition, and about the righteous resort to violence which abolishes reason as swiftly as it takes life. We should not have needed the return of the Balcombe Street gang to remind us of the central realities of what Sinn Féin stands for, what it is, how it thinks; but we did. By God we did.

Michael Collins, Éamon de Valera, Seán Lemass and Seán McBride are just a few of the individuals who made the journey from that perverse and morally delinquent Sinn Féin-IRA culture which sees no ethical disorder in violence, and which discerns only victimhood in its own condition. Each achieved the personal liberation which results from abandoning violence, and each actually increased the freedom of the Irish people by that abandonment.

For the greatest serfdom in this country, throughout this century, has been the enslavement by the gun. The gun intoxicates, it thrills, it weaves enchantment upon those who bear it, it glorifies, in their own eyes, those who use it. It is addictive, and only those who have used the gun would have been given the rhapsodic response which was given to the IRA killers at the Sinn Féin special ard fheis the other weekend.

And here lies my problem. That devotion to the gun is a core-cultural value of Sinn Féin-IRA. It is as vital to the existence of that tradition as fields are to cattle farming. Their real heroes are not the peace-makers, not the trojan workers who toiled that the killing may stop, not the nurses who nursed the shattered bodies, or the doctors who repaired the broken limbs – but the opposites of those people, the men and women who have killed.

The Balcombe Street gang was the worst and the most abominable of the units the IRA unleashed on London. It specialised in spreading terror amongst the uninvolved. Merely to eat in a good restaurant turned innocent people into legitimate targets; to drink in a pub where off-duty soldiers, in their own country, also drank, was to risk death. This was homicide at its most random, its most nihilistic, its most profoundly immoral. It was violence for violence's sake. Those whom the Balcombe Street gang caused to die were not just the dozen or so they actually killed, but those who died because one of the greatest cancer specialists in the world was one of their victims.

'These men are our Mandelas,' said Michael O'Brien – who is serving a sentence for attempted murder – at the ard fheis as he welcomed the Balcombe Street heroes. 'They are fit and strong, unbowed and unbroken, humorous, politically astute, and they still believe in unity after 23 years in the belly of the beast.' And of course there was uproar.

Such gibberish does not require refutation, for how can one possibly refute a statement in which all the ordinary meanings within human communication are stripped of value, and words are rendered almost meaningless? Gravity becomes anti-gravity; light becomes dark; to be a killer is to be a victim; to be murdered is to convey legitimacy upon those who murdered you.

It is bizarre, yet the words are useful, because they are the quintessential distillate of the Sinn Féin philosophy. Boil down all that you hear from Sinn Féin-IRA, and the liquid you have at the bottom is what Michael O'Brien said to those soon-to-be-ecstatic Sinn Féin supporters. It is the key sentiment to their existence and the fuel which has powered the moral engine of carnage and destruction through the decades, and which drives Sinn Féin-IRA unrepentant into the future.

I truly believe that Martin McGuinness and Gerry Adams want a settlement and an end to violence. I said they didn't before, and I am now convinced that I was wrong. But merely wishing for something is not enough; and in the democratic world they now wish to inhabit, awareness of how those who are not your immediate allies will react to what you do must be a guide to your actions. It seems that the Sinn Féin leadership has not even learned that much.

They have made a rod, and that rod will first of all be for the back of David Trimble. I pray it lands softly tomorrow and the No vote is overwhelmed by the Yes. I fear that the No vote will be substantial and that even if there is a Yes majority in the North, it will not be enough to confer a compelling moral authority on the Good Friday accord. And then the rod will fall on the Sinn Féin leadership.

We know that simple majoritarianism doesn't work in the North; yet on the other hand, all-party agreements are impossible. No shopping basket can accommodate all the political groceries in the Northern supermarket. The UKU and the DUP are already out of the basket. Even if Sinn Féin-IRA can shut up over the next 24 hours, is it not likely that sooner or later it will revert to type, so brutally exhibited at the ard fheis, and scare the unionists out of the basket for good? In other words, is it possible to reconcile the cultures of unionist orangery and of green gun-worship? It is not.

Complete solutions do not work. They are attempts to make submarines which double as orbiting television satellites. The Sinn Féin leadership must soon do as others have done before, and lead its followers away from the gun, leaving it to the mad, crooning guardians who have minded it down the years, and who always will.

PARSNIPS

The day was December 1st, not April 1st, when this newspaper carried a report on Sinn Féin policing proposals, so I can only presume it was not a leg-pull; and anyway, Sinn Féin's hurley-carrying friends don't pull legs, but dismantle them at the joints. Therefore we must assume that the Shinners' suggestions that firstly the Royal Ulster Constabulary must be disbanded completely and be replaced by a new force which is 45 per cent Catholic, 50 per cent female, 15 per cent homosexual, 2 per cent ethnic minorities, 3 per cent vegetarian, 1 per cent sado-masochist, 12 per cent red-haired, 0.5 per cent blind, 2 per cent wheelchairbound, 1.5 per cent mountainy farmers, 17 per cent unemployed, and so on, is serious.

Well, sort of. Everything after the 2 per cent ethnic minorities is my own contribution to policing. The rest is genuinely part of the Sinn Féin policing document – though I see no reason on earth why my recommendations should not be, ah, taken on board, as we say in the business. Why should farmers in the Sperrins fond of sprightly Merino ewes called Gladys or Mabel be excluded from contributing to society at large? Why should lentil-munchers not get their quota on the force? And since one in 500 of the population of Northern Ireland has been killed in the Troubles, it stands to reason that 0.2 per cent of the new force – the Proportionately Allocated, Radically ethno-Sensitive Northern Ireland Policy Service, or PARSNIPS – should be dead too.

Alas, not everyone shares my scrupulous zeal for representationalism, but no matter. We should be grateful for the Sinn Féin document, for it adds to the gaiety of nations and has brought a little smile to our faces as the days shorten to a few minutes of wan, grey daylight around noon. Just the sort of thing to give to the troops, if you'll pardon the expression. I'm not alone, I'm sure, in feeling a deep gratitude to the bright lads and lasses of Sinn Féin-IRA for pausing amid the flurry of leg-breaking and expulsions – all of which show how dear to their hearts the Mitchell Principles remain – in order to cheer us in our midwinter gloom. God bless their kneecapping little green hearts.

But a few questions need answering. Firstly, what happens if you can't get your proportions right for PARSNIPS? Take homosexuals. Research shows that 1 per cent of the population is homosexual, but Sinn Féin wants to have 15 per cent of PARSNIPS members attracted to their own sex. All very sapphosodomophilic, you might say, but is it? Not many people actually want to be policemen or women, yet now the poor old homosexual community is expected to supply 15 times more recruits than its numbers would justify. Which means, of course, if somebody hurls a brick at a PARSNIP peeler – and, as the nightly forays to smash kneecaps prove, old habits die hard in Northern Ireland – the chances of beaning a homosexual are 15 times greater than they should be. Sounds suspiciously like what those politically correct characters in Sinn Féin would call 'homophobia.'

And what about the ethnic minorities? Presumably they arrived in Northern Ireland in order to be doctors or run restaurants, and suddenly they find they're expected to provide 2 per cent of the police force. That being the case, they are presumably meant to supply 2 per cent of the lesbians too. A lot of ethnic minorities – such as the Bangladeshis, say – might have some interesting opinions about such expectations; after, that is, the equal-opportunities Sinn Féin PARSNIPS recruiting officer – lucky devil – has carefully explained what lesbians are. (They do *what* together?)

Poor devils come to Northern Ireland to open a curry house, and suddenly they find the womenfolk among them are expected to have sex with each other and stand in uniform on street-corners bobbing at the knees and murmuring 'Evening, all' to passing strangers. Don't be surprised if the Bangladeshis up saucepans and come down to Dublin. PARSNIPS might well end up playing merry hell with Balti cuisine in the North.

And what are ethnic minorities? Are they the politically correct, Afro-Caribbean-Asian minorities so beloved on US campuses, or are they the genuine ethnic minorities of Northern Ireland – the English, say? The English, after all, are probably the largest minority in the North. Will Sinn Féin-IRA be complaining because English people are under-represented in PARSNIPS? What about the Ulster-Scots? Do they count as a minority? And will the chuckies be demonstrating outside PARSNIPS headquarters with their 'Brits In' placards?

They will, it seems, certainly be complaining if 'human rights violators' within the current RUC are employed in its replacement force, though ex-RUC members might just be allowed to join PARSNIPS. However, Sinn Féin is opposed to former para-militaries being excluded from PARSNIPS. In fact, the integration of former combat-ants into the security forces 'is a significant feature of many conflict resolution situations.' So the happy, happy Six Counties can look forward to a blissful future in which policing falls to lesbian kneecappers and gay pub-bombers, plus, of course, Fatima from Dacca, looking decidedly unhappy on the beat with Sharon, a transsex-ual serial killer from Ballymena. And the silence of the new police force!

For as they say down the country, PARSNIPS utter no fine words.

The future of the RUC

It has been depressing indeed to read the unrepentant, aggressive tone of those who have been criticising the RUC at the Patten hearings, as if whatever police violations of law there were did not occur in a context; yet that same context is consistently adduced to justify both special status conditions in the North's jails and the early release of prisoners. One could quite easily believe from the Patten hearings in South Armagh that here was a peaceful, law-abiding community that was subjected to unpro-voked and ferocious assaults by the forces of law and order. For IRA apologists, it is a not displeasing image: the oppressed people of South Armagh valiantly, and largely successfully, opposing armed, imperial tyranny.

You can put the picture another way: of a police force which had to operate in simply inoperable circumstances in which it was, overwhelmingly, the victim. To be sure, the security forces did not invariably behave like Little Orphan Annie; the infa-mous shoot-to-kill policy of suspected terrorists, or the summary execution of Peter Cleary, the IRA commander taken from his girlfriend's house by the SAS and shot 'while trying to escape', were unAnnie-ish indeed.

But such murderous events do not compare with the atrociousness of the IRA campaign waged against the security forces, the local Protestant population and Catholics who were seen to be 'equivocal'; the only place in Northern Ireland in which Catholic ex-servicemen were, as a matter of policy, singled out for murder, disappear-ance or expulsion was in South Armagh.

Nobody conversant with the realities of the North over the past quarter-century is unaware of the particular realities of South Armagh; of the massacre of 10 blameless Protestant workmen at Whitecross; the Tullyvallen Orange Hall massacre; or the murder of Sir Norman Stronge, a survivor of the first day of the Somme, and proba-bly the last soldier from the First World War to be shot dead, killed with his son in their isolated mansion near the Border.

And we all know the scale of the war in Armagh in which 69 police officers and

114 soldiers have been killed. How does one even begin to sift through the human tragedy involved or measure one atrocity against another? Is there a human heart which does not sink at the fate of Louis Robinson, a policeman from Newtownards who had been off work for two years through mental stress? He was known as Louis the Lip because he was an incorrigible talker. While on holiday in Dingle with a group of Northern prison officers in 1990, Louis the Lip presumably told some local hero that he was a policeman. The necessary machinery was put into action, and he was abducted from his minibus as it crossed back over the border in South Armagh.

What did Louis the Lip tell his captors? How long did they talk to him and bleed him dry of all the information he had about police officers he knew? Did he weep and plead for his life? What were the last hours of this man's life like before that life was ended by rifle fire through the back of the skull? And what, dear God, do his killers dream of now?

Some people – such as poor Louis the Lip – have lives almost without consequence, and their deaths pass unremarked and unremembered. Other deaths trigger consequence through the decades. The killing of the Catholic Reavey brothers of South Armagh, murdered by loyalists in 1975, was followed by the Whitecross massacre, in turn prompting one local Protestant lad, who had been so apolitical that he used to play GAA, to join the UVF. His name was Billy Wright.

The killing strands reach down through the decades, and the consequences are condign, ubiquitous. The very first police officers to be murdered in South Armagh in these Troubles were Constables Donaldson and Miller, blown to pieces by a booby-trap bomb outside Crossmaglen in August 1970. Sam Donaldson's brother Alexander was killed in the massacre of nine RUC officers in Newry 15 years later. Their nephew Jeffrey is today the lightning conductor of opposition within the Ulster Unionist Party to the Good Friday Agreement, and its resulting release of 200 prisoners with not an ounce of Semtex handed in or a flintlock surrendered.

Nobody who claims to have any understanding of the North would seriously maintain that the RUC must face the future unaltered. It is in part a para-military force which must in time be disarmed and civilised. But the RUC is now being portrayed in places such as Crossmaglen as the sole begetter of these Troubles, whose members have kicked down doors and knocked nationalists about, almost for entertainment.

Count the bodies – the Louis Robinsons, the scores of dead policemen who breathed their last amid the drumlins of South Armagh. Did these men and women behave any worse than any other police force in the world would have behaved in such circumstances? They did not. For the most part they did their thankless and horribly dangerous duty with extraordinary discipline, courage and skill. It is not fashionable, and certainly not wise to say it in places like South Armagh, but they are amongst the true heroes of the Troubles.

ROAD RAGE

Caution: baby on board

Yes, I know it is a truism that nobody ever lost money by underestimating the taste of the general public; but even the wisdom of that truism could hardly have anticipated the deplorable vulgarisation which afflicts about 17.7 per cent of personkind when they buy a motorcar.

I once knew a man who made a fortune out of car accessories, and he awaited the arrival of the latest car accessories from Italy and Hong Kong with a peculiar mixture of relish and horror. There was a kind of deplorable pleasure to be derived from seeing what the human imagination could come up with as a suitable decoration for a motor car, as well as a deep sense of dread at what the accessory buying public was capable of.

When he got his first set of furry dice, to be hung, of course, from the rear view mirror, he was convinced that the inventors of the cornucopia of tastelessness had finally got it wrong. Nobody, but nobody, could possibly be enchanted by kitch which lacked both kitschish charm yet also managed to be so thoroughly lethal, for the dice could obscure a fully-grown juggernaut at fifteen paces, by which time it is of course far too late.

But the dice skittled out of the shop door on their first day; replacement orders took months because of the huge demand for the acrylic-lined cubes. They were still selling well by the time he left the business with his fortune made and some little of his wits intact.

There is, perhaps, a PhD to be done on the amount of pedestrians who have had the opportunity to examine the cubes from close range, having been propelled through the windscreen after the car driver had failed to see them because their presence on the road had been entirely obstructed by the very same friendly, furry cubes.

Could anybody have foreseen that fortunes would have been made by selling little stickers – 'Caution: Baby on Board' – to be placed on the rear window of motor cars.

Surely that was as bad as you can get. Twee, sickly, and insulting; as if the only reason the rest of us would have for not ramming the car concerned and finishing off any survivors by reversing over them and hitting them with our jacks was that there was a subtoddler inside.

In fact, I suspect the people who run the National Lottery are responsible for the 'Baby on Board' stickers – excuse me for a moment while I just get sick. Baby on Board indeed. It was when I first saw 'Caution: Baby on Board' that I began to do the

National Lottery. I had understood for the first time why it is that some people want to be millionaires.

A millionaire could buy a turbo-charged bulldozer and go round ramming such cars and not be too worried about the financial consequences. As for legal consequences, there would of course be none: no jury would possibly convict merely because one had reduced to metallic pulp a car containing such a flagrantly inflammatory sticker.

I have not given blood since I saw a sticker 'Caution: I am a blood donor – one day you might need me.' The idea of even being in the same building as such a person is unnerving; as for wanting their blood, why, I wouldn't be seen dead with it. I would prefer to be injected with live sheep brains than have any of their dimwitted, vulgar corpuscles loitering in my cardiovascular recesses.

Yet, it has to be said, even the worst such motorists do not compare for sheer brainless stupidity with the hordes of cyclists who feel no obligation to have lights on their bikes at night. The closest I have ever come to murder was a couple of years ago when by braking and dramatic steering, I did not kill an unlit cyclist; in return for my warning horn, he gave me a v-sign. Murder entered my soul: I stalked him through the streets of the capital, determined to convert him into something thin enough to fit under a microscope glass slide. Alas, he got away.

Miles? Kilometres?

Is Ireland the only place in the world which uses two completely different measurement systems on its highways? I must say I think a double system like this is to be richly applauded: the thing that one must deplore is that we have limited ourselves to just two systems. If it is the desire to baffle foreigners – and I presume that it is – then I can only ask why not employ such a variety of systems that not even visiting Germans and Japanese can work out how we govern our roads and our traffic? If we really wanted to outwit our visitors, the least we could do is to also use some traditional Polish measures casually about the place.

The outwitting of foreigners to this island begins at Dublin Airport, where they can collect their hire car. If the visitors are Americans, they are more easily duped, because they have just spent about three hours more than necessary flying to the capital, courtesy of the Shannon stopover, and are accordingly shattered.

It is perhaps typical of these squeamish times we live in that passengers for Dublin are no longer forced out of their slumbers and made to slouch around the Shannon duty-free area for a few hours, without being allowed to buy anything. This is absurd, of course. They should be made to squander more hours of their vacation in Ireland, not merely in Shannon, gazing at plaster thatched cottages and leprechauns, but also in Knock, Farranfore and other airports in the West, that region where, as we all know, *real* Irish people live.

You can recognise the Americans leaving Dublin Airport because they look as if somebody has been doing open-cast coalmining under their eyes and the front-seat passenger has a map the size of the airport open across the windscreen.

This does not, of course, mean that they miss the speed limit sign on the edge of the airport, the sign which says that the maximum speed limit throughout the Republic is 75 kilometres an hour.

'OK, Martha, 75 kilometres an hour maximum speed limit. How much is that in good old American miles, Martha?'

'I don't know, Jack, but this little round thing is marked in miles and kilometres so I guess that will do.'

And thus relying on the speedometer, which is conveniently marked in miles as well as in Napoleon's contribution to weights and measures, they set off on their tour of Ireland, frequently veering on to the wrong side of the road as Martha pores over the map and Jack, exhausted, forgets that he is no longer in a place where people drive on the side that God ordained they do, the American side.

The problem for Jack and Martha, Jacques and Martha, Johann and Martha, Giovanni and Martha and Juan and Marthas is that the 75 kph sign outside Dublin Airport is the last they will ever see in Ireland. All the others are in the imperial system. But our visitors do not know this. And everywhere they go they see maximum speed signs indicating that they should go no faster than 30.

Thirty what? Well, Jack, the road sign outside Dublin Airport was in kilometres an hour: and all the modern signposts give the distance in kilometres, too, Jack. Look, you can see the little km letters just under the number. So, when they say the maximum speed limit is 30, they mean 30 kilometres an hour.

After a few minutes of a law-abiding 29 kilometres an hour, Jack remarks to Martha that they don't seem to be getting very far. Martha, who has got out to enjoy the view, waits for the car to catch up with her before agreeing.

What baffles her and him is that Irish cars hurtle by, clearly ignoring not merely the 30 kph limit as well as the 75 kph limit and indeed every speed limit known to man or woman. This is not the only problematical piece of signposting that they encounter, because once they have become addicted to the placename signposts they will find that they will soon encounter a crossroads where their destination is mysteriously no longer named: and so they crawl at 29 kilometres an hour looking for a village they will never find.

And, if they are in West Cork, the one thing that is signposted unfailingly at every crossroads is something called Ambush Site. For, aside from being the only place in the world which has two measurement systems for its roads, are we alone in advertising places of killing in the way other countries direct visitors to picnic sites? Kilmichael is perhaps the most comprehensively signposted landmark in Ireland.

At least visitors there are spared the information that at that spot, amongst other things, disarmed men were killed and their bodies mutilated, which is the truth about the final deeds in that place. But I suspect we are as good at facing up to our history as we are at signposting in the Republic.

A modest proposal about drink-driving

It is unlikely we shall learn the lessons available; that as usual we will look at the example of others, see their mistakes in all their ghastly entirety, and then sedulously, and with great attention to detail, repeat them every one. We have seen planners and developers ransack the capitals of Europe and then permit their Irish equivalent to do the same. We observed the calamity which results from tower-block housing developments and faithfully produced our own.

Other countries experimented with new housing estates far outside the city centres from which their populations were drawn; and once it was discovered how socially disastrous they were, we did the same.

There is small chance that anybody will take any notice whatsoever of what follows next, since its proposal has no moral high ground whatsoever. Beware the moral high-ground, is all I can say; from such lofty vantage points have planners justified Kilbarrack and Ballymun. From such virtuous altitude did people justify Knock airport. All the falsities of health faddism are pronounced from that stratospherical perch.

To state the obvious: rural communities are dying all over Europe. Not just in Ireland, where the illness has been chronic and where the patient is gravely ill indeed, but everywhere. One of the reasons why the French are so exercised about the GATT deal is that they fear the way of life of the French countryside will be swept aside by the economic stringencies of free trade.

In England there is virtually no rural community left. Most villages are populated by abstemious, non-drinking commuters who have moved in from the cities. Country pubs, one of the glories of English civilisation, can no longer depend on local trade to stay profitable.

Much the same is true of Irish country pubs, though for different reasons. The Irish countryside has not been urbanised by townies. But rural public houses are threatened because of emigration. They need travelling drinkers. And this is where we abandon the high moral ground and go wallowing in the mud of low moral bogs of practicality.

The entire drift of law enforcement in the past few years has been to punish people who drive after having had a few drinks. Increasingly people are becoming more and more terrified of going to a party and enjoying themselves, especially on Saturday nights and at this time of year. If they drive they cannot drink; if they drink they cannot drive, and they certainly cannot get a taxi, because Dublin doesn't have enough on Saturday nights and rural areas have none at all at any time of year.

The issue for the law is not whether you are capable of driving, but whether you have had alcohol. At the moment the law stipulates that you should not have in your blood the amount of alcohol which results from consuming say about two and half glasses of wine.

I hazard a suggestion – and hazard is right, because by this time the morally righteous are already rolling up their sleeves – that nobody is killed on the road because somebody has drunk even six glasses of wine. They are killed on the road because a driver cannot keep his or her vehicle straight, or more likely, is driving too fast.

All over England pubs are closing down because energetic constabularies are posting bobbies outside country pubs to breathalyse people driving away from them. It does not need much of that sort of stuff to cause people to abandon going to pubs altogether.

Similar things are beginning to happen in Ireland, especially at this time of year. People are being flagged down purely at random (and not because of any driving irregularities) and asked by gardaí if they have had a drink. If they say yes, or if they give the appearance by general contentment or by fragrance of having taken liquor, they will be breathalysed; and then bingo. Ruin.

And doubtless the statisticians will at this point reel out all the facts and figures about the number of people killed in accidents involving drink. Never mind that many of the killed are drunk pedestrians: these will be numbered in the 'drunk-driving' category. Never mind that a very large number of the killed will be drunken teenagers driving down country roads at 90 m.p.h. at four in the morning and for whom the threat of law has proved no deterrent anyway. Never mind that the real killer in all such cases is not the drink; it is the speed.

The Diary's simple answer to this is that nobody who had had alcohol *to any degree* should be allowed to drive at more than 25 mph; all such drivers must stay on the left hand lane of all roads, driving with their hazard warning lights on. Provided their driving gives no cause for concern to gardaí, they should be allowed to proceed unimpeded. If they are seen to be driving erratically then the gardaí should arrest them and subject them to the necessary tests to ascertain that they are capable of driving. But otherwise there would be no prohibition on people drinking and driving.

Nobody, of course, will pay any attention to this modest proposal, because there is no lobby for it. Meanwhile country pubs will continue to face bankruptcy as the simple pleasures of driving down the country for a few pints in the evening will be denied one. Meanwhile, the real killer, speed, will continue to kill several hundred people a year in Ireland. And the right to drive at speed and to imperil life is seen as a more basic and inalienable right than the right to have a couple of drinks and then to drive slowly and harmlessly home afterwards.

Placebo crossings

One of the most fascinating devices to be seen in Dublin streets are placebo pedestrian crossing buttons which have no influence whatsoever on the lights they appear to control; they merely appear to change the lights. The lights themselves are on a pre-ordained sequence, such as that on the island where Tom Moore points loowards. Nothing the button-pushers can do will change those lights, which change in a sequence of eight seconds for a pedestrian and 96 seconds for cars. Those little buttons – which no doubt cost hundreds of pounds each – are merely devices to convince the pedestrians growing old at the lights that they have power. Other such pedestrian lights work on the reverse principle: they only come on when the button is pressed, but are wholly redundant, because the traffic is halted already on a red light.

Would it not make sense to have lay-bys at traffic lights, with condom-vending machines, and caravans selling hot dogs and hamburgers and enterprising youngsters peddling hot chestnuts in winter and ice creams in summer? We might have the most bizarre red lights in Europe: this way we would also have the most entertaining, a tourist attraction where people could actually holiday, with Germans grabbing the lightside deckchairs shortly before dawn.

Irish roads

Back to our roads – and I make no apology about returning to this. Yet is it not quite incredible that two capitals on the one European island are, nearly a quarter-of-a-century after both joined the European Community, united by roads which have barely improved since Independence?

In the early 1970s, when RTE had to send newsfilm from Belfast to Dublin by taxi, the Oxford taxi crews used to pride themselves on their ability to get the film to the Montrose studios in under two hours.

Twenty-five years later, and despite the extensive net of motorways connecting Belfast with the Border areas, there is no way that a driver could get to the southern suburbs of Dublin in that time. The volume of traffic on the roads south of the Border is such that the small improvements introduced here – an interesting peregrination through the suburbs of Drogheda, an intriguingly lengthy circuit of Dundalk, in order, perhaps, to breathe the diesel fumes the better – are more than negated.

My journey to Balbriggan from the centre of Dublin the other day took 40 minutes. I spent 20 minutes in that fair town, and by the time I left I was in no doubt why the Black and Tans burnt the place down. I was fingering a box of matches thoughtfully and gazing hungrily at a petrol station, wondering how much they would charge for a couple of bottles of their highest octane – and a few rags please? – when the last traffic jam released me to join the leisurely convoy for Drogheda.

The truth is that Dublin governments have regarded road-building as some politically profitless exercise that can never reward the party which engages in it. Road-building is long-term strategy stuff. It is not a question of a quick stroke here, a factory started up there. Road-building is the true hallmark of political vision, the mark of visionary pedigree. Only grown-up societies build roads, which can spend today's money not on today's future, or even tomorrow's, but the day after tomorrow's, and the weeks beyond.

The truth is – and it is a truth you are in no doubt of as you sit in a sweltering car and in front of you hundreds of other sweltering drivers inch towards the North, motorways, cheap wine – that nobody regarded serious road-building in Ireland as important. The traveller to Cork today will travel over pretty much the same road as her great-grandfather drove in his Model T to meet Michael Collins there in 1922.

Cahir now is by-passed. There is a dinky little bit of dual carriageway outside Cork. Otherwise, the road is largely unaltered. This is unique in the Community. The two main cities in any other country in the Union – in any European country apart from Albania – would this time be served by a multilane highway which does not pass through towns, on which a non-stop cruising speed of 70 mph is possible, and which dramatically cuts down on travel time and driver stress.

Road-building in Ireland from the 1960s to the 1980s consisted of one great project. It was called the Naas dual carriageway. Naas folk – including my uncle Jim Teevan, manager of the Ulster Bank, and one of the grandest men who ever lived – used to proudly refer to it as the motorway.

Jim and his fellow-Naasers were being a little previous. It would take another quarter-of-a-century before a motorway was bolted on to the end of the Naas dual carriageway. From the very beginning, with its unbelievably badly synchronised traffic lights, the dual carriageway was a model of bad roadbuilding: and recent additions on the Dublin end, with traffic lights and roundabouts, have merely served to create a road-slum.

Road-engineers wanted to spend money to build decent roads, knowing full well that traffic lights and roundabouts create knots of congestion. There was no political will to spend money on serious roads: a 'Sure 'twill do' culture, ensured that the tens of millions spent on the road were wasted.

But we should nonetheless rejoice in my Uncle Jim's motorway, because it does seem to represent the high-point in rural road-building endeavour. Other bits and bobs can be described about the place. Let us take our hats off, ladies and gentlemen, as we pause and gaze in respectful awe at the Athlone by-pass. Let us similarly doff our hats and say a decade of the Rosary in honour of that strip of road which links Dublin to its airport. A moment, too, while we reflect upon a quite majestic strip of road between Drogheda and Dundalk, which is called M something or other, and which no doubt causes our German visitors to yodel with joy as they embark on what they believe is an autobahn, with major service stations, fast restaurants, rest areas.

It is not. Car-park ramps in Germany are longer than that strip of motorway, which does not of course prevent the erections of gleefully boasting signs warning you that you are about to enter a highway heaven, a turnpike paradise, seemingly into a vast distance. Our German in her Mercedes is in third gear, sinking siz is wunderbar, only to see the warning sign that the brief and ecstatic encounter with motorway driving will soon come to an end. Next, ze cowtrack.

How much time is lost on these wretched roads? How much damage is done to business and to human health as a result? And worse, how much odious self-satisfaction is derived from the woeful incompetence, which mistakes this economic and political ineptitude for a highly desirable and loveable national characteristic?

Yet the deplorable truth is that the moment anybody gets a strip of roadway, Dáil Éireann will be promptly infested with an outbreak of that fell affliction, Me Tooery. Everyone wants a mile of motorway in their constituency: and in a nation where everybody gets their disconnected mile of motorway, all the nation gets is traffic jams and convenient little runways for invaders.

Thank God for Garret FitzGerald [LUAS]

Thank God for Garret FitzGerald. He has said about Luas what I feared to say: that we have the makings of an urban calamity that will cost us and our generous German friends millions and might well cause more problems than it solves. Even if his arguments are faulty, he has at least enabled us to discuss a project which has been protected from analysis by its relative 'cheapness', by the piety that surrounds anything which purports to be a public utility, by the alleged need to get our hands on the deutschmarks pronto, and finally by the extra cladding of an Irish name, Luas.

Luas, as we all know in this great Irish-speaking nation of ours, means *speed*. To judge from Garret's forecasts, it might well mean Limiting or Urban-Arresting System: because the streets of Dublin are too narrow to permit both Luas trains and reasonable traffic-flow, and perhaps more compellingly, the very density of buildings in the city centre does not permit many route-options for cars or trams.

That is the legacy of the Wide Streets Commission, which chose to insert an extraordinary number of important buildings and squares into a very small area. There is no way of pushing a new road through that heart of the city without killing it. And, instead of recognising that reality, and committing ourselves to a transport policy which would take the expensive but realistic long-term option of going underground, we did what we have done repeatedly in transport policy; we compromised.

Have we not learned by this time that structural compromises with traffic do not work? Have we not learned that policy has to be created and implemented with clear goals? And that in all traffic problems, there cannot be shared primacy between public and private traffic and pedestrians? And most of all, will we never face up to the hideous truth that there are no cut-price solutions to dealing with problems which require strategic planning?

No. There is no area in public life which reflects the culture and competence of political planning than road construction. In 1994, the Netherlands, which is the size of Munster, built 800 kilometres of motorway. We built 40. The main road between the capitals of Ireland remains a national disgrace south of the Border. Travellers must still pass through numerous pretty villages like Balbriggan, plus the suburbs of Drogheda and the suburbs of Dundalk. A journey which should last an hour and a half takes a good hour longer than that, with a disproportionate amount of stress involved too.

Astonishingly, for part of that route, a motorway exists, unused and unusable, because it has been built over bog, and our bright planners are not sure whether there is going to be subsidence on the road; *so they are waiting to see if the road which has cost millions is going to vanish in the bog.*

We react to the crisis when it is upon us. The urgency of the Luas scheme is in part because the European funding is only available by a certain time – though Garret convincingly points out that the proponents of Luas have exaggerated the need for quick decision-making here. What is not in doubt is that Dublin traffic is in crisis. As it is in Drogheda, Cork, Galway. These cities need action not soon, but now.

But there is no *now* in planning. The present tense does not exist, only the future. And that is the tense we have most difficulty with in Ireland, especially at Government level. No doubt we have the fastest-growing economy in Europe, but that is almost solely due to the energies of the private sector and an IDA which has absorbed the culture of the private sector. Roads are not built by private commission. They are planned and built by Government, and it shows.

Apart from the enduring blight of unemployment, no area in Irish life is as deficient as our response to traffic. The quality of that response is indicated to the new arrivals leaving Dublin airport in their hired cars, with a sign indicating that the general maximum speed through Ireland is 100 kilometres an hour. And that is the last time they will see a speed sign in metric. All other speed signs are in imperial measurements, which co-exist with distance signposts which are in metric. And this is not the confusion which results from changing systems, when there is bound to be crossover of old and new. This is policy being implemented. New signs still record speed in imperial, distance in metric.

I can't imagine what the reason is for this. I do know the reason for much other poor traffic engineering. It is the c-word. Compromise. We wanted a cheap intersection at the bottom of the Naas dual carriageway, not an effective one: so our politicians told our engineers to build a roundabout, and not an expensive cloverleaf.

The roundabout did not work, simply because traffic flows were too vast and fast for drivers to be able confidently to enter the system. Thrombosis. Cure? Traffic-lights.

We have two systems controlling traffic-flow; and far from being complementary, they are contradictory, and dangerous; because the green light which permits you onto the roundabout can be followed mid-system by a red light round a bend, on which cars are following you at speed. Do not blame the engineers for this. They respond to the specifications of our political leaders.

The same is true of the roundabout outside Dublin Airport, and the roundabouts on the National Travesty leading to Belfast, born of cheap compromises; but traffic management is expensive and requires political will – the central span of the newest bridge being built for Paris is *taller* than the Eiffel Tower.

We should be grateful our problems are small in comparison, and grateful to Garret FitzGerald for warnings where our short-term solutions might lead us. Luas is a cheap compromise which could turn out to be hideously expensive.

Hitchhiker from hell

It was mad, but I did it nonetheless. I picked up the hitch-hiker, something I seldom do. There could be no particular reason, other than that it was two days short of Christmas, and night had fallen.

But hitch-hikers are not what they were. The rules were very clear in that distant epoch when I hitched: the hiker's duty was to make conversation in return for the gift of a lift. My sense of gratitude from that time lives with me still – to the Austrian ex-wartime paratrooper who rescued me amid the snow near Klagenfurt and who fed me strudel and chocolate coffee; or the Frenchwoman in Switzerland who, while her husband drove, secretly stuffed crispy bread-rolls and Camembert into my rucksack; or the young German driver who fed me lamb chop sandwiches and made me promise, absolutely swear, that when my time came, I would give lifts.

I repeated that promise with an unquenchable passion at an autobahn entrance outside Vienna, where I waited for two days without a lift – and where I nearly resolved to become a lifelong homosexual in protest at the way girl hitch-hikers so shamelessly refused to honour the hiker's code of moving downstream of existing hikers – and invariably would get lifts within moments of undoing a shirt-button or two. That second near-resolution, mysteriously, came to nothing.

Yet I kept my promise to give hitch-hikers lifts, and in return they kept the conversation going. But over the years things changed, as I noticed most powerfully one Sunday morning in Co. Galway when three teenage girls from Kerry spent their entire journey giggling at my expense – until I threw them out, many miles short of their destination. Only my legendary willpower of steel prevented me from reversing over them, uttering wild cries of joy.

Then last summer I picked up a local lad near Ballyconneally; he spent the entire journey in aloof and sullen silence and departed without a murmur of thanks. I am to this day tempted to scour Connemara, find him, and bury him in a bog. Never again, I swore. Never again.

So why, with night fallen, did I pick up a hitch-hiker on a back road near Clonee? Maybe the last residue of the goodness of Klagenfurt, the remembered Camembert, the oath over the chop sandwich. The hiker got into my car and said: 'Clondalkin, please.'

'What?' I cried in disbelief.

'Clondalkin. You can go over the new motorway.'

A pause to breathe. 'Excuse me. I'm not going to Clondalkin. I'm going to Phibsboro.'

'You're some ——in' taxi driver', said my guest. 'And where the — am I now, anyway?'

Oh sinking heart, the hitch-hiker from hell is in my car. He is young and unkempt and looks perfectly capable of sticking a hypodermic in my eye.

In as low a tone as I am able to muster I report that he is not in a taxi, we are in Clonee, Co. Meath, and I am heading for Phibsboro.

'Fine, so.' Then he falls asleep. The smell of drink from him would make a breathalyser stand on its hind legs and bark.

Suddenly he is awake again and eyeing me. 'Why did you give me a lift?' A good question, a very good question indeed. 'Because I thought if I didn't, nobody would.'

'And here's me thinking you were a taxi. Would you like some wine?'

Oh no, dear God no, this drunken homicidal beast wants me to go drinking Cyprus sherry with him. I reply in a voice of odious piety: 'No, indeed not.'

'Does your wife? I mean, I won this bottle here in a pub raffle, and I don't drink wine myself, and nor does Michelle. The girlfriend. And you're giving me a lift. And it's Christmas. It's not bad – it's Rioja. Would you like it? For the wife, like?'

I turned and looked at him. I was in the company of a thoroughly decent but drunk young gentleman. I said, a little more amiably: 'You've had a few.'

'I have. I was with me mates, we've been drinking in the pub since ten this morning after we got off the building site, and Michelle got the bus up and joined us, but I got pissed and fell asleep, and when I woke up, they were gone.'

'Any of your mates fancy Michelle?'

'They all do, but she wouldn't mess around with anybody else, only me.'

'How'd you meet her?'

'At a mate's christening.'

'How old's the mate?'

'Seventeen.'

'Rather old to be christened,' I observed. It was not the funniest thing that was ever said, but he sat back and roared, tears rolling down his cheeks. He told me his name, Lee. His mate and his girlfriend and their baby lived in a flat, and maybe he and Michelle would move in together.

'And have babies?'

'I don't know about that. I'll have to find her first. I'll ring her when I get home. Will you take the wine, as a Christmas present from me and Michelle, for picking me up when loads of fellas wouldn't? Will you? Just to please me? Please?'

I took the wine from him with pleasure, and I drove him into the centre of Dublin to the Clondalkin bus-stop. 'Merry Christmas to you,' he said, shaking my hand.

Merry Christmas, Lee, I replied. And a happy new year. Somewhere in this universe, the spirits of a Frenchwoman, an Austrian and a German nodded in approval.

Brutish, Merciless, Witless

I have the shrewd suspicion this column isn't going to win me a free trip to Bavaria, though what follows is a compliment to the car manufacturer based in that perfectly lovely German state. For we should be deeply grateful to BMW for producing cars which declare their owners to be Bullying, Macho Wastrels. How else could we spot such people instantly unless they paraded their Brutish, Merciless and Witless qualities in a car apparently named after the drivers rather than the manufacturers?

This of course need not apply to all BMW drivers – after all, the very first BMW motor car was a licence-built version of the Austin Seven, a sort of pram powered by a petrol-driven shaver, which, with a following wind and a raised sail, could sometimes reach speeds nudging double figures. That BMW, made in 1927, was called the Dixi, presumably after the French word for the numeral 10 (its maximum velocity), and it was completely without any of the qualities which attract modern drivers to BMWs.

To be sure, it was not without its particular merits – for example, provided the wind were from a suitable quarter, its top speed in reverse was every bit as high as its top forward speed. It was light and easy for nanny to push through the park if she wanted to give the children a bit of air. It was a wonderful shopping basket and, suitably equipped with a parasol, great-grandmother could sit out in it to enjoy the Alpine breezes.

Actually, it wasn't just the Austin Seven-BMW which was a joy. Until the outbreak of the second World War, BMW made cars of great elegance and subtlety; and even after the war, the baby-buggy school of car manufacture lingered within Bayerische Motoren Werke. The BMW 501 of 1962 certainly did not look like a pram, but it behaved like one: it took half-a-minute to reach 60 m.p.h. Shortly after that – and it is hard to believe now – BMW introduced a three-wheeler bubble car, the Isetta, a sort of motorised skate which could double as a handbag. Its top speed was much the same as that of butter that has been left in the sun, and its wheels were the size of teapot lids.

Ah, dem were de daze.

But the genesis of the woes which beset us today occurred at about the same time, when BMW engineers produced the 1500. Previously, in the push-chair culture of BMW, in which movement was of secondary importance, the engine was an afterthought, a sort of now-hold-on-haven't-we-forgotten-something-here, and at the last moment installed in whatever cavity it could be crammed into by lopping off a few cylinders here and leaving out the odd spark-plug there.

The 1500 was different. It was about engine, performance, speed. Most of all, its promotional colour was the one most of us dread in BMWs: red. With the 1500 of 35 years ago, a new breed of motor car and a new breed of driver were born. BMW no longer stood for Bayerische Motoren Werke, but Bonkers, Manic and oh yes, utterly, insanely Wild.

No doubt there are some courteous BMW drivers around. In fact, I'm sure there are. I just haven't seen them, just as I haven't seen griffins, unicorns or phoenixes, which almost certainly abound in other places, just as, I'm sure, kindly, courteous BMW drivers exist in corners of the planet I have not yet visited. But in the bits I have been to, BMW would not often stand for Benign, Mannerly and Wise.

Which of you have *ever* been waved on by a BMW driver? Which of you have ever seen a BMW driver give way? Which of you have ever seen a BMW driver slow down to let an elderly pedestrian cross? Which of you have ever seen a BMW driver acknowledge a kindness? Which of you have ever seen a BMW driver drive with care, concern and courtesy? Which of you have gazed on a BMW and murmured: that is driving as it should be done?

Good, OK. Not a hand moved. Now, then. Which of you have seen BMWs accelerate in order to prevent a car leave a side-road to enter a main road?

Which of you have seen BMWs weave in and out of lanes without indicating? Which of you have seen BMWs sounding their horns and flashing their headlights just because the lights have just gone green and the car in front has not departed like a bolt from a crossbow? Which of you have seen a BMW losing it at speed on a corner while its driver uses his mobile phone? Which of you have seen BMWs roaring down one-way streets on which children are playing?

Good. I think that's clear enough. It confirms what we all knew about an extraordinary number of BMW drivers, regardless of sex.

Boorish, Mannerless Wretches. In fact, the mere possession of a BMW should normally be considered evidence of a personality disorder so great as to disqualify the owner from having a licence; and even to desire, never mind own, one of those blood-red BMWs, before which wise people flee as if from rabid wolves, suggests therapy in a padded cell, to be supervised by muscular warders bearing blackjacks. In fact, we should be grateful to BMW for manufacturing a car which describes its owner to perfection: a Bad, Mad Wannabe.

Bemused, Misunderstood, Weeping

Bemused, Misunderstood, Weeping. I had no idea BMW drivers were such a sensitive lot – after all, who takes anything said in these columns seriously? BMW drivers, apparently. I'd have thought the vapourings which occur here are beyond notice, beneath contempt, and hardly worth pistols for two and coffee for one at the Phoenix Park gallops.

A lot of bruised BMW drivers do not agree, and have said so – which merely proves BMW drivers, conclusively, are not what I was suggesting they were. Forgive me for causing offence – it was meant in the most knockabout kind of way. No doubt in my heart of hearts I am secretly a BMW driver, and my BMWlessness has made me cantankerous and crabbed. Of course, all car-drivers – not just of BMWs – are susceptible to unfair parody. Maybe it is one of those wisdoms which Jane Austen meant to utter, but which she never got round to; that it is a truth universally acknowledged that each kind of car seems to draw from its drivers an extension of their personalities which might not otherwise be evidenced.

Take the top-of-the-range Volvo. It is normally driven as if it is as unassailable as the continental drift. Why? Because top-of-the-range Volvos are invariably company cars. Behind the wheel is the boss. This means he doesn't mind the odd scratch on the side which would normally have the rest of us chewing our tongues in grief.

And Volvos are constructed on the lines of the Alps. The driver doesn't expect to be crying after a crash – that is, if he even *notices* it. Volvo drivers tend to feel collisions with other cars in much the same way jumbo jets are retarded by collisions with gnats. That is why Volvos enter howling maelstroms of traffic as if they are nuclear-powered aircraft carriers entering the Sargasso Sea. Being in a car which is immune to every impact this side of a comet-strike gives the men behind the wheel a blissful sense of immunity.

I say men. I mean men. Has anyone ever seen a woman behind the wheel of a top-of-the-range Volvo? No, never. Volvos and their drivers command the road; they are proof of the theory that the safer the driver feels, the more risks he takes, for he is immortal. He is surrounded by air-bags, seatbelts, side-impact systems which can absorb the charge of a mother steamroller which has seen the driver interfere with her brood of baby steamrollers.

The men behind the wheels of Toyotas have a different sense of immortality, perhaps because very large numbers of them are taxi-drivers. This means that upon approaching green traffic lights with a fare aboard, they slow until a satisfactory red appears. This gives them the opportunity to excavate the interior of their ears with a specially constructed Yale key, and to contemplate the result with a steady glow of satisfaction while the lights go green, then amber, then red again.

There is a special plant at Dublin docks which removes the indicators on all cars, of whatever marque, destined to be taxis, thereby excusing all such drivers of the tiresome responsibility of informing other drivers they will be turning left or right. The taxi-drivers of Dublin do not indicate; they simply turn. It is as if they have been implanted with part of the brain of a Volvo-driver, and assume immortality is assured whenever they approach a junction.

Heigh ho, just turn.

There are lean, low sporting numbers from Japan – Mazdas, Toyotas, no doubt, others – which are painted red, with spoilers on the back like a surf-board rack. They burble at traffic lights, and lane-weave down motorways. Their drivers steer them with their palms while listening to rock music, their heads keeping time with the idiot-rhythm. When they emerge from their homes, it's a day for staying in bed.

As it almost is when the Metros came out. Metros have the style, elegance and *élan* of bedpans, which they resemble in every respect, except in matters of speed. Bedpans move faster. Metro drivers know only one gear, second, one place on the road, the middle, and one speed, 20 mph. They are apparently excused the need to use their rear mirrors for any purpose other than adjusting the tea-cosy on their head which they bought on the mistaken impression it was a hat.

The name Fiesta is as appropriate to Ford of that marque as it would be to call Nobber the Venice of Meath. It recruits its drivers from the ranks of the petrified who have not mastered the synchrony required to change gear and depress the clutch simultaneously. And therefore the progress of a Fiesta is marked by shed cogwheels and sheared-off clutchplate linings, while the driver, rigid with terror and nose against the windscreen, cruises into a Volvo, like a moth on a windscreen.

Red-faced, cigar-puffing Mercedes drivers tend to share that Volvine sense of inviolability. Nobody ever said of a Mercedes-driver: *He has an inferiority complex. He is full of uncertainty. He lacks self-belief.* Mercedes drivers move through traffic like a bishop passing through the Confirmation class, airy, confident, assured, with maybe an episcopal pat on the head for a mere Hyundai, and an odd question or two of a scarlet-faced, mumbling VW Polo, trailing a whiff or two of incense.

And as for Rover, the pride of the British motor industry, it was until recently a Honda and will soon be a BMW. Sorry, remind me again: just who exactly won that war? Which brings us, of course, full circle, back to Beatific, Majestic, Wise. OK? Friends now?

Cyclists of the world, unite!

There are many things more dangerous to cyclists than pedestrians, but pedestrians have a special place in that dark part of our souls reserved for hatred, though they do not crush us with casual left-hand turns the way that container lorries do, nor do they bear ridiculous little signs warning, Do not overtake on left-hand side while this vehicle is turning left (which is like saying, Do not put barrel of shotgun in mouth and pull trigger, or Do not place head on railway track while train is approaching or, Do not step over edge of cliff if you are allergic to the effects of gravity).

But lorry drivers, the fine fellows who think the yellow boxes at traffic lights are things you ease into when the green light goes to amber and there exits are blocked, and who then sit there picking their noses while they block four lanes of traffic during rush-hour, feel perfectly free to tell us not to hurl ourselves and our bikes under their rear wheels with a 20-ton loading per axle. Thank you, lads.

No, indeed, pedestrians are not lorry drivers; nor are they bus-drivers; whose favourite sport is to pull diagonally into a bus-stop just as cyclists are about to pass it. Nor are they BMW drivers, of whom I intend to say nothing.

Nor are they teenage motor-cyclists, whose particular joy seems to be to overtake you at 90 mph within the two-inch margin between your nearside pedal and the pavement kerb, which they normally manage only by gouging out much of your Achilles tendon as they do so.

All these things, I grant you, are scourges to the life of the cyclist, but nothing enrages us quite as pedestrians do. Sheep are graduates of the Massachusetts Institute of Technology, *cum laude*, compared with pedestrians. Search the world for something more stupid, and you search in vain. The rotten, dead skin left after an attack of athlete's foot has more intellect than a distillate made from pedestrians' brightest brain-cells.

The tobacco stain on the teeth of a comatose wino is brighter than anything you will find in the skulls of pedestrians. Seagull droppings are like rocket scientists compared with pedestrians. You will find more wit and wisdom in the sweepings from a horse's stable than you ever would from the conversations of pedestrians. Dandruff is Bach, armpit hair is Schubert, badger's toenails are Shakespeare, camel's footprints are Joyce compared with what goes on inside pedestrians' brains.

It is not that nothing goes on in pedestrians' brains; in the absence of thought, invariably, the right decision must sometimes occur, merely by accident. In fact, a quality entirely different from a vacuum is present in that lame organ we might call the pedestrian brain; it is anti-intelligence, a virus which compels its owner to do the most irritatingly stupid thing possible.

Mere stupidity would cause pedestrians to walk out in front of a thundering juggernaut and be turned into loganberry mousse, to the massed cheers of watching cyclists. Mere stupidity would prompt pedestrians to clamber over the parapets of O'Connell Bridge and head for Wales. Mere stupidity would make pedestrians imitate the Charge of the Light Brigade every time the lights turn red.

This does not happen. Alas, alas, this does not happen. Pedestrians are guided in their imbecility: there is purpose in their cretinism; in their idiocy, there is a point. When the lights are against them and the rules of the road call on them to stay on the pavement, who do pedestrians very deliberately choose not to see, and to walk out right in front of, but cyclists?

And the loser in such encounters is always the cyclist: a frail, 84-year-old Poor Clare tottering into the path of a Stephen Roche will barely notice the impact as he hits her, but by a perverse inversion of Newton's Third Law of Dynamics, he is sent flying and loses a third of his body weight, and a good many of his body parts, in a skid-smear the length of O'Connell Street.

I loathe pedestrians; I loathe them with every fibre of my being, every follicle I can command, every cell at my disposal; I loathe their brute stupidity, their herd-like witlessness, their dumb, bovine meanderings, like wildebeest migrating after a mass wildebeest-lobotomy. That is why I once fixed a yacht foghorn to my bicycle; there are few things more satisfying than sounding the earth-shattering roar of a juggernaut about to turn half a score of jay-walkers into tomato pot-noodle when in reality you are a mere cyclist.

At the very least, you know that you have ruined a few sets of underwear, and few pleasures compare with watching soiled pedestrians making the tiny steps homeward to the knicker-drawer. At best, you can stop the odd ventricle beating in its nest, and that is heaven indeed and he or she who would blithely have walked into you is now flapping and gasping on the road like a netted trout.

The problem with the old fog-horn is that it is far too cumbersome for everyday bicycle use; it cannot be easily fitted, and cannot be left – and to carry it around is too inconvenient. But now, in the greatest boon to cyclists since the drop-gear or the brake, a Canadian company has produced a bicycle horn which will drop an errant pedestrian stone-dead at 20 paces and double the laundry bill at 70. It could just as easily be used to disperse a besieging army, but instead is intended just for cyclists.

The device is the Air Zound. It is removable, renewable and handy, and so far as I know is available only in one bike shop, which also happens to be Dublin's best – Cycleways in Parnell Street. I have just cycled down O'Connell Street, putting three Sisters of Mercy, four pensioners, a mother with her four children and two unidentified targets into the Mater Coronary Intensive Care. Cyclists of the world: your moment of freedom is come!

Dublin taxis

'Where're you going to spend Christmas holidays this year?'

'We thought we'd try something unusual. You only live once.'

'You never said a truer word. So where'll it be?'

'In the queue for the O'Connell street taxi-rank. We spent the past few festive seasons in the Dame Street rank, and made loads of friends there, some really lovely people, share their turkey with you and everything. But we thought we'd have a bit of a change.'

'Well, we took the family to the O'Connell Street rank for Christmas three years ago, and we had the best Christmas ever. We arrived early – well, you need to there, otherwise you find yourself joining the queue in the Phoenix Park. So we got there on the 19th, and there were only 500 people in front of us. And you know what? On Christmas Eve, we even glimpsed what might have been a taxi! The excitement of it!'

'A taxi, begob! Did it stop?'

'Did it stop? It was a Dublin taxi. Of course it didn't stop. And to tell you the truth, I'm not even sure it was a taxi, but the youngest, Dolores, insists it was. Of course she still believes in Santa Claus.'

'But you're not going there this year? That's a shame.'

'It is. The wife's mother's bad with her varicose veins, can't spend Christmas queuing for taxis, so this year we're going abroad.'

'Really? Tenerife? Gran Canaria? Morocco?

'No. Quarryvale or Blanchardstown or the Square, Tallaght. The gridlocks there were looking promising in November, so by Christmas there should be a lovely atmosphere, nobody moving, traffic jams reaching to link all the suburban shopping malls of greater Dublin in a single traffic thrombosis. You could walk on car roofs from Quarryvale to Cornelscourt. The Christmas of the future!'

'I've got used to the traditional Dublin Christmas. Go for a few drinks. Try to get something to eat. Fail. Go for the last bus. Doesn't stop. Head for a taxi-queue. Wait a week. Walk home.'

'Ah yes, the good old days. Well, I can see your point, but you've got to keep up with the times. Shopping malls. Vast carparks in which nothing moves. Trolleys colliding with one another, grannies pulling one another's hair out, children throttling one another in the back seat. And on Christmas day, us all gnawing on a raw turkey. The modern Yuletide cheer.'

'Well, maybe we'll try the suburban Christmas when the kids are a little older. But they've got used to the traditional Dublin Christmas, standing at midnight with their arms full of shopping behind the entire population of Santry, Coolock and Artane, waiting for a taxi. And I mean, A Taxi. Which never comes. Sure it'd destroy the mystery of Christmas for them if we were to spend Christmas in a car in a car park in a suburban mall instead of where they always have it, in the freezing cold of the city centre, soiling their underwear, getting trench foot and frostbite. And singing carols.'

'The carols, ah the carols! It's true, you don't get the old-fashioned carols in the suburban shopping-mall gridlocks. God rest you absent taximen. The folly and the hackney. I saw three cabs come hailing in. Gives you a lump in the throat.'

'Exactly. Takes you back to your childhood, standing there, covered in chilblains, not eating in maybe a week, shivering in the sleet, and mumbling Christmas songs. Oh queue all you doleful. Once in Dublin's cabless city. Oh mythic cab of Dublin town!'

'Stop! Sure you'll have me in tears next. And remember the corpses at dawn, curled up beside the lamp-posts, maybe their taxi-fares held tightly in their pathetic little hands?'

'Well of course I do, and glad enough I was of them. The only blessed reason why the queue ever moved, the lads from the Corpo collecting the bodies in their hand-carts each morning, and us shuffling forwards to take their places. Ah, Christmas in Dublin. Sure there's nothing like it.'

'Where're you heading for now?'

'I'm not heading anywhere. I'm staying here indefinitely. I'm waiting for a taxi.'

'Same here. Merry Christmas.'

Women drivers

Hello? Hello? Anybody there?

No. Nobody there. The eerie sensation of writing a column for Christmas Eve in the certain knowledge that no-one's going to read it. What's the word count? Thirty-one. Another eight hundred or so words to go.

Bless me, but it's lonely here. No readers, no critics, no friends, no passing strangers, nothing, nobody. A vast and noiseless vacuum.

HELLOOOOOOO? IS ANYBODY THERE?

Silence. God, but it's eerie. I've often wondered what it would be like to be marooned in your space suit in outer space, and now I know. It's like this. Alone. Completely alone. Wonder if even the editor will read this? Probably not. What's the word count so far?

One hundred and thirteen, I think. Seven hundred to go, not one of which will ever be read by a single human being even in a century of February 29ths …

What was that?

- Nothing. It's your nerves. Calm down.

- Don't tell me to calm down. If there's one thing which makes me need to be told

to calm down, it's being told to calm down. I was calm until you told me to calm
down. Now I'm not.

- Good. So now you can calm down.

- DO NOT TELL ME TO CALM DOWN. EVER. DO YOU HEAR ME?

- Temper, Temper. I'll tell you what. In order to calm down …

- I'M WARNING YOU! …

- … why don't you take advantage of the situation? Why don't you say the things
you'd never have the nerve to say if you thought people were reading you? Now that
nobody is reading you, so have a go. Shout your head off! Bawl obscenities! Mention
the unmentionable!

- What? You mean like about women drivers?

- Exactly that. Woman drivers. Now if the sisters were to read your opinions on
women drivers, you'd be able to join the Vienna Boys Choir. But they're not going to.
So speak out. Tell me what you were saying about that Lexus driver.

- You mean the woman?

- Well it was a bit unusual, because (a) it was, as I say, a woman, but (b) it was a
big car driver. You've noticed – we all have, I suppose; my wife certainly has – that
women drivers hardly ever let you through. You know, you're stuck on a side road, and
there's a steady but slow moving stream on the main road. Very, very few women drivers will wave you through. And big car drivers of either sex, hardly ever. Yet there I
was, trying to get out onto the Foxrock Road, when this Lexus slowed down and
waved me through. And it was a woman driver. Incredible!

- They do say the Lexus's understated but sophisticated elegance attracts a better
class of driver.

- Do they indeed? Never been in a Lexus. Rather pricey, I believe. Well, this
woman not merely let me through but waved me through cheerily. And she was young
and good-looking too. That's another thing about women drivers. Good-looking or
not, they're never cheery. And when you let women drivers through, they never
acknowledge you. Ever. Men wave, smile, beep their horns, flash the old hazards, that
sort of thing. Women just sail through as if it's their right. Especially one with the sunglasses on the head in red BMWs.

– You're not going on about BMWs again, are you? After that last thing you
wrote, you were dropped from their race-day guest list.

– No I'm not, a mere aside. Happy to be dropped, incidentally. All those BMW
drivers in the one place. Ugh. But you know the kind of woman driver I'm talking
about. When you're stuck in traffic, you're passed by some blonde illegally driving a
red car down the bus lane. She's got sunglasses on her head and she's smoking
Marlboro Lites. The sort who'll never give way to you and never thank you for giving
way to her. Probably works in property or financial services. What I wouldn't give to
run a chainsaw through her tyres as she's revving her engine in the bus lane at the red
lights.

- Why do women drivers behave so differently from men drivers?

- It's not just a question of driving. Often, when you open a door for a woman, she says nothing. Passes on through, talking to her friends, as if you're invisible. Do it for a fellow and he's all over you with gratitude.

- Again: why?

- Completely different species. That's the point. Woman take courtesy for granted. On the other hand, men are far more dangerous. You only have to read your newspapers to see that. Lethal. It's this simple: men of military age cause fatal road accidents. Women generally don't cause accidents, except when they dither – shall I, shan't I? Dither and slither followed by bent bumpers. Men don't dither. Men go for vroom and doom. Much worse.

There! Did you hear something? Is somebody listening? Is there a reader out there? A feminist, mayhap, sharpening the knives to ready me for the Vienna Boys' Choir?

- Hush. There's nothing out there. No readers. No audience. All is still. All is quiet.

- So there'll be no complaints?

- None. No readers, no complaints.

- Good. Happy Christmas.

- Same to you.

Clamping

The only really surprising thing about the decision of Dublin traffic wardens to challenge the legality of clamping is that something comparable didn't happen earlier. Garda tow-away units have been operating for years now on a very dubious legal basis but nobody has opposed them in law because (a) the Department of Justice would use its big naval guns to sink them, with survivors finished off in the water with the flats of oars; and (b) nobody sensibly takes on the police, anywhere.

So gardaí are content to just to tow away and then to collect the tow-away fee of £100, thereby sparing the officers the trouble of the due processes of law. Such actions might well be *ultra vires* or even unconstitutional; for the executive arm of the law in such matters is also the judiciary, and is beyond appeal, with a courtless process in which the 'fine' is £100 (though not, I imagine, if you are a member of the Garda Síochána).

Do you detect some personal hurt here? You do. Some years ago, I parked my car bearing an *Irish Times* sticker in an area marked 'loading' outside our offices, adjoining a series of metered parking spaces, and otherwise identical to them. I assumed it was loading area for *Irish Times* use. The moment I was away from the car, a tow-away vehicle moved in.

Tipped off, I ran out and explained my business. The crew was adamant: my vehicle did not have a commercial licence, and only vehicles so licensed could park there. My car was towed and it cost £100 to recover it. No court proceedings followed. Had a traffic warden ticketed me, the fine, through due and constitutional processes of law, would have been £15. The extra-legal process cost me £100. No legal appeal was possible. Had I had the nerve, and the financial support of the Sultan of Brunei, I would have sued the State. Neither was the case.

Furthermore, are there two sets of laws here, one for streets outside Garda stations and one for the rest of the city? This newspaper ran an editorial a couple of years ago complaining about the situation around Pearse Street Garda Station – double-parking, parking on double yellow lines, parking on the pavement. There was an instant response. Suddenly, parking outside the station was orderly and law-abiding, though now, once again, it resembles a dodgem ring when the electricity dies.

Not just Pearse Street. Fitzgibbon Street, in perhaps the poorest part of the city, rejoices in cars parked on the pavement, cars parked on double yellow lines, cars parked apparently wherever the mood takes their drivers – a fine example indeed of law-abiding behaviour to set to the young (and desperately poor) people of the area. Name your Garda station; does the rule of law apply outside to the gardaí as it would to you or me?

Of course gardai want to park their cars outside their place of work. We all do. But we all can't. This is the way of all cities today. We have effectively banned on-street parking, and we compel motorists to leave their cars at home and resort to public transport (collapse in mirthless hysteria, and die sobbing), or park in multi-storey car parks.

A question: which would I rather be, the Sultan of Brunei or the owner of a multi-storey car park in Dublin. No contest. The Sultan, poor bastard, has to keep his people happy, and own an air force and so on. Car park owners have to do nothing. The State's resources – police officers, traffic wardens, clampers, tow-away vehicles and the courts – cattle-drive business towards them. They don't have to advertise, they don't have to strike competitive rates; they are State-enforced local monopolies. Use them or else.

So is it surprising that car park impresarios behave the way they do? The Temple Bar Car Park, now, I especially loathe, for it is run with a predatory and profitable inefficacy. Only one exit lane is virtually ever open, and long queues form trying to get out. I recently arrived in the exit queue having spent less than three hours in the car park, but during the long wait to get out my time in the place reached a minute or so over three hours – for which I was then charged for a full four hours' parking. How sweet it must be to charge people extra because you're saving money by not employing an extra person at the exit; what you won on the swings you gain on the roundabouts.

If the State creates such local monopolies, it might at least insist that consumers are only actually charged for what they use. Parking spaces are not like hotel rooms. The space for which I am charged for an hour, though I have used it for merely a minute, is then rented out again to someone else the moment I am gone. Though the State presumably licenses these car parks (and I don't mean just to print money) and protects their local monopolies, confiscating or clamping the cars of people who try to park elsewhere, it does absolutely nothing to protect the unfortunate consumers from monopolistic multi-storey price-gouging.

Charles: did you ever think of touching a car park owner for a few million quid? You should have done; and you know, they'd have never squealed. They know which side their butter is breaded on.

Driving lessons

It would be logical – would it not? – to assume that when the 100,000 people in the Republic waiting to sit their driving tests are finally tested, there will accordingly be 100,000 new and unaccompanied drivers on the road. Ah; would that it were that simple. Drivers with provisional licences can already get into a car on their 17th birthday and drive away, though they possess the automotive skills of a dog, have the eyesight of a mole, and the intelligence of a car-jack. Merely the possession of a provisional licence, for which no test whatsoever is required, enables anyone to sit behind the wheel of a ton or two of moving metal and vanish into the wild blue yonder or the casualty wing of St Vincent's Hospital.

'It is highly irresponsible of the deputy to suggest that, because a person holds a provisional licence, there is a danger to people travelling on the road,' puffed Bobby Molloy indignantly the other day to Brian Hayes TD, who had had the outrageous temerity to suggest that having so many unqualified drivers on the road was having a detrimental effect on road safety. Well spoken Minister! Stand by the right of the untested, the untrained, the unskilled, the unqualified to be free to drive however they want on our roads. To suggest that driving requires specially learned techniques which are difficult to master is clearly absurd.

We should all take a leaf from the book of the driver of a pick-up truck who was recently (and by our standard wholly wickedly) arrested by police in the Argentinian city of Trelew. He was completely blind. However, he had the visual skills of his 13-year-old daughter in the passenger seat to assist him. 'The blind man was driving fairly well, although he made some pretty abrupt manoeuvres which attracted the attention of a patrol car,' a police spokesman said.

I see. And this is what passes for freedom in Argentina, is it? A chap can't go out driving with his daughter without the heavy hand of the fuzz descending on the shoulder? Caramba! Thank God we order these things better in Ireland, and have done ever since that golden day 20 years ago when Sylvester Barrett, Bobby Molloy's illustrious predecessor, blazed a path for liberty by declaring that anyone who had had two provisional licences could claim a full licence without doing a test. That is to say, people who had repeatedly sat tests, and who had scared generations of testers into gibbering witlessness by their utter and incontrovertible proof that they were incapable of driving, were, without more ado, now entitled to drive unaccompanied.

So Prudence Entwhistle, that venerable granny from Kingstown who had first yearned to drive when watching the Gordon Bennett rally in 1903, and had been sitting tests since the time gels got the vote, failing every year since, suddenly realised her hour had come. She could leave behind her that unfortunate collision involving a crocodile of girls from Holy Child Killiney (but how pretty the massed wreaths had looked!). And the unlucky occasion when she'd chosen reverse instead of first and had backed into the day-trip of the pensioners from the Kingstown and District Presbyterian Sewing Club, crushing five – now mere history! And as for the time when the driving instructor had vaulted out of the car, even though they were bowling along at 70 mph northward on the southbound lane of the Naas dual carriageway? Lord, how she laughed.

Prudence's heirs are everywhere to this day, and they have, thank God, their defender in Bobby Molloy. The freedom-loving spirit of Sylvester Barrett and Prudence Entwhistle still informs so much of our attitude to roads and driving. We still erect road-signs which employ two measurement systems, metric for distance and imperial for speed, but sell cars whose metres measure distances in imperial only. About half of our drivers think the outside lane is for having a good natter in, with maybe the possibility of a right turn in about 20 miles, oops, 38 kilometres, meanwhile continuing the conversation with the hand gestures of a Neopolitan knitter.

Fully 10 per cent of drivers either think that signalling on roundabouts is a frivolous waste of energy, or even worse, they indicate in the wrong direction (the most common error being to indicate left simply because one inevitably turns left on entering the roundabout, and then leaving the indicator on during the jolly circumnavigation which follows).

A vast body of laws seem never to be enforced at all. How many JCBs have road-plates on? If they are not registered to be on the road, they cannot then in law be insured. When has any JCB making its stately passage down the centre of the road, without road tax or insurance, ever been stopped and its driver prosecuted? When has the cheery dumper truck which zips platelessly all over the President's highway ever been flagged to the side of the road and its operator been given a touch of the Argentinian treatment?

Never. It doesn't happen. We live in Barrettland, its principles of freedom stoutly defended to this day by Bobby Molloy. By Jove, sir, it makes you proud. And sometimes dead.

Tailgated

I have written often enough about traffic, about our politically frivolous, institution-ally inert, morally indolent attitude to the carnage on our roads, and also referred often enough to the cause of so much carnage – the young male driver – to fully deserve the condign punishment visited on me recently.

Returning from the west one Sunday evening, we were halting at one of the pre-dictable bottlenecks when our car was hit from behind. We were violently propelled into the car in front; and that car was itself then, by whatever peculiar laws of physics command the behaviour of moving objects hitting stationary ones – snooker players understand the process rather well – sent sideways, blocking the path of oncoming cars. By the divine providence which superintends these matters, there were at that precise moment no cars coming from the other direction. Otherwise there would have been bloody massacre.

As it was, there was mayhem on the road. The car I was travelling in – a BMW – was a write-off. The car in front, which was densely populated with passengers, was badly damaged, but its inmates seem to have escaped injury, though they might have interesting dreams about sitting peacefully in a car in a traffic jam at one moment, and being expelled from the jam into the path of oncoming traffic in the next. The car behind received less serious damage than one might have expected, especially as so much damage had been done to its two victim-vehicles. Its front was completely wrecked; but it could manage to creep away after the necessary investigation – if that is the word for the laughable procedures which followed – had been completed.

It had left 30-yard skidmarks before impact. Now at this stage, we may as well ask about the offending driver. Was it Prudence Sidewhistle, concluding a frantic after-noon at the knitting needles with a visit to the local church for evensong? Was it Sister Concepta Freebody on her way to a Revival Prayer Meeting Because Jesus Loves Us? Was it 55-year-old insurance salesman Augustus Peahen on his way home after watch-ing a GAA match? Or was it some young male in his mid-twenties with a young woman sitting beside him?

Step forward young male: the young gentleman who drove into the back of our car and nearly caused a massacre; the young gentleman who was driving so fast on a congested country road on a Sunday evening that even after a thirty-yard emergency braking he could write one car off and cause a multiple-car collision: the fine young fellow who did not even express regret or apology at what he had done to us.

Ah yes, what had he done to us? Well, my friend who was driving is constructed on the lines of an ox which had gone in for weight-training since it was a mere slip of a calf, and is so strong that he has been commissioned into FCA as its only tank. He seemed relatively unhurt. Me, I am built to a more delicate design: porcelain comes to mind. The initial impact had hurled my head against the headrest; the poor bonce had then been thrown forward, then back again. Our car had then hit the car in front, propelling my head forward; we were then hit again by the car from behind, by which time my poor neck felt like a fishing rod on the end of which was an angry great white shark making its opinions felt in no uncertain terms.

As a result, I have severe pains in my spine and neck, reduced feeling and power in my arms, numbness, tingling and weakness in my fingers. My young friend might well have altered the rest of my life, and very much for the worse.

A single garda duly arrived, took statements from the three drivers, looked at me, asked me whether or not I wanted an ambulance, and then, having seen a corpseless countryside, without any blood to be seen, declared the car which had hit us was the culprit, but also announced he would not be prosecuting anybody. Now this is good. It is by no skill of the young driver who hit us that there was no major slaughter; yet he was allowed to leave the scene of the accident with the certainty that no court case would follow.

So is it Garda policy that prosecution in such circumstances depends on the body count? If the gods smile, and no innocents are butchered by testosteronic idiocy, the owner of the testosterone is allowed to take his testosterone out on the roads again, to practise his vehicular lunacies upon other unfortunate road-users; but if the gods frown, and innocent and blameless blood is shed, then prosecution follows? Is that it? Law-enforcement by lottery?

If you removed young male drivers from our roads, our death toll would be cut by probably 90 per cent. That much is obvious. So is it unjust to ensure that just as the blind, the mad, the retarded, the old are either restricted in their rights to drive, or banned completely, young males might expect comparable limitations? Testosterone is endocrinal plutonium: is it wrong to expect those who are most subject to its homicidal impulses should be subject to rigorous controls? Is it wrong to insist that males under twenty-five be limited in the speeds they can drive at?

Wrong or right is barely relevant. We cannot manage to have a single-measurement system for speed and distances on our road. We cannot erect proper signposts. We cannot even remove the temporary 40 mph signs erected during the widening of the Naas dual carriageway, even though the roadworks have been completed for over a year. And most magnificently of all, a couple of years ago the general speed limit, applicable to country lane and to dual carriageway alike, was raised to 60 mph. A magic wand was waved over the mad the bad, and they were urged: go faster.

The Ansbacher affair, and all the other matters preoccupying Dáil Committee, tribunal and Jersey courtrooms are undoubtedly scandalous. They deserve to be investigated thoroughly; but these thefts of our public money are in real terms a moral zero in comparison with our tolerance of murder – and murder it is – on our roads. We know it happens; and we with studied deliberation ignore it. And for that, we truly deserve to be damned.

Signposts, Irish style

The sun was setting on The Absent Signpost & Almost Permanently Red, the pub favoured by the road administrators of Ireland. The senior administrator led the young apprentice into the bar, which was filled with other members of their calling.

'Excited, lad? You should be. There are men here who are masters of their craft. Listen to them. Learn at their knees.'

The boy felt grateful indeed. Not just any pupil in his class could qualify for an apprenticeship as an Irish road administrator. Firstly, you had to fail every exam throughout your entire school career. Ideally, you should have been expelled from at least two schools for sheer bone idleness. And thirdly, you should have no civic sense whatsoever.

'How did the pub gets its name?' the boy asked breathlessly. 'I'd have thought road administrators wouldn't approve of signposts that weren't there or traffic lights that are nearly always red.'

'In other countries you'd be right. But here in Ireland road administrators pride themselves on such little negative triumphs. Our day isn't made unless we can go to bed in the knowledge that we've left a tourist stranded in The Land That Time Forgot, just south of the Bog of Allen, or blocked an entire major artery at rush hour with a traffic light which shows green to a deserted country lane.'

'Golly,' said the boy. 'How exciting.'

The administrator looked at him with approval. 'That's what I like to hear – enthusiasm in the young. Now. What are you having? The cocktails are rather good here. I'd recommend The Signless Roundabout, a house speciality. Packs a hell of a kick. A couple of those and you haven't a clue where you're going. Or maybe you'd like another Irish invention, a Lights on a Roundabout – absolutely deadly, because it's mixing your drinks; one measure of individual initiative plus one measure of State command – a complete contradiction in terms, which you can have shaken, stirred or best of all, rear-ended.'

'Rear-ended? Is rear-ending allowed in this pub?'

'All right? All right? Why, you can't qualify for membership of our professional body, SMASH, unless you can prove your work had caused at least one serious crash, and you have at least 10 cases of misleading people with your road signs.'

'Who checks up on whatever accidents you cause?'

A terrible hush instantly fell on the pub. The barman came over and said: 'I'm sorry gentlemen, but unless you can mind your language, I'm going to have to ask you to leave.'

'I'm sorry,' whispered the engineer across the counter. 'He's young and doesn't know the rules here.' He turned to the boy and declared with deadly ferocity, 'Never let me hear you saying the 'a' word again. Never. We do not allow it here. We like to think there are no …' he looked around, lowered his voice and half whispered, half-mimed, 'accidents, *qua* accidents' – he raised his voice again – 'but car smashes caused by stupidity, arrogance and incompetence, qualities which we pride ourselves on.'

He gestured to a collection of portraits on the wall. 'Past presidents, and an inspiration to us all. This man here now,' he gestured, 'is responsible for the signage on the road from Dun Laoghaire to Tallaght, a highly complex itinerary with maybe a dozen major junctions and connecting two large towns, plus the N81 and a seaport, and only a few signposts along its entire length. A work of pure genius. Hundreds of motorists get lost every day because of his handiwork. I, nay, *we* revere him.

'Let him be your inspiration and guide.'

'And who is the gentleman asleep over there?' asked the boy.

'The current president. And a noble figure indeed. If you ever see a road-sign pointing in the wrong direction and leaning over sideways, if you see one which is obscured by branches, if you see one in a visual clutter which can only confuse, that is his responsibility. His job is signpost maintenance, which he attends to by sleeping. By Gad, sir, just to see him there, having 400,000 winks, makes you proud.' He stifled a sob.

'And who is that creature?' asked the boy of an odd character, sitting alone and cackling.

'You have a good eye for talent, boy. Another of our stars, a man of genius. He is a traffic light co-ordinator. He ensures that on roads right across the country you will invariably get a sequence of reds. Not merely does he add hugely and needlessly to people's journey time, but he puts them in bad, often dangerous form, so that they are more likely to have crashes. He is our ace of aces, our Red Baron, and no one can count his victories over ordinary motorists.'

His young companion paused. 'Bad traffic management really is a lethal business, isn't it? Do you think I'll have a future in it?'

His earnest tones caused a manly tear to start in the road administrator's eye. 'By Jove, sir, your enthusiasm reminds me of myself when I was young. Now, what would you like to drink? A Multiple Pile-Up on Ice? Or maybe a nice little Needless Tragedy On the Rocks?'

MORE PEOPLE

Con Howard

It was in Paris five years ago that I realised I would never be in Con Howard's class. Never. Live though I may, till lime trees flourish in Stavanger and walruses caper in Nevada, I would not ever be the man that Con Howard is. Nature made Con and, appalled and astonished by its own temerity, broke the mould, shot its designer and personally garrotted all the workmen involved. It was too late. Con was released on to the world, and the world would never the same again.

Con made the Brendan Society, and by definition, its trips were intensively perilous affairs. Scott was on one, and he never came back. Amundsen was tempted to stay on the South Pole rather than make the return journey in the company of Brendan Society people, who subsist on about three minutes' sleep a night and wear funny hats and blow party thingummies even at family funerals.

Livingstone was invited on one and was so appalled and terrified at the prospect that he hid in Africa until Stanley, who had a similar and subsequent invitation, also fled there on the pretext of looking for Livingstone, and accidentally found him, accosting him with the famous words, 'Fleeing the Brendan Society, I presume' – a salutation which later generations have bowdlerised.

If you look at some of the most reckless events in human history, you will probably find the Brendan Society behind them. The reason why Alcock and Brown flew the Atlantic 75 years ago was to flee a Brendan Society party which had just begun in Newfoundland – which within a decade was to halve the population of that treeless meridian and which was only interrupted by the outbreak of the second World War.

Ten years previously the Brendan Society had begun a little party in Calais, prompting a despairing and sleepless Blériot to clamber aboard his monoplane and head for England. Five years later, a Brendan Society visit to Vienna prompted the Archduke Ferdinand to make for the peace and quiet of Sarajevo. The only reason the insurgents of 1916 took over the GPO was to prevent a Brendan Society party which was scheduled to begin there the moment Fairyhouse races were over, and as patriotic subjects of the king they were determined to prevent the kind of excess with which the Brendan Society bashes were imperishably associated.

In 1920, the British Government was in such despair at the revels of the Brendan Society that it raised an entire force of special policemen called Black and Tans to subdue the ceaseless revelry in which the society was engaged. They dashed themselves against the rock of Brendan pleasure in vain: defeated, they retired home, the sound of Brendan Society rollicks ringing across the Irish Sea at their departing backs.

Partying was going on and ringing across Europe so that Herr Hitler, a notoriously prudish man who had trouble sleeping, decided to end it all personally by getting his armies to terminate the Brendan Society with prejudice. They got as far as Calais and, fuming with impotent rage, heard the din of Brendan Society capers ringing on the western wind. They got no further. Attempts to get at the Brendan Society the long way around proved equally futile.

At the epicentre of all these upheavals was normally to be found the figure of Con Howard. Con was a veteran of the '98 Rising. Con was a veteran of whatever event that caused sore heads in the morning. And there were sore heads the morning in Paris five years ago, when I was on a Brendan Society trip. One woke up feeling that somebody had crammed one's skull full of sharp-sided rocks and when I gazed in the mirror, an aged albino stoat with eyes like raw crumpled lungs gazed back at me.

And so that morning we made our way downstairs, trembling, draped in blankets, barefoot and being helped by pretty nurses, like survivors from a pleasure trip on the *Achille Lauro* – which I suspect was, in fact, on perpetual hire to the Brendan Society.

And there, in the open-air café, the sun beaming down on his similarly beaming face, was Con Howard. It was about ten to nine in the morning. He was drinking a beer. Several of our number squealed, rather as the *Achille Lauro* survivors did at the suggestion they get back on board and continue the party there. Three fainted. Two had species-change operations and now eke out their days as teetotal Friesian cattle. Four became Carmelites. Two walked into the Seine and were recovered several days later by police divers. None of us will be the same again.

But Con will. Con never changes. Con sees everybody to bed, cherubically beaming as another pint goes to its eternal reward. When those who actually survived the night trickle downstairs, like raindrops who expect a hostile reception at the bottom of the windowpane, there they find Con, a bottle of beer open and another couple at the ready, just in case, the big grin on his face assuring the world that he has had his five minutes' nap, thank you, and now he is raring to go.

Ten years ago, Con and his nearly-as-lethal friend, Bob Ryan, decided there were not enough perilous days in the year; and on the Feast of St Stephen, they noted that here seemed a day designed for devilry yet which was largely spent by the natives of this land, in bed and groaning, with maybe a totter along to Poolbeg Lighthouse a possibility. This seemed to them to be a shameful waste of liver. What point was there to that organ unless you put it over the jumps first thing in the morning?

Thus they came to revive the feast of the Wren Boys on that day. Ever since, they have been taking strangers' livers and shaking the living daylights out of them. They will be doing the same the day after tomorrow. They gather at Sandymount Green at noon, with music, dancing and livers to the fore, proceeding to the Mill House in Kilmacud and Monkstown RFC for liver transplants. Needless to say, I will not be there.

Denis Bethel

It was before the Fall from Grace, before UCD was banished to the Sinai beyond Montrose. University College, Dublin in those days was a truly Catholic university – Catholic and still infused with a ceruleocamisian authoritarianism. O'Duffy ruled the boardroom. Theology was lifeless, arid, and purely Thomist. Vast flocks of nuns – austere, supercilious, aloof – arrived in limousines each morning and repaired to their common room. The rest of the students had to make do with the main hall or the rain.

And the main hall on a wet morning would be dense with the vapours of moist wool and wet shoe leather and the odd fragrances of lanolin liberated when scalp and hair and rainwater mingle.

The canteen kept odd hours. Essentially, if you felt hungry, that meant it was closed. It was in the bowels of the building and seemed capable of serving about five students an hour. The queue for it stretched round its internal circumference, up the stairs, into the Great Hall and out towards the suburbs.

Small, famished students curled up and died in some of the remoter precincts while waiting for the queue to edge forwards, their little bodies swept up from the streets each dawn and carted off to kennels. Small proud farmers in Monaghan and Kerry would wait for news of their scholarship sons or daughters above in Dublin at *uni*, and each morning would gaze hungrily at the postman on his rounds, but in vain.

Art or Nuala or Fedelma had perished and had long since nourished hounds, who were said to favour classics students, though it was reliably reported that Kerry first arts could be especially toothsome, and there was an incorrigible old Scarteen hound whose particular weakness was for female pre-meds. He reserved the highest opinion for their femurs – one many of us shared, incidentally, especially in summer in Iveagh Gardens when vast stretches of thigh emerged like animals out of hibernation.

Food was also to be got in Newman House, in the basement, where the Commons Restaurant now dwells. Or otherwise, there were the neighbouring cafes – Robert Roberts or Bewley's on Grafton Street which, unbelievably, were closed on Saturday afternoons, as was all of Dublin. There was an Italian chipper on Stephen's Green just next to Rice's which, on my first day in Dublin, did me the signal honour of being the first pub to bar me: 'A coke please.' 'Get out, you're barred.' 'But, but, but …' 'Out, you're barred.'

What had my doppelganger been up to? I never knew. Rice's was, I discovered later, in part a gay bar and was one of the few places in Dublin – Bartley Dunne's was another – where the word 'gay' was then commonplace. I have often wondered about the reputation the other me was sedulously carving for me.

One can say one dwelt in Elysium in Earlsfort Terrace, but academically it would not be true for most students unless, that is, one had the great good fortune to be studying history. Then did a galaxy of great teachers fill the firament – Kevin B. and Frank Martin and Francis Bourke and Peter Butterfield and Dudley Edwards and Donal McCartney and Hilary Jenkins and Desmond Williams and Art Cosgrove and Ronan Fanning.

It is true that Dudley was not always at home; and it was also true that Desmond spent much of the time smoking three cigarettes simultaneously while looking for a fourth, and at times his study resembled a forest fire.

But there was an excellence in history teaching at UCD then which has refreshed and delighted those who had the good fortune then to be there through all our days. And this is the time of year when those who briefly browsed in Elysium are moved to remember Denis Bethell, another jewel in the gallery of Earlsfort Terrace.

Denis Bethell was an odd man. At the time I never thought about him in the ordinary sense – whether or not he had a girlfriend, or whether he even possessed that kind of hormone: it seemed wildly improbable. Maybe he was one of those eccentric creatures, a true celibate, for whom the flesh held little or no temptations. His was happy with his books and his scholarship, and that was that.

Denis was an English Catholic, a creature entirely dissimilar to an Irish Catholic. Catholicism for him was not an identity but a religion, and a religion which filled his life. He was genuinely a good man, liked by his students, who relished his bumbling English ways. In many senses, he was the one creation of P.G. Wodehouse whom P.G. forgot to create – innocent, enthusiastic, immensely clever. But though liked by his students, he was adored by the staff, who were in a better position to perceive his astonishing erudition and to enjoy his enormous kindness.

Denis lived in a flat in Monkstown, a vast metropolis of grand decay and magnificent eccentricity, where his friends gathered to revel in his scholarship and his gentle good humour. He possessed that wonderful quality of personal magnetism which put people at their ease. He was assured, learned, clever and lovable, like a fat little boy who escapes bullying at school because of his charisma and wit.

Denis died of cancer in 1981, aged 46. It was a terrible blow for UCD and his friends, who could not imagine life without him. And so it was that the Denis Bethell Memorial Lecture came into existence, to retain and restore the memory of Denis and the scholarship he held so dear.

Brian Clark MC

Each August we gathered in that perfect place in Kilmacanogue and the divinities Brian and Brendan Clark consulted beforehand, whoever they may have been, always ensured that the weather was irreproachable. Year after year it was thus, as sunlit evenings proceeded into twilight and the deadly fruit punch circulated in the seemingly endless benignity of the annual Clark party.

That party will soon gather for the last time, this time in Enniskerry Church for a memorial service for Brian. An annual fixture, much cherished and anticipated with deep pleasure, is gone. So is much more.

It was so like Brian that he should have left his body to medical science. No doubt he learned in North Africa and on the evil approaches to Monte Cassino, where the Irish Brigade left so many young Irish bones, the true value of a body uninhabited by life.

Frankly, I am glad I never crossed Brian Clark. As he himself assured me, he could in his time have been a right bastard. Soldiering often calls upon the sterner qualities of human nature; though to see him in his final decades, especially with his beloved dogs, was to be convinced that he had lived in the company of carpet slippers and flowerbeds all his life.

Brian Clark served with the Royal Irish Fusiliers throughout the last World War. He adored the regiment and the men who served in it. I suspect that was where he first met Irish Catholics in large numbers. My own suspicion is that he preferred the company of such people. Certainly his August parties in Knocknagow were full of ex-officers of the Irish Army.

The Army he once corrected me when I referred to it as the Irish Army. *The* Army. In this Republic, he said, there is only one army. *The* Army. He would say that he had the good fortune to serve in an Irish regiment of the British Army; but when he referred to *The* Army, he was referring to Parkgate Street.

He was born of a Northern Irish family in London. His father had served in the Irish Fusiliers in the Great War. The regiment was to unite him with Ireland and the plain people of Ireland to launch him on a military career of distinction. He won a Military Cross at Monte Casssino; though what he did there in the terrible fighting in 1944, I never found out. 'I engaged in infantry fighting with all that that entails,' he told me. No more. His great ambition was to survive long enough to return to Monte Casino and to meet the German paratroopers he had fought and learned to respect there and who he later befriended. Last year he did.

Later in the war he met his wife Brenda, a Dubliner serving as a volunteer welfare worker in Italy. That happy union not merely brought him a fine family but also permanent links with Ireland, to which he was to return with his regiment.

He was serving in Northern Ireland when the IRA left a bomb in the barracks early in the 1950s campaign. He carried the bomb out of the barracks and it exploded harmlessly. For that deed he was awarded the George Medal, but the incident made him all too aware of the axiom of: 'There but for the Grace of God …' The officer commanding the barracks, Dermot Neill, was dismissed for the breach in security and retired, in semi- (though innocent) disgrace to live in New Zealand. His son Sam thus became a New Zealand rather than an Irish actor.

When Brian retired from the Irish Fusiliers, a respected Lt. Colonel, he and Brenda came to live in Kilmacanogue. 'There's no point in my dying,' he would say. 'I'm already in heaven here.' He was in charge of the Royal National Lifeboat Institution for years. One of his objectives there was to hibernicise it more – he was not at ease with the Posh Prod image. It was he who caused it to be known as Irish Lifeboats and gave it a wider recognition beyond the narrow world of plucky coxswains and gallant fundraising Heathers and Hazels.

His other ambition was to remind nationalist Ireland of the contribution made by Irishmen and women in the two World Wars. It was a difficult task. His role in the British Legion invited unworthy and contemptible innuendo that he was attempting to subvert Irish independence, that he was some sort of spy.

Rubbish. All he sought was a frank recognition of the realities of history this century, and he understood the magnitude of his task more fully when the Government, led by Charles Haughey, chose to cancel all State representation, including that of the Army, at Remembrance Day Services. It was an ignominious and ignoble day for Ireland. Yet Brian persevered in his task of reviving memories of the forgotten men of 20th century Irish history, and was rewarded triumphantly in recent years when the State accepted responsibility for maintaining the Islandbridge war memorial and chose to remember the Irish dead of the second World War on the anniversary of the opening of Belsen.

'Wotcha cock,' he said to me when I visited him in hospital nearly a year ago. 'Just a mo, can't quite remember your name.' Seeing his vacant stare, his uncertainty about where he was, I was sure he was doomed then, but his heart was stronger and his will was even stronger, and he pulled around.

When I last saw him in Kilmacanogue earlier this year though much recovered, he was not the man he was. His memory was going, he had slowed considerably; his heart had proved stronger than his health.

It would have been cruel indeed for this man to have experienced the humiliations of infirm or dependent old age. He was spared that end. Last Monday, that great old heart ceased to beat.

So, students of medicine, you have there the heart of a good man. Guard it well and learn from it, that others might profit from his death as those who knew him profited from his life.

Gus Martin and Aidan McCarthy

Two deaths within a week remind us how much a part luck plays in life – Gus Martin in his 50s and Aidan McCarthy in his 80s. Gus should have been good for 25 years and Aidan should never have even reached Gus's age, never mind the grand old age he did.

Gus was lucky and he was not. He was lucky in his wife, Clare, and in life he made his own luck: he worked hard and he was a wonderfully enthusiastic teacher and a singleminded, singular politician. Perhaps hundreds of thousands of students owed much of what they knew of English to Gus's writings; through them he has sent a wave into the future which can never be extinguished. It is a noble monument; none nobler.

Yet Gus always appeared to be recovering from some injury or other. Even if he was sound in limb and rib, one sensed he was grinning mischievously above a swathe of plasters. He was the only adult who fell victim to a school's sports day, in which he was anchor in the boys'/fathers' tug of war. Unfortunately, Gus tied the nylon rope round his hand. As the boys began to tug the fathers boywards, other fathers joined in, grasping the loose rope behind Gus. But it was already wrapped around his hand – and slowly it began to cut through his fingers. All his screaming was taken as noisy encouragement. First, he lost one finger; and then another, blood spouting everywhere.

I met him shortly afterwards, his hand as mangled as if he had put it into a blender. Typically, he was laughing as he told the story. A couple of years ago, he was mugged as he walked through St Stephen's Green. Then he fell off his bike and broke his leg. Then somebody slammed a car door on the broken bit. It caused him much agony: I once saw him white with pain, sweating through pallid flesh, but uncomplaining throughout.

Aidan McCarthy was a Cork man who had joined the RAF before the last world war. He was evacuated from Dunkirk, where he had to avoid the rifle fire of indignant British soldiers being left behind quite as much as he had to dodge the attentions of the ever-vigilant Luftwaffe. Not long afterwards he ran into a blazing bomber and pulled out the crew, for which deed he was decorated – and even now he had not come close to enduring what Gus had suffered in a cycling accident in Belfield. Aidan's next stop was the Far East, where he was one of 10 Irish doctors in the RAF in one area alone. He was captured by the Japanese, who singled him and other Irish prisoners out for especial brutality because of their nationality.

After two years the good news came that he was to be taken to Japan. He rejoiced, and joined 1,000 thousand men in a small merchantman. It was so crowded that men suffocated to death in the hold, and remained there, stuck. One night, while some slept, an American torpedo struck. Those sleeping on the deck had their backs broken by the whiplash and, threshing helplessly, went to their doom. Aidan, having had a dispute with a rat, was awake and upright. Uninjured by the torpedo, he made his way on deck and dived overboard.

When dawn came, a few survivors were circling around in the grey waters. One of them was a Korean guard who had been notorious for his cruelty. Some Australians swam over to him and silently strangled him. They all then swam around for 12 hours before a Japanese destroyer arrived and rescued them.

The Japanese sailors lined up the survivors on deck and began to beat them before throwing them overboard into the propeller wash, where they were promptly pulped. So Aidan jumped right back into the sea, where he again swam around for a long time before being rescued by whalers, who took the survivor ashore. But the Japanese military then ordered the whalers to take Aidan and his few fellow-survivors back out to sea and dump them there ...

The whalers declined and Aidan and the dozen other survivors from the initial thousand were sent off to a prison camp, where they saw out the war.

I think that Gus, given his luck, would not even have survived one of Aidan's earliest experiences in the RAF, when he was ordered to give a medical inspection to a new draught of women recruits. He walked into the hangar where 200 of them were lined up waiting, naked and to attention. Because Gus was unfortunate in the little things, always stepping on the prongs of garden rakes which would slam up and hit him in the nose, then appearing at the next party grinning gamely on either side of two flattened nostrils. If he'd walked into the hangar, he would probably have encountered 200 elderly nightwatchmen with haemorrhoids.

But, no matter what happened to Gus, he was always grinning gamely, full of energy and fun, breaking into *Just a Song at Twilight* at the thwack of a garden rake – irreverent, cheerful and disrespectful, yet full of the love of Anglo-Irish literature, which guided his life and which he transmitted to many thousands of his students. Gus was the living proof that enthusiasm is the best teacher.

We do not know what killed him. Bad luck, at a guess. He contracted massive septicaemia last week, for whatever reason – none was found – from which there was no recovery. He is dead, and that is that: we who knew his endless ebullience should be pleased and happy that we did. However heartbreaking it is for Clare and her family, he left this life painlessly and quickly, unburdened by age or invalidism or dependency. We should all be so lucky.

Enthusiasm for life was what had enabled Aidan McCarthy to survive to his journey back to the safe camp in Japan. He was in that camp, famous for its ease of condition, shortly before war's end when he noticed a single silver object high in the sky. The object was a B29, and the camp was at Nagasaki.

Yet he still lived to a glorious old age.

Gay Byrne

You might be surprised to hear that Gay Byrne is actually quite disliked by a certain class of journalist – usually the right-on, the hip, the cool – who think that he takes a patronising tone to women, to the working class, to the poor, etc., to whom he should be showing a more ideologically sound and seriously caring approach, sort of on the lines of *A Beggar's Oprah*.

What those few critics either do not know, cannot see, or choose to ignore, is that Gay Byrne is a fiercely moral man. There is no more rigorous interrogator of personal honesty than the radio microphone, no more ruthless exposer of the fraud, the humbug, the deceiver. Gay Byrne has the hearts of the Irish people because in those hearts they know he is not morally feckless. He tells no lies; does not express feelings which he does not feel; misleads nobody; and most of all, is what he is, warts and all.

Being what you are, endlessly, day after day, is usually not merely wearing on the spirit, but wearing on the audience too. No ordinary soul can, morning after morning, talk to the plain people of Ireland at a serious level without one or other losing interest sooner rather than later. Yes, yes, it requires great powers of inventiveness, versatility, and energy: but these are relatively commonplace commodities. What makes Gay Byrne a great broadcaster is his simplicity.

Simplicity is one of the greatest and most elusive of virtues. Like mercury, it escapes those who enthusiastically try to capture it, for simplicity is complex. It is not stupidity, it is not narrowness, it is not ignorance. It is harmony between intellect and the heart, the mind and the emotions, conscience and desire.

Simplicity results when the normally lopsided energies of human nature achieve an equilibrium and remain locked in balance.

Gay Byrne is simple in that sense. All the complexities of nature seem to mesh within him, and he transmits a sense of ease; not of complacency, not smugness, not self-contentment, which are qualities which will kill a broadcaster more quickly than a claw-hammer between the eyes. Ease of being, and simplicity of thought and emotion reassure the listeners; they are not being misled. What you hear is what you get: no falsehood, no artifice, no deceit, no showiness.

Great broadcasters are rare, just like great goalkeepers are rare, and for the same reason. For each, astonishing simplicity and unwavering integrity are the key. Those qualities do not fade with age: that is why both species have careers which last decades. A broadcasting station which doesn't have one great broadcaster is in trouble; and a football team without a good goalkeeper wins no medals. And between the posts for the past quarter-of-a-century on RTE Radio 1 has been Gay Byrne.

It is his honesty, his transparency, his lack of a hidden agenda which have enabled Gay Byrne to tackle the issues he has tackled, for it was clear that his only motive was his own insatiable appetite for honesty. It was this transparency of emotion during his now-famous-interview with Gerry Adams which was attacked by the witless, right-on school of hey man, I'm so kyool.

For such fools would not recognise that the great thing about Gay Byrne is that he can't feign affection and didn't even try – and rightly. In times of conflict, false emotions are the road to certain tears, for the peace they bring is a phoney peace without base beneath or principles to build upon. Would Gerry Adams have been better or wiser, and would peace have been the closer, if Gay had fawned all over him? What would Gerry Adams have learned about the feelings of the plain people of Ireland in the face of such worthless ingratiation?

We know from his absences from the airwaves, both on radio and television, that Gay is simply irreplaceable. Nobody comes near him, either in the quality of his presentation, his humour, his self-mockery, his sympathy and his genuine, indeed Olympian modesty. It is that last quality which has been shield and armour for his simplicity, which might otherwise have been overwhelmed by both the national adulation and the isolation that have been his portion for almost his entire adult life.

No walking down Grafton Street; no quiet dinners with his beloved wife Kathleen; no popping down to the supermarket for a bottle of wine. His every move is a matter for public record and public comment. He cannot pick up a copy of *Playboy* at a newsagent or pop into the cinema to see a movie with sex in it or go to Lansdowne Road for an international match. The price he has paid for his broadcasting career would be for most of us absolutely unpayable; and politicians who have spent their wretched lives dissembling and deceiving and who now query his salary might reflect that whatever Gay Byrne earns, he deserves twice as much.

It is perhaps too soon to grasp the importance of Gay Byrne in public life in Ireland, but I am confident that when historians look back on independent Ireland in the 20th century, they will see two epochs, each 40 years or so long. In the first epoch, the towering figure was Éamon de Valera. In the second it was Gay Byrne; and of the two, the latter was the finer man by far.

Liam de Paor

FOR whatever reason, I did not know Liam de Paor was dead until I read about his funeral – an ignorance which he would probably, but in that ineffably kind way he had, regard as a rather typical piece of sloppiness on my part. Liam was not sloppy, not lazy, but always keen and diligent and blessed with a mind which ranged far and wide for nourishment.

That mind was accompanied by a quite wonderful attentiveness to other people. He always kept an unwavering look of interest on his face, even as he had to digest what might be drivel. That attentiveness was born of a vast politeness which was both personal and representative of an older way, an antique, pre-urban and almost vanished Irish culture.

And with that attentiveness invariably came a smile – a puzzled smile, an irritated smile, a knowing smile, an agreeing smile – a smile for all occasions except one: he never offered, because he would not have known how to manufacture one, a superior or supercilious smile. That old courtesy again; it guided his life.

His was indeed often a silent smile, for Liam was a great man for the silences, during which he would rummage through the finery he stored in his cerebral ware-house. Those silences, those smiling silences, might be a little unnerving – though they weren't intended to be – simply because you could be sure they were the precursor to something infinitely wiser and more knowing than whatever you might have been saying. And that something would always be offered with such delicacy and gentle-ness, in tone, word and expression. In other words, you didn't hit the ground with a bump. All right, you weren't as smart or as knowledgeable as he was, which was fine: he had merely given you the benefit of his mind. It was a transaction, a deal, in fact a favour; it was a true gift, not an act of condescension or of show.

And that, of course, is the mark of a great teacher, which is what Liam was: a truly great teacher. The assembly of letters, *entrance,* spells two words; one a verb, meaning to captivate, the other a noun, meaning a doorway or opening. Liam's mind magically captured the two meanings. When he spoke, it was quite captivating, a doorway open-ing before you into the treasury of his mind. For he and it had travelled widely through word and world, and on those travels he and it had filled their pockets with the wisdom and lore of everywhere. There seemed to be nothing he could not talk about – at various times he taught me Chinese history, American history, Japanese his-tory, Irish history, archaeology, and all with equal ease.

I remember having a bet with an American student at UCD whether or not we could catch him out on some recondite part of Chinese history. By consulting a par-ticular book we were sure he could never have seen, we prepared a perfectly impossi-ble question, on the lines of 'What was the name of the Emperor Chin's favourite concubine?' Not merely could he name the concubine; he gave reasons why the emperor preferred her to the 30 others in the imperial seraglio.

And he did so with that gentle but knowing smile, slightly hesitant in his deliv-ery, as if volubility of reply might be boastful or showy. But of course that was the other characteristic of Liam's, which was I suppose a key to his politeness, but was a rock-hard part of who he was: he was so unbelievably modest, and in a very Irish way. There are, of course, post-colonial forms of Irish modesty which are self-denigratory out of some sense of cultural inferiority, but that was not Liam's modesty. Liam's mod-esty was a mark of the self-confidence of his culture, his identity, of his assuredness of Irish values and Irish ways.

He was modest because he was polite; polite because he was modest. The circu-larity of those virtues is as unbreakable as the relationship between Liam and the cul-ture of which he was part. He truly embodied a way, a style, a set of civilised values, which are all but gone – yet he was not ostentatious about this. Indeed, it is only by thinking hard about it that I have made the connection between the man the thing that created him: Ireland.

It was an old Ireland, almost an extinct Ireland, which made him. He was proud of his nation without being narrowly nationalist; proud of his culture without being closed to others; proud of his race without being racist.

He certainly wasn't old-fashioned or reactionary – his mind was open and eager and enthusiastic. It's just that that mind, that moral character of his, were guided by values which are hard to put into words, but are more easily understood when you see them personified in the way that Liam personified them. It always comes back, I think, to his Irishness: it was so unqualified, so confident, so sure, so tolerant, so benign, so generous, so scholarly. Only two other men I have met have possessed that wise, scholarly, genial and generous Irishness – Cearbhall Ó Dálaigh and my uncle, Judge Tom Teevan. They are, all three, together now: I would that I could hear their words (but without actually joining them).

ISSUES

804353 or 2804353

There has been a revolution in Dublin in recent months, infinitely more silent than all that nastiness in St Petersburg, but ten times more effective. An entire class has been overthrown; the swaggering rentier plutocrats in their mohair coats, their vile wives with their cigarette-holders and dead animals draped around their necks have now been humiliated, shamed, their riches turned to ashes.

Trotsky must be capering with rage that he did not try it; that evil genius Lenin must be dumbfounded that its glorious simplicity never occurred to him.

In a single stroke, Ireland has become a classless society. Allow me to explain. Class in Ireland has for a long time been defined by one thing, and it is not simply the way you speak or the size or expense of your car, or where you were sent to school, or your standing in the A-B-C-D categories beloved of people who analyse newspaper sales. True class has been defined by something else. It has been defined by the opening digit of your telephone number.

The rule was terribly simple. If your telephone number began with an 8, or better still an 88, you were the biz, you were icing on the cat, you were the cake's pyjamas. Ditto a 69 start to your telephone number.

People whose telephone number began with 8 or 69 had a nonchalant swagger, they possessed that curious lady, a certain Joanney Saikwa. They owned long, shining Mercedes and BMWs with car-phones, and stand tickets for Lansdowne Road. They called their sons Rupert and Jonathan, their daughters Emma and Emma and Emma, with just the odd Jessica thrown in. They were friends of ambassadors. They voted Fine Gael. They owned yachts. They owned country homes near Schull or Roundstone. In the last couple of years they started taking an interest in soccer, and flew to Rome in corporate jets to see the Ireland-Italy match, either flying back that night, champagne corks popping in the stratosphere, or staying overnight in a top hotel.

And, outside that hotel, or sprawled in small heaps alongside the airport, drinklessly slumbered and snored the soccer supporters who had followed Ireland from the beginning but had been unable to afford the black market prices for tickets for the quarter-final. They probably had not washed since they left Ireland. They had slept on campsites, where they were munched by mosquitoes. And, at home, if they had telephones at all, and they frequently didn't, their numbers began with a 2 or a 3 or a 4, instantly conjuring up images of vast estates around Blanchardstown or Tallaght or Cabra or Finglas. A mobile phone for these people is one that has been stolen from the kiosk.

And, as for Lansdowne Road, most of them had never been to the ground before the Irish soccer team started playing there, though some had made it to the terraces for the rugby internationals, where for years they were treated as if some glorious genetic mutation in areas with telephone numbers beginning with 2 or 3 meant that they did not need ever to use a lavatory.

Meanwhile, revolution was being planned by a subversive in Bord Telecom under the pretext that Dublin had grown to such an enormous size that people needed to be given seven digits rather than retain the old six.

Now the simplest and most logical approach to this would have been to have told everybody beginning with 8 to start their number with an extra 8, ditto the sixes. A double six nine would be socially acceptable, once one had explained the situation to one's friends. Perfectly acceptable, old chap, shan't hesitate to ring you, prepared to ring a double six nine number any day of the week, no disgrace in that at all.

But the Trotskys and Lenins in Bord Telecom did not go for that simple solution at all. All over the southern suburbs in recent months telephone subscribers have been opening their mail, uttering little shrieks and fainting dead away. Telecom had officially informed them: their telephone numbers now begin with a 2.

In the last dying days, when their numbers still began with eight and they could ring one another, the soon-to-be-six-niners were frantically discussing their new status. Worried women were asking whether they must have chips in their hands when they have sex, and where could they buy fake jewellery?

Now it is done: the eighters have become two-eighters. They smoke small untipped cigarettes, held between thumb and second finger. Their daughter, Emma, has mysteriously become Sharon. Their lovely Daimler has been transformed into a 1972 Ford Escort on breeze blocks outside a house festooned with outside plumbing.

Meanwhile, in the estates outside Blanchardstown and Tallaght, palm trees are mysteriously shooting up. Second bathrooms are appearing out of nowhere. Yachts grow in front gardens, BMWs materialise. 'What do you call a Monkstown man in a suit?' guffaws one resident. 'The *accused!*'

'What do you say to a Killiney man with a job?' cries another. 'A big Mac and Fries!'

Haw haw haw. And meanwhile, in Bord Telecom, an individual rubs his hands in satisfaction; but his work is only beginning. He is redesignating the area codes: Belmullet will soon be 01, and Monkstown is to go manual … A small cry, and a bag of chips hits the ground.

Unmarried mothers

The year closes – and the biggest surprise of 1994 for this columnist – was not being lynched for remarks he was sure would lead to certain, self-righteously inflicted disembowelment. Subjects which touch upon the moral-indignation button include AIDS, money for Rwanda, drink and driving, racial differences, trade with dictatorships, itinerants, equality in education, the Irish language, positive discrimination for women in employment – and so on.

The column which I thought would cause the Left and the sisters to lynch me said that the growing trend amongst teenage girls to have babies as a career option was a truly reprehensible social development, both for the individuals concerned and for society at large.

The fact is that very large numbers of young girls think it is perfectly all right to choose to bring into existence another human being as a means of expressing themselves, or of asserting their individuality, or of moving up the housing ladder and gaining all the benefits unmarried mothers are entitled to from the State. The truth, the bizarre and astonishing truth, is that there is virtually nobody who is actually neutral on this matter. Everybody in authority in the State will privately agree – but not publicly – that the trend towards teenage pregnancies is perfectly deplorable.

Yet equally, this profoundly anti-social and potentially disastrous trend is actively encouraged by the State. The 17-year-old unmarried mother is rewarded by the State in a way her more responsible and more caring sister is not; and it is a universal human rule that if you pay people to do things, those things will be done.

It is easy to see how Irish society has been led towards this social and moral imbroglio. It is barely a generation since pregnant teenage girls were hounded from society, were vilified and abused, and treated as skivvy labour by convents.

Teenage pregnancy was merely the most obvious example of a profound Irish aptitude for creating exceedingly harsh moral norms to be enforced by authoritarian and often barbarous sanction. (It is hardly coincidental that Irish schools, run by Irish religious orders, had a code of conduct enforced by the most astonishing violence, often randomly administered.)

That tendency towards extremist response to difficult problems has been again witnessed in the drink-driving laws, which were framed with a morally impeccable and intellectually trivial enthusiasm. A previous set of laws drawing upon comparable inspiration was the unenforced and unenforceable dog-leashing and dog-muzzling laws of a couple of years ago.

Of course there was finally a reaction to the disgraceful treatment of pregnant young girls. That reaction has not merely abolished the punitive response to pregnancy. It has not merely ensured that a full measure of welfare benefits is as available to the unmarried as to the married. It has also prevented anybody saying out loud, how thoroughly and completely dreadful it is that young girls think nothing, absolutely nothing, of getting pregnant the moment they leave school, almost as a means of filling in the time.

And the girls return to their schools the year after leaving, mere children with their babies in their arms. Teachers gaze on mutely, unable to comment while the next group of soon-to-be-school-leavers gathers round and makes gurgly noises and, no doubt, makes private resolutions that they too should all soon get pregnant – for what fun it is!

You get to be the centre of attention; you soon might get a corporation flat; you will soon get all sorts of financial assistance from the State to buy buggies and clothes and prepared foods which are normally too expensive for their responsible, married sisters to buy.

Now baby-producing for such motives is truly bad decision-making. Babies are not merely filthy, incredibly noisy nuisances who require constant attention, who are monomanically selfish and thoroughly unreliable, but the State benefits do not even begin to compensate for the huge personal disadvantages which result from mother-hood – the loss of freedom, the unendurable responsibilities and the loss of carefree youth.

Yet somewhere, somehow, the argument of a woman's right to choose has perco-lated down to such girls. The very logic which was deployed to allow a teenage girl ter-minate a pregnancy has been redeployed to justify this insane teenage fecundity. If her body is capable of producing a baby, and she wants it, why should she not have a baby?

The argument is unanswerable. And from the traditional guardian of moral authority in the land – namely, the Catholic Church – silence. Of course, silence – what other course of action is left the diminishing band of clergy? How can any Catholic prelate make any comment about the sexual conduct of the laity at the moment? Even if the moral ground of the Catholic Church in such matters had not been eroded, if not destroyed, by the prominent role of the Church in the hurt and isolation suffered by earlier generations of teenage unmarried mothers, the Church would be obliged towards a prudent silence after the recent scandals involving so many clergy; and others, believe me, yet to come.

So who is there left to say that this trend is deplorable and must be deplored, not merely for the sake of the young mothers, who are making frivolous, life-changing decisions; not merely for the children, who must grow up in a fatherless society, pos-sibly surrounded by fatherless peers; but for the country as a whole?

America is a generation or more ahead of us here. It has refined the maleless, wel-fare-supported ghetto society of unmarried mothers. It has been a perfect catastrophe. Those who predicted this outcome were called racists.

Their prediction, nonetheless, was right. The same prediction will come true here unless this trend is halted; and the first step in this halting process is to identify the trend and admit that potentially, it is a disaster.

Telefís na Gaeilge

The day of Telefís na Gaeilge draws near, and the sad truth is that it will not cause a single person to speak Irish who does not already speak the language. But since Telefís na Gaeilge is clearly a good thing, the subject is almost undiscussable.

We know the sad truth. To oppose Telefís de Lorean is to be against the Irish language, for the Union, in favour of the parachute regiment and the Black and Tans, and is almost tantamount to an admission that the Famine was a useful exercise in supply-side economics which might have been a little more beneficial if the dashed natives weren't so bally indolent.

There is another truth. The economic realities have already dictated that the station's broadcasting time has been reduced to the point where the audience will consist of that specialist, dedicated variety who would, if its interests were somewhat different, tune into odd satellite television stations at 3.30 a.m. to catch a programme on train-spotting in Lithuania in the 1930s or the mating habits of the nuthatch.

Just because somebody in Government decides that we should all become experts in Lithuanian railways or the nuthatch and that, therefore, television stations will be conjured into existence to promote these admirable projects – this does not mean we will in fact become experts, as intended.

Quite the reverse. When we discover that millions of pounds of *our* money are being squandered on television programmes about the nuthatch and Lithuanian choo-choos, we might find ourselves thoroughly cross and wishing nothing but mischief to them both.

Such stuff should be for specialised television, crank TV, where eccentrics are able to indulge themselves at odd hours. There was even a film made about such television stations. It was called *Wayne's World.*

But Telefís de Lorean is not crank TV. It is not *Tír uí hUaine.* It is serious money – capital costs remain high at over £17 million with annual running costs of £16 million for the station and another £5 million subvention through RTE programming.

RTE will, of course, just love that. Now, it might just be, as Joe Lee recently said, that though Telefís de Lorean – I believe he used some other name – could not save the language, without it Irish would die. That is frightening.

But, of course, there is no limit to that kind of spend, spend, spend logic. I can solemnly declare that if Joe does not give me his life's savings, I will assuredly set fire to his home; though if he does, I am afraid, it is no guarantee that I will not sooner or later get busy with the petrol-bombs.

And once you accept this logic – that the Irish language is in such a frail condition that without the life-support system of a television station with millions of pounds of taxpayers' money it will certainly die, is there any line you can draw on the expenditure required?

For it is clearly a good thing that the Irish language should survive. If £20 million will not save it, maybe £200 million will.

Okay. Just how many unbuilt hospitals, how many unconstructed third-level colleges, how many old people's homes remain on drawing boards, how many ...

What? You don't like this kind of arguing? No doubt. Who does?

It is unfair, it plays to the worst kind of gooey sentimentality, panders to the lowest instincts, calls for the most simplistic kinds of logic.

Which is what many in the Irish-language lobby have been doing for years. The argument has been revived every decade about the priceless cultural heritage which it represents and how Ireland wouldn't be Ireland without it and that any proud and independent people should cherish the language of their land.

All this would make sense if all the people who don't speak Irish, but profess a wish for it to be revived, actually wanted the Irish language to succeed for *them* personally, not as some abstract for other people, or some engaging personal fantasy, like winning the lotto.

I am like that. I would love to speak in Irish, to read Irish, to denounce anglophone language-detractors in Irish; but like those who want to become rich only through winning the lotto, I don't want to work at it.

Who does? Well, the people who already speak Irish. The presence or absence of a television station will not change that. As in all matters of political importance, it is a question of will. And there is no genuine political will to save the Irish language as a living language to be spoken by ourselves.

There is, however, a political will to appear to be concerned about the language. Indeed, it is almost mandatory if you wish to survive in the upper echelons of political life in Ireland to subscribe to the myth that the language is a salvable force of great potency if only we spend more money on ...

Spending State money in an economy profoundly statist is normally the first response of any politician who encounters a problem. But will spending any more money on the language – and thereby certainly depriving other, deeply needy areas of the money concerned – do anything but create jobs in certain areas?

And maybe subliminally, as least, spending the money in such areas is the main motive behind Telefís de Lorean; maybe it is merely another wheeze, like Shannon Development and Udaras, to give State-subsidised jobs in the few reservations where it lingers like lichen.

The truth is sadder. The truth is that as a vernacular language Irish is dead. Such pronouncements are normally regarded as a wish that it be so. This is unjust. The physician who pronounces life extinct does not wish it to be so. I wish Irish well. But it is doomed. Telefís de Lorean is set to add to the hundreds of millions of pounds already squandered on a life-support system for the dead.

Travellers

These Travellers ... insinuate themselves everywhere. The worst dwellings are good enough for them; their clothing causes them little trouble so long as it holds together by a single thread ... The worst quarters of any town are inhabited by Travellers. Whenever an area is distinguished by especial filth and especial ruinousness, (one) may safely count upon meeting chiefly traveller faces which one recognises at first glance as different ... and the singing, aspirate brogue which the true traveller never loses ... The Traveller deposits all garbage and filth before his front door ... and accumulates the pools and the dirtheaps which disfigure working people's estates and poison the air ... The filth and comfortlessness that prevail are impossible to describe ...

The Traveller is unaccustomed to the presence of furniture; A heap of straw, a few rags, utterly beyond use as clothing, suffice for his bed. When he is in want of fuel, everything combustible within his reach – chairs, doorposts, mouldings, flooring, finds its way up the chimney ...

Drink is the only thing which makes the Traveller's life worth having ... so he revels in drink to the point of the most bestial drunkenness. The facile character of the Traveller, his crudity, which places him but little above the savage, his contempt for all human enjoyments, in which his very crudeness makes him incapable of sharing, his filth and his poverty all favour drunkenness ... when he gets money he gets rid of it down his throat.'

Had Mary Ellen Synon written these words, she would have been subject to yet further calumny; and had I defended her *right* to say those words, never mind whether or not I agreed with them, likewise for me. She did not write them. They were written by somebody whom many of the self-appointed spokes(wo)men for the Travellers probably admire – Friedrich Engels; but he was writing not about Travellers but ordinary Irish emigrants to England. I merely substituted 'Travellers' for 'Irish'.

Engels did not make those observations in order to vilify or generate hostility against the average Irish emigrant. Quite the reverse. He was writing for a German audience and was deeply moved by the appalling plight of the Irish in English towns; the quote above, about drink, concludes – 'What else should he do? How can society blame him when it places him in a position in which almost of necessity he becomes a drunkard; when it leaves him to himself, his savagery?'

We are back to the issue of Travellers again because there is no getting away from it, and we must deal with it without public effusions of meaningless piety; and even more important, without tolerating the voices of hatred. We heard the voice of hatred last week from Waterford: had such sentiments been issued about Jews, we know the speaker would have been ejected from the chamber. They were not and he was not; the only useful thing that gentleman has to teach us is that there are others with such disgusting and intolerable opinions.

In her controversial article in the *Sunday Independent* Mary Ellen Synon clearly abominated Traveller-life. What is wrong with that? Engels clearly abominated the life of the Irish working-class emigrant in England. But for the Irish individuals concerned, he felt every sympathy, just as she felt admiration for those able to escape the dreadfulness of the circumstances of so many Travellers' lives. As well she might, for who truly finds the prospect of life as a Traveller appetising? She certainly did not urge discrimination or violence against travellers – she merely spoke of her thorough dislike for the circumstances in which they live. That is her right; as Travellers may disdain and deplore her way of life too, and mine.

There is no more difficult issue in Irish life than this one. I have written before about the monstrous discrimination which Travellers must face; but the High Moral Grounders have always chosen to ignore that and to concentrate on what I think undesirable about Traveller-life. But we know the problem can only be solved by honesty, and not by the kind of putative piety of a letter-writer in Dundrum who disassociated himself from membership of a putative group 'who live in hope that a Travellers' halting site is not constructed next to their houses.'

I have land next to my house which conceivably could be turned into a halting site; the pious letter-writer lives in a densely built estate where no such site is possible. His virtue is therefore unlikely to be tested.

Now, I see, the National Union of Journalists has weighed in with instructions not to refer to Travellers as itinerants, knackers, traders or tinkers. So what are we to call them? If they deal in horses, are they not knackers? If they work tin, are they not tinkers? If they trade, are they not traders? If they are itinerant, are they not itinerants?

A rose by any other name … The first response of feel-gooders to a problem is to change the language associated with that problem. So tell me: is the position of American blacks improved or altered by the repeated change in the vocabulary we are commanded to employ about them? Nigger gave way to coloured; coloured gave way to negro; negro gave way to black; black gave way to African-American – yet how many bigots actually had their minds changed by such nomenclatural switches?

Linguistic dodges don't avoid disdain; they mask it. The term 'remedial' was devised to prevent the retarded child from being stigmatised by its peers: now the term is itself stigmatic. We can call the nomadic minority of Ireland whatever we like; it will not alter the nature of the profound problems which they already face and which will almost certainly get worse.

Those problems will not be diminished by non-traveller traveller-spokes(wo)men who have a nice line in sanctimoniously accusatory waffle directed at those with whom they disagree. Travellers are perfectly capable of speaking for themselves; they don't need self-appointed Political Lady Bountifuls speaking for them.

Litigitis

In other societies and other legal cultures it would be possible to identify judges whose rulings are bizarre, absurd, insulting to the commonweal; but not here. We have instead a system which allows a judge to be his own judge, counsel, jury and executioner.

If a judge slumbers through a case or by his consistently crazy awards is a huge burden on the public purse or on insurance companies – which alas comes to pretty much the same thing – it is not possible to identify him. Or her. Were we to say that Mr Justice Caomháin Uí Midhir is a blithering idiot who could not be safely entrusted with the trial of a hamster, that fine gentleman can order his critic before his court, and sentence him at his discretion alone, and almost without limit; though I understand that beheading is no longer quite the thing.

The point is of course that the peculiar world that the bench has created for itself permits only expressions of approval. Judges remain above criticism; though not above approbation, no doubt for the same general reasons that they expect counsel to collapse in uncontrollable hysteria at their jokes.

Anyway, having thus scared the living daylights out of the unfortunate *Irish Times* solicitors who read this copy so we don't all end up in jail, let me here commend Judge Lynch, who recently told a litigant who had been blocking a road and who was hit and injured by a car that the accident was 90 per cent his own fault. Lynchie, old thing, I love you; you're an absolute dote, the yolk to my egg and the butter on my toast.

Fortunately he is not alone. Maybe the floodtide of profitable *litigitis* which has been washing through the courts in recent times is beginning to hit the breakwaters of prudent jurisprudence. Judge James Carroll recently rejected a claim for £30,000 from a woman who was hit by a flying shoe during celebrations in a pub after the Egypt-Ireland match in 1990. And more to the point, the fine judge ruled that the costs of the defendants, Meagher Inns, should be paid by the plaintiff. Oh bliss, bliss; if I took sugar in my tea, Judge James Carroll you'd be it.

Recently this column wrote about the elderly lady who slipped on a piece of potato at a Dublin Corporation lunch centre which provided almost free meals, with the assistance of unpaid helpers, to pensioners. She was awarded several thousand pounds. Now it seemed to me at the time that there is no way that any public body can protect itself against litigation on such grounds.

And so it appears to be. A 63-year-old woman was recently awarded £13,500 after slipping on a soft-drinks spillage on a DART train and injuring her back and knee. But no organisation which deals with the public can reasonably be expected to take provision against every spill of Club Orange or every dropped potato. Trains would have to be patrolled by squads of spill-police to protect against litigation-provoking accidents and then there would have to be sneeze-police to prevent costly spread of diseases, and smell-police to ensure we were not traumatised by our fellow passengers' armpits, and possibly requiring counselling.

Yet happily it is not always like this. A break-dancer who fractured his ankle during a competition sued the Penthouse pub in Ballymun the other week, alleging that he had slipped on a spilt drink. No spilt-drink police were to hand, but the judge dismissed the case. And the judge? My old chum Judge Lynch.

Not that litigation in itself is wrong. Not at all. One can only sympathise with Thomas Craig, whose nose was broken by Zebedee Moore because the latter thought he was kissing his girlfriend. Moments later the assailant apologised, realising that his eyes had misled him because of the alcohol he had drunk. I trust that you realise in the USA the pub would have been sued for serving Zebedee the drink; though one can't help wondering whether it was the drink or the Magic Roundabout which affected his eyesight.

Neither the Magic Roundabout nor Zebedee Moore could in any way be held accountable for the tragic fate which befell a group of lawyers who attended a Sligo discotheque. They were, observed the judge at the court case which resulted from the fate which befell these unfortunates, a distinctive group, unlike other patrons, formally attired in suits and ties.

What happened in the hotel seems rather like *Deliverance* but without the love scene. One of the regular patrons began to eyeball the boogeying barristers who, knowing an eyeball when they saw one, referred the matter of said eyeballing to a bouncer, who assured them there would be no problem.

Before you could say wigs and braces, the locals were on the barristers and doing a war dance about their earlobes. One barrister was knocked to the ground and suffered a fractured jaw and other injuries. He shouted for help, got none, and crawled into the lobby of the hotel between the legs of a bouncer. Another lawyer attempting to leave was kicked, knocked to the ground and suffered a broken jaw and other injuries.

Yet another lawyer, seeing the Revenge of the Hill Billies enacted before his eyes, requested the Bouncers to end the massacre. They did nothing. And did nothing when his turn came, which resulted in him being thrown into a corner, kicked in the head and suffering cuts and bruises to various parts of his body.

Damages of £12,000 were recently awarded to one of the lawyers; and though we might have difficulty keeping a straight face when we read of what befell possibly an entire generation of future judges, scrambling between bouncers' legs on hotel floors, it is sobering nonetheless to reflect on the innovative hospitality of the Grand Hotel, Sligo, where the assaults took place.

Has Bord Fáilte awards for places like this? I think it should have. It seems to compare rather favourably with the Holiday Inn in Sarajevo; the perfect place for an adventure holiday, and these days, not a lawyer in sight.

Immigrants

The number of black faces in Dublin increases by the day, and my heart sinks; not because of the people themselves, but because society here is probably incapable of making the mental and social adjustments to accommodate our new immigrants. We can't even use honest words about them. Immigrants are not immigrants but 'economic refugees' or 'asylum seekers', which are merely terminological denials of the truth that these people are simply migrants seeking better lives for themselves, just as millions of Irish people once did.

They will bring with them different skills, different religions, different diets; they could enhance Irish life enormously, as did the Huguenots, the Jews, the Chinese. But they are not like the previous generations of black immigrants, who were, archetypally, intellectually and often socially superior to most of the host community.

Our latest newcomers are different. Many will be entering at the very bottom of the economic ladder; and from the way we seem unable to assimilate, or even come to terms with, the humanity of Catholic, Irish stock already milling helplessly at the bottom of that ladder, we might fairly wonder how we shall cope with the rising number of poor Bangladeshis or Jamaicans – or whatever – who will sooner or later be assembling there as well.

Anne Power's recent report on the truly abominable estates which Irish society has manufactured has, to judge from newspaper accounts, apparently laid blame for these 'white ghettoes' on the economy, with the media also being used as a scapegoat for creating stigmas about their residents (a standard and rather tiresome canard: which media, please, where and when?).

But it is not the 'economy' or newspapers, or television, which generated the attitudes behind the creation of such estates, and which sustain a prejudice against their residents. You can lay blame for that fairly and squarely on the cultural and political priorities within Irish society, which pre-date the Lemass economic boom, and which seem to be surviving, with a virulent vitality, into our tigerishly bright new future.

Irish life is riven with a thousand snobberies and shibboleths, Irish people seem profoundly insecure away from their own type, or even sub-type. Estates like Jobstown and Neilstown are merely a socially marginalised form of the estate construction which characterises Dublin generally. Journalists and barristers like to live in an estate called Ranelagh; sad, middle-aged trendies in one called Phibsboro; architects in one called Sandymount; fitters in Finglas, factory workers in Coolock, and so on.

The social structures within such local communities are largely self-enforced. It is not the wish of Irish universities that working-class students attending them are just about as rare as Bushmen in the Broderbond. The communal pressure in working-class estates is towards conformity. Be what your parents were; and if you are working-class, do not rise above yourself. Do not get notions. What was good enough for your parents should be good enough for you. Snobs, not real people, go to university.

We have the worst record of educating working-class people to university level in Europe. It is not the Irish economy, which increasingly resembles economies found elsewhere, which is responsible for that, but an extraordinarily powerful social conservatism which seeks internal continuity, which seeks to exclude outsiders, especially of lower rank, which seeks to discourage insiders from achieving upward mobility, which seeks a geographical reassurance that families are not departing the economic and social consensus. It is not coincidental that 'losing the run of yourself' is one of the most powerful terms of social opprobrium in Irish life.

And we are not even aware of this. Quite the reverse. Our self-image contrasts starkly with the reality. We think we are broad-minded and tolerant, but we are not. We think we are not snobbish, but we are profoundly so. And this snobbery is not merely the worker-as-victim stereotype, as any brickie's labourer who tries to eat his 'piece' with brickies on a building site will tell you.

Equally, we probably declare that we are not racist – a laughable belief considering the conduct of Irish emigrants in the US and Britain. Certain forms of racism are already quite socially acceptable here – such as abusive epithets about 'Brits' or 'unionists'. Those so free with such language today will probably within a decade be talking about niggers, Pakis, coons.

We face huge problems in the coming decade, as immigrants – who legally and morally have every right to come here – compete for jobs with the professionally unskilled people from the estates which we have so scandalously neglected and where life anyway does not dispose one to tolerance. The recent decision to cut Government spending on sports and recreation centres in such estates … from £20 million to just over £1 million, with the same hand that was giving £20 million to the GAA, the paradigm of monoculturalism, is beyond parody.

A multi-racial Irish society is a certainty, and one we must get used to. We might take a lesson or two from our neighbours on how to pre-empt problems, but the chances are, we will do no such thing and will opt instead to repeat their mistakes; and then we could have another jolly little tribunal of enquiry to help out the residents of Ranelagh with their mortgages.

Asylum seekers

There is one term which we should have banned long ago in the discussion about racism in Ireland. It is the sanctimonious weasel-term 'asylum-seeker', with its implication of refugeedom from tyranny preventing any reasoned conversation about the actual growth of both immigration and of racism here. Of course, it makes the *bien-pensants* who use it feel morally superior; and moral superiority has always been one of the most high-mindedly popular and insidiously dangerous aspects of the race debate anywhere.

In Britain, arrogant, middle-class liberals attributed the upheavals in working-class areas after the arrival of huge numbers of people of a different culture, race, religion, diet, shape and smell to the intolerance and racism of the natives.

Hampstead socialists might have wondered how it was that the working classes – in whom they ideologically reposed so much faith – could so unfailingly let them down; but instead they preferred to blame Enoch Powell, who, with his infamous 'rivers of blood' speech, had become the single most popular politician among the English working classes.

Why? Because he spoke for them. He uttered the heretical truth that the face of urban Britain was being changed for ever, that new and irreversible forces were being released by massive immigration into old, tight-knit, mono-cultural and mono-racial working-class communities. To denounce the perfectly understandable human incomprehension and confusion at these changes simply as 'racism' was bourgeois condescension at its most arrogant and insensitive.

Enoch Powell facilitated that condescension. The language he used was both inflammatory and inaccurate. It shifted the authorship of racist violence from whites to immigrants, when the traffic was overwhelmingly in the opposite direction. Between them, Powell and his liberal opponents made it impossible to discuss the gravest and most enduring changes to have occurred to the English proletariat since the industrial revolution.

In the largely liberal-enforced silence which resulted, poisonous racist sub-cultures emerged like unlanced boils among the young, white working class, spreading into, and often corrupting, local police forces. This happened in large part not in spite of, but actually because of, middle-class, liberal sneers that to be unhappy about the changes happening in your area made you a racist. Thus 'racism' for those so labelled became a badge of honour, a mark of realism and of national identity. And the ideological, linguistic and moral tyranny of liberals was made even more odious and hypocritical by its imposition from districts where outsiders were few and where a black face meant a GP and an Indian face an accountant: such faces did not mean the virtual eradication overnight of neighbourhood cultural norms which had been in existence for generations.

We are far from having immigration on that scale in Ireland, but already the debate is steeped in censorious highmindedness and linguistic dishonesty on the ship's bridge, even as the secret fires of racist bigotry spread through the coal-holds below.

Taxi-drivers are already mouthing the brainless 'asylum-seeker' anecdotes which are the symptoms of emerging social tensions; and I regretfully believe the letter on this page last Saturday from a dark American visitor who told of hostile stares from young Irish people.

People are not fools all of the time. We cannot pretend that black people coming here generally are 'asylum-seekers'. They are immigrants, legal or illegal, looking for economic opportunity, just as tens of thousands of Irish immigrants, legal or illegal, are in the United States for precisely the same reason. Let us call these people immigrants. And let us be absolutely sure that even while middle-class liberals – whose residential areas are immune to large-scale immigration because of property prices – loftily denounce racism, in poor, working-class areas where immigrants are arriving, genuine racist tensions are starting to grow.

I haven't got a clue how to defuse these tensions, but I'm sure a good start is honesty – and honesty is not something we're particularly good at, even as 'niggers go home' graffiti deface walls in red-brick, working-class areas of Dublin. The immigration which is occurring now is drastically different from the sort of immigration we have received before – which was largely of white Christians.

It is simplistic to dwell on our debt to that assimilable and racially indistinguishable immigration of the past when we know that poor Muslims from Bangladesh and Rastafarians from Jamaica are a different kettle of genes and culture altogether.

That is the kettle that is arriving, and we must accept it. It is both practically purposeless and morally unacceptable to have immigration officers standing at Amiens Street looking for dusky complexions arriving on the Belfast train. Such filtration procedures are primitive, racist and insulting for all concerned.

We simply must accept that people travelling from the UK should have automatic right of entry here. If a few thousand illegals get in, so be it.

Yes, and there will be the D & D problems – dole-fiddling and dope-smuggling – and no doubt various other disagreeable aspects to immigration, just as Irish builders virtually pioneered the 'lump' in Britain and smuggled hooch into prohibition America. Equally, there will be the advantages of cultural and culinary diversity – but these might not be so obvious to poor, bewildered people in the Liberties (or wherever) who will dislike the changes happening to their areas. To dismiss such unhappiness as racist, and not heed it, is to repeat the errors in England. Just for once, are we capable of learning from the experience of others?

Opening hours

The Minister for Justice, Mr Zero Tolerance O'Donoghue has, I presume, a bin under his desk; he should fill it immediately with the 130 pages of the report from the All-Party Committee on Liquor Licensing Laws, and start again. It is clearly a soft-shoe shuffle between the politicians' compulsive instinct to interfere in our lives, and yet not too grievously offend that mightily powerful lobby, the licensed vintners.

Not that it's likely ZT will go so far as to take a principled stand against the political instinct to meddle in other peoples' lives – after all, that's what impels men and women into politics in the first place. Not that there's much power in native politics anyway, these days. Authority has shifted east, and soon we shall be governed from Bonn or Berlin. What is left for our native politicians to do, but tinker with and intrude on our private habits?

There are two conflicting philosophies at issue here; one accepts that the state has the fundamental right to exercise authority almost at random over its subjects; and the other grants to citizens the right to behave as they wish, free of the authority of the state, provided no unconsenting person is unreasonably discommoded. Subject, citizen; Hobbes, Locke. Locke and citizenhood are the boys for me.

This is a republic. Did the nannies on the All-Party Committee ask themselves what right they have to regulate the drinking hours of the citizens of a republic? Did they ask what right they have to forbid, on pain of penalty, one person to sell drink to another person at one particular hour and not another? Did they ask themselves about the philosophic difference between a man buying a bottle of stout at 12.29 a.m. on a Thursday, (no offence) buying one at 12.31 a.m. on a Thursday (offence) and buying one at 12.31 a.m. on a Friday (no offence)?

Did they? Probably not. There's little enough evidence of abstract thought in political life in Ireland at the best of times; and now, as they see power slipping away from them, our politicians seem more thoughtlessly addicted to the minor manipulation of our lives than ever before – hence the idiotic proposal above.

In Britain, where the libertarian revolution has been far more complete than here, politicians are contemplating 24-hour licences for bars. And other things being equal, why not? The issue should not be whether or not the state has a right to interfere in the private transactions of individuals, but whether those transactions interfere with the rights of others – the most obvious right being the right to sleep, to enjoy peace and quiet, the right to be spared drunkenness in the street.

These are reasonable considerations, the relevance of which in part changes according to geography. Nobody who lives in the city centre expects to have the same tranquillity that they might find on Croagh Patrick. But, provided people leave and enter a hostelry in good order, why should they not be able to buy drinks at any stage of day or night? Why should the huge apparatus of the state be positioned to outlaw people from drinking in pubs, but not night clubs, at one a.m.? What possible cause is being served, what good is being done, what considered philosophical principle being maintained?

None, none whatever. And whatever actual practical points might be raised in opposition to late night drinking – rowdiness, insane intoxication, drunk-driving – are pertinent at any time of day. It is illegal to serve drink to someone who is conspicuously drunk; yet who has not seen the nearly comatose being served in pubs until 'nearly' no longer applies? Who has not seen clusters of drunks weaving and swaying at street corners? Who has not seen why Temple Bar is now Temple Bladder? Who has not heard the news each weekend of the latest high-speed motoring slaughter of yet another bunch of drunken teenagers?

Such delinquency should not justify the undelinquent, the happy reveller, the holiday-maker, being prevented from having a drink at one, two, three in the morning, as they do in Madrid or Barcelona, where one never sees drunkenness or rowdiness. Provided their houses are orderly, publicans should be able to serve drinks through to breakfast and beyond. IF THEY WANT.

But not, according to the All-Nanny Committee on Liquor Licensing Laws, whose 70 recommendations seem to be a gigantic exercise in witless and obsessive statism. The committee has laboured long and hard to propose that closing time (from Sundays through to Wednesdays be 11.30, winter and summer, and from Thursday through to Saturdays it should be 12.30). What a committee of giants! What intellectual colossuses to have come to such a decision!

Why those times? Because the All Party Nanny Committee drew from some deep well of chrono-alcoholic sagacity? Or because those times are a simple incremental increase on the old rules, devised when the State really did think it knew better, and when it intervened at all sorts of levels to prevent people getting their hands on 'pornography' and literature and condoms and vast amounts of innocuous film. In 1998, we know that there's no justification for the State deciding that a deed moves from legality to illegality, merely because the hands of the clock have shifted a quarter of an inch.

ZT, the thing at your feet is the bin. Time to use it.

Giving Bray a miss

Perhaps you noticed the case in which Detective Garda David Byrne was awarded £116,347 in damages for assault. He didn't get a penny too much. If the award were trebled, I'd shake his hand, tell him he deserved every groat of it and murmur politely, Mine's a pint. Of the Dom, seel voo play.

David was on plain clothes duty in an unmarked car in Bray in 1992 when he came across a traffic accident. A certain female Traveller had been hit by a scooter and the lady's gallant menfolk – her husband and his brother – were setting about the scooter-jockey so robustly that David, being a copper and all that, felt compelled to intervene, ushering the said scooterer into his car.

Did he but know it, the best place for David was in the car as well, provided, that is, the car was anywhere – Grozny, say – but not Bray. But David wasn't in the car, and he certainly wasn't in Grozny, which must have seemed an attractive place indeed when one of the strapping young male Travellers lifted the scooter over his head and smashed it onto the ground. Heavy things, scooters.

The two young gentlemen then turned their attention to the nearest living-and-breathing human being to hand, i.e. David. This is beam-me-up-Scotty time, but there is no Scotty, just David Byrne, detective, by himself with two indignant young Travellers. Why did he not urge gentle persuasion? Why did he not seek the non-confrontational, I-feel-your-pain approach, and jettison the rude discourse of male physicality?

Why not? Because his two companions, apart from being hopping mad, were stone-deaf. So they kicked and punched him in the kidneys, arms and chest, trying to get his gun from him. A word here, David. Was there not a strongish case for introducing that device a little earlier in the disagreement? Though maybe, you'd almost certainly have had to use it, and then where would you have been? Few enough people would have been saying that here you were, faced with two raving madmen and in real fear of your life, and what else could you have done but shoot them?

Enter a passer-by with a lavatory seat. An interesting place, Bray. Scooters being flourished over heads like bandsmen's batons, bold chevaliers seeking instant physical redress for their injured damsel, an armed police-officer being walloped by deaf scooter-brandishers, yet not even reaching for his gun. And now, to judge from this tale, there are apparently all these citizens wandering around the town with lavatory seats in their hands. Is this because everyone's always stealing lavatory seats in Bray, and you have to take your own with you wherever you go, just as in the old Soviet Union you had to have your own plug for wash-basins?

And what happens in restaurants? Does the waiter say, 'May I take your lavatory seat sir?' and you say, 'No thanks, I'll keep it with me,' and then of course the only place to put it is on the real seat. Hmm. Does merely sitting on a lavatory seat trigger associative reflexes, so that there you are, tucking in to your dinner in Bray, when you suddenly find yourself simultaneously having a number two and bawling for the Andrex? Bray does not enjoy a reputation for haute cuisine; now I think I understand why.

But stay. I digress. As I was saying, one of Bray's many lavatory seat-bearing citizens intervened in the fracas, smashing it so hard over one of the two Traveller's heads that it, the seat, smashed, whereas it, the Traveller's head, didn't. In fact the owner of the head didn't even blink, but kept on fighting.

Exit, one former-owner of a lavatory seat, seatless. By this time, David is somehow or other safe and sound back inside his umarked garda car. Safe and sound are of course relative qualities. Most of us would say that garda cars are solidly-made affairs, but then most of us don't live in Bray. Or go around with lavatory seats, just in case. Or send young ladies flying with our scooters. Or have stand-up fights with deaf and dumb Travellers, one of whom now decided to punch David. But David is in the car, no? Yes.

The fist went right through the windscreen – you know the laminated shatterproof windscreen? Well, it went right through that, shattering David's nose and jaw and blinding him with blood. So now, his car, one scooter, one scooter-pilot and one lavatory seat, were in bits. So was David. And then a passer-by (with or without a lavatory seat) breaks the good news to David. Passer-by: 'Those two men, they've gone.' David: Phew. Passer-by: To fetch a shotgun. Tell me. Have you ever noticed that there are some days when root canal treatment with a Black and Decker would have been a better option?

Actually, things got better at this point, because another garda car arrived before the scooter-twirlers could return with their shotgun.

I'm giving Bray the miss this Christmas.

Germica Jeer

Good morning and welcome to An Irishman's Chatshow, and our first guest is the renowned feminist Germica Jeer, whose latest book, *A Burden Grown Greater: The Tribulations of Woman in the New Millennium*, is published this week. Good morning, Ms Jeer. It's nearly 30 years since your first book, *Fear of the Flying Eunuch*, first appeared. Have you ever in all that time experienced a remotely critical interview?

'The world is a deeply misogynistic place. Hatred of women is everywhere. Governments not merely tolerate rape as a social means of controlling women, but approve of it. It explains why there are no female generals in the US Marine corps, no women in the soccer World Cup or the baseball World Series. There's a lot of anti-womanness out there, and after more than three decades of feminism, it's time to confront the massed anti-feminist movement head on.'

You've visited Ireland many times during those past three decades. Has a radio or television interviewer ever given you a difficult question? Has one, just one, ever disputed any of the many modish fatuities from which you have made your fortune?

'That's a good question. Let's put it this way. Far from the feminist movement actually breaking through the patriarchy which has stifled woman's creativity, which has chained us to the sink, which has prevented us from expressing all our commercial, sporting, military, sexual and artistic selves, the oppression has actually grown worse. In many US states, courts regularly sentence women to be gang-raped. Female circumcision is now mandatory in Canada. In Britain, the army uses women for live target practice. In Spain, matadors practice sword strokes on orphan girls who are then beheaded. The Finnish parliament has outlawed the female orgasm. In Italy, they're so afraid of women even discovering their sexuality that by law they must sleep with their hands manacled behind their necks. Here in Ireland, women may not be seen in public without written permission from their husbands or fathers. In France, women found on bicycles are summarily strangled by special police. Things have got worse, not better.'

Listen. Does no interviewer anywhere ever say you're talking rubbish, inventing oppression where it doesn't exist and creating a wholly fictional victimhood? Or are they all coiffed and fawning cretins who agree with your every witless utterance?

'Right. In the States that's what we call the glass-ceiling syndrome. Women can see the higher positions in society, but we can't reach them. Why can we see them? Because we're allowed to. And why are we allowed to? Because it's an extra torment devised by the patriarchy, like a starving prisoner in a cell being shown food through the window, but not being allowed to eat it. Being allowed to see the highest positions in society, but not being able to get near them – just another cruelty among the many torments women must suffer.'

Do these simpering buffoons who interview you never say, look you stupid cow, what you're complaining about is called life, and every five years or so you visit upon this poor unfortunate bloody world your particular discontent with whatever stage of life you're at, only dressing it up in the guise of feminist politics?

'Exactly. Women know oppression in a cultural and institutional way that men cannot understand. Our lives are threaded with loss, with suffering and with feelings that men do not know. It's a well known fact, for example, that women are more prone to mental illness and suicide throughout the Western world because of that.'

You *what?* What's that organ you're talking out of? It's certainly not your mouth. Mental illness is predominantly a male phenomenon. Nearly 90 per cent of all suicides in this country are male. When one columnist – chap by the name of Waters; don't always agree with him, but he was spot on with that one – attempted to highlight this, he was, of course, promptly vilified.

'That's a valid point. I agree with you. So long as the political establishment denies women access to the highest powers in the land, what hope is there? I look across Europe; where do I see an elected woman head of state? Where do I see a woman party leader? I see sexual oppression, marginalisation, and you know, outright hatred of women everywhere. It is perhaps the single most potent feature of Western culture.'

What tree have you just fallen out of? We're on our second female president here in Ireland. Our deputy prime minister is the leader of her party. What drivel are you going to come up with next?

'Precisely. And as you've just pointed out, while women are treated as slaves, we cannot fulfil our true potential. This is what my book is all about. It's about the violent male conspiracy, against women in all its forms.'

Christ alive. OK. So will you do me one tiny, tiny favour? Will you please not tell me that women are survivors?

'But you know, we women are survivors.'

AAAAaaaarrrggghhh.

FOOD AND DRINK

French cuisine

Every now and then news comes from the health industry which should fill the hearts of all right-thinking citizens with joy. Such citizens are aware that the health lunatics are set on causing misery throughout the western world, and there seems to be no stopping them. But there is never a time when the health police are quite as officious and interfering as at Christmas, when people are preparing to enjoy themselves – there burns the beacon of hope.

In a couple of months time the French National Institute for Health and Medical Research – Inserm – will publish the four-year study of 600 cardiac patients in Lyons. Half of the volunteers in the study followed the conventional recommended diet of the health fanatics, a virtually vegetarian regimen which was high in poly-unsaturated fats such as margarines and sunflower oil, and completely free of alcohol, while the others ate a normal diet with wine very day; in one sense only did the latter group depart from the norm, and that was in the higher than usual consumption of olive oil.

The study was supposed to last five years, but was abandoned after four on ethical grounds. The organiser considered it immoral to continue a programme which was proving fatal to so many volunteers. Needless to say, the fatalities were occurring amongst those who had embraced the healthy diet and who were dying at a rate five to six times higher than those who were eating meat, gorging themselves with cheese and drinking wine every day.

Indeed, the reassuring truth is that the French, a most intelligent race whose cuisine is the single greatest glory of civilisation and which alone marks us out from the brute beasts of the field, are a living refutation of everything the health fanatics have tried to force upon us. They consume vast amounts of fat every year. Their alcohol consumption is such that they have dedicated the greater part of their countryside to the manufacture of wines. They have invented virtually every single spirit and liqueur worth drinking, and those they have not invented, they import huge amounts of. Not surprisingly, after the US, they are the world's biggest importers of scotch whisky, and Pernod-Ricard regarded whiskey as so important that they bought the entire Irish whiskey industry.

The French smoke almost indefatigably. They eat nothing but white bread; and merely to visit a French patisserie is by the standards of the health police to invite a coronary.

Conversely, the French are the least fit people in Europe. They do no unnecessary exercise. The blight of jogging is unknown in French cities. French motorists do not have to swerve to hit runners on the roadway, as one does in Ireland (three last week and one winged: not bad).

Needless to say the French do not suffer from heart disease as the health fanatics tells us they should. French women suffer the lowest number of heart attacks of any of their sex in the industrialised world. Only Japanese males have fewer heart attacks than French males.

Now. Let us turn our attention to Toulouse, where the low-heart attack rate of the French reaches such glorious depths as to cause our health fanatics to attempt suicide by secondary smoking or eating a lamb chop or even having a second glass of low-alcohol wine. A lingering death. Actually a quicker way of doing away with yourself is to eat wholemeal pastry or brown rice.

In Toulouse death-rate from heart disease is 13 times lower than in Glasgow. Belfast is marginally healthier than Glasgow in this category. Not in other regards, perhaps, but in coronaries, yes. Why are Glasgow and Belfast and doubtless Dublin and Cork so much more dangerous than Toulouse? Because they eat more fat? No.

There are a couple of factors. One is the people of Toulouse eat more vegetables. Lots of meat, oodles of saucissons, wine by the gallon, but lots of vegetables. And also cheese. The French eat lots and lots of high cholesterol cheese; and with the cheese, yet more wine.

But there is a further factor, the most important of all. The French enjoy their food. They eat it with relish. The only group – the *only* group in France amongst whom heart disease is growing are young people who, having heard the nonsense of the health police, have given up wine and fatty foods and generally any sort of pleasure in food, and hence are dying off as if it were Dien Bien Phu all over again.

Jean-Pierre and André and Louis-Marc sip their low-calorie mineral waters and nibble on their high-roughage lettuce and gradually, losing the will to live, one by one slide under the table, dead with boredom.

Meanwhile, overweight middle-aged Frenchmen and women tuck into foie gras and potatoes fried in duck fat and cauliflower au gratin and great helpings of goose stuffed with chestnuts, bacon and pig entrails, followed by pounds of cheese and another litre of wine, patron, *s'il vous plait,* and perhaps some choux pastry to follow, accompanied by a Muscat de beaume de venise, perhaps, and to conclude, with the coffee, some of your admirable calvados; and then I must go, for I have some brain surgery to perform this afternoon. And I too, agrees a companion, for I have a cabinet meeting this afternoon. *Eh vous aussi?* cries a third: why I thought that I alone was busy – some more wine, Louis? – for I have the talks on GATT to conclude this afternoon. A busy week, to be sure, agrees the fourth, for I have to finish the design of the new 500-seater Airbus by dinner, and so far I have only designed half a wing. Still, there's time for more of this excellent cheese, I think, and is that wine all gone already? *Sacré bleu.* Patron, two more litres of your excellent house wine, and might I point out that the superlative *chèvre* you were kind enough to serve us is gone? Perhaps another half kilo, with some bread? Good. Here comes the wine.

A glass with you, Michel, and good luck with the heart transplant you are performing on your wife this afternoon. She never drank, I believe? A grave error. I am glad to see you rectifying that omission, madame, so shortly before you have this operation. Might I suggest some of this brie? It is a most excellent companion to the *vin de pays* the patron favours us with here, and is particularly recommended for patients about to receive a new heart ...

God bless the French; the saviours of humankind, and the despair of the health-police everywhere.

Galway oysters

One hundred thousand oysters went to their doom, gallantly and unflinching, a week ago at the Guinness Galway Oyster Festival. The world might not yet have learned that this is a choice year for oysters, but it most certainly is. The pity of it all is that unlike the grape, the oyster cannot be bottled and stored, and precious oyster vintages be kept for future years, to be tasted and relished in less fortunate times. The time to eat oyster is now, always now, or not at all; and never was there a more blessed now than now.

This year's Galway oysters are quite superb. They are fat without being fatty, which is often the condition of that intrusive Pacific oyster to be found throughout the year. In high summer it is an acceptable substitute, when the native oysters are busy about their sexual duties. But sometimes one finds oneself eating a Pacific oyster as it is in the middle of its own unpredictable season. It is like biting into a condom full of cold mayonnaise, or whatever.

But this year's Atlantic oysters are fat but never fatty, and are lusciously nut-flavoured in the way unique to the Atlantic oyster. Their texture is firm; soft to the tooth, but pluckily resistant in the way that I'd like to think I'd be if I were being eaten alive. Unlike my own modest cadaver, the Galway oyster yields a briny juice which washes through the mouth as you bite into it. The oyster might emit a protesting gurgle as it slides down one's throat – but then wouldn't you? – and then it is gone where all good oyster go, leaving behind it a powerful nut-flavour and an even more powerful desire for more of same.

The shrewd observer will have noticed two features about a good oyster, as referred to above. One is that it is alive and kicking when it is consumed, and two, that it has a nutty flavour. The two features are related. The regrettable habit of spraying lemon or tabasco on oysters came about in the olden days, when oysters could not be kept cool and might die within their shell. Eating a dead and mildly infected oyster can cause hallucinations, vomiting and distressed laundresses.

To test whether an oyster was alive or dead, oyster eaters would pour a drop of lemon juice, or some other acerbic like tabasco, into the soft-flesh. If it puckers, it's alive, and consumable. If it stays as unflinchering as the eye of Tutankhamen, eat it by all means; but don't be surprised if you wake up in the middle of Sunday mass, with a chainsaw in your hand and the bishop in neat little slices by the altar. Shellfish poisoning is the oldest poisoning there is. You can end up thinking you are Pope Pius XII, calling for nuns.

But with modern refrigeration, and speedy transport of oyster from tide to tongue, there is no need to test its flesh, no need to put unnecessary testers, like lemon-juice or tabasco, into the oyster-flesh. For such oyster-testers take away from the full nutty taste of purest Irish oyster. Eat it unadorned, unflavoured and perfect, and you will face only the slightest chance that you will cause any modifications to the college of bishops. There is only one proper Irish stout companion to proper Irish fat oysters, and that was being consumed in heroic quantities in Galway.

The odd thing about the oyster is its curious reluctance to be eaten alive – though this is the very reason why this ingrate is bred in such huge numbers every year. The only time I tried to open any number of oysters in a short time, I ended up in intensive care with a posse of priests chanting glumly at my bedhead and much wailing from the Pro-Cathedral. I have never had much faith in this thing called decommissioning, but in the event of it happening just a *little* bit, I'd be grateful if the lads could spare me the old RPG? Or two, merely as an oyster-opener.

Others are made of more intrepid stuff. This year's Irish oyster champion is Gerry Grealish of Moran's of the Weir, perhaps the greatest seafood pub in Ireland. In less peaceful times, Gerry is the kind of fellow who disables tank-columns using his bare hands and an oyster-knife; now he whiles away the years between wars practising on oysters, a distant glint in his eye as in his mind, he prises a turret off its chassis and hurls it aside. He emerged from his brief personal encounter with 2 1/2 dozen oysters, unbloody, unbowed and triumphant, while his opened oysters bivalves in the air, were led off to a short-lived captivity, concluded, one hopes, without the use of lemon juice.

It is with the greatest of deference that I suggest that four – or was it five? – bands and a single Macnas float do not constitute a parade within the meaning of the act. It was perhaps a little unfair of nature on the sunniest September in decades to rain on the oyster festival; but whatever it did, it did not rain on a parade. It fell instead on a few ambling players, and a few hearteningly unclad Macnas mermaids, with Neptune is his travelling oyster. A parade, it was not.

No doubt future oyster festivals will have longer and grander parades – for how much longer will they have Garreth Phillips? The festival rightly prides itself on its entertainers – the absurdly youthful Linda Martin, who must now be up to her tonsils in middle age, but doesn't look, sound or seem like it; and Margaret Heffernan, whose name suggests she will not get many bookings from Mandate. Different woman. Less money. No tan. But great voice.

And there was Garreth Phillips. He is young – only 23, I hear – but is a quite superb singer of big band classic songs. He can take on Sinatra, Nat King Cole and Righteous Brothers numbers, ones you were sure could never be sung again by any other singer, and make them completely his. His range is astounding, his voice is strong and sure and true and sounds 10 years older that it is. It gets worse. He is absurdly good-looking – one maturish woman at my table was only prevented from having her way with him on stage by a suicide bodyguard of trained oyster-openers, oyster-knives flashing. Has he ever made it to RTE? If not, why not?

Vins de France

There are three bottles of unfinished wine on my kitchen counter. And if they are unfinished, what does that mean? Either that I am a master of self-control, or they're French. Which explanation do you think is correct? If you opt for number one, you're a cretin, and can I borrow a couple of grand? If you opt for number two, it probably means that you, like me, are tired of buying third-rate French wines which end up in the gravy.

This is uneconomical, but it is better than doing the only other thing you can do with the *plonque,* which is to pour it down the drain. I'd leave it out for the slugs and snails, only they are far too fastidious, and leave haughty trails of slime as they head off towards something more delicious.

Writing this pains me. I love France, and I love good French wines, and I love Sopexa, which promotes Food from France; most of all, I love Dominique Geary and Jacinta Delahaye, whose promotion of French foods and wines through Sopexa has not merely widened Irish tastes enormously but has also encouraged the development of similar food products in Ireland.

Trade is one of the wonderful human inventions. It civilises and opens us up to the civilisation and the culture of other people. The essence of trade is the buyer's belief that his money is buying reliable quality, to be repeated on each fresh deal at a fair price. And that essence is nowadays too often missing when I buy French wine.

Like many people, I spend between £5 to £6 on a normal bottle of everyday wine. For that money, I normally know what I am getting from most countries, and not just from the new world whose wines are rightly trumpeted. Once I get to the £5 threshold, I can also be sure that wines from Romania and Bulgaria will be drinking now, with loads of character, a bit of structure, a good nose, and a complex flavour.

But I do not have to go outside the EU for this – Italian wines are a little expensive, but many Iberian wines are extremely good value: the Don Carlos range of wines offer superb value for money, and at an extremely competitive variety of prices.

The point is, with those wines at moderate prices, I know what I am getting. Not with French wines – and not just at the £5 or £6 mark. I can buy a claret or a burgundy for £8 or £9 and the chances are it will taste like stewed tea mixed with industrial alcohol and an infusion of sad and sorry grapes, the identity of which, or the blend, I know nothing – for French winemakers assume that we do not need to know these things. And they assume it because they have been allowed to assume it. We still buy their dreary, listless wines, and they no doubt think we are celebrating French culture.

Wrong. Wine might very well be part of French culture, and be both the adhesive of the French agricultural economy, and its creation – certainly, when one visits French vineyards one always feels that something profoundly important to producers is involved, something beyond our understanding. A god we do not know is being worshipped; and if the wine produced in the course of this worship is good, good: and if not, not good. There is nothing more to say.

But there it is, it seems, if you are French. Vineyards all over France produce a vast lake of thin, tanniny grapejuice which they bottle and label inscrutably, incomprehensibly and almost identically, and then sell to us. And why do we buy it? Why do supermarkets continue to stock their shelves with scores of French wines whose names I can't remember, which look identical, are completely without character and whose only proper destiny is to make gravy or the dog drunk?

Now I really hate saying this; but here goes. The promotion of French wines is still governed by the mystique of France, and the mystique of viticulture, not by ordinary commercial rules of quality and price. Those involved in that promotion, and those captivated by the ethos of French viticulture, normally assume a popular knowledge which simply isn't there – for example, wine-guides invariably list French wines not in some index to which you can instantly refer, but under the region from which the wines come.

Sorry. Most Irish people do not know whether Chateauneuf du Pape comes from Burgundy, Bordeaux, Loire or the Vatican, and more to the point, do not care. Equally, the promotion of French wine in Ireland has depended on the granting to Irish sommeliers the right to wear funny hats and gowns and to call themselves by grandly named titles such as *maitre de vin* this or *grand cheavlier de vin* that, as if some magic part of French culture is thus magically transmitted to Ireland.

Wrong again. The standards of Irish sommeliers in the Sopexa contest last year – announced with huge pomp and even hugher speeches over a very expensive and classically statist dinner at the Shelbourne last year – were extremely poor. We are still learning about wines – but maybe at least we are beginning to learn that a wine should not be chosen for the country it comes from, or because of any cultural associations it brings to our tables, but for two things only – value-for-money and reliability.

Everyone else – the Spanish, the Romanians, the Down-unders and the Chileans appear to understand this. Not the French. Fine. So let's teach them a lesson. Since I am no longer prepared even to try and remember one indistinguishable *chateau* label from another, when there are 20 or 30 alongside one another on the supermarket shelves, I simply will not buy French wine any more, not unless I know the wine is extremely good indeed, or I have beside me one of Alex Findlater's excellent wine-experts like David Miller.

For it is surely time to tell the winemakers of France: the rules from now on are as we make them. And these are the rules – a reliable and recognisable product, please, with an intelligent label which explains things in English, at a right price. Otherwise, no sale.

Foie gras

Not so long ago I scornfully dismissed suggestions that the production of foie gras involved cruelty to the geese. Show me the goose that dislikes eating even in flight, geese take a packed lunch with them and munch like airborne cows so that they can generate the vast amounts of by-product which comes out of their southern end. Pigs after an extra-strength vindaloo washed down with ten pints of bad porter are anally retentive compared with a goose which just had even a Jacob's Cream Cracker.

No matter how little a goose eats – and it *never* eats little – its opposite end generates vast volumes of green-brown wet matter which makes pig-slurry look like something you'd put on a billiard cue. Leave a goose in a field and by dawn you will have a swimming pool of emerald-dun porridge in which you could hide the Americans' submarine Pacific fleet.

Geese's alimentary conduct has, I regret to say, caused me to be cavalier about a goose's innermost feelings. A goose has a heart; it has a soul; and most of all it has a liver, which, after a goose has been gorged on chestnuts, is most tasty fried, fresh and pink, but will more than answer when turned into a paté and consumed with toast.

Admittedly, some people complain about the treatment experienced by the goose when being fed on chestnuts, which consists of its head being inverted and chestnuts being poured down its throat, glug glug glug. Sounds terrible, I know, but a friend who worked on a foie gras farm insists that, come feeding time, geese are incorrigible guzzlers and brawl so much to get first in the chestnut-queue that they have to be kept in line with horsewhips and snarling guard-dogs.

This was how I came to believe that I could eat foie gras with impuntiy; and on a recent trip to Bordeaux – of which more on another date – I can modestly say that at least I did not brush my teeth with it. Otherwise, geese by the gallant battalion surrendered their vital organ for my hourly sustenance – greater love hath no goose than to lay down his liver for a fiend, some might say – until the final day when I consumed a slice of foie gras the size of an elephant's ear.

And so to bed, and odd things began to happen. When I drifted off to sleep a battalion of geese promptly stamped into the bedroom and defecated on my bed; I awoke screaming, threshing away at the bellies and squatting haunches, only to find the room empty.

To sleep again, and this time the geese were in my bed, inspecting the old vitals. The old vitals might not be as vital as they once were, but still … A gallant rearguard action ended up beside the hotel bedroom mirror where I was about to succumb to a sabre-toothed goose which used to prey on dinosaurs – and then I was awake again, gooseless as ever, but gibbering. My next attempt at sleep concluded when a goose built on the lines of a combine harvester was force-feeding me chestnuts still in their prickly skins.

The geese withdrew at about 6 a.m., and a vague, troubled cousin of the thing called sleep took their place. I awoke with a squiche of easy virtue, namely, a start. There were no geese in my bedroom, but I did not need any. I felt as if I had been the dance-floor upon which a herd of overweight rhinos had been lumbering through a high-impact aerobics class. My brain was working with the alacrity of Dememara sugar on its way to the firing squad. My mouth tasted not unlike the squashed solids in a gosling-nappy. My stomach was heaving like the bilge-water in a banana-boat butting out of Calcutta in a mad monsoon. My eyes, ah my eyes; they were tight and small as a pair of goose anuses during an exceedingly rare outbreak of goosely constipation. I have known better days.

My taxi dumped me at Bordeaux airport much in the way that Chicago gangsters abandon the body of a bullet-riddled rival. Miraculously, I made it to Paris. A quick cup of coffee and then to the duty-free (proof of how witless I had been made; to judge from its prices, the Paris airport duty-free is run by the French branch of NIB) before heading for the Dublin flight.

It is 15 feet from duty-free to the boarding gate; and in those mere five yards, a goose apparently swept down and seized my boarding pass from my hands. Certainly the pass was gone, totally, utterly, completely, as the last passengers were shuffling into the Dublin plane, on which my bags were loaded.

As hosts of goosely ghosts cackled in glee and slapped their thighs, panic consuming my decadent old frame, I dashed back to Air France, who issued me with a fresh boarding pass in somewhat less time than it took earth to create the Alps. A thermonuclear flash from my fellow passengers finally welcomed my arrival aboard, 10 minutes late.

I have in the past been so quick to castigate airlines for their time-keeping, never thinking of how blameless they actually are.

Now I know. Blame the goose guzzlers, of whom I am no longer one.

I have had my Damascus. Apologies, my fellow passengers and CityJet; and foie gras, farewell.

Xmas fare

The true season for turkey and ham and pudding falls not on Christmas Day but on those mellow and melancholy days which follow, when one can reflect on the waning season, the imminent year, and on life. Then is the turkey (and its companions) at its best, somewhat freed of its grosser companions of alcoholic excess and noise which tend to obliterate both taste and memory. Even aside from the distracting intensity of Christmas, the food we provide on that day is, like revenge, best taken cold. The flavour of the brown meat of a free-range turkey reaches heavenly proportions after a day of contemplating the wisdom of its juices; ham is royally enriched by the mucus of its own gelatinous devising; bread sauce, left on its own like Mozart with 24 hours to produce a score, can devise some truly delightful palatal melodies; and as for Christmas pudding, brandy butter, rum sauce – ah well now, does the Choral Symphony not come to mind?

The Stephen's Day walk to blow the yulewebs from the frontal lobes is one of the great rites of this time of year. The stomach juices churning like a washing-machine on a slow cycle, the dogs bounding and yelping after illusive or elusive quarry, the sun setting as the chill rises from the icy December clay – and one can almost hug oneself at the thought of the feast ahead, consumed in peace beside a crackling log fire. It was during such a walk, amid an alimentary reflection over the imminent prospect of dark nutty meat, sucked from the generous and juicy confines of a turkey wing, that suddenly the trees around me bowed like dress-uniformed dragoons at a ball as the dance begins.

Have you ever been in a wood when a hurricane comes to call? It is quite beyond my power to give appropriate advice with the power I would wish. But in essence, what I am saying is: in preference, be in Kosovo, be in a balloon with Richard Branson, coat yourself with honey and consort with bears, open up an Israeli tourist office in the kasbah in Algiers or enter the Iraqi national song contest with a little ditty called 'Saddam Hussein is a Zionist Sodomite.' In other words, be elsewhere. For when, as far as the eye can see, trees are touching their toes, and huge boughs are whirling past you like freshly-flung maidens in a polka after the dragoons have had a rum-punch too many, elsewhere is the only place to be.

Of course the problem is that elsewhere can often be an extremely hard place to find, especially when one is trying to cajole five – yes, five – ecstatic dogs out of a howling arboreal typhoon, for such conditions are pure liver and bacon to a dog's taste for fun. All those sticks to fetch – though the sticks were of course 100-foot beech trees, bounding across the landscape like cricket-stumps off on their summer holidays.

Finally, with the dogs scooped, scraped, bawled, beaten, whipped and flogged into the jalopy, we set sail for home. I speak literally. At one point we were overtaken by something large and dark and swirling, yet somehow vaguely familiar. Of course.

Offaly. Followed by largish tracts of Tipperary. Bits of Thurles – the cathedral, say – are very recognisable, even at 100 mph and heading for the Hebrides at 500 feet. I even paused in the fond hope of seeing bits of Kerry containing Jackie Healy-Rae making a similar journey, en route for Inverness, where he could swiftly embitter the pill of Scottish Home Rule, but in that fond hope I was sadly disappointed. Ah, well. Maybe next time. Now, onward to home.

Home. Ah yes, home, a journey of many diversions due to felled trees and crackling ESB cables. Home turned out to be Muroroa Atoll, with doors to the outhouses flapping off hinges like tea-towels on a washing line, even as a neighbouring farm unloaded the odd barn or two onto my lawn. Being a man of rare decision, I locked the hounds, all five of them, in the boot-room, and tried to shut the outhouse doors. When that didn't work, I tried to jam them open. When that didn't work, I tried to furl them.

And when that didn't work, I ran in the kitchen door, so avoiding the dogs, in order to ring the ESB and inform them their electricity was leaking out of their cables all over the place and forming in big pools on the road. Even as I dialled, I was able to see the Rock of Cashel pass right by my kitchen window. By now it is probably the Rock of Aughtermuchty.

At the very second that I reported my findings to the ESB, I heard a contented belch from the boot-room. A micromoment later I had the connecting door open, and recumbent on the floor with huge bellies, with satisfied looks on their faces and with post-prandial cigars in their mouths were the five resident dogs. Beside them, licked perfectly clean, were the dishes which minutes before had borne almost an entire turkey, the greater part of a huge ham, and a positively imperial Christmas pudding; gone, all gone.

Dogs agree. Turkey and ham and pudding are at their best after Christmas. Spam, not. I know.

IRISH OUTINGS

Railway journeys

Railway journeys are not what they were in the good old days, when the original Victorian soot on the windows of Heuston station reminded people what life had been like in the steam age, the epoch when most of the staff appeared to have been recruited.

Appeared is perhaps the wrong word, since few if any staff were ever in evidence and those who were had as clear an understanding of railways as Hottentots have of gas central-heating boilers. At least Hottentots have a language. It was often the case that employees of Heuston responded to no known human language at all, but were lost in some reverie which engaged their attention in the middle distance.

The middle distance did not include the timetable board, which promised you railway departures to places like oscommon and allo and Ga ay and C rk, at times which might once have been present on the board but which had since vanished in that fate which with catholic and generous embrace had engulfed the pharaohs, the firbolgs, Nineveh and Tyre.

A few railway carriages might be found sulking glumly beside platforms, graffiti on their windows recalling the contemporary reaction to the Tay Bridge disaster, the unhappy reverses at Alma and upon the Balaclava Heights.

Inside, they smelt of how one imagines a mushroom factory in a cavern in Monaghan smells, the air immobilised by dense thickets of vertically stacked dust which you could bite lumps out of and chew into a quite passable mud. One could sit in one of these compartments and wait for a locomotive to be appended to the train; and wait, and wait, and wait, while news filtered through of the birth of your child, his first day at school, his leaving, his first-class honours at UCD, his fellowship at Harvard, his marriage, his first child, his divorce, and so on; and meanwhile you too could sketch on the grime on the window your own opinions of the news of the departure from the gold standard, the evacuation from Dunkirk, the formation of the inter-party government, the Mother and Child Scheme, the return of Dev to power; and so on, until your bones were found by another generation of traveller who would sit down and read in his newspaper of the Munich disaster and as years rolled by, hear whispers from other travellers of discord in Algeria, the emergence of de Gaulle, fresh war in Vietnam, etc.

The prudent visitor could always choose to leave the bones of earlier generations of disappointed travellers and repair to one of the two centres of refreshment which

Heuston then sported. One, situated near the main concourse, appeared to have been left over from the Crusades. The history of dietary deficiency through the ages could be traced in the sandwiches, which lacked virtually every vital nutriment known to science yet were still able to be passed off as food.

This deception was not aided by taste, since their flavour was a cross between athlete's foot and fishbait, with perhaps just a touch of carbolic soap.

There was the other centre of refreshment, a canteen painted the colour of a cow's colon, where curious furtive humans, with low brows and little squinting eyes, would gather and wait for news of trains which never arrived, meanwhile smoking cigarette ends which were stored behind ears and drinking mysterious ales which smelt like a tidal estuary after a fish-kill. Meat pies composed of pastry made from bleached shoe-leather and containing brown glue and tiny traces of what was presumed to have been animal protein were obtainable, with the tremendously reassuring prospect that if you did not eat them this year the very same pies would certainly be available next year, or whenever.

Then one day the world changed. CIE, the sovereign master of this little paradise, learned that not everybody was prepared to endure the unendurable. Railway locomotives were bought. New carriages arrived. And Tom Mythven, the railway catering manager, decided that there was no reason why railway passengers and others should not have access to decent meals in a decent environment in Heuston station.

A young architect called Karin O'Sullivan was commissioned, and she took the little den once occupied by dark, brooding troglodytes washing down slurry-pasties with enteric beers and speaking a dialect of Albanian; and opened up and transformed the place so that it more resembles those splendid railway restaurants one finds in France.

It is difficult in this cynical era in which we live for a journalist to be complimentary about anything without suspicions that he is being bribed. Deplorably, this is not the case: I have not met Karin O'Sullivan, and know nothing of her. So it is not even a question of giving a friend a puff. Alas, nothing of the kind. She has simply designed one of the most elegant restaurants in Dublin and which is as much intended for the outside trade as it is for travellers.

The food is really excellent, as unrelated to the fare once available in the former dungeon as a Chopin nocturne is to the sound of a tooth being sharpened with a broken bottle. Lunch is served every day throughout the week, including Sundays, and the set menu is only £9. Car-parking is of course no problem. It really is quite wonderful.

This is uncommonly like a puff. Are you sure you are not being bribed?

Certain.

Hmm.

West Cork in September

'Oh', they said, 'do not bother with West Cork in September. For September is autumntime and the seas are grown cold. The sun barely shines. Fogs come up and fill the air. Oh, do not bother with West Cork in September. Go instead, they said, in high summer, when the seas are warm and the days are long and the harvest is still in the field, before the swifts have vanished for Africa, before winter closes in.

'Even in Schull, they said, Oh what a shame, you've missed the good weather. Still it's nice now, nice and quiet, even if it's too cold for swimming. You can walk to heart's content; but it is too cold to swim. Far too cold.'

And, true enough, that first day in Schull it did seem that the best of the weather was gone. There were great grey clouds scudding autumnly around the skies and the sun had that worn and pallid look which tells you that even on cloudless days it will never warm, never tan, never burn the bared hide of a human being. Yet that first day I dipped a querulous toe into the waters of a deserted quayside near Schull. It did not seem cold, merely no longer warm, and had that soft tingle of soda-water on the lips.

A quick look around and then off with the clothes – all of them, no point letting inert garments sense the pleasure of water when your skin is so much better equipped – and then into the water. A moment's chill and then the glorious sensation of zesty clean water all over the body. All over.

Listen here. Do not believe them when they tell you it is all much of a muchness whether you wear togs when you swim. Something completely new happens when you feel the flush of cold water surging along your unclad keel and tingly liquid ozone splashing over the bare fo'c'sle, the naked afterdeck. It is only when you have immersed yourself in the bubbling waters of the Atlantic that you understand how tramp-steamers last so long churning through pounding coastal waters. It is pure joy. The only way to swim. And, as it happens, not in the least cold, in the waters of West Cork, this September, this early autumn.

Not cold at all – in fact it was addictively wonderful. And far from the sun being archly and winsomely pallid, it was radiant and strong. Each day we gloated as we looked at the weather map and saw that the length and breadth of Ireland there was cloud cover, drizzle, perpetual sunlessness. But in West Cork a different dispensation ruled. Day after day dawned bright and brilliant, the sun sizzling above in the heavens.

In the bank of fuchsia outside the kitchen windows bees choired their keen monotone of industry, the undulating hum of the hive, like monks plainchanting their ways through a ceaseless compline. Blackberries sat like grapes, the hedgerows transformed into vast untamed vines.

Swallows gathered on the telephone line and grumbled about their imminent return to Africa and discussed hiding from the swallow-monitors, the ones that shoo them off to Zimbabwe each autumn, until they had finished their last patrol and vanished too. No doubt, then, the untruant truant swallows might then emerge and learn what it is to spend a Christmas in West Cork.

No fear of Christmas just yet, or Christmas weather, not in West Cork this September, with a sun brilliant before we awoke warming the seas for our morning dip. It only struck me during my morning dips how much the men of the Forty Foot must resent the stupid larceny which prevented them from enjoying their morning swim as it should be taken – naked, quite naked. How they must keen as they watch the cold refreshing breakers lapping over the rocks of the Forty Foot and know that they can no longer swim there in the way that once they did.

No doubt it was anachronistic that men only were allowed to swim there. Women who wanted to bathe there should have been allowed to, on the same terms as the men – naked. And if they did not like those terms, too bad. But each year certain silly women complained that it was wrong that men alone were allowed to bathe at the Forty Foot. Each year they told the media they were going out to swim with the men. Each year these prudish, ostentatious infants duly turned up, in their bathing costumes, amidst naked men, acting as if they were being oh so daring, *Assumpta, look at me,* and while cameras clicked, flung themselves in the water.

So now the Forty Foot is virtually finished as a place where people can swim without regard to clothing. A shame. There is nothing like it in this world. It is the only way to swim and to sunbathe. What psychic damage has been done to people that they feel the need to don clothing in order to undress? On one all-but-deserted beach I saw three people changing beneath huge towels like buffaloes wrestling beneath a collapsed marquee. Who were they hiding their bodies from? What great secrets have they that they must conceal them from the world?

It is not true, as some say, that what is objectionable about nudity is that it only encourages the beautiful. It is not about beauty. Nor is it true that nudity encourages the ugly to expose their ugliness; the ordinary swimming costume does that anyway. What people object to about people bathing naked is their *freedom.* Those enchained by inhibition resent the liberties of those not so inhibited; they yearn for others to share their chains.

In vain in West Cork. Day after day we visited the numerous coves and swam in their enchanting seas. Winter bared its teeth at us one day, with grey lashing seas and cold slate-skies, and then departed as we returned to the Indian summer of this great summer of 1995. And at night the full moon, as bright as a sun, its cerulean light illuminating the land from the mountains to the sea.

'Oh do not go to West Cork in September,' they said. I agree. 'Do not go to West Cork in September. An odd, nude man gambols happily in the surf in September. Oh, go nowhere near West Cork in September. For he is mad.'

Looking for Temple Bar

If you haven't read Nuala O'Faolain's column last Monday on the behaviour of Telecom and Dublin Tourism, do so. She points out that the new phone cabins in Dublin have no information or operator services, and Dublin Tourism's telephone service to tourists depends on a pay-while-you-wait principle, not dissimilar to a sex-line, which in both my case and Nuala's must depend on what we *imagine* happens.

Sometimes it seems our entire administrative culture is based on the notion that we shouldn't expect help from the administration of the state or its services, but should simply ask a citizen. Which is what happened to Nuala. A foreign tourist, unable to find out anything about the Casino in Marino, asked her to help out. Nuala obliged, poor fool.

She embarked upon a long day's telephonic journey into the night, which ended up with her shovelling pounds and pounds into a payphone, trying to find out about the Casino, Marino. All she got was a series of recorded messages informing her about sporting events, bungee jumping, hedgehog steeplechase, cow handicap, or whatever.

The culture that a) people know or b) can ask, infuses the attitude of the state and semi-states towards the people of the State. Any Irish person driving from Dublin to Dalkey will soon realise that the wretched signposting which brought them halfway to their destination, and has abandoned them at a ten-exit roundabout in the middle of a housing estate, is a spent force; now is the time to ask.

I have written about this before. I expect to write about it again. And again. The notion that the duty of those who erect signposts is to make the signposts sufficient unto themselves, without the need to ask for further assistance, is foreign to our signpost erectors. Instead, they like to encourage social inter-activeness halfway through the journey, by obliging us to ask for directions.

It is impossible to follow any series of signs in Dublin all the way through to one's destination, unless it is to Dublin City Port, which for some reason is well signposted – perhaps to enable demented tourists to escape before they slay the signpost erectors of our land by an adroit use of stout metal posts.

On the Continent, they assume that visitors to cities a) will not know their way and b) not be able to ask their way. In dear old anglophone Dublin, we assume that visitors can speak English and will get to their destination, one way or another. Hence the scores of baffled tourists standing in the rain, turning maps around, and twisting their heads to get the proper orientation. They were to be seen all over the capital city in recent weeks, looking for the unsignposted Temple Bar or the unsignposted O'Connell Bridge.

Many tourists looking for Temple Bar will opt for Dublin Bus; there they will discover an ark from the past, buses which use cash. But the old-fashioned buses had conductors to collect fares. The modern Dublin bus compels the passengers to pay in coins and be given change as they enter; and the queue shuffles slowly on to the bus.

If, that is, the bus had stopped in the first place. Dublin buses are by request. People at a stop must indicate to the approaching driver that they want his bus. But nowhere on Dublin bus-stops is this information given. I have seen so many tourists standing, slack-jawed, while buses thunder by, no doubt wondering what sort of company Dublin Bus is. A good question. It is the sort of company which introduced two-door buses some twenty years ago, at huge expense, but still does not use the second door, *even though the buses instruct the passengers to exit from it.*

Of course Ulf and Sigismund, our foreign tourists, who have actually managed to get on to a bus for Temple Bar after a wait of several days, cannot possibly know that the second door is a special and expensive ornament, without any utilitarian function whatsoever. After their bus has taken half-an-hour to travel a distance it would take a pedestrian five minutes to walk, U & S will cluster expectantly around the rear exit, ready to bail out when Temple Bar is reached, and will remain expectantly there until they are back at the terminus, with the last bus of the night gone.

They might choose at this point to get a taxi to Temple Bar, a vain endeavour in Dublin these days. There are no taxis at night. The entire taxi system is a government-run, monopolistic conspiracy against the public. The purpose of the system is to ensure a return on expensive taxi-plates, not to provide a cheap, flexible service to the people of Dublin.

Ulf and Sigismund, our stranded tourists at the bus depot (if they can find a phonebox which has a list of operator-services) will be able to call a hackney. But the administrative system which has so little regard for the bemused foreigner, here comes into its own. That system has made it illegal for hackneys to have fare-meters. Instead, the driver has to look at a chart he alone possesses, and read the tachometer he alone can see, come up with a fare which he alone knows the meaning of.

And Ulf and Sigismund must pay the fare. They are finally at Temple Bar. But it is closed. Nothing is open. The administrative system which cannot manage to put up a logical sequence of signposts, and which makes it illegal for hackneys to have meters, also decides that it is a criminal offence for a pub to sell Guinness at ten-past-two in the morning.

Time to go home. But Ulf and Sigismund cannot remember the address of their B & B. There is no phone book in the kiosk. They phone directory enquiries with the name of the B & B. Though the B & B's addresss is listed in the phone book, Telecom operators decline to give it, or any other address over the phone. Instead, Ulf and Sigismund will have to knock on a door, and do what the driver looking for Dalkey must do. Ask a citizen; because the State won't help you.

Castle Leslie

Monaghan and Cavan people will assure you they are two distinct and different species, as alike as wallabies and seals. But what actually divides them are merely those tiny differences you find between close kin, and the kinship is to be measured in what they have most in common – their enterprise – they do not complain, they do not whine, they do not call for more grants.

Some people say it is the influence of Protestant Ulster which causes this self-reliance and industry; which hardly explains the absence of those qualities within certain areas of Northern Ireland.

Monaghan, for example, has some of the poorest land in Ireland, it is unfortunately located along a bloodily disputed border, and largely has no natural resources. As a tourist venue, it is not causing sleepless nights in Thailand.

Its beaches have yet to be located. Its sun is intermittent, and seldom raises palm trees above ground. The Gulf Stream is at its weakest here. The coral reefs of Monaghan are a negligible quantity. Not even its most lurid laureates are moved to compare it to Hawaii.

Surfers waiting with their boards to ride the white rollers on Carrickmacross's sea-less shores must learn patience. All in all, what Monaghan has, Monaghan must make, in luck as in all matters.

And it has been a hard quarter of a century or so for the county, and not least for those whose melancholy duty it is to make Castle Leslie turn a penny or two to pay for its keep. Big houses such as Castle Leslie are good ideas for Saudi princes, and not bad ideas for most of us to spend an idle weekend in, and coming over all languid and Bridesheadian – what ho, Bertie, care for a spot of croquet, what?

Fantasy over, we return to our small and comfortable homes where draughts are a game played on a black and white board, and bedrooms are *not* deep-freezers with a single-bar electric fire glowing sulkily in the corner.

Sammy Leslie knows all too well about the truth of a big house like Castle Leslie. Yes, it is beautiful, and set amongst the most beautiful woodlands and overlooking one of the most enchanting loughs in Ireland; but such things, like racing stables and ocean-going yachts, have to be paid for.

Castle Leslie sucks up cash as a vacuum-cleaner inhales dust. Its vast Gothic roof is in fact a device for distributing internal heat to Monaghan at large. Those great stone floors could extinguish the fires of hell without breaking into a sweat. And the vast windows can lose money faster than a group from Alcoholic Gamblers Anonymous cutting loose on a daytrip in Las Vegas.

Castle Leslie has been kept going by furious energy and courage over the troubled decades. It has served as a hotel and as an equestrian centre, and Sammy has somehow or other contrived to keep the place together.

She has even managed to renovate the rooms and warm them for paying guests, without turning them into early experiments in cryogenics. Her latest venture is a Gourmet Circle for Monaghan, using largely food produced in the county and wines, thankfully, which are not.

The heart does not lift at the thought of *Chateau Hackballscross,* and lies still in its bed at the mention of *Scotstown Cabernet Sauvignon* and refuses to leave it. Wise old heart.

Yet Monaghan does produce most of the other ingredients for a banquet, such as the one Sammy plans for the opening night of the Castle Leslie Gourmet Circle. Permit me a few column inches to regale you with *canapés* of yakatori mushrooms, quail, smoked duck and something called Others to be decided.

Dinner will consist of quail eggs set in consommé, warm salad with smoked duck in citrus vinaigrette, mushroom soup, *timbale* of Glaslough pike on a bed of spinach, pear sorbet, chicken *crepenettes* with *lardons, croutons* and mushrooms, marriage of venison or pheasant and turkey, with orange and cranberry *jus* and turnip *gratin,* trio of desserts of yoghurt with ice cream and red berry coulis, *petit pot de cremé* with praline, and blackberry cobblers, plus tea and coffee, and not a drop of Sauvignon Blanc de Ballybay to be seen. Instead, every course will be accompanied by a different wine from Woodford Bourne.

Why all this space for a gourmet circle? Two reasons. One, everybody benefits, as Kinsale has shown and others have since discovered, by an improvement in culinary standards. Two, Castle Leslie has been home to one of the most bizarre and unpredictable families in Irish history.

An early Leslie, a bishop, married a woman about forty years younger than he, and proceeded to father about a dozen children before he dropped the mitre, aged one hundred.

One might jest about Monaghan wines, but in the last century, the Leslie greenhouses produced vast amounts of exotic fruit – a *Chateau Leslée* would have been then perfectly acceptable.

The Leslies were among the few landed families to come out ardently for Home Rule, at a time when it was not socially fashionable for them to do so, and even became Catholics, for whatever reason. More recently, one Leslie spent five years in a German prisoner-of-war camp and another flew Spitfires. Both, happily, are with us still, alive and no doubt intending to emulate the bishop in the longevity stakes, though not, Sammy is probably the first to wish, in the paternity stakes.

One can have too much of a good thing, even when that good thing is a Leslie. The only thing certain about the tribe is its complete uncertainty about what it will do next.

A question, though, and one I will be coming back to soon. No doubt the wines consumed in Castle Leslie will be lawful and duty-paid. But how many people in the Border counties actually buy their wine in the Republic? How much money is given over to the British Exchequer every year because of our punitive, idiotic alcohol duties?

Several friends from Britain came on holiday this summer with their cars stuffed with enough wine to last them their visit. The time has come – we must harmonise alcohol duties. It is costing us money, and tourists.

Hunting

THE silhouette, dark, low and vulpine, slithered across the road like a snake on legs, paused to look over its shoulder at the distant huntsmen and women on their horses and at their hounds, turning in baffled, snuffling circles, then slid with anguilline ease through the hedge, 'Away, away,' came the cry as the brush of their quarry vanished into the undergrowth.

The huntsman tootled the odd despairing yelp from his horn, the howl of a bitch in heat, and the hounds moved towards the gapless hedge across the road where the fox had found a gap as effortlessly as an eel finds a hole in mud.

At the top of the field, where the riders had been looking in the wrong direction, the horses turned, all dilated nostrils and wide eyes and prancing hooves, their breath steaming as if from the boiler of a locomotive. The hunt spiralled down the field towards the gate opening onto the lower road as hounds galloped up and down the impenetrable hedge, behind them the huntsman's horse cantering handsomely, muscles moving like large regulated pistons under his noble buttocks, as his rider searched for an entrance into the estate in which the fox had vanished.

A hunt is a fine thing to watch. It is primarily about hounds and their master, the man (or woman) who trains them, who feeds them and disciplines them, who keeps them on lean commons so that they remain peckish for the fray, yet not so promiscuously carnivorous that any passing sheep will do. A hound that separates for long from the pack will not be allowed back, and probably has a limited future.

There is a tale of a hound which would not obey the rules of the kennel and was sent packing. Kindly neighbours took pity on it, and gave it a home. Shortly afterwards the cat disappeared. The cat's full and sorry fate became evident only when the hound passed the cat's collar undigested: the rest of the cat, being digestible and probably delicious, was less identifiable.

It is a hard life being a hound; but if hounds are not hounds, what are they but memories and prints on walls? It is a hard life being a fox, too; but not made hard so much by the odd hunt which comes its way but by the vicissitudes of having to live on its wits. To the slow, the old, comes the grave of hunger, of disease, of exposure, and not soon enough. How long does it take a fox to die of natural causes? Might not the swift hunger of a pack of dogs, whose individuals can dispose of a cat in seconds, collectively deliver to a fox a hastier and more merciful end?

But that is not why people go on hunts; nor is it as a means of pest-control. The hunting lobby did a bad day's work when it topped it the virtuous and suggested that it was no more than vermin-controlling cavalry. Hunts are not. They are people who love riding horses and they adore the thrill and the uncertainties of a chase where the quarry is as artful and as blessed with guile as a fox in its prime.

They must learn patience too – the patience which comes from the lost scent as the steaming horses clatter and clomp and the huntsman reassembles and rechoruses his hounds, which snuffle with eager stupidity in every hedgerow cranny. The truth is that the combined wit of horse and hound and huntsman and hunt is barely a match for the wickedly devious mind of the fox, the most perfect proof of non-verbal intelligence that we can find in Ireland outside a zoo.

And so it proved. The gates of the estate were closed, the hedges too high to jump. The fox reappeared, loping casually over its far fields, graceful as an Ethiopian, almost as if it knew what entrances were locked and which ones would be opened upon the command of a bell. And this brings us to the point of the hunt; it is not hunting. The point is companionship and uncertainty on horseback. While the huntsman hurried off on his small, lean horse to investigate a possible opening, the huntsmen and women circled affably, some of the men inhaling on cigarettes in the odd, emphatic way of riders.

The horses were not grand by any means. A couple resembled the offspring of pit-pony-out-of-camel, shaggy things with strange, glued-on legs and wandering eyes, as if they had not seen full daylight before. Others seemed to nourish ambitions to bear a hussar; others were from that arrow-straight guardian of Irish stock, the brood mare, sound of neck and strong of heart and steady over the fences.

The huntsman chivvied his hounds through a lane, and in the amber light of a November noon horses and hounds vanished down it, mud splashing in wet crescents around them, dogs lolloping, tongues lolling, the horn tootling, enough to scare a wise fox well clear of them. If they get a fox, it will be a lucky fox, one that this night or next will not now die of cold or famine or disease, but will be instantly despatched. It is nature, sort of: and it is part of the Irish countryside. Long may it flourish.

OUTINGS ABROAD

Florida

Watching the recent television pictures of hurricane-ravaged Florida only left one question in one's mind. Why does any single person live there at all, never mind the millions who appear to?

The weather is simply appalling; they appear to have just two seasons – microwave and hurricane.

There is, in fact, much to recommend the hurricane season, because in addition to reducing the temperature to below boiling point, it also disperses the mosquito population.

Admittedly, there are some negative aspects to the hurricane season, not the least being that, in addition to destroying – for the time being – the mosquito population, it destroys the state in its entirety.

This seems a high price to pay to get rid of the mosquitoes, since they are back within days, but the state takes several years to recover, at which point it is time for another hurricane.

Perhaps Florida is testimony to the unquenchable optimism of human nature. Only optimism could cause people to attempt to inhabit a place which makes Mars seem like Kinsale. Many people in Florida live in what Americans call mobile homes. Mobile is right. Most of them are now in Texas.

In fact, Texas is so habituated to windborne architecture arriving out of the blue that they have even collected it all and called it Mobile, made up of buildings which started out in Florida.

Mind you, even homes that are not called mobile are in Texas as well, which makes one wonder what causes people to choose one variety of home over another. Maybe the presence of wheels on a house is one of those design features such as concrete balustrades which in Ireland make neo-Georgian homes irresistible to certain buyers.

But the regular appearance of thermonuclear hurricanes windblasting the entire state into the world's largest billiard table is not the only reason for regarding Florida as a baffling place to live. When it is not hurricaning, the temperature is seldom below the fervid nineties, with humidity weighing in at about blood temperature.

Even aside from the mosquitoes, which in Florida are about the size of Irish magpies and which set about their victims with lump hammers, life outdoors in Florida is unbearable. One of the reasons why the residents of the state generate such huge bottoms is their unbelievable consumption of sugar-laden soft drinks to compensate for the catastrophic liquid loss which occurs within seconds of going outside.

That might not be so bad if the sweat were able to evaporate, thus creating a cooling effect, but in conditions of 100% humidity this is not possible. Instead, the sweat gathers around people's feet in small pools in which mosquitoes can lay their eggs.

Much of Florida that is not Miami is in fact swamp where mosquitoes can lay their eggs without even bothering to look, dumping them like bombers cascading incendiaries. The mosquitoes in such areas have teeth only slightly smaller than the teeth in the jaws of the alligators which abound there.

The reason why alligators are so common in the swamps is that they are the only form of legged life which can live underwater.

On land, legged animals are promptly mugged by mosquitoes and hauled off to the mosquitoes' lairs, where they are turned into banquets, with mosquitoes carousing through the night, tossing gnawed animal thighbones over their shoulders and generally imitating Henry VIII.

Alligators are spared this fate because they spend their entire lives just beneath the Florida swamps, with only their eyes blinking dolefully above the surface. A gloomy lot, the Florida alligators, made all the more unhappy by their knowledge that their cousins in Africa can lie in the sun and grab passing villagers and generally party the entire time.

No parties for the alligators of Florida or for anybody else either. You can hardly party if there is not a single intact building in the entire state or if you are working all the daylight hours to rebuild your home after the last big blow.

And anyway, who can feel like partying when you live in a state which collects old people from all over the US, either for recycling or to give young hoodlums some strangling practice in the state's own throttle bank, and which has entire communities whose average age exceeds their blood temperature?

Admittedly, not everybody in Florida is in their late nineties. The Cuban criminals, whose recreations with chainsaws make them such persuasive interrogators, are not in their nineties. Nor are the Colombians who conduct massacres and mutilations much in the way that Americans in other states have cookie parties.

And nor, indeed, are the legions of black and white junkies in the state in their nineties. Their age is more likely to be close to most adult's shoe size.

Being mugged by a nine-year-old is no sweeter than being mugged by a 19-year-old. Schoolteachers in Miami feel so strongly about this that children going into school have to be body-searched to make sure that they do not reprimand teacher with the help of an Uzi or a Browning 9mm, or settle their differences in the playground so as to leave it resembling a Colombian cookie party which has recently been discussing some missing crack.

If there is anything to be said for global warming it is that one of the first places to disappear will be Florida. The entire state is about two inches above high tide; they get flood warnings if more than one hundred people swim in the sea simultaneously.

But this seldom happens because there are so many terrible inhabitants in the sea – barracuda and shark and jellyfish which can stun a nuclear submarine and large sargassoes of human poo – that everybody swims in swimming pools.

And the truth is that nobody likes Florida. New York, New York, yodels the Manhattanite. There is nothing finer, cries the lady from Carolina. Nothing plain about the state of Maine, is the happy riposte. I'd rather pay a load of moose debts than leave Massachusetts, opines another. I'd sooner dwell in a yeti hut than leave Connecticut, warbles the Yale student. There is nothing more horrida than the state of Florida, moos the Miami man as he watches mosquitoes making off with his children in their beaks and hurricane Bertram disappear over the horizon with his supposedly immobile home.

Air crashes

The year's crop of aircraft accidents began early enough in 1994 – a Russian Tupolev crashing upon take-off before the New Year had even brushed its teeth. It was the kind of crash which is most common – some fault of pilot or machine in those awful, hazardous moments soon after take-off. It was not the kind of crash which is the only kind for which passengers all over the world are given advice. The reason for this is that the accident for which people in airliners are briefed does not happen, has virtually never happened and will never happen. Yet, nonetheless, the hypothetical accident which virtually cannot happen is the only one for which passengers are prepared.

Why is this? I cannot say. Perhaps the preparation which airlines engage in is some form of displacement activity; since they can do nothing, and we can do nothing, about the form of air disaster which claims most lives in a year, except to yell a brief act of contrition, they can console themselves with pre-flight 'safety' procedures which are nothing of the kind. If these displacement activities have any purpose, it is to convince the people flying with the airlines concerned that they are in the hands of professionals. This is done by creating a fiction.

The fiction runs thus. If the aeroplane runs into difficulty flying over the sea, the pilot will probably try to ditch his plane on to the water, using all the skills and training acquired over the years. The plane will come splashing down, bouncing in the way which we have all seen in the cinema, while the passengers are braced in the 'crash' position.

Once the plane has bounced to a halt, the flight attendants leap to the emergency exists and haul them open; we meanwhile, having been briefly educated at the onset of the flight in the ways and wiles of the life-jacket, don these little yellow affairs and dutifully file out on the wing, from which we all jump into the sloshing brine. Once in, we inflate our jackets and swim around in circles, possibly singing sea-shanties and merry little tunes we learned beside the old campfire, our spirits being kept up by the sterling young flight attendants.

Night begins to fall, and we light the little lamps on the life-jackets the airlines have provided us with; then, just as we begin to lose faith, just as the little old lady in the print dress who has been such a, well, *brick*, since the plane put down, begins to wander in her wits a little, a rescue plane is sighted! We are saved! And, as we scramble into flying boat which lands alongside us, we cheer our gallant skipper and her doughty crew and flight attendants. Hip, hip! Etc.

Now. Let us be frank. This cannot happen. OK, perhaps, for a 1930s de Havilland bi-plane; OK certainly for the film-makers; rubbish for us, the regular flyers. It is nonsense (and nonsense to which I was treated for a recent Budapest-Zurich flight which overflew nothing more maritime than a lidless lavatory cistern).

Most planes that crash do so at landing or take-off. Some perform what is called a controlled flight into terrain – that is to say, the pilot flies into the ground thinking it is the sky. In such circumstances, life-jackets are as much use as dental floss in saving your life.

But what about something happening at altitude? Can the pilot not then steer his craft and splash down on the waters of the friendly Atlantic?

No doubt, no doubt, on film. In reality, something happening at altitude will cause the plane to break up, probably close to the speed of sound, six miles up, in which case we are back to dental floss again. But what if the plane runs out of fuel: can the pilot not glide his craft down to seas and there enable us all to follow our intrepid stewardesses on to the wings?

No. Because there is no ground effect beneath a plane flying over the water; it plummets much more steeply than the pilot can do anything to avoid. If he/she has trained over water, it was with an empty plane with engines, not a full one with no engines. It is virtually impossible for a plane to glide on to water. What would happen is that the plane would crash into a probably violent sea with neck-fracturing momentum and break up and sink; no bonfire ditties as we paddle in circles, no stewardesses swimming around to check if we are OK, just a few empty life-jackets to tell the corpse collectors about which full-fathom five marks our graves.

Why are we then briefed on an accident which cannot happen, and not one which will – say fire on take-off? Is it because the reality of fire is that the young, the strong, the violent – the ones who fight their way to the exits – will survive, and the old, the infirm, the pregnant, die? Perhaps the advice we should get – that the slow are doomed and should sit back and accept it – is not the message which airline companies like to give their passengers.

Oh, very well. Can't argue with that. But is it not time that airlines did the sensible thing which air forces do all over the world, and insist that we all fly in seats facing backwards, thereby lessening the disabling effects of both impact and turbulence? It is only my opinion, and a remarkably modest one, too, considering the volumes of common-sense it incorporates: but would not Aer Lingus do wonders for its market share if it decided that all its seats faced backwards?

Would it not be incredibly wise if it told its passengers: 'Look, we are grown-ups and you, for the most part, are grown-ups, and we really don't believe any of this garbage about life-jackets, but we do believe that sometimes things can go wrong, so we have placed your seats facing backwards, so that the seat backs absorb as much undesired impact as possible?'

As rescue plans go, it is modest: but if I were to be given a choice between an airliner which gave me free baby bottles of gin and smoked salmon that looks – and tastes – as if it were made from reconstituted condoms, and one which said 'Look, flying can be dangerous: let's be sensible about this and fly backwards', the latter would get my money – or rather, this newspaper's – every time. Look Up, it's the airline with its priorities right.

Paris

Paris again, and the heart lifts. It is no more spring there at the moment than it has been here. The daffodils are late, the grass is scalded brown and grey by a winter which has not yet quite lifted its siege, and the skies were as drab and lifeless as clotheslines draped in old fleeces.

But Paris is Paris. It remains the capital of European culture, the heart and soul of the Continent, and those who govern Paris, whether it is through their own egotistical impulse or because of their reverence for the greatest city in the world, have a view of the future of their city which no other planners in Europe possess.

They do not fumble from one set of confused blueprints to another; they seem to have a certainty about the future of their city which is absent in its entirety from the process of planning in Ireland. Perhaps our greatest natural vice has been to see the future and the past as convenient objects of happenstance upon which to rest the plank of the largely accidental present.

Paris is the truly great human invention it is because it combines the structure of planners who know their minds with the inventiveness and fertility of the imagination of French civilisation. It has been the most enduring and the greatest imagination within that thing which we call European civilisation, and it is no exaggeration to say that the new Louvre Museum extensions are classically within that tradition.

That the famous Pyramid within the Louvre was designed by an American-Chinese architect only serves to reinforce the point. The great enduring civilisations of the world have been enriched by learning and wisdom from other cultures. All that is required is the cultural self-confidence which allows them to absorb that learning and wisdom and to regard the past and its inheritances not as a prison, but as an opportunity.

The original Louvre, dating from 1793, was the second most visited museum in the world, but it was locked into the quarters it had inhabited for two centuries along the Seine. There was virtually nowhere for it to expand, other than underground and into government buildings. But to go underground was to intensify that sense of oppression caused by the three million annual visitors.

What the museum needed was light and space, height and air. People needed to breathe. The solution was sheer architectural genius. The now-famous Pyramid, with its elaborate rigging of steel hausers supporting a transparent angular cone over a central connecting underground cavern, is only part of the solution. There has been an elegant conceit based upon the creation of roofed areas of permanent open-air.

Former car-parks behind old Ministry of Finance buildings have been covered with transparent roofs; marble and tiles have been laid where Citroens and Renaults once dozed through the day, and instead equestrian and outdoor statues have been erected in broad but weatherless daylight. Two great open-air, protected vaults have been created, abolishing that sense of footsore, sweaty oppression which people inevitably experience when gathered in great numbers beneath low ceilings and electric lights.

This marvellous extension of the Louvre must be one of the most architecturally clever and thoroughly humane transformation of a building which has yet been devised. The original building, the Aile Richelieu, dating from the 1850s, combined offices with predictably extravagant quarters for the enchantingly preposterous Napoleon III.

All but the Napoleonic quarters was gutted in the conversion of a bureaucratic beehive into a vast and airy place for the public to gather. The three courtyards within the Aile Richelieu were roofed, and the creation of sunlit areas within the Louvre, pioneered by the Pyramid, was turned into a central feature of the museum.

Huge numbers now file into the covered auditoriums connecting the three wings of the museum; already the turnover has been virtually doubled since the erection of the Pyramid, and with the recent opening of the Richelieu wing, certainly there was the other day no sense of being crowded in a museum, although thousands of people were filing through in awed and airy piety.

There is, of course, an air of imperial loot abut any Western museum; one wonders what any Iraqi visitor to the ground floor of the Richelieu wing makes of the ground floor and its oriental antiquities. Well might one translate the name of the former French chief minister of Louis XIII as *wealthy place*. For in this wealthy place is wealth others might claim to be theirs, such as the Mesopotamian collections from thousands of years before Christ.

Myself, I would say they should stay where they are. The civilisations which grew among the alluvial gardens of the Tigris and the Euphrates are no more the property of present-day Iraq than the shamrock; and the cuneiform script on stone and statue, written in Assayrian and other languages, tells us soberingly of the transience of empire and the folly of might.

Those who constructed the famous winged bulls of King Sargon II housed within *le cour Khogsabad*, dating from 720 BC, no doubt thought they were dealing with eternal verities. All around those evocations – two of which are superb copies – are artefacts bearing inscription after cuneiform inscription referring to local kings who were declared to be lord of land, master of the skies, eternal emperor of the oceans, and whose kingship and whose empires are now mere dust, forgotten everywhere but in the bright and sunlit rooms of the Louvre.

This epoch will pass; not much of cultural or artistic merit, I suspect, of the past 50 years will endure. Most will vanish into the dust which engulfed Sargon and his empire, and be forgotten. But I suspect that the visionary work done in the Louvre in recent years, the brilliant compromise reconciling the architecture of revolutionary France, of the Second Empire and of the final decade before the third millennium will stand out virtually above all.

Croyland Abbey

Dark was seeping in from beyond the Dogger Bank that evening as we drove through the flatlands of Lincolnshire, away from Croyland Abbey.

Croyland was once an island in the wetlands and fens beneath The Wash, that great gash in the ribs of the east coast of England. In other parts of Lincolnshire, place names end in -by and -thorpe, proof of the rule of Danes. There is even a Scandinavian cast to the dialect and a slow lugubriousness in demeanour brought down from the Skaggerak in the longships a millennium and more ago. But around Croyland the placenames end in -ston and -well, Anglo-Saxon toponymics that show that the Vikings did not settle close to Croyland.

By the time the Northman came to Lincolnshire, worship in Croyland had been well established by a young Mercian nobleman, Guthiac, who had found seclusion there in 699. The foundation stone of the abbey was laid in 716. The Danes fell on the place in 870, destroying the abbey and butchering the monks. And when the invaders were gone the surviving monks regathered and refounded their abbey in the Saxon style under the rule of St Benedict. The reformed abbey had the first tuned peal of bells in England, and they were named after celebrated monks of the community – Guthiac, Bartholomew, Beccelm, Turketyl, Tatwin, Pega and Brega.

Fresh invaders, cousins of the Norsemen, arrived, and the area round Croyland proved as resistant to them as it had been to the Danes. Hereward the Wake led his guerrilla war against the Normans and was buried in the Abbey, along with his wife, Torfrida, and his mother, the gallant Lady Godiva. Inevitably, the Norman French triumphed and in 1109, Joffrid of Orleans became abbot and an extensive monastery in the Norman style was constructed.

The abbey became a centre of learning and one abbot founded a college at Cambridge, known today as Magdalene. Fires regularly visited the abbey and it was frequently rebuilt, the perpendicular style being added by the predominant early Norman. Through the centuries the Benedictine rule was adhered to, the day beginning at 2 a.m., with breakfast six hours later. That rule and the civilisation of which it was a centre came to an end on December 4th, 1539, when Henry VIII dissolved the monasteries of England and Ireland – to my mind one of the great cultural and social calamities in the history of the two islands.

Much of Croyland was destroyed; choir, transept, tower and monastic buildings levelled. But the nave remained and it continued to serve as a parish church. And as Croyland had stood against Norse and Norman, in time it stood against Roundhead too, and the nave and the ramparts around were besieged for three months.

But as deadly a foe to the church was time. The nave roof collapsed, the south aisle was removed to provide stone for buttresses and for local housebuilding. Yet the church survived as a church, though with only a fraction of the great building it had once been. It retained a curious arch alongside the present nave, a relic of the old Norman Abbey, when four such arches existed. Those others were felled by the Henrician barbarians.

The church survived other vicissitudes too; at one stage both its rector, James Benson, and its sexton, William Hill, were completely blind: and it survived the vigorous meddling of the Victorians, so that it remained a still-wonderful building, standing great against the skyline of the fenland, the Wash and the distant North sea that Sunday evening we were there, in time for service.

We crept in, the vast stones echoing to our tentative footsteps and the guilty metal clink of eased bolts. Inside, the rector was conducting evensong. His congregation consisted of a single old woman who tremulously sang the responses.

No doubt they felt they were worshipping God; and no doubt in such worship, numbers do not count. Yet evensong is a public ceremonial, and our visit felt like a grotesque invasion of privacy, a cumbrous and burly trespass upon a discreetly commemorated family shame. And not just in Croyland. The Church of England, whose forlorn spires peer above the oak and beech of countless hamlets, possesses hundreds of churches which are locked and unvisited, tenanted by web and rot and occasional curates preaching to stone.

It was a sobering thought as we left and the sun set on the fens and on the steeples of a now abandoned religion. Is that it? Is the creed established in the wetlands of Lincolnshire 1300 years ago now expired? The truth is, the astonishing truth is, that more people attend Muslim mosques each week in England than attend Anglican,

Catholic or Methodist churches. The muezzin cry might soon be more commonplace than church bells in England.

In Lincolnshire, where farmers plough vast acres amid wheeling clouds of lapwing, where holiday-makers from the English industrial midlands hurry past the churches to the caravan parks and the amusement arcades of the east coast resorts, the old stones of Croyland are no doubt as mysterious to tourist and to tiller as the ruins of Nieneveh and Tyre are to the residents of Southern Lebanon.

We had, we felt, intruded not upon evensong, but a secret funeral by the last devotees of a vanished rite, and they alone, unseen, unknown, remember the meaning of the names Guthlac, Bartholomew, Beccelm, Turketyl, Tatwin, Pega and Brega.

Skegness etc.

It was that fatal, lingering contemplation of Croyland Abbey which did the damage, which left us sleuthing around the flatlands of Lincolnshire looking for a home for the night. Flocks of starlings circled in the dying light, gathering friends and nattering about their day. Dark descended. Those few places which advertised accommodation were full.

We had only one option – to head for Skegness, where there was bound to be a bed of a sort. Skegness. Could it be as bad as it sounded? Skegness, a famous resort of the working classes of the English industrial midlands for a century or more, celebrated by one of the Victorian era's most brilliant posters, a portly mariner-type in sou-wester skipping along the beach, crying: 'Skegness is so bracing!' Nowadays, was it Tabloid-on-Sea, where people with satellite dishes go on holiday?

As it happened, virtually every single B & B in Skegness offered as an allure the fact that Sky TV was available there. Up to that moment, I had never even met anybody who had actually seen Sky; it was only then that I realised the huge gulf which can exist within the human spirit.

En suite was the word used by the proprietor of our B & B to describe the first B. En wardrobe is the term most of us would use. It cost £30 a night. My mind went back to Mrs Stack's sumptuous bed and breakfast in Listowel – thatched, huge clean rooms, and busy, genial Mrs Stack serving scones and tea at every opportunity, all for £27.50 a few weeks ago; and now, in contrast, we had this.

This is hard to describe. It was a tiny room, small enough to give a mouse claustrophobia. I was reminded of a certain bedsitter in Harcourt Street earlier this century. You could, if you were skilful, put a paper-knife between bed and wallpaper. At the end of the roomlet was a wardrobe in which perched a shower and a lavatory. What made the lavatory a particular delight to use was that the wardrobe doors did not meet in the centre, leaving a handsome one-inch gap between them. There was a symmetry in this elegant wood-working, for at each hinge, too, there was another one-inch gap, just to ensure that anybody sitting on the WC never lacked company. Which can be important. In Skegness, apparently, people need companionship at all times.

We wandered the town that night. Every pub exceeded every other pub in the density of the cigarette smoke and the din of its jukeboxes and video machines. Large middle-aged couples, she in floral prints, he a positive symphony of artificial fibres – brinylon shirt, polyester shorts and imitation polyester baseball hats – sat speechlessly exuding tobacco smoke and *inhuding* Bacardis and Watney's Red Barrel with no evidence of joy whatsoever. The men had tattoos, the women perms in nut-brown or fire-engine red hair.

We fled to our double wardrobes of the gaps, trailing other people's bronchial fumes. This was not so much secondary smoking as secondary Chernoblying. Morning. Ablutions. Tried to work out whether the space in the wardrobe was bigger with the doors open or shut. Then downstairs.

The breakfast room opened at 9 a.m., precisely. Not before. In the front room – no doubt the lounge, in their words – sat a small army of our fellow-guests, festooned in acrylics, draylons, polyesters, crimpolenes, tightly drawn over huge bellies. They were all smoking as if a firing squad were limbering up outside, their mouths open and their eyes glued to breakfast television as if word of their reprieve might come through any second.

A banquet of saturated animal fats followed, washed down by an effluent I believe our landlord termed tea: Peter Barry would more willingly have swaggered down the Shankill Road brandishing a copy of the Anglo-Irish Agreement and bawling 'Deep in the Panting Heart of Rome …' rather than use the word about a wash which might have been wrung from a sheep's withers after falling in a drainage ditch.

We commando-crawled out of the breakfast room through the six-inch gap above the floorboards, where cigarette smoke had only imperfectly penetrated, and took the air, the stuff shipped in from the North Sea by the bucketload. We were soon joined by our fellow-guests, who were still licking various forms of grease off their lips.

The first thing they did after several entire minutes of abstinence from lards or suets of any kind was to buy hamburgers, hot dogs and doughnuts which dripped pools of tallow. Some, having thus restored themselves, went to the newsagents. Every single newspaper on sale there was a tabloid. No alternative was possible, save for the *Daily Telegraph*. That he would be read and savoured by such a clientele is a thought which might have Auberon Waugh yelping through the night.

The funfair had opened up, and the temporary population of Skegness filtered inside, all tattoo and Park Drive and perms and *Suns* and baseball hats and bellies bursting through T-shirts. Coaches arrived and disgorged fleets of puzzled and arthritic old people, who leaned against one another in clusters and who seemed to yearn to get back in their buses. The coaches drove away. The new arrivals tottered in little circles of confusion and regret, keening for the departed buses.

The funfair machines started. We got on the Big Dipper, which started off about 15 feet from the ground and conveyed all the terrors and all the perils of Musical Chairs in the annual Little Sisters of the Poor knees-up. Loud, indeterminate music numbed the eardrums. Dodgems bumped one another with listless weariness.

It was time for more frankfurters, hamburgers and adipose tissue and rendered fats in all their shapes and forms. So the holidaymakers politely formed their bellies in queues; and, as they forced their roughage-free, vitamin-free, vegetable-free diet past their tonsils, the full and awesome implications of a lavatory with doors which did not do their duty sank home. It was time to leave and we did, never to return.

Paris encore

One of the great divisions in the western world is whether the Louvre pyramid is an affront to civilisation or one of its glories. Functionally it is quite superb. The vast glass edifice with its elegant geodesic construction open up the underground reception of the museum into a huge and airy vault, full of light and clean air which sucks up and dissipates the din of the unwashed hordes shuffling below.

One of its merits is its transparency which makes all four sides of the courtyard visible. But there is no time when one can be unaware of this vast, great, modernist protrusion rising from the ground; and whereas today it might not be too offensive, can we say that in 20 years it will not be?

One of the glories of the Louvre is that it came to pass by a series of accretions of almost syncretic diversity which all conform with classical concepts of architecture. I.M. Pei's pyramid does also; but in quite drastically different materials.

I doubt we will ever see it as part of that integral whole of central Paris, from the Place de la Concorde with its 3,000-year old obelisk from Luxor to the elegant coolness of the Tuilleries or the gracious spaces of the Rue de Rivoli.

The Eiffel Tower, of course, is materially disconsonant from classical Paris; but then it is not part of it and seems an odd, whimsically vulgar imposition when viewed from the Tuilleries. It is there, and imperishably part of Paris, but only because it does not violate the rules of the area which it inhabits.

A decade or more will tell whether the Pei pyramid is appropriate. It certainly will never be the reason why people visit the Louvre, which is one of the great and most lustrous diamonds in French civilisation.

No doubt much of the contents is booty from empire, tut, tut, tut: but is it so bad that the artefacts of Assyria or Babylon can be seen in the centre of Paris rather than dear old downtown Baghdad? And anyway, what claim have today's Iraqis over items from a civilisation with which they have nothing in common, other than geographical accident?

A standard cliché about the Louvre's most famous item is how disappointing it is. I did not find the *Mona Lisa* the least disappointing; quite the reverse. I found breathtaking, full of wondrous subtlety, the famous smile almost moving on the face as her eyes followed me. No wonder it is the most protected item in the Louvre.

In the history of the world, there has probably never been a more sublimely crafted object than this, transcending the human skills of mundane genius into something almost unearthly. The *Mona Lisa* is one of the wonders of the world, if not the greatest wonder of the world: it alone is worth a trip to Paris.

It draws huge crowds, seemingly at the expense of the Leonardo nearby – the painting of the Virgin, the child Jesus, St Anne and the lamb. That I found as quite as transfixing and transforming as the *Mona Lisa*; its beauty is ethereal, elegiac, almost supernatural.

Love – or fear – of God has produced some of the greatest works in creation and this is surely one of them. Because of the divided focus on the four figures, it is not as singularly captivating as the *Mona Lisa*, but the smiles are individually as haunting, and the whole is infused with an extraordinary sense of unsanctimonious worship. It is pure genius.

To view this work is to experience a genuine spiritual liberation.

It is worth visiting Paris for it alone. It used to be the case that the restaurants of Paris were a reason for a visit. Generally speaking, this is no longer the case. Irish restaurants have so improved and their prices are so moderate that it is only in the area of *haute cuisine* that Paris remains *sui generis*.

Since most of you are unlikely ever to eat at Guy Savoie's, allow me to run through the little dinner I had there the other night. We began the meal with an amusing little Moet et Chandon rosé as an aperitif, accompanied by tiny *amuse-gueules*. A tiny cup of carrot-scented warm cream followed, mouth-watering and light.

The first substantive dish was a confection of ray and caviare in a cool oyster sauce which miraculously retained the zingy freshness of uncooked oyster.

Quite superb; but not as superb as the salmon which followed, which was cooked crisp brown on the outside yet slightly underdone inside, as is right, and bathing in a sauce made from puréed parsley. In composition a simple enough dish, but in execution quite astounding.

A brief pause before lobster, simply cooked and dressed in a sauce made from lobster entrails and accompanied by crisp mange-touts. Too many people ruin lobster with cheese sauces and garlic butter and other rubbish. But lobster is a delicate meat which benefits from lobsterly delicacy.

We drank a strikingly handsome chablis, deeply structured with late fruity notes, with the above, but at this point began to move into rouge territory, accomplished with the aid of a Pommerol of rare complexity and finish. Veal sweetbreads in a nest of wild mushrooms provided the first of the meat dishes. They were close to perfection – crisply sizzled on the outside, soft and tender within, and the mushrooms reeked of wild woodland.

Then came the *pièce de resistance,* layered breast of duck in its own sauce, cut thinly and cooked rare, accompanied by slices of *foie gras* that vanished in the mouth like mousse, accompanied by spinach in a vinegar dressing and thin-cut potatoes, fried deep brown. Astounding.

What next? Ah yes. Cheese. A vast cheese board whose inhabitants smelled of cholera and typhus, Wanderers' changing rooms and bad feet. Quite wonderful. Then a dessert of crème caramel, with toasted slices of apple in a green apple coulis, followed by another dessert, this time of chocolate ice-cream in a *tuille,* accompanied by chocolate sauce.

Followed by coffee. Followed by the bill. *Eeque.* Followed by men with big hammers to widen the doorway so that we could leave. *Magnifique.*

Belgium's claim to fame

Belgium. What, why, how is Belgium? What historical miracles occurred that led to the creation of a country which has as much right to exist as a duck-billed platypus? And then what divine miracle burned this beaked, egg-laying mammal of a country into the political and economic heart of the EU? For if Belgium, why not Lurgan?

Socrates never said a word about Belgium, until his last treatise, when he wrote 'Belgi …' – and promptly died of it. Hamlet briefly began to speculate about a flight to Belgium, but got no farther than 'To Be …' before chickening out. Dante proclaimed in his *Divine Comedy* that the innermost and most unspeakable ring of hell was a dreary mudcovered plain. To the Tuscan mind, Belgium.

This Belgium: has it got a tourist board? Apart from freaks such as myself, who else goes to Belgium for their holidays? Do foreign universities have departments of Belgian Studies? Is there such a thing as Belgophile? Has any Belgian abroad ever been vigorously cornered at a party by a wide-eyed stranger who is yipping with glee at meeting someone from exotic little Belgium?

You're Belgian? How absolutely *ripping.*

Name a famous Belgian. Okay. Magritte. He lived and worked in Belgium. He was a Belgian Belgian, and was, mad, mad. There's Jacques Brel, who hated Belgium. And Simenon, whose master-creation, Maigret, was French. It took an Englishwoman to invent what any Belgian knows to be impossible, a clever Belgian detective. Who else?

Leopold, of course, who owned the Congo. Frightful bounder. Name the present Belgian prime minister. Can't.

Belgium is a rice pudding. Trying to define its unifying essence is like trying to

serve it with a knitting needle. It is perhaps most famous for the IQ of its police officers, usually about the same as their shoe size. If the RUC was recruited in Belgium,
its sleuths would probably have difficulty detecting a lambeg drum in a confessional.

That is good. Beware a state where the elite run the police. Plodocracy OK. So I
like the Belgians. They are amiably baffled; they know they get things wrong, but their
navigational equipment is so faulty that they can't see how or why. Take the inn outside Mons (delightful town) where we were shown our en-suite room by a cheerful
youth, who gestured around it with extravagant pride – see this elegant salon! – before
hurrying below. Then we discovered that the lavatory opened directly and doorlessly
onto the bedroom, being separated solely by a waist-high strip of curtain, over which
an enthroned guest could merrily chat with her loved one. Very romantic. *Ah. Il n'y a
que du papier. As-tu quelque pages des* Irish Times *là? Ah. Le golfing coverage! Excellent.
Tough mais absorbent.*

How very Belgian. As was the Eurotoque conference in Brussels for Europe's great
chefs some years ago, in which we were harangued by Belgium's finest about the
absolute need for Europe to return to pure and natural and unadulterated products.
Then we had coffee, served with condensed milk, and with Belgium's finest beaming
on approvingly. *Carnation, c'est beau, n'est-ce pas? Oui, absolument, surtout avec les
tinned peches.*

Yet who but the Belgians make such a splendid feast of *crevettes,* the fresh-water
shrimps on which I feasted in the very hostelry where en-suite actually means ensem-
ble? Served in a cream sauce on fresh and succulently crisp asparagus, they were quite
exquisite, the very lad to banish anorexia nervosa.

The young restaurant manager sat down and talked to us with an affable unaf-
fectedness which would have been perfectly inconceivable a few miles south in France.
The next morning, his fat, genial father sat waiting at our breakfast table, anxious to
advise his Irish guests on local sights.

Belgians are neither uncouth nor couth; merely demi-couth, a nation of Tony
Lumkins – nice, genial, curious, clumsy, extremely good at some things (chips, choco-
lates, beer), awful at others (Belgian lavatories – oh, dear me), yet not quite knowing
the difference. And perhaps that failure not quite to understand the world about them,
the inclination to get things a little wrong, has made possible the miraculous relationship between Walloon and Flemish. Belgium, uniquely, is the state where Teuton lives
with Gaul in enduring accommodation and perpetual friction. Perhaps this nation of
Lumkins fully understands neither insults nor compliments, and that is the secret.
Belgium is a braille-land where everyone is missing some fingers.

Why should one go to Belgium? Because the Belgian people are decent and
honest, as summed up by their national dish of chips and mussels: unpretentious and
utterly delicious. No man or woman who loves beer can fail my humanity test; and
the Belgians adore their beers, in vast variety in every pub, with local breweries

abounding. And as for intelligence, don't the Belgians wisely say *huitante* for 'eighty' rather than the idiotic French *quatre-vingts?*

We Irish once went to war for Belgium. I'm not sure I'd go that far again: no matter. But I have never met a Belgian I disliked; the food is excellent, and far better value than in France. And of course there are so many of our lads lying there, in Ypres and at Mons – the St Symphorien cemetery there is perfectly enchanting - awaiting your visit. They'll be glad of the company.

FOREIGN AFFAIRS

Holocaust denial

Were any of the mere 20 MEPs who voted against the 420 MEPs who approved the lifting of the immunity from prosecution of Jean-Marie Le Pen last week Irish? I hope so. The vote was to make Le Pen amenable to a law which might make a certain bizarre sense in Germany, but otherwise is a denial of a basic intellectual right – the right to be horribly and hideously wrong, the right to espouse foul ideas, the right to justify the unjustifiable.

That law, part of the special German criminal code for the suppression of Nazism, makes it a criminal offence to present as inoffensive any act committed by the National Socialists; and Le Pen apparently offended that code by declaring that the Nazi gas chambers were a detail in the history of the second World War. He might be vile, but he is no fool: he was being deliberately provocative in uttering those words at a launch of a biography of him by a former Waffen SS member, Franz Schonhuber MEP, in Munich. He wants free publicity; and the vote in the European parliament has guaranteed him just that.

Of course there are no laws anywhere which demand the prosecution, imprisonment and criminalisation of anyone who denies the atrocities of the Soviet Union, which, in numbers who were either butchered or worked to death or starved to death, exceeded handsomely the total killed by the Third Reich. Yet for whatever reason, those who had a soft spot for the Gulag's industrialised murder machine for 30 years are not judged as harshly as those who trivialise the crimes of the Third Reich.

This is not the first time that Le Pen has said that the gas chambers were a detail of the second World War. Morally, he is of course wrong. The Holocaust is morally the single biggest event in European history. But in geopolitical terms, he is probably right, though this assessment will not accord with the post-war popular mythology. Who really believes Britain would have gone to war in 1939 if Hitler had confined himself to the genocide of Jews in Germany and Austria? Would the US have gone to war with Germany in 1941 if the Nazis had condemned the Japanese for the attack at Pearl Harbour – an attack by non-Aryans on Aryans – and declared that the Nazis now had a duty to deal with their own non-Aryan problem, which they would do with finality?

The second World War was not about the racial policies of the Third Reich. It was about the repeated violations of international law, of international treaties and of international boundaries by Hitler, who, if he had restricted himself to murdering Jews, homosexuals, gypsies, socialists, democrats, etc. within his own domain, as Stalin did with other categories of human beings, would most probably not have found himself at war with half the world.

The war certainly wasn't about the gas chambers; up until the liberation of the concentration camps in 1945, only the rulers of the Western powers had an inkling of what the Germans were up to, and they did virtually nothing to stop it.

RAF Bomber Command and the USAAF Eight Air Force could have destroyed the infrastructure of industrialised murder, but they did not. Jewish leaders pleaded with the British and American governments to bomb the camps and the railway connections which fed them their fuel of human bodies and slave labour, but both governments preferred to devote their bombers to defeating Nazi Germany rather than militarily limiting its criminal excesses. Who knows, possibly, even if only at a subconscious level, Western leaders preferred the idea of German rolling-stock bearing Jews eastwards to German rolling-stock bearing tanks westwards.

Certainly, there was little or no appetite for sending bombers all the way to Poland, with possibly catastrophic losses, in order to save Jewish lives.

In our lifetimes, the world – including little us – has stood by and watched mass murder in Cambodia, Algeria, Iraq, China, North Korea and vast tracts of Africa, and done virtually nothing to prevent it. The brutal reality is that epidemics of homicide, if domestically confined and not impinging on the vital interests of outsiders, do not trigger foreign wars. As it is today, so was it 60 years ago.

Is this what Le Pen meant? I don't know. He does seem a remarkably disgusting man: catholically anti-Semitic in despising all the offspring of Shem, and not just Jews; an Afrophobe and a hater of homosexuals; and a sneaking-regarder of the Third Reich. Yet we should not deal with such venom by repressing it, for such repression inevitably curbs our own freedom not merely to debunk his falsehoods but to debate whatever truths people like Le Pen must inevitably include in their wider programme of lies.

Holocaust denial is today a crime in Germany; but in 1945, it was Irish government policy. Censors rigorously removed from our newspapers all reports of the discovery of the death camps. We officially denied the Holocaust, even as de Valera offered his condolences to Herr Hempel; Irish history has known more glorious moments. Once our politicians worked to prevent the Irish people from hearing the truth about the Holocaust. Their heirs should not now be voting to enable the prosecution of someone for restating what was, after all, public government policy in 1945.

Third World debt

It's probably pretty kyule at the moment to support the cancellation of Third World Debt. If Bono's supporting it, then it must be roit awn at the very least. He's not alone.

There are some pretty powerful people who are in favour of such a humanitarian move – such as British Aerospace, Fabrique Nationale, and the Colt Division of General Motors.

Why are Third World Countries facing starvation and infrastructural calamity? Because those big bad banks, white, Western and wicked, are squeezing the lifeblood out of them, because that is the way banks behave? Or because they have been run into the ground by cruel, incompetent and corrupt ruling élites, who have freely borrowed money from anyone who would give it, in order to buy themselves Mercedes to drive up and down the 15-mile motorway built by East German engineers 20 years ago, and which connects their capital with a termites' nest in the middle of nowhere?

That the West is somehow responsible for global ills informs almost every decent conversation about 'The Third World'. But that assumption is merely a relic of imperialism, with a comically obsolete terminology. There is no Third World anymore. The Second World, communism, has vanished, and its components have migrated to the two available worlds remaining.

One is where there's a rule of law, harsh as in China or liberal as in Scandinavia, but at least predictable; where political leaders do not confiscate the greater part of the GNP; where the political culture promotes economic activity by its citizens, who in turn see the benefits of working hard and *saving* because it makes *sense*. Then there's the world without a predictable rule of law, but governance by tyrannical whim; where corrupt leaders loot the national treasury; where the political culture discourages enterprise and where citizens accordingly resort to philosophical inertia and feckless *improvidence* because it makes sense.

Just as the Victorians were driven to improve the lot of 'the lesser breeds', so the modern uplifter of the Third World thinks it is the white man's burden to do for Africa (for which Third World is a code name) what the native cannot do himself; although of course that sort of racist, sexist language is not employed by the roit-awn, the kyule. So forget the language; we're talking ideas here, and the idea basic to all the roit-awn, kyule assumptions about that misnamed planet the Third World is that it needs special rules which contravene rules elsewhere and special economic models which ignore the oh so expensively acquired lessons learnt elsewhere.

The result? Take your pick: Sierra Leone, Uganda, Congo, Tanzania, Eritrea, Sudan, Ethiopia. Maybe soon Kenya, Namibia, KwaZulu Natal – who knows? What have they in common? One thing is that they have been repeatedly misgoverned by slovenly despots or serial killers; the other is that they would almost certainly welcome a cancellation of national debts by the World Bank. Such a move, the UN declares, could save the lives of 7 million children a year across the continent.

Why? What on earth makes the UN, Bono or any of the kyule or the roit-awn think that the élites of those countries are suddenly going to start thinking about the infants whose lives they have been so careless of so far? Is it not more likely that whatever money is saved in debt repayment will be spent on Mercs, and that their armies will find an excuse to buy fighter planes (only to rust in hangars for want of proper maintenance) and assault rifles to keep the citizenry in its place? Big smile on the faces of British Aerospace and Colt Firearms Manufacturing Co. Inc., no smile at all on the faces of dysenteric children in sun-seared villages without wells.

Of course, it sounds kindly, this business of cancelling debts; as it does to cancel the debts of an addicted alcoholic or gambler. But the payment of debt is perhaps the only discipline such people, such countries, have in their lives; the certainty of foreclosure is more likely to concentrate their minds on being grown-up than would an absolution from the consequences of reneging on those debts. We know this for certain in Ireland. So recklessly had we been governed for over a decade that 12 years ago, the IMF nearly moved in. We were obliged to place our affairs in order, to pay our debt, and to live in the real world. We grew up.

In other words, a simple cancellation of debt is the worst service we can do the hungry of the earth and their debt-addicted governments; it would guarantee that their children would grow up in a world as vile as the one they inhabit.

Furthermore, banks do not lend their own money. Never. Bankers are hard, ruthless bastards who lend the money of eejits (aka their depositors) impartially either to the masters of Kinsealy or of Kenya. But no doubt Bono would be quite delighted if one morning his bank manager cried: Good news! We've lent all your savings to that nice man, CJH! And as a decent, humanitarian gesture – after all, the poor fellow's getting on – we've just cancelled the debt! Hello? Mr Hewson?

Rupert Murdoch

Last Sunday, News International, the newspaper company owned by the Australamerican magnate Rupert Murdoch, successfully brought professional disaster to the career of the English rugby captain Lawrence Dallaglio with a piece of journalism of quite breath-taking nastiness. That same day, the reputable wing of News International the *Sunday Times*, published a deeply intimate photograph of the former taoiseach Charles Haughey passionately kissing the journalist Terry Keane. As an act of personal treachery, it vastly exceeded any of the revelations we have heard about the man.

The two scoops had more in common than the grubby fingerprints of Rupert Murdoch. Both of them involved betrayal. The Keane-Haughey photograph was never intended for publication. It was a private moment, either recorded by a friend or by themselves on a camera-timer. She is semi-recumbent on the floor, he kneeling down and kissing her deeply on the mouth. This was not my business; it was not the business of anyone outside their families (and God love them this hour); for merely to see such a photograph transforms even the inadvertent viewer into a voyeur.

I felt soiled by the picture, not because a deeply intimate and private act had been turned into a public event, but because though not enriching me in any degree, it must have emotionally impoverished the families of the two participants hugely. Grave personal hurt must have been done to people who had no part in the affair; and that, no doubt, was the intention. The purpose of the Dallaglio revelations was slightly different. It was to wreck his career as England rugby captain: and as they say in another code, game, set and match.

This mucky affair was stage-managed by the now commonplace tactic of having a young woman approach the intended target pretending to be other than what she in reality is: a perfectly vile journalist rummaging around the bottom of the professional barrel of our trade. (The worst kind of tabloid journalism is nowadays almost a female preserve: by jove, ma'am, that must make the sisters proud.)

In poor Lawrence's case, the hackette pretended to be an executive of a shaving-products company trying to get her victim promote its goods. In the course of a 'business' meeting, the entrapping sleuthette spoke of her own drug-habits, the better to provoke her victim into doing likewise; and the poor dolt duly obliged. Thus the *News of the World* got its story, and England a new captain.

I am not at all sure which newspaper is the more reprehensible; the *News of the World* because it is a vile rag? Or the *Sunday Times* which has so degraded itself with the publication of such a personal photograph? The latter probably, because it sets high standards for itself, and its Irish staff are without exception first-class journalists who generally speaking are a credit to the business.

Which makes the decision to publish this photograph all the more incomprehensible, all the more inexcusable, and on the face of it, all the more inexplicable.

But of course it is not inexplicable. Somewhere above the Irish staff there is a line manager close to God, i.e. Rupert Murdoch, whose duty is to ensure that the demands of vulgar and tasteless populism, in which the decent bourgeois standards of reticence, decorum, and restraint are repeatedly violated, are pandered to throughout the kingdom of God.

For Rupert Murdoch is an ideologist. He hates the class system, and he detests in particular those values which he associates with the middle-classes of the imperial Australia of his childhood. He especially loathes the British monarchy and the value-system of the social system of which it is the pinnacle. So, just as all state organs in the Soviet Union had party hacks at every decision-making level to impose a secretly divined politburo policy, so News International has its Murdoch-commissars, ensuring that the base appetites of populism are regularly stoked, in order that they can then be slaked.

In this terrible world, the principles of privacy are extinct; in this terrible world, young women, with fluttering eyelashes and whirring tape recorders concealed within some perfumed crevice, flatter and deceive that they might bring personal ruin to some celebrated sap; in this terrible world, the minor indiscretions of life are shaped out of recognition into the front-page fare of tabloids; in this terrible world, there are no standards or rules which prohibit disclosure; in this terrible world, the discretion which makes life endurable, which divides the properly-knowable from the properly-concealed, is eradicated. All of our lives become a peep-show for others' delectation. In this terrible world, all honour is dead.

It is not just the famous, or the families of the famous, who are potential victims of this abominable culture which wrecks lives and reputations. At a pinch; anybody will do. Short of a film-star snorting coke? Then a GP, a teacher or journalist will do. Three-in-a-bed romp? Spice it up, and even a brickie's mate, plus, of course, two other mates, will suffice, regardless of the distress being caused to the blameless uninvolved. The story's the big thing; all other standards may safely be disregarded.

Journalism is sinking into a vat of manure; and the Lord of this journalism is Vatman himself, Rupert Murdoch.

Herr Haider

We are it seems, 'associated' with the partial boycott of Austria by EU states if the Freedom Party under Herr Haider enters government. The reason for this unprecedented move? Because Herr Haider has praised Hitler's economic policies, and has declared that Waffen SS men were brave men and patriots. The 14 EU states – plus Government Buildings – should prepare to boycott this column: Herr Haider was right on both counts. Hitler's economic policies were, for a while anyway, a triumph; and the Waffen SS, loathe them as I do, were nonetheless perhaps the best soldiers the world has ever seen.

Economic policies first. In 1933, the year Hitler came to power, Germany produced 118,000 cars. The British figure was 286,000, the French was nearly 190,000 and the American was short of two million. Five years later, the German motor industry had nearly trebled its output to 340,000 vehicles. The British and increased their output by a mere 60 per cent, the Americans likewise, the French by 25 per cent. Now, who is achieving the economic miracle here – the western democracies or the fascist state?

Right across the economy, Hitler had wrought extraordinary changes – coal production almost doubled in five years, iron production increased five-fold, gross sales of motor vehicles also up five-fold. Unemployment, which stood at over six million in January 1933, was a mere 72,500 by September 1939. Is it any wonder that Hitler was adored by the German masses? And is it any wonder that today some fool should admire his economic miracle?

No doubt Hitler's command economics violated many basic economic tenets, and no doubt the only way he could sustain growth was by replacing market realities with a war economy: inasmuch as I am able to understand Richard Overy's *War and Economy in the Third Reich* (from which the above figures are taken), that might well indeed be the case. That is merely an argument; not a cut and dried case. But if we subtract the numerous vile sides of Hitler – the pathological anti-Semitism, the pagan adoration of violence, the exaltation of a spurious but lethal tribalism – it is possible to see that his regime achieved a great deal, before it began to unleash its pent-up evil on its neighbours. The means by which unemployment was driven down – the abolition of free trade unions, and the actual reduction of wages – were in fact the tools used by communist regimes to achieve economic take-off. Do I approve?

Irrelevant; but I would not diplomatically boycott a country which had communists in government – such as Italy, say. And communism has been a far more recent foe of freedom, more persistent, and bloodier by far than fascism.

Now for the Waffen SS. Yes, its *einsatzgruppen* were the butchers of East European Jewry, and the *Totenkapfverbände* – Death's Head Band, who were largely despised by other sections of the SS – ran the concentration camps. But for the most part, the Waffen SS – *waffen* means 'armed', as in 'weapon' – was a *corps d'élite* unique in war. It remained aloof from and disdainful of the concentration camp thugs. Even when, under an order from Himmler in 1941, all the various arms of the SS were to be amalgamated, the *einsatzgruppen* remained separate from the main body of the fighting SS. The SS were not gentlemen, and some were responsible for dreadful atrocities. That doesn't mean they all were. Is this not the way of war? Does being a member of the IRA in 1922 necessarily implicate one in the pogrom of Protestants in Cork? Does membership of the Black and Tans mean one was responsible for the slaughter in Croke Park? And might each group of men not, by their own lights, be regarded as patriots?

So can one say that SS men were patriots? Of course one can: that they volunteered for the most dangerous duties in the service of their country defines them as such. Which merely raises another question altogether: what is patriotism and what is so patriotic about it?

But that is barely the point. Jorg Haider said that SS men were patriots; some no doubt were. Most, I dare say, did nothing to be ashamed of by their own peculiar standards of ruthless warriorship. They expected no mercy, and by God were seldom shown it: Allied soldiers invariably murdered those relatively few SS captives who were taken alive.

That is one historical kernel of the issue. Here is the other. Would the member states of the EU boycott a state which refused to extradite suspected terrorist murderers because those murders were done in pursuance of a supposed constitutional imperative of that state? We are not talking about Iran and its fatwas, but about the IRA and its fatwas. The Supreme Court of the Irish Republic ruled – to its endurable shame, and under now-extinct constitutional provisions – that a suspect may not be extradited from Ireland for a murder committed in pursuit of a united Ireland, provided that the murder *was done with a hand-gun*. With that dispensation supplied by the highest court in this State, terrorists then pistol-killed an army recruiting sergeant in England.

For all its delinquencies, Austrian democracy has never embraced a legal definition as barbarous, depraved and wicked as that one. On the issue of Herr Haider, frankly, we should shut up.

African issues

How I dread the arrival of another story of genocide in Africa, - not merely because of the unbelievable human suffering involved, but also because it will trigger the why-doesn't-the-West-do-something about it school into another frenzy of moral pulpi-teering. These are probably also the very people who say we should cherish our neutrality, and the US is a vile and wicked world empire, and NATO is a military con-spiracy against the Third World, and intervention in Kosovo was no more than a cyn-ical piece of imperialism. And having said all that, they still want somebody to go charging into Africa.

Who nowadays actually is able to keep track of what occurred between Hutu and Tutsi, Hema and Lendu, Huanga and Shute, Ngdwange and Ruhuya? I confess I am not. Apart from the pulpiteers conjuring imaginary troops with imaginary peace-making skills out of imaginary barracks in imaginary countries with a wholly imagi-nary political culture of self-sacrificial virtue to send to this imaginary African land which will respond with a wholly imaginary cordiality, relief and docility to this thor-oughly imaginary outside interference, almost no-one has the least idea what to do about it.

Here is a horrible question. Brace yourself. Do we care? Do we really? The death of a single elephant keeper in England three days ago merited a sidebar story in this newspaper alongside a comparably sized report about the appearance in court of an African gentleman charged with the massacre of over 100,000 Africans six years ago. Most of these poor people were not even shot, but hacked to death: it does seem to be one of the peculiarities of the greater Congo area that tribal butchers, even when they have access to Kalashnikovs, prefer to kill their victims – usually in perfectly astro-nomical numbers – with their crude, machete-like pangas.

Here is another horrible question. Is it more fun that way?

We must recognise this awful truth: most of us are not irredeemably past caring about these human calamities. A tribe being chopped to death by their nearest and dearest neighbours in their African rain-forest will make less impact in Europe than an earthquake in California in which no-one dies. Usually the most vociferous people in Ireland who respond to Africa's calamities with demands for intervention by armed outsiders are middle-class breast-beaters whose sons or daughters will not die trying futilely to impose order over African swamplands.

For the rest of us, we know we can do absolutely nothing about the human calamities being visited on Africa. How is it possible for the outside world to impose its will on any country on that continent? The combined mass of NATO and sundry other countries – including a highly-skilled and much-praised contingent from our own Army – is unable to impose its will on Kosovo, which is about the size of a couple of largish Irish counties, and which has numerous NATO air-bases a short flying time away. Which country is willing to sort out a continent which is the size of the European land-mass from the Arctic circle to the Mediterranean, from the waters of the English Channel to the Caucasus mountains?

Well, plucky Zimbabwe is having a go: is it because it wishes to bring democracy, WCs, nice toilet-roll holders and honest local government to the Democratic Republic of Congo? Possibly.

On the other hand, is it because Robert Mugabe and his generals have an eye for the unprotected diamonds and gold their troops might find there? And if we were to send the Army in to help out, which square mile of rain-forest would our lads and lasses be bringing peace to? And who would then be minding the other 905,364 unpoliced square miles of the place?

But of course, somebody will then have to ensure that trouble doesn't spill over into the neighbouring – but slightly confusingly named – Republic of Congo, which, at 132,000 square miles, is a mere postage stamp of a country: the size of Germany, 40 per cent larger than Britain and 26 times larger than lovely, cuddly Northern Ireland.

Dear me; and that's just two African countries, with lots and lots still to go. But will the logistical enormity of Africa's problems, their sheer intractability and their utter incomprehensibility silence the pulpiteers who call for armed outside intervention? Probably not; for Africa is not the issue.

The issue is their own self-esteem. They have opened a morality competition over Africa, a Fantasy Football of Good Works, in which they buy all the great virtues on the transfer market of their mind and in which they are the certain champions.

So be it. And ask yourself, when next you hear mountebanks demanding 'action' over Africa, how deep they are prepared to dig into their own pockets to help that continent? When such people sermonise, they are merely being casual about other lives, other treasuries. There is in fact not much we can do for poor bloody Africa, other than helping cope with short-term disasters, as we would anywhere, and providing technical assistance in backward areas, and most of all, giving Africans visas to work and settle here. Not out of goodness: but out of self-interest – the most logical and comprehensible motive of all.

David Norris and Robert Mugabe

If you read the letter on Monday from cuddly, much-loved Senator David Norris which, amid much politically correct froth and frenzy, accused this column of being obnoxious, you might well wonder what monstrosities I had perpetrated. His letter, I admit, was not obnoxious, merely silly, hysterical and inaccurate.

On the one hand, one is on a hiding to nothing taking on David Norris; he is the media pet, Joycean, boatered, yet right-on in every regard, with a perfectly-pitched sanctimony, yeasted with the right amount of wit and victimhood. And of course, who could fail to admire his tenacity and his courage in almost alone ending the barbarous laws against male homosexual acts. Who would ever take him on? On the other: into the valley of death …

Senator Norris: 'He [i.e. K.M.] attacks people who got themselves into a fine old lather blaming the west for arming Hussein … As one of those people, I refuse to retract a single word … Weaponry of all kinds, including the means to manufacture chemical and biological weapons, were made available to Saddam Hussein by the West.'

I know you're a busy man, Senator, but you'd probably scribble 'Could do very much better,' beneath an essay from a student who presented such a dysfunctional, counterproductive argument as that. What I actually said was that both West and East sold Saddam weapons. Yet in his letter the Senator pointed his finger at the West alone, even though Saddam's air force was Soviet-supplied, as were his Scuds, as were his tanks, as were his infantry weapons. So why does the Senator not even manage to mention this in his reply? Why is the West held solely responsible for the evils of the Hussein regime?

'Not only that, but the political opposition was betrayed into his hands *so* [my italics] that they could be murdered.' Leaving aside the singular noun commanding a plural verb – after all, the Senator lectured in literature, not in writing correctly – he uses 'so' as a conjunction meaning 'in order that'. Is that what the West intended? That the opposition be rounded up and murdered? Which not merely makes the West thoroughly evil, but also one of Saddam's best friends. This a) makes all those sanctions and downed Iraqi aircraft rather puzzling or b) suggests the Senator doesn't understand the role of a conjunction.

That's more than possible. He speaks of my 'nonchalance' in opposing the sale of Hawk aircraft parts to Robert Mugabe's air force. Nonchalance? What is nonchalant about the words I used – 'vile', 'majestically cynical', 'wholly wicked'? Is he writing in a dialect of Martian? He adds: 'I have consistently opposed such deals for precisely the same reason as I opposed them in East Timor. Then I would, wouldn't I, being a liberal gay critic of certain aspects of American and European foreign policy?'

Leaving aside that curious final question-mark, which performs no grammatical duty other than tell us that this former lecturer in TCD doesn't know a subordinate and rhetorically interrogative clause when he writes one, I ask myself: what is relevant about his homosexuality? Why bring that into the sale of Hawks to Zimbabwe? Why can he be relied on to introduce this now-thoroughly tedious aspect of his life into almost every conversation – even at a Bosnian solidarity meeting I attended several years ago? A word of advice, Senator: proclaiming your homosexuality at a meeting which is discussing rape-camps and mass-murder is mere attention-seeking self-indulgence.

The Senator's letter went on: 'Kevin Myers objects to "liberals" resisting Mugabe's mindless and vicious persecution of gay people in Zimbabwe.' Tell me, Senator: Were your lectures as complete a farrago of misrepresentation as that single masterpiece of the genre? I do not and did not object to 'liberals' resisting Mugabe's 'mindless and vicious persecution' – if that is indeed what it is – of homosexuals. Persecutions should always be resisted. What I said – are you attending here, Senator? – was that 'it says something about the disordered priorities of the Holland Park Lefties of London that what really disenchanted them ... wasn't the (corruption) ... or his £2 million wedding, or his lunatic war a thousand miles away ... or even his slaughter of the Ndebele in 1982. Nope: what did for Mugabe among the *bien-pensant* was his dislike of homosexuality.'

The Senator says 'He [i.e. K.M.] can well-afford to be cavalier about what he light-heartedly described as Mugabe's 'dislike of homosexuals'. The Senator clearly has as little regard for the meaning of words such as 'cavalier' and 'light-heartedly' as he has for grammar. Of his regard for the largely heterosexual people of Matabeleland butchered by Mugabe's troops while he was in public life, I cannot speak, having been unable to find one single condemnation by him. Maybe he would care to enlighten me in my ignorance.

One does not need to be light-hearted or cavalier to see this obvious truth: measured against his numerous sins, Mugabe's dislike of homosexuals – such idiotic phobias are common amongst the pathologically authoritarian – is as nothing compared to the murderous monstrosities he has visited on the peoples of Zimbabwe and the Congo.

Try harder next time, Senator. And most of all, please, please, spare us your sexuality at very bloody turn, all right?

IRISH POLITICS

Tribunitis

So there I was, sunk in the leather, thinking of this and that, while Blenkinsop, the old club servant, lingered in a shadow in that obedient way he has, when who should totter in but Montmorency, whimpering for beakers of ambrosia.

Before he collapsed in a heap, his face in his hands, I noted, rather sharply, I thought, because I'm never at my best much before sunset, that he looked unwell. 'You look wan, old fellow,' I said, for wan just about summed it up. He said nothing but raised his face – still wan, I noted – from his hands and clicked his fingers impatiently at Blenkinsop, who was sailing with purposeful majesty towards him, bearing the restorer of the old tissues.

Monty took the drink and drained it to its lees, inhaled deeply, and again sank his f. in his h. After a while, he turned the old phys towards me. Still wan, I noticed. I lined up a crack about wan of those days, but when I saw his eye, and the dangerous glint within, I thought better of it. Monty can be a bit of a handful when riled.

'What is it, old fellow? Anything a chum can do?' 'No,' he told the carpet and was silent for a while before he muttered: 'You clearly haven't heard the news.' 'News? What news?' 'There is,' he said in a low voice, and enunciating each word with great care, 'to be another government tribunal.' I lofted my drink clear out the crystal glass, hitting Blenkinsop neatly in the eye.

'A what?' I whispered. 'A tribunal. Another tribunal.' 'I thought we were done with tribunals. That was the deal. No more tribunals.' 'Who said that there were to be no tribunals? Who actually promised it? Nobody, that's who. So we've got another tribunal.' 'In a good cause,' I whispered to nobody in particular.

'Of course. That's the damnable thing about the wretched things. They're always in a good cause. That's why nobody has the nerve to say, Stop. That's why this poor unfortunate land is afflicted with tribunitis. Piety. I blame piety, the Catholic conscience and all that.' 'Another tribunal. I'm emigrating.' 'Where to?' I thought about that for a bit. 'You have a point,' I conceded.

'Another tribunal. I don't think I can take it. I really don't.' 'I know.'

Blenkinsop arrived with a replacement drink for me. 'Have you heard the news, Blenkinsop?' I asked.

'News, sir? What news?'

'Did you not hear Monty here with his tidings?' 'I am not in the habit of eavesdropping upon the conversation of club members sir. In certain circles the practice is rather severely discountenanced.' 'No doubt. Would you care to sit before I ...' 'I think not, sir. Club rules ...'

'Quite, quite. Well, the truth of the matter, Blenkinsop old fellow – are you standing comfortably?' – 'Perfectly sir.' – 'is that we're about to have another tribunal. Catch him, Monty!' Too late. Blenkinsop keeled over like one of those Californian redwoods, and hit the floor with a bang which dislodged the painting of the Fourteenth Duke of Leinster from its moorings.

'Missed,' said Monty without remorse.

'Yes, you did rather.' 'Had other things on my mind. Such as this tribunal.' 'What's it about, this tribunal of yours?' 'It is a tribunal of ours,' he said with some asperity. 'Its task will be to find out why every time this State fails to do its job properly, it calls a tribunal. It's an amazing thing. The State doesn't ever manage to arrange criminal proceedings against major wrong-doers, but is an absolute whizz at convening tribunals.'

'I see. Let me get this straight. This isn't a tribunal of the ordinary sort. This will be a tribunal of tribunals, is that right?' 'Sort of. It'll look into why it is that whenever anyone in power blunders, or is corrupt, or is stupid, or lies, there isn't a criminal investigation, with an examining magistrate, as there would be in France, with people going to jail and so on, but there is instead an attack of RTS.' 'RTS? Don't tell me. Scottish television.'

Monty looked at me in that way he has. 'Repetitive Tribunal Syndrome. Its primary symptom is an overwhelming itch on the part of the Government to distribute millions to the legal profession.' 'The poor dears.' 'Quite. And after each attack of RTS, everyone promises never to have another tribunal again.' 'As I do with booze each morning.' 'Precisely,' said Monty. There was a groan from the floor and Blenkinsop began to rise.

'And then somebody in public life does something wrong again, and TDs get cross and start shouting at one another. All very self-righteous,' Monty continued dolefully. 'Instead of heads rolling, the Government announces, Another Tribunal.' At the sound of those words, Blenkinsop fainted again, and there was the sound of a clunk as his head hit the floor. The Duke of Ormond fell off his perch with a clatter.

'I think I'll join Blenkinsop,' said Monty, and after briefly reciting the Open Sesame of unconsciousness, 'Another Tribunal,' promptly fainted.

That's another thing about tribunals. Always leaving a fellow with no one to drink with. Wonder why that is? Perhaps the Government should announce a tribunal into why a tribunal about tribunals causes a chap to drink alone. But it never, never, ever, causes anyone to go to jail.

Odd, that.

Legal fees

Another tribunal! How absolutely spiffing! And I thought my chances were blown after the homobenignal beef tribunal. God, it was pure bloody murder to see my entire generation from UCD pass through Dublin Castle for month after month, turning up at the beginning in an Austin Seven and leaving at the end in a Boeing 747 Jacuzzi, en route for whatever paradise they had made their holiday home.

One lawyer who in his youth was distinguished by his ferrety-face, his greasy hair, his shiny suit and a tie which, if boiled, could render a quite passable pigswill, at the conclusion of the beef tribunal was able to buy a couple of islands. By the name of Hawaii, I believe. He even bought a little craft to shuttle between them – the USS *Dwight D. Eisenhower,* complete with F-14 Tomcats.

Not everybody did as well as he did. One barrister was only able to buy a modest plot of land to build his little house on, namely, the Midlands, but most lawyers seem to have done the equivalent of coating themselves in glue and then diving into a swimming pool of gold-dust, day after day after day.

But not me, though I have been a beef-eater all my life. I have been to Brussels. I once even sat next to a Goodman accountant on a plane – surely these were grounds for a call-up? I waited and waited, all a-tremble with excitement, and mentally spending my money in advance. My first day's fee would be used as a down payment on a property I have my eye on, called Kildare, my second day's would perhaps buy me a little salmon stream I rather like, the Shannon I believe it's called, which comes complete with free electricity.

Not a word. Not a bloody word. Gazed at my phone for months on end as an entire population passed through the portals of Dublin Castle en route for the pastures of plenty and the field of the cloth of gold; by their expenses claims shall ye know them – The Cost Generation. By the time the beef tribunal came to an end, a completely new class had come into existence: not since the Normans arrived has so much flowed from so many to so few. And amazingly this huge transfer of resources from the many to the few was done at the behest of the Labour Party, the very people whose careful regard of public resources gave us TnaG as well.

After such a generous use of taxpayers' money to benefit a minority, it was generally assumed that we were done with tribunals, which would henceforward be as redundant as parchment and quills. The reverse has been the case. The legal profession has since been gorged on tribunals like geese on chestnuts, and their livers have grown large and tasty.

This is where the more cunning of us should seize our chance. So many established lawyers have become so fat on tribunals that they cannot pass through the swingdoors of the Four Courts. The slimmer, the trimmer the zimmerless of us can now finally make it to a tribunal, over the recumbent wheezing corpses of The Cost Generation.

Who is better equipped to help the Dunne tribunal than myself? I own a passable pair of St Bernard knickers, and I have seen Ben Dunne's house from afar. And as for Michael Lowry, what better fellow than myself? Have I not spent a pleasant afternoon in Thurles? Have I not rummaged gaily through the odd deep-freeze looking for frozen chips? In other words, I am what is called a perfect tribunal-performer – and thanks to the homobenignal precedents, I've got a shrewd idea what to ask for.

Taxing master, take note. From this moment I am on standby, ready to serve the State at the drop of a wig. My daily retainer while I await your call is a mere £5,000. I will be poised beside the rooftop pool at the Hotel George Sank on the Cap d'Antibes, my gold mobile phone cleared to receive calls solely from the Dunne Inquiry – rental of said phone adding a further £500 a day.

Ingrid, my Finnish masseuse, and her two friends Britt and Hannalena, will be in constant attendance, keeping my brain and mind fit with carefully administered unguents imported from Thailand. Needless to say, these companions must be reimbursed for the skill, knowledge, complexity and difficulty for the task in hand; and taxing master, take note, if you please, their fees will be necessary and appropriate.

We might as well agree on these fees now – perhaps £100,000 for the aforesaid skill, knowledge, complexity and difficulty, and another £100,000 for effort and responsibility, which for simplicity's sake we will round off to £3.2 million. This, needless to say, does not cover my three assistants' personal expenses, such as catering costs, fresh toast in the morning, etc., etc., etc. – call it a further round million. Okay? No point in creating unnecessary headaches for the accountants.

Now. Let us deal with the serious fees once you have whistled me up before the tribunal. Needless to say, it would be entirely inappropriate for me to disclose to you the hourly rate I charge. That would compromise the relationship between myself and the plain folk of Ireland, who have no business knowing such details. Essentially, my fees come down to the notional rate I myself devise – it most certainly should not be a sordid hourly matter, open to examination by any Tom, Dick or Larry. It stands to reason – such information is confidential and enjoys absolute privilege.

The same must be said about my three companions, Ingrid, Britt and Hannalena, who will need full reimbursement for the long hours they expect to put in. Needless to say, I cannot reveal the hourly rates Ing, Britt and Hann charge; concerns that some might have that you will end up paying me more than I am paying them are a complete red herring, and an unwarranted intrusion between a chap and his masseuses.

We will be putting up in the Shelbourne during our stay in Dublin. You cry, why the Shelbourne? Because there is nowhere better, TM, my old fellow. I await your call *anxiously.*

Mary McAleese for President

Only a few more days of this poison and rancour to go; and we might well ask how we got to this pretty pass. Simple. The stakes were once too low, and now they are far, far too high. Mary Robinson turned the office into a stepladder and now we are paying the price.

Is it surprising that the most ambitious and most capable woman in Ireland, Mary McAleese, wants to be the next to put her foot on the bottom rung of the Aras? Does she wish to be President, merely to be a good President? Or does she wish to be President because the Presidency is another step towards the international stage, as pioneered by Mary Mark I?

That is the real issue in this election. The Sinn Féin-gambit was a neat little hand grenade for a while, and it did some injury, but the long-term effect of it was to gather more souls solicitously around the intended target. John Hume and Brid Rodgers, who presumably would otherwise have stayed silent, felt it necessary to intervene. As the dust settles, and the ambulance goes wailing back to the hospital, we can see Mary McAleese standing at the scene of the explosion, not even shaken, while the other candidates are making sure she's all right or are in the ambulance, groaning.

The gentlemen who tossed in the Shinner smear – and that was a perfect little Stalinist tactic, with a sticky pedigree all over it – seem to have done more damage to just about everybody else than to Mary McAleese. Throughout she stood tall and unbending, handling herself with the composure of the woman she most resembles, Margaret Thatcher. I was frightened of Mary McAleese before the hand grenade; now I am terrified of her.

She is, like Thatcher, tougher, more able, more single-minded than those around her. No other candidate could have coped so imperturbably with the leaks, and the artfully constructed falsehoods, as she has done. She was rock-steady, giving strength around her when others were failing. She is in a class of her own.

That is why she scares the living daylight out of me. She'll make mincemeat of the elected politicians of Dáil Éireann, none of whom come near her in ability or single-mindedness. She has not put herself forward as President in the amiable-old-duffer mould, an Erskine Ó Dálaigh, nor even in the mould of the Mary Mark I we saw seven years ago, who – remember? – asked us to dance. That was the presidency as minstrelsy (though it wasn't what we got).

Mary McAleese's visions make me tremble, for before she moves on to a post-presidential post, she will not settle even for the Robinson presidency. She is far more driven and has far more composure than Mary Robinson had. I once saw Mary Robinson break into tears in the Seanad because she missed a debate. Can you imagine Mary McAleese breaking into tears over anything?

Mary McAleese does not want to be President in order to become the lord of the dance. With her ferocious energy and ambitions, she will soon tire of the presidential round, and she will not have the clever hand of Bride Rosney to steer her. She could be a constitutional crisis waiting to happen.

That she is a Northern nationalist per se troubles me not one whit. Northern nationalism needs good strong people to express and represent it, most particularly because it is in a permanently adversarial role with unionists. If the latter are right to defend their identity, and I believe they are, nationalists would be insane not to do the same. I do not grudgingly concede this.

The declaration of identity and the cherishment of the details of that identity are commonplace through the civilised world.

What is not so commonplace is the presence within a small area of two identities, competing and rival – and until recently in a state of war. This doesn't mean that a representative of the Northern nationalist community shouldn't be. President Seamus Mallon, for example, is as brave and tolerant a gentleman as you could wish for, an exemplar of the virtues of the broader Irish nation; if he were President, he would both adorn the office and settle for its limitations.

But I don't believe Mary McAleese would. I don't even think she can help herself as she strides through life, the earth shaking beneath her feet. She is what she is. She marched into the smugly unionist bastion of Queen's University and before you could say Mary McAl ... the bastion was in pieces, and unionists were sheltering in the rubble while she turned south, towards the Park, thud, thud, thud. John Alderdice, nice, amiable Alliance John Alderdice already feels threatened by the prospect of her Presidency. How do you think the *real* unionists feel?

If this were an American or French presidential election, she has the ideal qualifications: intelligence, ambition, charisma. Her eyes flash on the television screen and at home I faint in terror. She is the most impressive, most dynamic and most purposeful person in public life in Ireland. She is simply incomparable.

Which is why she would make a bad President for this Republic.

Footing the bill

Helplessly, we watch through trembling fingers as news emerges daily of how we are being dealt with by those whom we have traditionally trusted most of all. Our helplessness is compounded by our impotent indignation, because in our heart of hearts we know nothing will come of the injustices which are repeatedly inflicted on us by the rich, the powerful.

One page in this newspaper this week told us much of what we needed to know about this society. Filler stories told of how several men, no doubt from low-educational backgrounds, were fined in connection with cigarette smuggling; and the top story on the same page reported how the legal fees resulting from the cases of three women who sued the State over the Hepatitis C scandal were four or five times the amount actually given to the women in compensation.

That is not the astounding thing; what is truly astounding is that when the legal bills were submitted to a legal cost accountant, they were promptly reduced by £800,000 – almost as if £800,000 were the small change at the end of a bill which you round down for book-keeping purposes.

And that little figure of £2.3 million in legal costs is merely the crevice down which the dog chases a rabbit; follow the dog and you will behold a vast subterranean chamber of gold and gems which have come the way of the legal profession from the scandals which grow in this State like stalagmites and stalactites.

The legal profession is not responsible for this; the responsibility lies with the law-makers who have systematically abandoned their duty to run this State. For nearly three decades, the powers that be in Dáil Éireann have preferred to hide behind the wide-brimmed skirts of costly tribunals than to deal with abuse, corruption and white-collar criminality through Dáil committees.

We are seeing a new subterranean chamber of bank fraud open up before our eyes even now; and before us is the grisly prospect of another tribunal of inquiry, to follow the beef tribunal, the McCracken tribunal into the Dunnes scandal, the Moriarty inquiry into Haughey and Lowry, Flood into planning, and the Tom Cobley an' All Enquiry. These inquiries essentially involved abuse and corruption by politicians, and instead of the political establishment cleaning out its own stables, it has whistled up the expensive services of lawyers, who will pay themselves well and who will change very little.

They do not need to. They are not electable; they are not answerable to the public – but they have the sovereign effect of *appearing* to resolve problems. And politicians can take their reports and find in them whatever they need to declare their own innocence; meanwhile, the fundamental problem, the transfer of power to law-interpreters continues unabated.

There is another problem in Irish life which appears to result from a profound cultural characteristic – and that is that people do not complain until problems have come to a crisis. We are poor at defending our own interests. This is evident in even the humblest of transactions. When we are mournfully munching a thoroughly third-rate meal and the manager comes up and asks how is everything, we chirrup cheerfully: 'Fine, thanks.'

Americans and Germans do no such thing. And we let little things like bank charges go by without complaint; yet those charges are a mockery, for they are often purely discretionary. If the banks think they can get away with charging Client A but not Client B, A is charged and B is not: we are punished for our pusillanimity, and we hardly breathe a word of complaint until our grievances accumulate and become insupportable.

Banks have been getting away with murder because we let them. There can be no justification for bank charges for frivolous transactions such as using ATMs. The banks have our money, a lot of it at zero interest: to be charged for taking out some of that money is plainly ludicrous, but we let it happen because we prefer not to ruffle feathers. Is it any wonder, therefore, that AIB profits are £580 million and Bank of Ireland's £500 million annually?

And now we learn that, as with National Irish, some trusting, naïve clients were 'over-charged' by their banks. But we know there is another word for this. It is robbery, premeditated, intentional and systematic: and we know also that, unlike the little cigarette-sellers of Henry Street, nobody will find themselves in court for this criminality.

Meanwhile the transfer of resources from the people, via the State, to the legal professions on foot of political delinquency or inertia continues day after day after day. There was, for example, no outcry when the High Court awarded four people £1 million in legal costs following what turns out to have been an unconstitutional attempt by the former taoiseach, Charles Haughey, to turn the Great Blasket Island into a National Park. The judge concerned also gave the plaintiffs the liberty to enter a motion regarding damages.

We do not need a tribunal of inquiry here. That wretched man Charles Haughey was, according to the plaintiff's counsel, guilty of 'an unprecedented abuse of legislative power', the judge opined that some of the provisions of the National Parks Act were 'very unorthodox.'

The outcome of this tiny, unnoticed scandal is that the plain, simple taxpayers of Ireland will pay for Charles Haughey's attempt to turn the island, though not his own Inishvickillane, into a National Park. And they will pay not merely in legal fees - £1 million to the plaintiffs, and presumably a comparable sum to cover the costs of the State's defence of the Haughey land-grab – but now, we hear, possibly in damages too.

No wonder the Government is silent. Most of its Ministers today faithfully served the man who is responsible for so many of the horrors besetting us now. The sound you hear is the rubicund din of lawyers, laughing.

Herr Johann Zwindler

'Gut mornink, herr manatcher. It iss most gut off yoo to see me. My name iss Herr Johann Zwindler.'

'Is it, by God? And my name's James Joyce, and I'm married to Martina Navratilova. How can I help you?'

'Tchames Tchocice? Za same name as za rhiter? Zat is amaxing! Und on Tchames Tchoice un expert I amm! Ja! Trulich! An admirer! But in Tcherman only. My Innglish is no gut enuff zoo read *Ulysees* in Innglish. In Tcherman only. "Statich drall Buck Mulligan," ja? Ha ha ha. Verr gut! Are you a rhelatif of Herr Joyce?'

'No, I'm not, and all this isn't necessary, you know. This is Tralee, after all. We ask no questions, look for no identification, just call you Paddy O'Sullivan, and there'll be no problem. Know what I mean?'

'Ja! I know! Und eet ees wunderbar! Your eye, it opens, zen it shuts – is it ill?'

'No it is not ill. All I am saying to you, Herr Schwindler, that this is Tralee, and we have more than roses here!'

'Ja, ja. Tralee verr pretty. Und you are Tchames Tchoice, ja? Und the great Tchames Tchoice was from Tralee, ja? I haff always sought that he from Dublin vos. Za Dubliners. Und setera.'

'Look, whatever your name is, cut the crap. It isn't necessary, you know. I'm sure I can help you out without this performance. A little bit sub-Colditz, don't mention the war, doner und blitzen, ve haff means of making you talk, you know? So, no more of this James Joyce from Tralee, okay? We both know he wasn't from Tralee.'

'Gut. My fhrends sink I am expert on Tchames Tchoice am. How shtupid me they wold sink if Tchames Tchoice from Tralee really vos! And Martina Navratilova, she is from Tralee allso! Inbelievable! Und a tcheck I thought she vos!'

'She is a Czech. Please. How can I help you? We offer a very confidential service here. We dish the dirt here, if you take my drift. Clean as a whistle if you like. No dirt here, okay? Doesn't matter where you're from, you take my drift, no real names, no pack drill!'

'Forgiff me, my English is not gut enuff zu follow you, apart from ze first bit. So. Martina Navratilova here in Tralle now liffs! Iss gutt! But, forgiff me. In Tchermany people sink it is ze vimmin she likes! In Tchermany ve say that she duss the jiggy-jig mit ze frauleinen und ze damen, not mit ze men. Vot dumbkopfen ve are in Tchermany! So. She is married to you and liffs here in Tralee. Gut news, ho ho ho. Haff you many kinder?'

'Look, this is wearing a bit thin. Are you going to mess around all day here or what? I'm a busy man, I've got a lot of non-resident accounts here to attend to, you take my meaning. NON-RESIDENT ACCOUNTS FOR PEOPLE WHO ARE NOT ALL THAT NON-RESIDENT. You understand?'

'Vot is the mater mit your eye? It opens then it shuts, opens and it shuts. Haff you somesing in it?'

'Not dirt, if that's what you mean. Is that what you mean? Are you asking me if there's any danger of dirt around here? Well, the answer is no. No dirt here. Okay? This is a dirt-free zone. Is that good enough for you?

'Off course. Duss Martina a clean bank like?'

'Martina? Martina? There's no Martina here, okay, just a dirt-free bank, and look, I haven't got all day, so are we going to do business or what?'

'No Martina here! Ha ha ha ha, Herr Tchoice! Yoo Irish! Vot senses of funniness you haff! Tchames Tchoice, your relatiff, he was funny like zat, no? But Martina, she is not full of funninesses, no, yes? She a Tcheck. Glum. I understand. Tchamberlain. Zer Munchen Agreement. Peace is our Times. Nineteen sirty ate. Sixty years on, und cetera. Okay. She not like funninesses. But she a clean bank she likes! Zat is gut. A clean bank also I like!'

'Look, my name is not Joyce, all right? Und Martina Mavratilova my vife iss not. WHAT AM I TALKING ABOUT? I meant to say that Martina Navratilova is not my wife. And equally, you are not Herr Schwindler. So who are you?'

'You Irish! So funny! Full of funninesses! Zat is why I want to open an account here while in Tchermany I liff. Za bank manatchers in Tchermany no sense of funninesses haff! I like funninesses, Herr Tchoice!'

'Who are you? You can be who you bloodly well like. Just tell me who you are. Please.'

'I am Herr Johan Zwindler, und I vish to open a non-rhesident account mit your bank, ja?'

'Good day, Herr Zwindler, it was pleasant meeting you. I'm afraid this being Ireland, our non-resident business is strictly reserved for residents only. Gut day. Ze door behind you open iss.'

Armistice Day, 80 years on

Today is the proudest in my professional career; and if I am henceforth assigned to prising impacted chewing-gum from the pavement outside the *Irish Times* with my teeth, I will remain a happy man. For this day, this Armistice Day, 80 years after the killing on the Western Front finally ended, this State and this country are recognising the sacrifices of upwards of 35,000 Irishmen – and not a few women – who fell in the Great War.

I wrote my first article on this subject for the *Sunday Independent* 20 years ago this week. I had been interested in the Great War since childhood, but my true sense of the missing dimensions of Irish history came from a letter in the *Belfast Telegraph* in the early 1970s written by a survivor of the 36th Ulster Division, who deplored the silence surrounding the equally brave soldiers from the South.

In October 1978, I went down to Tipperary to interview Jack Moyney of the Irish Guards, the last surviving Irish Victoria Cross winner. His week-long patrol, stranded in no man's land in Ypres in the winter of 1917, was a true epic of endurance and courage; but he said that he was never as scared then as he was during the War of Independence, when, he thought, it was the Victoria Cross which had kept him alive.

I didn't know what he meant. Because just as the *fact* that hundreds of thousands of Irishmen had served in the Great War had been elided from official memory and from all history courses at school and university, so too had one aspect of the Anglo-Irish and Civil wars of 1919-1922, during which ex-soldiers were convenient victims. Indeed, this aspect was regularly headlined 'the campaign against ex-servicemen' by this newspaper; yet despite this, no historian of the period ever referred to it. Jack Moyney felt his VC made him too famous to murder; many others in Tipperary were not so fortunate.

Murder was not the only tool used against these hapless men. Some county councils effectively introduced an employment boycott on them, even banning their children from county scholarships. Crowds of veterans wandered the country looking for work, and many were shot as 'spies'. Yet history books ignored their plight though the evidence was there to see, even in the unrepentant memoirs of IRA men.

What had they done to deserve this? They had followed the advice of their elected leaders who had supported participation in the war, urging young men to enlist. In all, including the Irish in Britain, some 300,000 Irishmen did, and they left Irish ports to cheering crowds and bands playing *The Wearing of the Green* and *Let Erin Remember.*

Erin didn't. A huge shutter came down in public memory, and the hundreds of thousands of Irishmen who had served in the war and who had not emigrated stayed silent. War service was not to be discussed, ever. When I determined to revive the memory of these men, I wrote to every provincial newspaper in Ireland, asking for ex-servicemen to contact me, hoping that I could collate their memories. Just three did.

I went to the Memorial Gardens in Islandbridge, built to honour the Irish dead; and their condition was an artistic and moral scandal. After they were completed in the 1930s, de Valera had refused permission for them to be opened. When I saw them first in the spring of 1979, they were a vandalised tiphead, covered in weeds and grazing horses, the great stonework festooned with graffiti.

So I started writing about the Irish in the Great War in this newspaper. I truly was a lone voice. Some people teased me; some mocked me. I got unexpected support from the late Eileen O'Brien, a republican through and through, who told me that in her Galway village, children, unreproved by their parents, used to throw stones at shell-shocked veterans.

Another sympathiser was the late Brian Clark, newly appointed secretary to the British Legion, who was determined to broaden the memory of these Irishmen, which was now largely retained solely by a largely Protestant community which furtively commemorated Remembrance Sunday each November. Brian's ambition, like mine, was to see the ordinary Irish people and the Irish State acknowledge the Irish dead, but most of all, to see the Army of Ireland officially do so.

The late Campbell Heather began his gloriously successful campaign to restore Islandbridge. David Fitzpatrick's history workshop produced an entire volume of local essays about the Great War. One of his students, Jane Leonard, has since emerged as a pioneering historian of the period. In St Patrick's Cathedral, Dean Victor Griffin was determined that the memorial service should be uncompromisingly Irish.

But even the process of spreading the message brought a harsh backlash. Brian had to endure obloquy that he was in M15; and indeed, so had I. The Army was in the habit of sending a couple of officers along to Remembrance Sunday as a military courtesy. When the then-Taoiseach, Charles Haughey, discovered this, he ended the Army presence. Indeed, there was one ignoble year when the Army was represented at the memorial service for the German dead of the second World War, but not at the service for the Irish dead of two world wars.

There is a tide taken in the affairs of men; and let us add, women. I wonder if the great events that are taking place today would have happened at all without Presidents Mary Robinson and Mary McAleese; would the humdrum run of conventional male presidential candidates have had the courage to transform Remembrance Sunday as they have done? Unquestionably not.

In this, the two Marys – whom I have traduced, God knows, often enough – have truly performed a signal service to the State, to the people of this country, and to our Irish dead who only did their duty. Thank you, Marys. At last, at last I can truly say: Ireland remembers, and my heart bursts with pride.

Political contributions

There have recently been churlish and begrudging remarks about certain cheques. Let me be frank (you can be bing). This is a matter easy of explanation. Firstly, the sum of £20,000 which the Hibernian Temporary Building Society made out in the name of the Mother Theresa Orphanage for Leprous and Palsied Infants in the late 1980s and which found its way into a bank account in my name in the Seychelles.

Let me state quite clearly, I have long taken a vigorous interest in the Mother Theresa Orphanage for Leprous & Palsied Infants, and personally organised several cash collections for it outside churches in my constituency, the proceeds of which I handled with the utmost probity. I am proud to say that it was Mother Theresa's express wish that I should regard these monies as contributions from the orphanage towards my political costs. The orphans themselves were most eager this should be so. Even in faraway Calcutta, the interests of this great political party of ours are close to their dear and dusky little hearts.

The late Mother Theresa, RIP, told me this personally. It is true that this was in the course of a telephone conversation to which there is no other witness. It is also true that I made the phone-call from a coin-box in the centre of Dublin, which of course explains why there is no record of it either in Dáil Éireann or from my own home. I used a coin-box because my conscience forbade me from making such a call at public expense. I am aware that Telecom insists that there is no record of any call from any kiosk in Dublin to Calcutta during the year in question, 1984. This is because, at

Mother Theresa's insistence, I simply reversed the charges. She was most anxious I should not incur further expenses in my extensive voluntary work for her orphanage. The orphans agreed, the little brown mites.

'You scratch my back, and I'll scratch yours,' was the way she put it. A rather neat expression, don't you think? In my position of influence, I was able to assist her orphanage in many subtle ways, and she was happy to defray some of my numerous political costs.

When I – at her specific request – opened up a general fund for Mother Theresa in Ireland, donors such as the Hibernian Temporary Building Society would naturally lodge contributions through me.

I was merely a conduit to India; and as you may observe from a map, the Seychelles are halfway to India. The allegation that I personally have been benefiting from the account for the 15 years of its existence is simply preposterous. I have merely defrayed my personal expenses while in the Seychelles supervising the account itself. How could I discharge such duties from Ireland? Did I not have to check personally on how the account was faring? Would you have me be the equivalent of the absentee landlord who brought so much misery to Ireland? Is this what the revisionist school has reduced us to? Not merely kow-towing yet again to the Brits, but praising absentee landlords too! What next? The oath of allegiance? Rejoining the Commonwealth? Never! Erin go Bragh! Up the Republic!

Now, having cleared that little matter up to everyone's satisfaction, let me consider the Tots of Chernobyl Fund, which I myself founded. It has been alleged that cheques made out to that fund were countersigned by me and then placed in the aviation company owned by family members. So what? Are we to deny the tiny tots of the Ukraine access to helicopters? Is this what our Brit-loving moral zealots want, that these poor, scalded unfortunates are not to enjoy the miracles of modern technology? Would you have them crawl to hospital on their hands and knees? Does that not remind you of those cruel British landlords during the Famine? Remember the Black and Tans! How can we think of those wretched children without remembering the men of 1916, and the cruel fate they suffered?

It is true that Hibernian Helicopters has not yet been able to assist in the Ukraine. This is due to operational reasons, which we regret. But we take the long-term view in such matters. Is there something wrong with taking the long-term view? Is short-termism not one of our besetting vices which I have striven throughout my career to overcome?

Here I am, preparing for the future by ensuring that Hibernian Helicopters is a lean, keen fit aviation outfit, ready to rush to the aid of the wee babes of Chernobyl or even Calcutta at the drop of a donation to my election expenses, and all I get is namby-pamby criticism. What next? The RIC back? Evictions? Aye, and followed by pitch-cappings! You won't be happy until the Penal Laws are revived, and our beloved holy priests are hunted from Mass rock to Mass rock!

Was it for this that died the sons of Oisin? Was it for this that ...

What? What happened to the gold dagger and diamond necklace given me by Crown Prince Abdullah Aswas Andstillis? A simple matter. It forms part of the Mother Theresa Chernobyl Hibernian Helicopter Bursary, of which I am treasurer and chief executive. But enough of these trifling matters. Let us get to serious stuff! What abut MI5's plot to discredit the most honourable man in Irish life? And most of all: What about Maggie Thatcher's teapot?

RELIGION

Sunday trading

With Christmas rounding the bend and hurtling at us like a greyhound, a hideous grin contorting its carnivore's features, we soon can expect yet another symptom of yulery to grab us warmly by the carotid and to shake us till our corpuscles yelp. Sunday opening.

We have had several years of Sunday opening in the run-up to Christmas. The fashion would make sense if it were confined to the couple of Sundays before Christmas Day, for we are an improvident, feckless race who cannot be relied on to do anything in time.

Very possibly that last-minute scramble to obtain those few inessentials – the turkey, the Christmas tree, presents for everybody and possibly that odd festive bottle of Paraguayan sherry – can only be achieved if supermarkets and stores open on a brace of sabbaths to compensate for our earlier listlessness.

But we are not talking about a brace of Sundays. Sunday Christmas shopping began, I believe, in the Square in Tallaght in October. Now it is not entirely beyond the bounds of possibility that this is indeed necessary. It is just arguable that Christmas presents bound by mule-train for Ulan Bator and Tristan da Cunha must be bought and packed in early October; though I remain unconvinced that this needs to be done solely on Sundays.

Otherwise there can be no excuse for Christmas opening on Sundays beginning in mid-autumn, other, that is, than as The Thin End of the Wedge for Sunday opening throughout the year. Is this what people want? If they do, why?

Irish Sundays are one of the joys of Irish civilisation. Admittedly they are not what they were since the Catholic Church, in its post Vatican II mood of heathen laxity, allowed all sorts of sloppiness to be accepted. That a Mass attended on a Saturday evening should be regarded as an observation of one's sabbatical duties seems to be a heresy of Albigensian proportions. And that the pre-Communion fast has been extinguished reminds one of the worst excesses of the Roman Empire. Yet these lapses into voluptuous self-indulgence and wanton depravity might be forgiven if they were sustained by and adorned by the old rite.

They are, apart from the glories of the Pro-Cathedral, not. It is hard to hear the linguistic banalities of the modern Mass and all modern services without thinking that Tiberius maybe had a point when he was feeding all those Christians to famished lions. He clearly had late 20th-century anglophone Roman Catholic Masses in mind.

If he had suspected the true horrors of what lay ahead – folk-Masses with guitars, nuns warbling *Blowin' in the Wind* as a theological statement, public therapy sessions accompanied by hugs and reassurances that I Feel Your Pain, all masquerading as Masses, he would not have shown so much restraint.

Just as the Papes ditched the glories of their liturgy and ransacked their churches too, bless me if the Prods didn't do much the same to the Book of Common Prayer and ended up with a liturgy that feels like a gruel you might spoon-feed to ancient, blind witless tortoises.

And yet ... and yet – the Irish Sunday is still a glorious thing, with the fragrance of that blessed thing, the Irish fry, filling the air mid-morning. We are the last population in Europe to regard church-going as a norm (and the wastrel sluggards who think Saturday Mass counts will find how wrong they are as they enter the fires of hell). All those double-parked Toyotas and Volkswagens outside Catholic churches, all those neatly aligned Austins and Rovers outside Church of Ireland churches, represent a cultural tradition which is uniquely Irish.

On this Irish Sunday all traditions are largely united: it is better as it is. There is no reason why supermarkets should open on the sabbath: people are intelligent enough to manage to buy on six days a week what they need on the seventh, other than frivolous items like newspapers and crisps and packets of rashers and pints of milk and in the evening, the odd bottle of wine for dinner.

Yet the long reach of Christmas opening stretching into the autumn months should make us all feel uneasy; and the false gods of Sunday trading will wheel out the predictable arguments to support their case.

Very well, Scotland once had a severe sabbath culture and now has Sunday opening, so why should we not? Why? Because ours is a sabbath culture of joy, of sport, of concert, of family pleasure. By introducing Sunday opening we would not be abolishing a grimly Knoxian regime as the Scots did: we would be destroying our weekly Christmas.

We are not the only culture which protects the Sunday by law. In Germany, the archetypal free-market society, everything is closed within one millimetre of the grave throughout Sunday. I do not say I rejoice, for a north German Sunday, makes Ballymena's look like the Rolling Stones in Rio during Mardi Gras: I merely say that even in Germany market forces are permitted to work only within politically established constraints.

Those politically established constraints are now being constantly eroded in Ireland. The checkout operators in supermarkets, who doubtless cherish Sundays as lions once cherished early Christians, might soon face the unbelievably dreadful prospect of a seven-day working week. If that happens in the suburbs, market forces will oblige city-centre supermarkets to do the same. Dunnes and Quinnsworth will cause Marks and Spencer to follow suit; Clery's, Brown Thomas, Switzers, Arnotts and all the rest will do the same.

We do not need to be able to buy beds and electric kettles and suits and televisions and computers on Sundays. But those people the market condemns to working on Sundays do need to get up late and have a heavy breakfast and brouse over burly wads of Sunday newspaper, to celebrate familyhood, to hear the cathedral bells of Christ Church and St Patrick's ringing in carillon as I do each heart-lifting Sunday morning, to walk on park on beach or mountain, to play Gaelic and hurling and soccer and rugby and cricket, to go to church, to lie in bed sleeping off hang-overs or joyously and splendidly fornicating their lives away. That is the Irish Sunday. It is a precious birthright. We should guard it carefully.

Mumbo-jumbo (C of E)

MARYLEBONE. It is one of those London names which brings a little thrill to the soul, a sense of the old London of plague and tenement, of Pepys and Wren and Johnson and Dickens, the great beating heart of a nation.

Shoreditch, St Clements, Old Bailey, Pall Mall, Lime House, Soho, Waterloo Station. The names come from fairy-tale and nursery rhyme and Monopoly board. They are redolent of childhood and mystery.

But Marylebone especially, Mary the Good. What Norman pillager made good his conscience in this parish? Did Dr W.G. Grace piously kneel to thank the Lord for an astonishing innings at the home of cricket, Marylebone Cricket Club? Did Londoners scurry into the church to pray for deliverance from Heinkel and from Doodlebug?

And did they, 50 years ago, drop to pray on hassock and in pew to thank God for an end to six years of war and fires which had consumed their capital and scores of thousands of their fellows?

No doubt. I thought, the church would be largely empty today; but few consolations equal the melancholy pleasures of a deserted church, its echoes, its shadows and the ghosts that walk beneath its columns, and up there an altar and a pulpit and the word of God which can appeal even to an unbeliever on a wet February day in London town.

But God has fled this church of the Church of England. There was no sign of him in the new temple of psycho-sexual counselling and therapy sessions to which the church of Marylebone has been dedicated.

What remains is a parody of the Church of England. All the warnings and jesting prophesies about a new and refined form of non-denominational, multi-ethnic, all-inclusive, concerned and caring, inoffensive, modern, relevant and most of all godless strain of Christianity, in tune with modern needs, have come true in the Church of Marylebone.

The church, the church: you do not have to be a Christian or even a believer to expect the word God to appear on the notices outside Marylebone church. So far as I could see, it did not. What the building did offer, I learned, was a café and psychotherapy group and a men's group and healing services and crisis listening and a National Health Service centre and a counselling service and a befriending and help service and a café and an art exhibition and a bookstall.

But no prayer. Not once did I see the words prayer or grace or redeemer or Christ or forgiveness or repentance. No. All I saw was a tabernacle to the new and dreary heresies of helplines and crisis listening and all the hocus-pocus of pseudocare; the creed of today.

I walked the vaults beneath the old church and found a tiny little chapel, a bolt-on after-thought to the drop-in centres and counselling rooms which fill the old church where the new non-sectarian mantras of I-share-your-pain ring out where once hymn and psalm were heard.

And for the sad and lonely, the concerned and caring godless religion of Marylebone offers a Befriending Service, '*The aim.* To provide support and a friendly listener. *Assessment.* This service requires an initial assessment which will be conducted by a member of our assessment team ...'

Well, obviously there are limits to the level of friendliness which the concerned and caring folk of Marylebone can give to the tiresome, the boring, the cranky; which no doubt is why those who need to be befriended need first of all to be screened, filtered, checked.

And if you really are too irritating and irksome to merit the full befriending service, no doubt you can benefit from the service called Crisis Listening, in which you 'talk face to face with a listener anonymously and in confidence for up to 50 minutes.'

And you will be happy to hear that, though the church of Marylebone seems to offer nothing in the way of godliness, eternity or – perish the thought – hell, it also offers courses to enable one to become a Crisis Listener or a Befriending Service Assessor.

I have been reading through the above, and it is like a joke. It is not a joke. You do not have to be a Christian to regard it as a terrible reality. Is the Church of England dedicated to becoming a kind of therapy-movement, with therapy outlets which used to be known as churches and non-denominational gender-equal counsellors who used to be called priests?

Is it merely nationalism which inclines me to say that the Church of Ireland, companion within the communion of Anglicanism, is too stoutly addicted to the traditional norms of religion to be seduced by the mumbo-jumbo which currently bewitches its fellows in the Church of England?

The church here has retrenched; scores of church buildings have been deconsecrated and bequeathed to the community at large. It has seen hard times; yet it remains a Christian church dedicated to the precepts of Christianity.

The churches of the Church of Ireland are among the great uncelebrated treasures of the Irish countryside. What civilised heart does not surge an extra beat at the sight of the spire rising above a stand of beech in the middle of nowhere, and at the thought of the small congregation of farmers and traders converging down sinuous bohereens on cold Sundays?

One of the most famous of all church-spires in Ireland is at Powerscourt, in Co. Wicklow, its green copper pinnacle a totem for hikers and walkers for generations. And now that spire is doomed. It is in such a terrible condition that insurers will not accept the consequences of it falling over and braining passing hikers.

Doomed, yet none the less under a protection order. It will cost £70,000 to rebuild the spire.

Protestant engineering

What is the relationship between religion and social skills? For example, why is it that Catholics in northern Europe are seldom great mechanical engineers? We tend to think of such religious differences as being Irish. I suspect that it is not so – that religion is an important vector in secular matters as well as the manner of one's worship. This can follow complex and not always predictable patterns – I suspect, for example, that Britain would not have a medical service for much of this century and indeed in the last century without the services of Irish Catholic doctors.

Scottish engineers tend to come from the Lowland Protestant culture which produces dour but effective football managers. One might not seek them out in a bar; but they build great bridges and assemble effective teams. It is perhaps not surprising that the most elegant and artistic British teams – the great Manchester United and Glasgow Celtic – were either managed by or largely composed of Scottish Catholics. Perhaps slipshod in defence, but glorious and profligate in attack.

This difference in culture depending on religion need not be a Scottish or Irish thing. Is there, for example, any relationship in northern European car-making countries between religion and that industry? Was a genius at car-engineering a largely Protestant thing? Were the car-makers of Belgium or Holland or north Germany in any way influenced by the religion? France – in parts anyway – is a surprisingly Protestant country; were its car-makers – Simca, Peugeot, Renault, Citroen – Protestant? It is worth noting, in passing, that Ferrari, I think, means simply Smith or McGowan. In the transport business a while, Signor Ferrari.

Certainly to judge from the record of Ireland, the ability to tinker with car-engines *tends* to be associated with Protestants; anyone who has ever visited Co. Antrim, where there is a car workshop at every crossroads, will be aware of a profound mechanical culture which does not exist in Connemara.

Mechanical engineering thrives in Protestant (effectively state) schools in the North. To all extents and purposes, it is absent from Catholic schools; and that was an absence which no doubt reinforced the inclination of many of the large companies not to employ Catholics. If no Catholic schoolboy had done mechanical drawing or metalwork, it was surely not hard to decide who was going to get the annual apprenticeships. The Catholic church demanded a monopoly of education for its schoolchildren; it then deprived them of the skills they needed in the workplace. And no doubt many unionists were happy that they did not have such skills.

(Of the two Northern Catholics I know who went on to become successful mechanical engineers, both had been asked to leave Catholic schools and they found education instead in state technical colleges.)

Is it just a process of education? Or are there other cultural forces at work? What car companies have resulted from Irish mechanical skills? There is of course Eddie Jordan, who seems determined to refute my point about Catholic engineers.

But stay. There is older evidence – Henry Ford, the Cork Protestant, who was the greatest magnate of them all, who was at different stages in his life behind Ford and Cadillac too. (And the construction of a Ford tractor factory in the 1920s in the Soviet Union was probably the first brick in an industrial programme which culminated in T-34 tanks entering Berlin.)

A rather more modest achievement – and one which I learned of recently for the first time – was that of another Irish Protestant, Frederick Wolseley, whose family came from Tullow, Co. Carlow. Frederick was born in Golden Bridge House in Dublin. He clearly was something of a mechanical genius, for he emigrated to Australia, where he invented the world's first mechanical sheep shears.

He returned to this side of the world and started the Wolseley motor car company in Birmingham. One of his engineers was Herbert Austin; between them they created the first motor car to be made in Britain. One hundred years ago this year that car, the Wolseley three wheeler, was rolled out. The British motor-car industry was born. [...]

One question: was Riley the company Wolseley amalgamated with in reality Reilly, thereby challenging my theory?

It was – at least in that generation – no mean family. Frederick Wolseley was the brother of Field Marshal Garnet Wolseley, one of the most famous of Britain's imperial generals. Yet they might not have retained their Carlow connection after the '98 Rising, when their home was burnt; by rebels, presumably.

Faith of our fathers

And we come back to the question again, as we have done so before: where did the Catholic Church go wrong? How is it possible that the most powerful and vibrant institution in Irish life could have so mistaken its essential cultural values that it ditched what people loved, and embraced the meretricious, the shallow, the ephemeral? The Church possessed a vast body of music, ancient and recent, and dumped the lot, and reached instead for a curious stew of trendiness and bogus folk.

Tell me: does your heart not sink when you hear the organist wrap his or her fingers around the opening chords of *Kumbaya*? Why? Because you know it lacks all authenticity. It is a bastard hybrid of the Catholic Church mated with *The Black and White Minstrel Show*, a musical piccaninny that presumably is meant to appeal to hearts which were once stirred by the thought of all those unbaptised Little Black Babies, millions of grinning, misfortunate samboes destined for limbo.

Maybe it is because so many people are retrospectively appalled by the old attitudes to Africans that the Church reached for the Negro Spiritual as a reassurance to our little Black brothers and sisters that We Am All Equal, and We Gonna Sing One of Dem Dere Slave Songs Using One of Dem Dere Phoney Slave Voices. One always senses that whenever a church choir breaks into *Kumbaya*, one is meant to sway – ethnically, of course, with a touch of mournfulness in our voices, Cause, Lord, We Am Just In From Pickin' Cotton, Yassuh, Indeedy, And Our Black Asses Is Plumb Tuckered Out.

If *Kumbaya* doesn't finish us all, *Michael Rowed the Boat Ashore* almost certainly will as we drown in a sea of simpering semiquavers and glutinous crotchets. And then, as we go down for a third time, we are clobbered across the forehead by some new Ecumenical Anthem, probably called a Hyrr, which offends nobody, is gender-inclusive, vegetarian and deals with the plight of Cross-Dressing, HIV-positive Lesbian Whales, and most unbearably of all, *has no melody whatsoever.*

Yet these dirges and politically-correct twitterings have replaced, almost in their entirety, the vast body of melodically enchanting music whose only crime – like the interior of so many lovely churches – did not suit modern liturgical requirements, and like the interiors, were unceremoniously dumped.

In 30 years' time, today's 10-year-olds will not break into whatever musical bilge they are being fed through the churches; but take any gathering of adults who were raised to the old music, give them a line of *Queen of the May* or *I'll Sing a Hymn to Mary* or *Soul of My Saviour,* and they're away, big grins on their faces as they lustily remember words unsung over three decades or more, but remembered as perfectly as they remember the names of their brothers and their sisters.

No doubt values and habits were different in those days. Processions and church services formed a bigger part of children's lives than they do today, and what's gone is gone. You will no more get today's 10-year-olds to shuffle in a May or Corpus Christi procession than you will get them to go to Mass at 8 on a wintry Sunday morning.

Yet children are children: they love strong and simple melodies, and that was the great merit of that body of songs which the Catholic Church disposed of in those few, fell years when it was also ransacking old churches and putting up monstrously ugly new churches which resembled airport terminals or, sometimes, in a fit of pseudolithia, pagan stone cairns.

This purely voluntary destruction of music and architecture only makes sense in the context of suicide cults in Guyana and mass *sutti* on the Ganges, yet it happened. We who spent our childhood in a darker epoch infested with sin, limbo-bound black babies and fine hymns should be grateful at least for the third of these.

It was when John Kearns heard an elderly priest break into these old heretical anthems at an evening Mass recently, and saw how the entire congregation relaxed, smiles on their faces, that he realised that the demand for this music remains; for not merely is it fine music, for most Irish people over the age of 35 it is childhood, innocence, and fond memories. He and his business associate Bernard Bennett rapidly assembled singers – Frank Patterson, Regina Nathan, the monks of Glenstal – shooed the lot of them, plus the RTE Philharmonic Orchestra, into a recording studio, spent £80,000 recording the lot of them: and produced the fastest-selling cassette/CD of the year, *Faith of Our Fathers*.

No *Sweet Sacrament Divine*, I notice; an oversight which might be corrected in the next cassette/CD. But otherwise, so many of the melodies which gave one a profound love of music in the days when sin was telling a fib or not saying one's prayers, in hymns which contained mystery-words and mystery-concepts like womb and seed and virgin, which we mouthed with blithe enthusiasm. Childhood was mystery; womb *et alia* were just another mystery, but surrounded by a vast firmament of music which we bawled out with infantile relish. And even as I write these words, I ask again – how could such a treasury have been so lost, so purposelessly squandered?

These hymns are not, as people might think they are, uniquely Irish. Quite the reverse – perhaps most of them are by English Catholics such as Frederick Faber and Edward Caswall. And one hymn which used to be sung at Croke Park has vanished because finally people discovered it was not what they had thought it to be. It is *Faith of Our Fathers*, the second verse of which explains how the GAA lost its appetite for it at All-Ireland finals:

Faith of our Fathers, Mary's prayers,
   Shall win our country back to thee.
And by the truth that comes from God,
   England shall then indeed be free.

Quite.

Free choice for Catholics

I regularily receive newsletters from an American organisation called Catholics for a Free Choice: and a more oxymoronically named organisation I will be unlikely to find until I run into a member of SS Simon Weisenthal or find myself in the company of the Gerry Adams Loyal Orange Lodge.

The point, surely, about being a Catholic, is that one doesn't have a free choice. The point, indeed, about belonging to any organisation, even an anarchist one, is that one doesn't have a free choice – even anarchists must agree to meet at the same time and same place, not wherever and whenever each anarchist feels like.

But for Catholics in particular, the choice is not free; and that there is a well-organised movement in America demanding a woman's right to choose abortion, demanding homosexual priests, demanding same-sex marital unions *as Catholics* suggests that an awful lot of people haven't quite got the hang of things. Because it is not what one personally wants which counts, but what the rules, style, intent and purpose of a particular organisation are.

If I want freedom of choice, the Presbyterians can be quite relaxed about the individual conscience; so too the Quakers; most of all, the Unitarians, who seem to demand nothing of their adherents save they follow their consciences. For Christians unhappy with Catholicism, there are many places to go – and many, indeed, in Ireland are opting for the Church of Ireland.

But I hardly expect such people who have made that journey to start demanding car maintenance classes in Church of Ireland services, or insisting that the Church of Ireland should permit ministers to have homosexual relationships. There are rules in all organisations – and obedience within the hierarchy of the Catholic Church is what is expected of adherents of Rome.

Freedom of choice is not an option anywhere in any organisation; and for Catholics to demand that priests marry same-sex couples or permit women to have the 'right to choose' is to misread and misunderstand the Catholic Church, which does not feel it is on this earth to let people do whatever they want. Quite the reverse. One of the few places in the world where people do genuinely feel free to do almost whatever they want to whomever they want - *and do* – is Africa; the reaction to that is for vast numbers of people there to flock to the disciplines and moral certainties of Catholicism.

Most civilised people today would agree that the criminalisation, marginalisation and ostracism of homosexuals has been one of the great crimes of Western civilisation. But that is not the same thing as saying that the Catholic Church should conduct marriages between homosexuals, for the first and most powerful reason that within its own rules it cannot, no matter what evidence of fringe-practices by certain priests is revealed in a book by John Boswell – the subject of recent writings by Jim Duffy and Senator David Norris.

Priests are as prone to stray from the rules of their calling as are journalists from theirs. The medieval papacy was at times so steeped in evil as to permit almost anything. In more recent times, Catholic priests have blessed departing Panzers, have showered holy water on tanks bound for Abyssinia, have revelled in the genocide of Serbs, and in this country have given absolution to murderers that they might further slay with a clean conscience (Michael Collins would send his killers to one particular curate, in order to cleanse themselves before they murdered again). Beside all this, the blessing of same-sex unions is benignity itself.

But of course the Catholic Church, when it is in its senses, and not seized by the sort of delinquency referred to above, cannot judge deeds by the standards of such atrocious departures from what Catholicism in its heart knows what it stands for. It is unreasonable to expect it to contradict the vast bulk of its own moral inheritance merely because it makes homosexual couples feel better. The Catholic Church is about a far vaster historical mission than catering to the particular requirements of some of its members; and that mission is served by its rules for all.

What do I think? Of course, I know some homosexual couples who are far more loving and devoted than many of their heterosexual friends. Should the Catholic Church marry them? Well, the truth is that by its own rules it can't, no more than it can 'marry' two extremely good friends who want the church to recognise the special quality of their friendship.

Marriage is a holy sacrament within the Catholic Church. Whether or not I agree with the emphasis it places on this sacrament is irrelevant; as indeed is my opinion on the tenets of Islam to a Muslim. For sacraments are not pleasing little playthings for the Catholic Church to toy with according to the mood of the moment: they are the very reason for the existence of the church and its priests, and the conferring of a sacrament is a divine occasion in which the priest is merely the human mediator of the hand of God.

This is what the Catholic Church believes. If you are a Catholic who understands the meaning of Catholicism, you are unlikely to want to trifle with occasions of such awful majesty without a monumental amount of thought and care.

That thought and care will, one day, permit the ordination of women priests; will also permit priests of either sex to marry. But there is nothing whatever in the moral theology of the Catholic Church which could permit the hand of God to confer divine and sacramental grace on homosexual acts, no matter how loving and loyal the couple concerned might be. The Catholic Church, being the Catholic Church and not the San Francisco Collective for Free Love, is obliged to defend and promote the primacy of heterosexual marriage. Only idiots who believe that Catholicism is about choice could believe otherwise.

WHERE DOES IT GO?

A bad Irish summer

Excuse me, but this clothesline which you sold me two weeks ago doesn't work. It simply doesn't work. I don't know how you have the nerve to sell such a clothesline. It's outrageous.

What do you mean it doesn't work? How can a clothesline not work? It can not work by not drying my clothes, that's how it can not work. I've had it for two weeks and it's dried nothing all that time.

Well, sir. I don't mean to appear to be impertinent, but it has been raining for the past two weeks. You can hardly expect to get clothes dry in weather like that.

What? Do you mean to tell me that you sell clotheslines which only work in hot weather? That's monstrous. How dare you? This is Ireland, chum, not Mexico. It rains all the time here. How can you have the nerve to sell a clothesline which only works in hot weather? You didn't mention that at the time, did you? You just said, here's your clothesline, sir, all very smarmy and smooth, and all the time knowing that it was a warm weather clothesline. It's outrageous. I've a good mind to call the guards.

But sir, you did not say you wanted an all-weather clothesline. I'm not sure we even have an all-weather clothesline, but unless you specified that you wanted one, you can hardly expect to get one.

What? I've a good mind to punch you in the nose. If I walk into a car showroom, I don't expect to have to specify that I want an all-weather car. If I walk out with a car, I expect it to be allweather. I do not expect to have to come back in two weeks time saying the car doesn't go in the rain. The same for spades. If my garden centre sold me a spade which doesn't function every time it drizzles, I'd know very well what I'd do with that spade, no matter the weather.

There is no need to be vulgar.

I'm not being vulgar. I'm being angry. I've got a heap of laundry which your clothesline refuses to dry. I'm running out of clean clothes, simply because you have sold me a temperamental clothesline which simply declines to do its duty. I want a replacement this instant. One that works, regardless of the weather.

Well, sir, I'll happily give you another clothesline, but I'm not at all sure it will do any better than the one you have.

What? You mean you make it your business to sell third-rate clotheslines which only function if they live in the Sahara? Listen, they don't need clotheslines in the Sahara, clothes just get dry of their own accord. Having a clothesline in the Sahara is like having an icemaker in the Arctic. And how do you think you can get by in business selling clotheslines in Ireland which only work in African deserts where they don't need them?

We don't just sell clotheslines, sir. We sell, for example, watering cans.

Oh really? I need one of them. Let me see what you have there. Yes, well, it looks rather nice. But where's the water?

Yes, sir, well you see, you have to put the water into the watering can yourself sir. We merely provide the instrument for distributing the water.

Is this some kind of joke? You have already sold me a clothesline which doesn't work in the rain. Now you try to sell me a watering can which doesn't water. Do you sell oilcans without oil?

No, sir. We do not sell oilcans at all. But we do sell petrol cans.

Ah. In that case, I'll have one of them. Thank you. Here, you bastard. What are you trying to do to me? There's no petrol in this petrol can.

Indeed, sir. By law, we are not allowed to purvey petrol. But we are allowed to sell vessels which may be filled with petroleum.

Or olive oil, for that matter, but you can't call them olive oil containers, now do you?

This is true, sir. We do not call it an olive oil can, perhaps the demand for a spare container of olive oil in one's car-boot is sluggish, at best.

Yes, well, I'd have thought the market for clotheslines which don't work north of Tangiers sluggish too, but you seem to be making a packet out of them. Also out of watering cans which only water when it's raining. I suppose you sell umbrellas which only work in the rain, eh?

If sir means, 'Do our umbrellas fend off rain when it is not raining?' I regret to say that they do not.

Hmp. Some operation you have here.

It is, sir, a perfectly sound operation. Might I suggest that you buy the umbrella for your clothesline, thus making it an all-weather line. Attach runnels to the umbrella, by which means you can fill your watering can, so that when the drought comes, your clothes will be dry, your watering cans full, and your umbrella can relax in the sun.

Excellent! I'll take the lot.

And the petrol can, sir?

No. Keep the petrol can.

Very good, sir. A pleasure doing business with you.

A word of advice about Dublin hotels

A word of advice. If you have adultery in mind, be very careful about which hotel you choose to engage in same. Some hotels by name seem disposed to that sort of activity. The Berkeley Court, for example, seems to be named after a technique for wooing. Sachs Hotel is perfectly dubbed, providing the naming ceremony was done by a Northerner. The Montrose and the Mont Clare merely cause you to speculate who Clare and Rose were. The Royal Marine Hotel might just leave you wondering if gentlemen in green berets do not kick the door in just as you relax in your bed of sin.

The Shelbourne seems to have been at the logical outcome to such activities being, of course, where Shel came into this world. In Blooms Hotel, of course in memory of Molly, *anything* goes. And in the new Davenport ... Well, in the new Davenport, nothing goes, and not because of the name. It is because of what it was.

The Davenport Hotel was once a mission hall. Stolid low-church folk gathered there in the last century to raise their voices in lusty denunciation of Satan and all his works, with fleshly temptation doubtless being the foremost of them all. Bonnets would have nodded in stern approval as the clergyman warned of the horrors of vice and beastliness generally.

A century on and the old mission hall is now Dublin's latest five-star hotel. Do pious old ghosts prowl through the corridors, an ear to the bedroom doors in the ceaseless vigil against vice? Do sanctimonious spectres tremble with rage as they hear happy cries ringing through the rafters which once echoed with the stentorian denunciations of the very behaviour now occurring in that very mission hall?

We need not speculate on how people enjoy themselves in the bedrooms of the Davenport. There is only one way to do it there: the missionary position, of course.

Hotels, ex-mission halls and otherwise, do not seem to feature on the Home Help Domestic Services guide, the clever little card which, by magnetic means, attaches to your fridge and which can tell you at the drop of a bag of chips the telephone number of a local plumber, driving school or flooring contractor.

This seems a mistake. Bertie Wooster used to find that when he had stayed in a house for a couple of days, far from his hosts imploring him to stay, he would find on his bed a copy of the railway timetable with early trains marked out with urgent recommendations. The same is pretty much true in my own case.

I frequently find that whenever I ring somebody down the country with the news that I shall be in the neighbourhood for a few days soon, the news is followed by a few strangled cries and the whimpered regrets that what shame, they are just leaving for Patagonia and will not be back until – when did I say I would be returning to Dublin?

The reason for this reluctance is, of course, clear. My company gives such pleasure that the agony of my departure becomes simply unbearable; so people avoid this torment by rather bravely foregoing my company altogether. Rather heroic, what?

Hobbies

Hobbies. Is there a more male and anglophone word anywhere? The very word is quintessentially English, and its etymological roots are sufficiently mysterious and linked to Norman French and Anglo-Saxon linguistic collisions (it is somehow derived from the personal name Robin) to render it distinctly archipelagic.

Do male francophone cultures have hobbies? Do women? Do French girls collect stamps and note the numbers of railway engines and spot aircraft and spend hours lying in mud waiting for the lesser garlanded twit-wit to land on some ice-blasted slob? Gentle reader, do you really believe that they do?

Well, I don't believe it. We are all good Europeans now and furthermore the equality committee has ruled that the genders – as the sexes are now called – are equal and doubtless a subcommittee is discussing why there are not more career opportunities for woman cigarette card collectors. They discuss in vain.

Women don't sit on wet canal banks waiting for a glum, inedible coarse fish to come slinking through pram and cow-cadaver to sink its teeth into worm and hook and to be hauled up, unhooked and ignominiously returned to pram and cow-cadaver. Women seldom buy model aeroplanes and laboriously construct and paint them, to the point of getting the right spinner-colour appropriate to the correct *jasta*.

Young women do not lovingly assemble the Tirpitz or the Ark Royal or the Junkers 88; indeed how many women are there in the entire world who have even heard of the Junkers 88, never mind have an opinion on my contention that it was the most versatile aircraft of the second world war?

Women do not discuss the relative merits of 2-4-2 engine layout as opposed to 1-3-3 on the old Great Northern line, and they do not outbid one another for tiny bits of adhesive, coloured papers called stamps, they do not assemble collections of matchboxes or beer-mats, they do not, well, collect, unless of course you count obsessive deviant behaviour, such as Imelda Marcos and her shoes.

Yes, women garden; but that is different from the pure hobby, which seems related generally to collecting, even if it is collecting the same poor bloody educationally subnormal perch, who after a dismal, much bullied childhood spends its adult years being lodged on the same hook 28 times each afternoon and each time being triumphantly counted as a fresh catch before being returned protestingly to the water from which it will soon again be so ignominiously abstracted.

So women garden but gardening, after all, is art and it is nurturing, which perhaps explains why so many of the best amateur gardeners are women. But the collection of objects – even objects of art – is normally a male past-time. Collection, allied with an obsessive attention to detail, is the essence of hobbydom.

Some hobbies are personal. Having personally seen the Blue Mallard train is not the same as having a cigarette card of it. The first is a spotting kind of hobby. The second is a collectible, and that will be the basis of the fair at the Royal Hospital, Kilmainham this weekend.

It comes as something of a shock to learn that to the collectiblophile, virtually anything is fair booty, even something as apparently spiritless and characterless as an unused telephone callcard. To the sentient and the quick, callcards must rank with parking tickets, chipshop menus and fingernail clippings as the least interesting items in all the world and beyond doubt outside the pale of collectibility. This merely proves that the sentient and the quick are also thick.

Perhaps fingernail clippings have not yet caught on, and the day of parking tickets has yet to come, but the era of the telephone callcard is with us now. Telecom has even produced a limited edition commemorative card for this weekend's fair, which provided it retains its virginity and is not used, is probably the surest bluechip investment one can make this year. By the end of this decade, a single card might cost the price of Meath.

Dealers and collectors from all over the world will be attending this fair – proof of the Anglophone nature of hobbies is provided by the nationality of these dealers – they are Irish, British, Australian, American and South African; not a Brazilian or Lithuanian or Turk in sight.

And the biggest inducement for attendance at the fair? According to its organiser Peter Sheen it is the specially designed Telecom Callcard, worth £4 face-value and for which collectors are already willing to pay £30.

There seems to be nothing which collectors won't sell their aged grandmothers into white slavery to obtain. Old postcards, valueless banknotes, elderly bayonets, uniforms and medals all have their aficionados. (I say valueless banknotes; yet who can look at the old notes, especially the 10 shilling note, particularly bearing that radiant and virtuous maiden, Hazel Lavery, and not yearn for such fiduciary elegance?)

'It's going to be bedlam at the fair on Saturday,' predicted Peter cheerfully. 'Crowds turning up at eight in the morning. You mark my words. Unbelievable excitement. Bedlam.'

And all for a few telephone cards, possibly a shoelace or two and maybe some late cans of tinned haddock from 1910. But why do women not become collectors? Well, says Peter, some do; but very few. One he knows collects lavatory chain handles, and these were often objects of great beauty. 'But I don't know, I'll get into great trouble for this, but do women get lost in things the way that men do? I do when I look at my coins and my military medals, and I retreat from the real world into complete abstraction. I'm gone completely, and all I want is to be able to revel in the beauty of what I'm looking at and the craftsmanship involved, and I'm away. Do women do this? Do they?'

Americana

An American reader rang in to say how pleased he was at recent criticisms of Telecom in this space, but it was the first time, he said, that he had ever agreed with a single word written by this writer. One particular criticism he felt especially strongly was of this column's anti-Americanism.

Now, far from being anti-American, I am an ardent Ameriphile. America is the most exciting country on earth. Even backwater towns have an excitement, an enthusiasm, a vigour which are intoxicating. Americans are hospitable, likeable, easy-going. They hate pretentiousness, snobbery and social reserve.

But what Americans especially understand is freedom in a way which the media in this country can only envy. It is inconceivable that the restraints upon the media which are making life for newspapers virtually impossible in this country could ever exist in the US. Indeed, they would be incomprehensible to an American journalist.

Far from having an appetite for freedom of information, we have a body of law, bad law mostly, buttressed by a series of decisions and guidelines by judges, which militates against the press in a number of extraordinary ways. Newspapers now live in terror of libel laws and of contempt of court judgments which make much of our work impossible.

Litigation has become so costly and so inhibitive that this newspaper is having to put every journalist through a special libel-awareness workshop which has caused most of us to leave, white and shaking. You out there cannot know how bad things are because I cannot under the present monstrous rulings of courts and precedents of case law, disclose details of them to you. I cannot tell you what eminent people in this land – and some of them are very eminent indeed – are in litigation with newspapers, over what and why. Gagging orders effectively accompany such litigation, and remain in place not merely while the litigation takes place but also after the plaintiff has successfully sued.

The laws of the land are lined against your interests; you cannot know what is going on. What have you, and your elected representatives, done about this? Have you demanded freedom of information about how you are governed? How have you protected the freedom of newspapers to do their job?

The chances are you, and your elected representatives, have done nothing. We have not the passionate belief in freedom which Americans have. Any Irish journalist who watches the film *All the President's Men*, made 20 years ago, can only weep in frustration. When we see Woodstein being given access to the Congress library records to what politicians are reading, then we know we are talking about a concept of freedom which would be impossible in Dáil Éireann, where TDs even now are not obliged to declare their interests in anything. And we are as likely to be told by a Dáil library employee what TDs are reading as we are to hear the archdiocesan press office disclose the secrets of the archbishop's confession.

The truth is that the senior party in the present Government up until quite recently espoused legislation which made it a criminal offence to transmit information about contraception and abortion, that as recently as three years ago an entire edition of the *Guardian* was banned in Ireland because of information it contained about abortion, that vast numbers of publications are banned in Ireland without uproar of any kind; even a harmless publication like *Playboy*, whose senior staff are now almost all women, is outlawed *for all time* without a peep of complaint by anybody (save me).

Americans would not put up with these violations of liberty. Americans would not put up with the sloppiness and incompetence which our semi-State monopolies have been able to get away with, by Government decree, for generations.

And Americans do not wait for their politicians to act. They take action them-selves. You want it done, do it yourself is the truly American motto. If America is the home of world capital, it is also the home of aggressive defence of consumer interests. God bless madmen, obsessed, lunatic, Ford-terrifying people like Ralph Nader and all the consumer watchdogs that have come bounding out of his kennel.

What I do not like is the Americanisation and Anglicisation of Irish society. I like Irish accents – though emigration caused my family not to possess the accents we might otherwise have, I do not like to hear the importation of foreign pronunciations at the expense of native ones. The new Anglo-American twang of south-Dublin sub-urbs fills me with despair.

But my dislike of Americanisation does not extend to my dislike of, say, McDonalds. Provided planning permissions are controlled within a city, as they must be, far from McDonalds being a bad thing, it is good. It gives people the freedom to choose whether they want something or whether they do not.

McDonalds has been successful all over the world because it gives people freedom of choice. It also gives them a standard of service which they want but seldom get else-where. How often does one feel in some establishments that one is interrupting the staff about their normal, every-day chat?

What is awful is the importation of the most trivial, superficial elements of American society – the neon-lit *nite-club, the hootenanny burger-bar, the Deep South Dixie-Fried Chicken* syndrome and, of course, normally getting everything wrong. The America I love is the America which loves liberty, an America which expects grown-ups to make their own decisions in life without state interference. If that is the America we can import, then I say, God Bless America.

At the embassy reception

It was a bit of a blow not to be invited to the reopening of Brown Thomas; something of a setback to discover that Habitat could contemplate opening their new store in my absence; but crushing beyond belief to hear that the American Embassy chose to celebrate their Independence Day by inviting every journalist in Ireland, every politician, every member of the Garda Síochána, apart from the half-dozen directing traffic outside the International Financial Services Centre, a load of cheerful IRA types, every TD elected since 1918; every sporting personality since Christy Ring, every parking offender since the first traffic light in 1924, and anyone who had merited a mention in the telephone directory since Prudence Entwhistle had her Edison communicating device installed in her home in Kingstown so that she could talk to her sister Primrose. Even Obadiah Haddock, who cannot be trusted in the same room with a bottle of mineral water and any female under the age of 98, was invited. Everybody was.

But not me.

Messengers in the *Irish Times* spent last Thursday crawling around in bemused circles and trying to remember their names, all as a consequence of Oh-say-can-you-see hospitality, which seems to have consisted of a Lake Michigan of beer, a Lake Superior of wines and a Mount Rushmore of grub. Many TDs are asleep to this day from the after-effects of the American booze. Most businesses in Dublin remained closed on Thursday because their proprietors were unable to get out of bed. Courts did not bother opening. Government departments were empty. The party of the year for all of Dublin and beyond, except one person.

Still, we are reliably informed that the party was but five minutes gone when Obadiah Haddock made a gallant endeavour upon the virtue of Primrose Entwhistle – which is not quite as intact as people like to believe: there was the long, burning look between her and Reggie Arbuthnot during the Kingstown and District Outing to Maryborough that time of the Relief of Mafeking, and there was the warm night when she woke up to find that she was ... But enough of that. Relatively speaking, Miss Entwhistle is chastity itself: yet that was no protection against Obadiah Haddock, whose disdain of personal hygiene is normally enough to give adequate warning of his approach so that the vulnerable self-respecting might disappear.

Alas, Miss Entwhistle has long been a martyr to hay fever, as Reggie Arbuthnot found when he carefully manoeuvred her behind a hayrick outside Maryborough, and found himself being showered with thousands of delicate little sneezes. So she did not notice Obadiah approaching her at the Independence Day party, though around her dozens of women were scattering like mice at the fruit cake when the cupboard door opens. She looked up from her handkerchief. Too late!

Not far away, the entire upper echelon of the Garda Síochána was – I am told – standing in companionable proximity to the massed ranks of the Army Council of the

IRA, having put their spades away for the day and for the moment not looking for all those pesky missing bodies. Somewhere in there too, no doubt, were members of the Army of the Republic, though whether or not the nice Americans have mastered the subtle differences between Óglaigh na hÉireann, defenders of the Republic, and Óglaigh na hÉireann, Semtexers and Kneecappers Inc., is an interesting question.

For I remain reasonably certain that when Lt.-Gen. Gerry McMahon, the Chief of Staff – the fellow whose soldiers, by their patience and courage and sometimes their lives, have helped to keep the peace all over the world – goes to the US, he will not find himself an honoured guest of the White House, with a welcoming presidential hand on the small of his back.

Mmm. With attitudes like these, I'm beginning to see that the Americans showed a certain common sense when they compiled their guest-list. Fortunately, the Salvation Army is less demanding when it sends out its invitations for the annual sardines-and-Mi-Wadi knees up for down-and-outs on Dollymount Strand, the highpoint of my social calendar. Obadiah assures me that it is infinitely superior to the American Independence Day party; this year he is bringing Primrose. No doubt her comely twin sister Prudence will cast a fond eye on the only unattached bachelor in Ireland not invited to the July 4th bash.

P. Picasso

Lord, how I laughed with joy when I saw that a Picasso had fetched $48 million in the auction of the Victor Ganz collection in Christies on Monday. Even now as I write, tears of ecstasy are running down my face and nervous colleagues are backing away with chairs raised towards me as if they were facing a lion who hasn't tasted a Christian in ages. May the idiocy continue and continue: this way lies happiness. Money squandered on modern art is therefore not money spent on real art, prices for which might otherwise be sent sky high.

I am actually rather tempted to dabble in a bit of Picasso-creating myself, for so much of what passes for appreciation in the art world could not differentiate between a Picasso and a pick-axe. There are so many unprovenanced Picassos on the market, with many thousands of actually provenanced Picassos, that in reality they should have the face value of a German mark, *c.*1921.

But they have not – partly because of the folly and brainless greed which drive the New York art market, the influence of which can be seen in almost every exhibition put on by young artists in Dublin. Witless daubing, without style, technique, sympathy, composition, seems to the first and last thing young artists have in mind when they create, if that is the word I want. And there, standing as their master-figure, the man who helped start the entire wretched heresy of modern art, is our friends, Pabs.

The Picasso which went for $48 million the other day was *Woman in an Armchair,* a hilariously silly assembly of bodily components which purports to represent Picasso's teenage mistress, Marie-Thérèse Walther. Since the creation of this world, few more beautiful things have been constructed by nature than a fine teenage female body. Picasso manages to turn such a body into a spare-parts heap in a mannequin factory.

One of the heresies adduced to justify the rubbish passing as modern art is that it is no longer necessary for art to resemble that which it depicts because a photograph can do that just as well, if not better. Three seconds' rumination would dispose of that argument, for would our walls not be covered in framed photographs of haywains, madonnas, English warships being towed to their watery graves, aye, and of naked girls too, if that were so?

It is not so. There is no end to the ingenuity of human artistry and creativity, as literature has shown. The novel is no more dead than the human imagination. Writers constantly are able to invent fresh ways of expressing themselves, and reinventing literary formulas which tell us the truth about ourselves.

And there is no end to the way one could paint a beautiful teenage girl's body. Only a fool would deny that. And only a fool would wish to dismantle it as if it had just been fed through a combine harvester and dumped in a skip – apart, that is, from a practical joker and a hoaxster, which is what Picasso was.

He was also a sublime draughtsman, perhaps the finest of the century. Technically, he was a genius, as was his fellow fraud, Salvador Dali. Between them they debauched artistic standards worldwide. No silliness became too silly for them to perpetrate, no traduction of standards too heretical for them to embrace.

Perhaps it was not coincidental that both went to live in Nazi-occupied Paris, when they could have lived almost anywhere else. But they chose to live in that same city where another great fraudster of the 20th century, Jean-Paul Sartre, was also living, and dutifully submitting his work to the German censor, who would have found nothing substantive to worry about. But clever J.P. had the wit to join the Communists as the Allied tanks were approaching Paris, neatly preparing his reputation as a hero of the resistance.

All three men became draped in the mystique of 20th-century intellectual creativity, when they were the opposite: they were the prime manufacturers of self, using an impenetrable plausibility to fool a gullible world. Picasso knew this about himself, and the extraordinary truth about his reputation is that it has survived his own searing appreciation of himself:

> The rich, the professional idlers desire only the peculiar, the sensational, the eccentric, the scandalous in today's art. I myself, since the advent of cubism, have fed these fellows what they wanted and satisfied the critics with all the ridiculous ideas which have passed through my head. The less they understood, the more they admired me! Through amusing myself with all these

farces, I became celebrated ... I do not have the effrontery to consider myself an artist at all ... I am only a public clown, a mountebank. I have understood my time and have exploited the imbecility, the vanity, the greed of my contemporaries.

He no doubt thought he did – but he could never had thought that the myth would survive his death, or that his influence would spread like a plague through a slave ship. But it is not just idiotic ignorance which generates such ludicrous prices for Picassos, and the sub-Picassos which have followed; the market is driven also by the great financial institutions of New York, which have invested so much money in modern art that they are obliged to keep the prices high.

The stock-market equivalent of this is a company buying its own stock to keep it high, and it is illegal. But of course it is not illegal in the demented, part-infantile, part-debauched world of modern art: it is hardly surprising that, at the auction which saw the disposal of a dismantled teenage body, a work of Eva Hesse, assembled when she was aged 30 and consisting of polyethylene, sandpaper and string, fetched $2.2 million.

Peanuts. The Picasso paintings in the Ganz auction sold for a total of $164 million. It was a triumph for one of the great frauds of the 20th century; but then so was the profession of Victor Ganz, the former owner. He was a psychoanalyst.

At the auction

There is a company somewhere which makes small signs for the back of juggernauts which read: DO NOT OVERTAKE ON THE INSIDE IF THE TRUCK IS TURNING LEFT. The sign does not add, GRASSHOPPER: for space reasons, presumably, and understandably – the signs are so small that you have to be overtaking the lorries on the left to read them. (When did anyone ever last see a lorry driver use his left indicator?)

The maker of the warning-plate presumably runs off all sorts of plates bearing comparable Zen-wisdom. Purdeys have little signs on the buttstock declaring DO NOT PUT THIS SHOTGUN WHEN LOADED IN MOUTH AND PULL TRIGGER, this sign only becoming legible when the barrels are in the mouth and the trigger is being pulled. Iarnrod Éireann has installed thousands of tiny warnings around the country: DO NOT PLACE HEAD ON TRACK IF TRAIN APPROACHES. These signs are activated by the approach of the train and are only visible if your head is resting on the rail itself.

There is no reason why similar such guiding profundities are not signposted everywhere to guide us through life. DO NOT TURN ON THIS TWO-BAR ELECTRIC FIRE WHILE IN THE BATH. DO NOT TRY TO WARM A COLD BABY IN THIS DEEP FAT FRYER WHILE

COOKING CHIPS; REMOVE CHIPS FIRST. DO NOT CLIMB INTO JUMBO JET INTAKE AT TAKE-OFF. DO NOT CURL-UP IN SLEEPING BAG ON FAST LANE OF M50.

The more sophisticated of you might contend that only the most irredeemably stupid would need such signs. Maybe so. But there are certain days in the calendar when people find themselves being impelled into doing the strangest things, which they would never otherwise do. So even as a tiny voice within you shrieks, *No, no, no*, you unfold your 'Lee Clegg is Innocent' banner in Crossmaglen main square and call for locals to come and sign your petition. And even as warning flares light the sky within your brain, you beamingly lower your trousers and expose yourself to the passing-out parade at Templemore.

These special days, by careful calculations based on the movements of the moon and stars and tides, are as predictable to experts as are the ley-lines which guide Chinese life. Auctioneers employ these experts to choose their auction days, when otherwise shrewd, conservative, tight-walleted citizens, like corpses from the night-of-the-living-dead leaving their graves, are drawn mumblingly towards the auctioneer's hammer, arms extended, eye-sockets empty, bank balances flapping open.

All right, it's highly likely that even if auctions had signs warning, DO NOT ENTER THIS PLACE UNLESS YOUR ARMS HAVE BEEN AMPUTATED AND YOU HAVE A CORK IN YOUR MOUTH you would still enter, gob unstoppered and arms flailing like someone trying to catch butterflies. But at least you could say someone had tried to rescue you: and that I cannot say. I went to my doom unwarned.

But of course, that's the thing when you open your 'Lee Clegg is innocent' banner in Crossmaglen, or as the trousers flop around the old ankles in Templemore and you're reaching for the elastic of the underpants: you know you're doomed. You can't help yourself. Compulsion, your honour. Uncontrollable compulsion. Guilty as charged.

Take this recent auction attended by Kildare's finest, including my friend Mairéad. Mairéad is a very shrewd businesswoman who nightly turns REM into YEN. She makes George Soros seem like Wurzel Gummidge; yet within half an hour of this particular auction beginning, she was bidding against herself, lustily bawling offer upon her previous untopped offer and was only silenced by a sharp rap on the forehead with the gavel.

As for her companion, the author of this piece: he found himself bidding for three watercolours he had never seen before – not merely bidding for, but in due and deadly course, owning. On a good day, in poor light and held up with their back to a setting sun, you might think them worth a couple of pounds. But at least I had the excuse that my £45 might have been about to net me a couple of hitherto undiscovered young Turners. It didn't.

But no such excuse could be made for my strenuous and ultimately victorious quest for an oil-painting which my absent (and soon to be utterly incredulous) wife and I had already agreed might have been executed shortly before the painter responsible for it most deservedly was.

There might be an explanation for that acquisition – that I liked the green bit in the middle – but there can be none at all for the purchase of a collection of forks with encrusted egg-yolk (c. 1957), or a dozen assorted socks, some nearly matching and perfectly acceptable if boiled for a couple of hours, or the selection of false teeth collected on the floors of pub lavatories, for which even now I am trying to find a home: but still, a snip at £50.

But I only became fully aware of my final and most crushing acquisition on that unspeakable occasion known as the morning-after. It was of a little sign, declaring: DO NOT OVERTAKE ON THE INSIDE IF THE TRUCK IS TURNING LEFT.

WHEN THE COLUMNS APPEARED

Abandoned churches: *July 95*
African issues: *February 00*
Air crashes: *January 94*
Alice: *January 98*
Alu-fenestreers: *December 95*
Americana: *May 94*
'An Abbess Ballooning': *July 98*
Armistice Day, 80 years on: *November 98*
As the writer said to the bishop: *January 95*
Asylum seekers: *April 98*
At the auction: *July 99*
At the embassy reception: *July 95*

Bad Irish summer, A: *September 91*
Bats and CJH: *June 96*
Before and after the Famine: *October 95*
Belgium's claim to fame: *July 99*
Bemused, Misunderstood, Weeping:
    February 98
Bienvenue à Irlande: *July 98*
Birmingham Six, The: *January 94*
Bluebottle: *June 92*
Brian Clarke MC: *August 95*
Brutish, Merciless, Witless: *January 98*

Captain Jack Aubrey and Dr Stephen
    Maturin: *September 94*
Castle Leslie: *September 96*
Caution: baby on board: *July 91*
Chaps, guys and chums: *October 93*
Church vandals: *January 95*
Clamping: *March 99*
Con Howard: *December 94*
Conference time: *October 95*
Croyland Abbey: *August 94*
Cyclists of the world, unite!: *April 98*

Cyril's Cinders: *June 98*

David Norris and Robert Mugabe:
    February 00
Denis Bethel: *May 95*
Discovering Patrick O'Brian: *February 91*
Dortspeak: *July 94*
Doubts: *May 98*
Driving lessons: *March 99*
Dublin old and new: *December 94*
Dublin taxis: *December 98*

Easter 1916: *March 96*
Ecclesiastical art: *July 95*
804353 or 2804353: *May 91*
Emdeeville: *October 97*

Faith of our fathers: *October 96*
Family that won't go away: *October 94*
Flann O'Brien: *February 94*
Florida: *September 92*
Foie gras: *April 98*
Footing the bill: *April 98*
Free choice for Catholics: *August 98*
French cuisine: *December 92*

Galway oysters: *October 96*
Gay Byrne: *August 98*
Gerard Hanley: *November 93*
Germica Jeer: *March 99*
Gerry Adams?: *September 96*
Giving Bray a miss: *December 98*
Golf and tennis: *June 91*
Golf-courses: *August 99*
Greengage summer: *August 25*
Gus Martin: *October 94*